INCLUSIVE EARLY CHILDHOOD EDUCATION

A Collaborative Approach

Suzanne M. Winter

The University of Texas at San Antonio

PEARSON

Merrill
Prentice Hall

Upper Saddle River, New Jersey
Columbus, Ohio

Library of Congress Cataloging-in-Publication Data
Winter, Suzanne.
  Inclusive early childhood education : a collaborative approach / Suzanne
M. Winter.
    p. cm
  Includes bibliographical references.
  ISBN 0-13-042335-1
  1. Inclusive education—United States. 2. Early childhood
education—United States. 3. Teaching teams—United States. 4. School
support teams—United States. 5. Home and school—United States. I. Title.

  LC1201.W565 2007
  371.9′046—dc22   2006022871

Vice President and Executive Publisher: Jeffery W. Johnston
Executive Editor: Ann Castel Davis
Editorial Assistant: Penny Burleson
Production Editor: Sheryl Glicker Langner
Production Coordinator: Dennis Free, *Techbooks*
Photo Coordinator: Valerie Schultz
Design Coordinator: Diane C. Lorenzo
Cover Design: Bryan Huber
Cover Image: Super Stock
Production Manager: Laura Messerly
Director of Marketing: David Gesell
Marketing Manager: Autumn Purdy
Marketing Coordinator: Brian Mounts

Photo Credits: KS Studios/Merrill, p. 1; David Madison/Getty Images Inc.—Stone Allstock, p. 9; Laima Druskis/PH
College, pp. 13, 274; EMG Education Management Group, p. 17; Scott Cunningham/Merrill, pp. 24, 47, 131, 139,
185, 191, 217, 304, 332, 336; Barbara Schwartz/Merrill, pp. 43, 145, 188, 318; Shirley Zeiberg/PH College, p. 49; Anne
Vega/Merrill, pp. 53, 107, 267, 330, 341; Krista Greco/Merrill, pp. 75, 123, 202, 254, 264; Todd Yarrington/Merrill,
p. 80; Michael Littlejohn/PH College, p. 82; David Mager/Pearson Learning Photo Studio, pp. 86, 241, 307; Julie
Peters/Merrill, p. 117; Valerie Schultz/Merrill, pp. 133, 195, 246; Anthony Magnacca/Merrill, pp. 148, 194, 223, 238,
253, 272, 296, 309, 312; Laura Bolesta/Merrill, p. 156; George Dodson/PH College, pp. 170, 243; Silver Burdett Ginn,
p. 215; Modern Curriculum Press/Pearson Learning, p. 220; T. Hubbard/Merrill, p. 224; Merrill, p. 259; Patrick
White/Merrill, p. 292; Lloyd Lemmerman/Merrill, p. 293

Pearson Education Ltd.   Pearson Education Australia Pty. Limited
Pearson Education Singapore Pte. Ltd.   Pearson Education North Asia Ltd.
Pearson Education Canada, Ltd.   Pearson Educación de Mexico, S.A. de C.V.
Pearson Education—Japan   Pearson Education Malaysia Pte. Ltd.

ISBN: 0-13-042335-1

Dedication

To my dear husband, Jim, who has been my best collaborator in life and supportive of all my personal and professional efforts. To my children, Lindsey, Scott, Andy, and Marykate, of whom I am so proud. I have been completely fascinated observing your development and participating in your life as you became individuals with your own unique strengths. To my parents, Chester and Agatha, for teaching me to read, write, and explore to learn. To Dr. Joe L. Frost, who continues to be a mentor for whom I have much admiration. Especially, to all the persons with disabilities I have known who have inspired me and have given conviction to my life's work.

Preface

RATIONALE

Teaching young children today requires teachers to acquire a variety of skills and competencies to meet the changing needs of diverse groups of children and their families. Children growing up in the twenty-first century are part of a technologically advanced, interdependent, global society. Families experience life at a rapid pace in highly industrialized, urban areas. People have greater mobility, making world travel seem almost commonplace. As a result, it is becoming typical for groups of young children to represent greater linguistic, cultural, and ethnic diversity than in years past. Moreover, greater numbers of children with disabilities and special needs are being served in community, early childhood settings that formerly served only children with typical developmental patterns. Federal mandates require attention to the educational rights of children and have set a precedent in favor of inclusive education. Further, technological advances have permitted children with more severe disabilities and medically fragile conditions to be included in general, early childhood settings, such as child-care centers and public schools. Including children with special needs in classrooms has widened the range of ability represented in groups of young children. These trends have increased the complexity of inclusive early childhood classrooms.

The key premise of this book is that meeting the care and educational needs of all young children and their families today requires inclusive education with a highly collaborative approach that establishes strong lines of communication. Collaboration and communication are necessary among early childhood professionals and, most importantly, between families and schools. Inclusive education is a philosophical and methodological paradigm for early childhood education based on an interdisciplinary perspective. Teachers are expected to integrate principles and practices recommended by professionals across various disciplines and fields, such as traditional early childhood, special education, psychology, sociology, and multicultural education. The success of children in inclusive classrooms depends largely upon the ability of teachers to effectively use a full repertoire of teaching strategies and practices to differentiate curriculum and instruction. Further, it is critical for teachers to facilitate differentiated instruction by matching the type and intensity of strategies to children, so that each child receives individually appropriate support for learning. Ensuring the success of all young children, including those with special needs, requires teachers to be prepared to

background of research knowledge about the types of strategies that are considered "best practices." An interdisciplinary approach gleans strategies and practices from across fields in an integrative approach. Chapter 9, Identifying Effective Teaching Strategies and Practices, discusses the implications of brain research for identifying teaching strategies. Further, this chapter introduces teaching strategies on a continuum from least to most intrusive. The chapter ends with a discussion of naturalistic teaching strategies. Chapter 10, Differentiated Instruction with Individually Appropriate Support, discusses how to ensure access to the curriculum for all children by embedding teaching strategies that offer individually appropriate support to children. The book concludes with a chapter on assessment to inform instruction and evaluate teaching effectiveness. In Chapter 11, Assessing the Effectiveness of the Inclusive Classroom, readers learn key elements of evaluating children's progress and using the knowledge gained from individual assessment to plan the curricular activities. Assessment to inform teachers about the need for possible accommodations, modifications of the curriculum, or the use of adaptive technology is addressed.

ACKNOWLEDGMENTS

I am very grateful to Lindsey Rausch, an inclusive early childhood education teacher, who assisted in many ways, and shared her experiences and expertise with me. Lindsey has taught inclusive early childhood and kindergarten classrooms in different roles. She shared her experiences with me as a general education teacher and also as an early childhood special education teacher. Her proficiency in each of these roles was very apparent to me and I benefited immensely from her ideas on collaborating with families, related services personnel, and teachers. Lindsey's ideas helped to keep this book practical and true to life. I am also very grateful to Susan Veitschegger and Jessica Christian for sharing their thoughts and experiences on collaborating with teachers and families in community early childhood settings. The insights I gained from listening to their stories and observations were invaluable.

I owe a debt of gratitude to Dr. Blandina Cardenas, President of The University of Texas–Pan American. Through her example and advice, I learned much about community collaboration. Dr. Cardenas is an expert in social policy and leadership in early childhood and her insights regarding my efforts were appreciated. I would like to acknowledge and thank Mr. Dennis Campa, Director of the Department of Community

> **Note:** For ease of reading, the term *teacher* is frequently used in its broadest connotation. Whereas the term *teacher* is usually associated with school contexts, it is frequently used in a more liberal sense in early childhood contexts, especially those that are inclusive. Consequently, unless otherwise specified, this book refers to teachers as individuals representing a range of early childhood professionals who may fulfill the role of teacher in inclusive early childhood settings. Depending upon the setting, caregivers, public school teachers, specialists, and related services personnel may constitute a team of individuals who may share teaching responsibilities or participate in coteaching arrangements.

Preface

RATIONALE

Teaching young children today requires teachers to acquire a variety of skills and competencies to meet the changing needs of diverse groups of children and their families. Children growing up in the twenty-first century are part of a technologically advanced, interdependent, global society. Families experience life at a rapid pace in highly industrialized, urban areas. People have greater mobility, making world travel seem almost commonplace. As a result, it is becoming typical for groups of young children to represent greater linguistic, cultural, and ethnic diversity than in years past. Moreover, greater numbers of children with disabilities and special needs are being served in community, early childhood settings that formerly served only children with typical developmental patterns. Federal mandates require attention to the educational rights of children and have set a precedent in favor of inclusive education. Further, technological advances have permitted children with more severe disabilities and medically fragile conditions to be included in general, early childhood settings, such as child-care centers and public schools. Including children with special needs in classrooms has widened the range of ability represented in groups of young children. These trends have increased the complexity of inclusive early childhood classrooms.

The key premise of this book is that meeting the care and educational needs of all young children and their families today requires inclusive education with a highly collaborative approach that establishes strong lines of communication. Collaboration and communication are necessary among early childhood professionals and, most importantly, between families and schools. Inclusive education is a philosophical and methodological paradigm for early childhood education based on an interdisciplinary perspective. Teachers are expected to integrate principles and practices recommended by professionals across various disciplines and fields, such as traditional early childhood, special education, psychology, sociology, and multicultural education. The success of children in inclusive classrooms depends largely upon the ability of teachers to effectively use a full repertoire of teaching strategies and practices to differentiate curriculum and instruction. Further, it is critical for teachers to facilitate differentiated instruction by matching the type and intensity of strategies to children, so that each child receives individually appropriate support for learning. Ensuring the success of all young children, including those with special needs, requires teachers to be prepared to accommodate the individual learning needs of children. Most critical for successful inclusion is the ability of teachers to collaborate with others to support the development and learning of young children. The key relationship to establish is with the family, the first teachers of children. Effective working relationships formed with other teachers, support personnel, and the community require team planning. Moreover, collaborating with related services personnel, such as speech and language pathologists, occupational therapists, physical therapists, and other specialists, may also be necessary to meet the educational needs of certain children.

PURPOSE

The purpose of this textbook is to prepare early childhood professionals to implement a highly collaborative approach to inclusive education in today's increasingly diverse early childhood settings. These professionals may include teachers in general early childhood, early intervention/early childhood special education, and general education early elementary teaching assignments. These teachers may work in community-based child-care settings, early intervention sites, and public or private elementary schools. Specifically, this book will address two major objectives:

- To promote an understanding of the major principles recommended by research and standards set forth by professional organizations for inclusive education in early childhood
- To prepare teachers to effectively use an array of best practices with diverse groups of young children who may differ in culture, language, ability, income, and other important variables

STRENGTHS OF THIS TEXTBOOK

The key strength of this textbook is the practical information regarding the ways to collaborate and communicate with families and other professionals. This text answers the call for teachers to develop skills in collaboration and communication. Practical information and examples are woven into every chapter. Another strength of this textbook is the interweaving of *inclusion* and *diversity* issues and practices across all topics. Teachers must be culturally competent and responsive, as well as sensitive to children's abilities and strengths. *Inclusive Early Childhood Education: A Collaborative Approach* is a textbook that offers the following major strengths:

1. **A Collaborative Approach.** This textbook offers a balanced view of inclusive early childhood education in culturally and linguistically diverse settings. Readers will be challenged to view inclusive education from multiple perspectives, representing philosophical stances and recommended practices

gleaned from across disciplines and fields of education. An interdisciplinary approach integrates the principles and practices of relevant disciplines within each topic addressed. The book introduces different philosophical stances and practices to help early childhood professionals view inclusion from perspectives of professionals from various backgrounds of knowledge. This multiple perspectives approach will encourage early childhood professionals to develop broad bases of thought that are likely to result in a more effective collaboration in team planning and teaching scenarios. Further, a multiple perspectives approach may facilitate collaboration with parents and families, a strategy considered fundamental to the success of children in inclusive education programs.

2. **Practical Approach.** This text is aimed at preparing teachers in child-care and early childhood education programs that include a full range of learners. Typical classrooms implementing inclusive education represent a wide range of ability, from children with high ability or giftedness to those with severe challenges to their learning. These classrooms are likely to include young children with identified disabilities and at-risk children in a culturally and linguistically diverse group.

   The book will emphasize practical teaching strategies that are based on sound principles. Care is given to helping teachers integrate strategies and practices from across fields. Implementing inclusive education in typical early childhood classrooms requires teachers to facilitate learning for children who vary in background, language, ability, and other characteristics. Teachers need to be prepared to select compatible strategies and practices to help individual children work with their strengths within a diverse group configuration.

3. **Coherent Set of Principles and Practices.** Rather than merging the tenets and practices of two fields, early childhood and early childhood special education, as is often done by authors of inclusive education texts, this book approaches inclusion from a cross-disciplinary viewpoint. The philosophies and strategies of multiple disciplines and fields are blended into a coherent set of principles and practices designed for today's inclusive early childhood programs. Standards developed by professional organizations for teaching in diverse and inclusive early childhood classrooms are integrated into each chapter.

4. **Realistic View of Implementation.** Preservice teachers and those in the field want to know how they can accommodate individual learners while ensuring that all children in the group have opportunities to optimize their learning potential. Teachers know they are responsible for the learning of all children, and they seek strategies and practices that will be effective in the busy, demanding, real world of early childhood classrooms. One-to-one instruction for extended time periods is not an option in single-teacher classrooms.

background of research knowledge about the types of strategies that are considered "best practices." An interdisciplinary approach gleans strategies and practices from across fields in an integrative approach. Chapter 9, Identifying Effective Teaching Strategies and Practices, discusses the implications of brain research for identifying teaching strategies. Further, this chapter introduces teaching strategies on a continuum from least to most intrusive. The chapter ends with a discussion of naturalistic teaching strategies. Chapter 10, Differentiated Instruction with Individually Appropriate Support, discusses how to ensure access to the curriculum for all children by embedding teaching strategies that offer individually appropriate support to children. The book concludes with a chapter on assessment to inform instruction and evaluate teaching effectiveness. In Chapter 11, Assessing the Effectiveness of the Inclusive Classroom, readers learn key elements of evaluating children's progress and using the knowledge gained from individual assessment to plan the curricular activities. Assessment to inform teachers about the need for possible accommodations, modifications of the curriculum, or the use of adaptive technology is addressed.

ACKNOWLEDGMENTS

I am very grateful to Lindsey Rausch, an inclusive early childhood education teacher, who assisted in many ways, and shared her experiences and expertise with me. Lindsey has taught inclusive early childhood and kindergarten classrooms in different roles. She shared her experiences with me as a general education teacher and also as an early childhood special education teacher. Her proficiency in each of these roles was very apparent to me and I benefited immensely from her ideas on collaborating with families, related services personnel, and teachers. Lindsey's ideas helped to keep this book practical and true to life. I am also very grateful to Susan Veitschegger and Jessica Christian for sharing their thoughts and experiences on collaborating with teachers and families in community early childhood settings. The insights I gained from listening to their stories and observations were invaluable.

I owe a debt of gratitude to Dr. Blandina Cardenas, President of The University of Texas–Pan American. Through her example and advice, I learned much about community collaboration. Dr. Cardenas is an expert in social policy and leadership in early childhood and her insights regarding my efforts were appreciated. I would like to acknowledge and thank Mr. Dennis Campa, Director of the Department of Community

Note: For ease of reading, the term *teacher* is frequently used in its broadest connotation. Whereas the term *teacher* is usually associated with school contexts, it is frequently used in a more liberal sense in early childhood contexts, especially those that are inclusive. Consequently, unless otherwise specified, this book refers to teachers as individuals representing a range of early childhood professionals who may fulfill the role of teacher in inclusive early childhood settings. Depending upon the setting, caregivers, public school teachers, specialists, and related services personnel may constitute a team of individuals who may share teaching responsibilities or participate in coteaching arrangements.

gleaned from across disciplines and fields of education. An interdisciplinary approach integrates the principles and practices of relevant disciplines within each topic addressed. The book introduces different philosophical stances and practices to help early childhood professionals view inclusion from perspectives of professionals from various backgrounds of knowledge. This multiple perspectives approach will encourage early childhood professionals to develop broad bases of thought that are likely to result in a more effective collaboration in team planning and teaching scenarios. Further, a multiple perspectives approach may facilitate collaboration with parents and families, a strategy considered fundamental to the success of children in inclusive education programs.

2. **Practical Approach.** This text is aimed at preparing teachers in child-care and early childhood education programs that include a full range of learners. Typical classrooms implementing inclusive education represent a wide range of ability, from children with high ability or giftedness to those with severe challenges to their learning. These classrooms are likely to include young children with identified disabilities and at-risk children in a culturally and linguistically diverse group.

   The book will emphasize practical teaching strategies that are based on sound principles. Care is given to helping teachers integrate strategies and practices from across fields. Implementing inclusive education in typical early childhood classrooms requires teachers to facilitate learning for children who vary in background, language, ability, and other characteristics. Teachers need to be prepared to select compatible strategies and practices to help individual children work with their strengths within a diverse group configuration.

3. **Coherent Set of Principles and Practices.** Rather than merging the tenets and practices of two fields, early childhood and early childhood special education, as is often done by authors of inclusive education texts, this book approaches inclusion from a cross-disciplinary viewpoint. The philosophies and strategies of multiple disciplines and fields are blended into a coherent set of principles and practices designed for today's inclusive early childhood programs. Standards developed by professional organizations for teaching in diverse and inclusive early childhood classrooms are integrated into each chapter.

4. **Realistic View of Implementation.** Preservice teachers and those in the field want to know how they can accommodate individual learners while ensuring that all children in the group have opportunities to optimize their learning potential. Teachers know they are responsible for the learning of all children, and they seek strategies and practices that will be effective in the busy, demanding, real world of early childhood classrooms. One-to-one instruction for extended time periods is not an option in single-teacher classrooms.

The realistic approach toward inclusion taken in this book sets it apart from other texts on the same topic. Preservice teachers require clear examples that illustrate how strategies and practices can be implemented within the contexts of real classrooms. Early childhood classrooms are complex, dynamic, social milieus. Teachers must manage classroom activities and facilitate the learning of all the children simultaneously. Preservice teachers must acquire the skills and confidence to be able to meet individual needs of children within diverse group contexts.

Given serious logistical barriers and time constraints, teachers want realistic answers regarding how to implement inclusive strategies and practices. Teachers in community child-care settings often have little or no paid time allotted specifically for planning. They often face budget constraints that hamper their efforts to provide an enriching environment for children. Training is frequently limited, especially concerning teaching children with special needs. This text will answer many of the questions that might otherwise undermine the confidence of teachers facing the challenge of providing inclusive education programs to young children in early childhood settings. The book will provide teachers with numerous vignettes that describe inclusive classrooms realistically. Case study scenarios with follow-up questions will be provided to aid discussion and in-depth analysis. Vignettes will help teachers gain a clear understanding of how teachers in inclusive classrooms structure the environment, facilitate learning, and manage classroom activities. Most important, the vignettes will give teachers examples of how they can meet the individual needs of children and maintain an optimal learning environment for all children in the classroom.

ORGANIZATION

Inclusive Early Childhood Education: A Collaborative Approach engages students with a wealth of information and practical applications. The narrative is highly readable with an abundance of examples using real-world situations. A variety of features make this text attractive and appealing to students. Each chapter begins with a graphic organizer and a list of chapter objectives or outcomes to help students gain an initial overview of the chapter contents. Chapters are organized around a set of principles to guide practice. These principles will be stated in a straightforward manner so they are simple to comprehend. Textbook sections that follow each principle will describe the strategies and practices that equip teachers with the attitudes and tools needed to successfully address each principle in their inclusive programs. As previously described, a key feature of this text is the use of stories based on real classroom scenarios. These vignettes will be used for illustration of key points in the chapter and for problem-solving exercises that students will ponder in small groups during class or independently as homework assignments.

Part I: An Effective Educator

For teachers, creating a classroom for all children begins with an understanding of the kinds of lives children and families lead within the contexts of their community and the larger society. This understanding becomes the foundational premise for setting professional and personal goals as an early childhood teacher. Consequently, Part I emphasizes the sociocontextual background that currently underlies inclusive education theory and pedagogy.

Chapter 1, Teaching All Children, informs the reader of the historical and sociopolitical contexts that continue to propel the movement toward creating classrooms that are inclusive of all children. The reader will learn about the myriad factors that exert an influence on the field of early childhood education. Chapter 1 also includes an examination of philosophical stances that have resulted in changes in pedagogical approaches to teaching young children. The major goals for early childhood education are identified for readers. Further, the various ways teaching professionals can address these goals are outlined with the introduction of eight key principles for inclusive education.

Chapter 2, A Professional Educator, describes the role of a teaching professional in early childhood education. Responsibilities for teaching children with a wide range of abilities who also represent diverse cultural and linguistic backgrounds are outlined. Chapter 3, Collaborating with Families and the Community, describes how teachers can meet the changing needs of children and families. This chapter provides information about creating positive relationships with families and ways teachers can learn about the community to which each family belongs. Part I ends with Chapter 4, Diversity and Inclusive Classrooms, which describes the characteristics of diverse groups of young children being served today in various early childhood classroom settings.

Part II: Creating a Classroom for All Children

This section helps teachers plan and set up an effective physical and social learning context for their inclusive classroom. Chapter 5, Planning Differentiated Curriculum and Instruction, makes teachers aware of critical selection factors and planning to ensure a "good fit" of curricular activities for all children. Chapter 6, Creating a Positive Social and Emotional Climate, helps teachers consider the social and emotional support needed by children. Chapter 7, Designing an Inclusive Physical Environment, discusses space, furnishings, equipment, and materials for an inclusive early childhood classroom. Safety and accessibility are key factors addressed. Chapter 8, Managing, Guiding, and Organizing the Classroom, provides teachers with effective strategies for managing daily tasks, scheduling, and setting up classroom routines.

Part III: Effective Teaching in an Inclusive Classroom

The chapters in this section of the book help readers gain the knowledge and tools to identify and effectively implement inclusive teaching strategies. These chapters build a

background of research knowledge about the types of strategies that are considered "best practices." An interdisciplinary approach gleans strategies and practices from across fields in an integrative approach. Chapter 9, Identifying Effective Teaching Strategies and Practices, discusses the implications of brain research for identifying teaching strategies. Further, this chapter introduces teaching strategies on a continuum from least to most intrusive. The chapter ends with a discussion of naturalistic teaching strategies. Chapter 10, Differentiated Instruction with Individually Appropriate Support, discusses how to ensure access to the curriculum for all children by embedding teaching strategies that offer individually appropriate support to children. The book concludes with a chapter on assessment to inform instruction and evaluate teaching effectiveness. In Chapter 11, Assessing the Effectiveness of the Inclusive Classroom, readers learn key elements of evaluating children's progress and using the knowledge gained from individual assessment to plan the curricular activities. Assessment to inform teachers about the need for possible accommodations, modifications of the curriculum, or the use of adaptive technology is addressed.

ACKNOWLEDGMENTS

I am very grateful to Lindsey Rausch, an inclusive early childhood education teacher, who assisted in many ways, and shared her experiences and expertise with me. Lindsey has taught inclusive early childhood and kindergarten classrooms in different roles. She shared her experiences with me as a general education teacher and also as an early childhood special education teacher. Her proficiency in each of these roles was very apparent to me and I benefited immensely from her ideas on collaborating with families, related services personnel, and teachers. Lindsey's ideas helped to keep this book practical and true to life. I am also very grateful to Susan Veitschegger and Jessica Christian for sharing their thoughts and experiences on collaborating with teachers and families in community early childhood settings. The insights I gained from listening to their stories and observations were invaluable.

I owe a debt of gratitude to Dr. Blandina Cardenas, President of The University of Texas–Pan American. Through her example and advice, I learned much about community collaboration. Dr. Cardenas is an expert in social policy and leadership in early childhood and her insights regarding my efforts were appreciated. I would like to acknowledge and thank Mr. Dennis Campa, Director of the Department of Community

Note: For ease of reading, the term *teacher* is frequently used in its broadest connotation. Whereas the term *teacher* is usually associated with school contexts, it is frequently used in a more liberal sense in early childhood contexts, especially those that are inclusive. Consequently, unless otherwise specified, this book refers to teachers as individuals representing a range of early childhood professionals who may fulfill the role of teacher in inclusive early childhood settings. Depending upon the setting, caregivers, public school teachers, specialists, and related services personnel may constitute a team of individuals who may share teaching responsibilities or participate in coteaching arrangements.

Initiatives of the City of San Antonio, Texas, for sharing his vision of family strengthening with me. I appreciate the insights he provided regarding collaboration with families involved in formal and informal care and education settings. I am grateful for the many opportunities I have had to be involved in community-based participatory programs for children and families.

The writing of this book was enhanced by what I learned through collaboration with various community agencies and organizations involved in the Early On School Readiness Project of the City of San Antonio, including:

AVANCE, Inc.
Family Service Association, Inc.
YWCA
KLRN Television
Positive Beginnings, Inc.
Parent Child Inc. Head Start Programs
Even Start Program, Northside Independent School District (ISD)
San Antonio ISD
Judson ISD
Harlandale ISD
South San ISD
Edgewood ISD
Northeast ISD

I would like to thank Mr. Victor Azios and all the members of the Making Connection San Antonio Site, Results Group #6, sponsored by the Annie E. Casey Foundation. The members are too numerous to name; however, I would like to give special thanks to Martha Castilla, Director of the Edgewood Family Network, for her willingness to collaborate and help us to learn more about collaboration with families in her community.

Finally, I wish to thank the editors and staff at Merrill/Prentice Hall. I would like to express my sincere gratitude to Ann Davis and Allyson Sharp, who guided me through this writing experience. I am most appreciative of the good advice, thoughtful analyses, and patience each of you offered.

I would like to acknowledge and thank all the reviewers of this text. I am grateful for the time and thoughtful ideas each reviewer gave toward the improvement of this text: Karen Applequist, Northern Arizona University; Geralyn Anderson Arango, Holy Family University; Barbara A. Beakley, Millersville University; Alice D. Beyrent, Hesser College; Janetta L. Bradley, University of Tennessee at Chattanooga; Marie Brand, SUNY New Paltz; Colleen Klein-Ezell, University of Central Florida–Brevard; Roberta Grawemeyer, Columbus State University; Ann Gruenberg, Eastern Connecticut State University; Joan Lieber, University of Maryland; Barbara Lowenthal, Northeastern Illinois University; Lorraine Martin, Grossmont College; Ruth McBride, Colorado State University; Maureen R. Norris, Bellarmine University; Rebecca B. Oekerman, University of Texas–Permian Basin; and Sharon Rosenkoetter, Oregon State University.

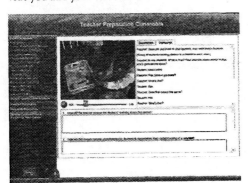

Teacher Preparation Classroom

TEACHER PREP

**MERRILL
PRENTICE HALL**

Your Class. Their Careers. Our Future. Will your students be prepared?

We invite you to explore our new, innovative and engaging website and all that it has to offer you, your course, and tomorrow's educators! Organized around the major courses pre-service teachers take, the Teacher Preparation site provides media, student/teacher artifacts, strategies, research articles, and other resources to equip your students with the quality tools needed to excel in their courses and prepare them for their first classroom.

This ultimate on-line education resource is available at no cost, when packaged with a Merrill text, and will provide you and your students access to:

Online Video Library

More than 150 video clips—each tied to a course topic and framed by learning goals and Praxis-type questions—capture real teachers and students working in real classrooms, as well as in-depth interviews with both students and educators.

Student and Teacher Artifacts

More than 200 student and teacher classroom artifacts—each tied to a course topic and framed by learning goals and application questions—provide a wealth of materials and experiences to help make your study to become a professional teacher more concrete and hands-on.

Research Articles. Over 500 articles from ASCD's renowned journal *Educational Leadership*. The site also includes Research Navigator, a searchable database of additional educational journals.

Teaching Strategies. Over 500 strategies and lesson plans for you to use when you become a practicing professional.

Licensure and Career Tools. Resources devoted to helping you pass your licensure exam; learn standards, law, and public policies; plan a teaching portfolio; and succeed in your first year of teaching.

Discover the Merrill Resources for Special Education Website

Technology is a constantly growing and changing aspect of our field that is creating a need for new content and resources. To address this emerging need, Merrill Education has developed an online learning environment for students, teachers, and professors alike to complement our products—the *Merrill Resources for Special Education* Website. This content-rich website provides additional resources specific to this book's topic and will help you—professors, classroom teachers, and students—augment your teaching, learning, and professional development.

Our goal with this initiative is to build on and enhance what our products already offer. For this reason, the content for our user-friendly website is organized by topic and provides teachers, professors, and students with a variety of meaningful resources all in one location. With this website, we bring together the best of what Merrill has to offer: text resources, video clips, web links, tutorials, and a wide variety of information on topics of interest to general and special educators alike. Rich content, applications, and competencies further enhance the learning process.

The *Merrill Resources for Special Education* Website includes:

- Video clips specific to each topic, with questions to help you evaluate the content and make crucial theory-to-practice connections.
- Thought-providing critical analysis questions that students can answer and turn in for evaluation or that can serve as basis for class discussions and lectures.
- Access to a wide variety of resources related to classroom strategies and methods, including lesson planning and classroom management.
- Information on all the most current relevant topics related to special and general education, including CEC and Praxis™ standards, IEPs, portfolios, and professional development.
- Extensive web resources and overviews on each topic addressed on the website.
- A search feature to help access specific information quickly.

To take advantage of these and other resources, please visit the *Merrill Resources for Special Education* Website at

http://www.prenhall.com/winter

Brief Contents

Contents

Note: Every effort has been made to provide accurate and current Internet information in this book. However, the Internet and information posted on it are constantly changing, so it is inevitable that some of the Internet addresses listed in this textbook will change.

PART I

An Effective Educator

Chapter 1

Teaching All Children

Objectives

After reading this chapter you will be able to:

1. Outline the legal, social, and historical contexts underpinning inclusive early childhood education.
2. Explain the basic principles of IDEA, such as zero reject, least restrictive environment, and procedural due process.
3. Discuss the changing needs of children and their families.
4. List the major factors that contribute to school failure.
5. Define the terms related to inclusive education.
6. State the rationale for a collaborative approach to inclusive education.
7. Explain the key principles for inclusive education.

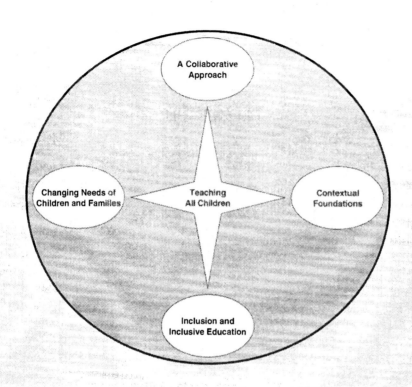

INTRODUCTION

This chapter addresses the teaching of all young children in today's increasingly diverse society. It is critical for teachers to provide inclusive early childhood education that meets the needs of all young children and involves their families in active, reciprocal partnerships. Teachers and other early childhood professionals approach collaboration from many different perspectives. This chapter identifies and explains these various perspectives. It specifies key principles to guide inclusive education in early childhood. Further, this chapter discusses the changing needs of families and the potential barriers that families often encounter in trying to care for and educate their children. The discussion identifies societal trends and changes that have exerted an impact children and families. Finally, this chapter traces how inclusive early childhood education has evolved to meet the needs of children. The implications of societal change and the evolution of the profession in which teachers who strive to help all children become successful learners are addressed.

A COLLABORATIVE APPROACH TO INCLUSION

Early childhood care and education settings serve increasingly diverse groups of children. It is rapidly becoming common to find that children in the class speak more than one language and represent culturally diverse family backgrounds. The inclusion of children with disabilities or other special needs has also become rather typical. Children who are gifted and talented further widen the span of ability levels served in inclusive classrooms. The early childhood classrooms of the United States are not alone in these demographic transformations. Schools of other industrialized nations in our global society are also experiencing similar trends (Stedman, 1997).

The complexity of teaching in an inclusive early childhood education classroom today requires innovative approaches to teaching. Few classrooms have single teachers assigned to meet the needs of all children. Typically, teams of professionals, who bring a collaborative approach to teaching, support most inclusive early childhood classrooms. Such teams actively pursue efforts to establish reciprocal partnerships with parents and involve families in all aspects of their children's care and education. Hence, collaboration, with an emphasis on teamwork and establishing strong lines of communication among all stakeholders, is emerging as essential to promote the development and learning of all young children.

Whereas logic and legislation might appear to support the notion of collaborative approaches to inclusion, forming such collaborations is far from simple. Theoretically, collaboration of teachers, family members, and related services professionals should be effective. However, in actual practice, many teachers find it difficult to develop collaborative relationships. Many barriers can impede good communication and the coordination of efforts necessary for success.

Practicing inclusion and collaborating with others requires professional commitment on the part of teachers. Understanding how inclusive early childhood education has evolved and understanding the underpinnings of the inclusive movement are critical steps toward successful teaching in inclusive early childhood classrooms. The following sections describe the foundation of fundamental concepts and principles that guide implementation of inclusive education. Gaining an inclusive education perspective also requires teachers to understand the historical and sociopolitical contexts that have propelled the inclusive education movement in the United States.

CONTEXTUAL FOUNDATIONS FOR INCLUSIVE EDUCATION

A confluence of interrelated conditions has provided the contextual foundation for the inclusive education movement in the United States. A variety of situational trends, factors, and variables have shaped theory, legislation, and practice, and have moved toward greater inclusiveness in early childhood classrooms. Some of these are social factors, such as popular beliefs and perceptions that underlie the social thought commonly held by people in society. Other variables and trends include the nation's political structure and economic status, and the increasing number of cultural heritages. Both past and present trends have shaped inclusive early childhood education. Consequently, many philosophies and practices in early childhood education have historical contexts, meaning either they are based on traditions passed on from prior generations, or that their influence can be traced to previous historical circumstances and events. In sum, past and current political, economic, cultural, and social trends or occurrences have become the contextual foundations underlying inclusive early childhood education today.

Historical and Sociopolitical Contexts

Providing inclusive education for all children is an innovation that is predicated by historical and sociopolitical contexts. Some of the factors reflect the sociopolitical contexts of the present, and others trace their roots to earlier times in history. These earlier events, influences, and subsequent legislation provide the historical context or foundation for the present-day concept of inclusive education.

Civil rights and educational equity. The roots of the inclusive education movement can be traced back to the beginnings of public education and the intent to provide an equal chance for immigrant children to gain an education (Olsen, 1994). Although educational equity has yet to be truly achieved, seeking equal rights and equal education has long been part of the American dream. Equal opportunities for an education were improved through the civil rights movement. *Brown v. Board of Education Topeka* (1954) ushered in an era of concern for equal rights for racial minorities. This landmark case was a turning point in civil rights and the education of minority children because it ruled that schools could not be segregated by race. The Civil Rights Act followed in 1964; however, racial and ethnic groups continued to face challenges as they attempted to achieve equal opportunities and equal education (Banks, 1993; Darling-Hammond, 1996). Box 1.1 summarizes major legislation and case law that influenced the social and political context and improved the education of minority children.

Rights for children with disabilities. The civil rights movement of the 1960s signaled a trend toward social consciousness of the rights of minority groups. In the late 1960s, a movement began to advocate for an extension of those rights to individuals with disabilities. The rights of children with disabilities and special needs to receive a free and appropriate public education have been established through federal statutes and court decisions.

The Individuals with Disabilities Education Act (IDEA) was the landmark legislation that mandated key tenets that are still enforced today:

1. *Free, appropriate public education (FAPE).* All children have the right to a public education that is individualized and goal oriented. An Individualized Education Program (IEP) is planned for each eligible child.

2. *Zero reject.* All children of school age are served in public education without exclusion.

EQUITABLE EDUCATION   BOX 1.1

MAJOR LEGISLATIVE AND JUDICIAL INFLUENCES
Poverty and Minorities

LEGISLATION/CASE	PROVISIONS
1954, *Brown v. Board of Ed. Topeka*	• Ruled against school segregation by race
1964, Civil Rights Act	• Ensured equal rights to minorities
1965, The Head Start Act	• Early education and comprehensive services for preschoolers in poverty
1965, Elementary Secondary Education Act (ESEA)	• Improved resources for schools serving economically disadvantaged children and families
1968, The Bilingual Education Act	• Provided for bilingual education in public schools
1972, The Economic Opportunity Act	• Enrollment in Head Start must include 10% children with disabilities
1974, *Lau v. Nichols*	• Language minority children entitled to assistance needed for school participation

3. *Least restrictive environment.* Children with disabilities have the right to be educated with their nondisabled peers to the maximum extent appropriate for the child.

4. *Nondiscriminatory evaluation.* To determine eligibility and monitor performance, diagnostic evaluations must be fair and unbiased. Assessments must be selected considering the culture and language of the child.

5. *Participation of parents and child.* Parents and adolescent students should be collaborated with in the decision-making process to determine the special education program needed.

6. *Procedural due process.* When parents cannot reach agreement with the school, they have the right to mediation or hearings to resolve differences.

Box 1.2 and Box 1.3 summarize the key legislation and cases that propelled the rights for those with disabilities and special needs, including landmark legislation that changed society and accessibility for individuals with disabilities to all aspects of society, including educational opportunities (H. R. Turnbull, III, 1993; R. Turnbull, 2002).

CHILDREN WITH DISABILITIES   BOX 1.2

EARLY LEGISLATIVE AND JUDICIAL INFLUENCES

LEGISLATION/CASE	PROVISIONS
1968, The Handicapped Children's Early Education Assistance Act, P.L. 90–538	• Initiated demonstration models for early intervention programs
1973, Section 504 of The Rehabilitation Act	• Prohibited discriminating against persons with disabilities enrolling in federally funded schools and preschool programs (e.g., Head Start)
1975, The Education for All Handicapped Children Act (EAHCA), P.L. 94–142	• Landmark legislation granted free, appropriate, public education (FAPE) to children with disabilities, aged 5–21 years • Granted assurances, such as individualized education program (IEP), least restrictive environment (LRE)
1986, Infants & Toddlers with Disabilities Act, P.L. 99–457	• Services to preschool children with disabilities, individualized family service plan (IFSP)
1990, Americans with Disabilities Act (ADA) P.L. 101–336	• Prohibited discrimination against people with disabilities in all community settings: child care, private schools, and after-school programs
1990, Individuals with Disabilities Education Act (IDEA), P.L. 101–476	• Reauthorized P.L. 94–142 and introduced child-first language (e.g., child with visual impairment)
1992, *Oberti v. Board of Education*	• Case upheld right of child with disabilities to attend general education classroom

Gender. The women's rights movement ushered in an era of concern in the 1970s about the equity of males and females in educational settings. Although the Civil Rights Act prohibits discrimination by sex, those rights did not extend to children in schools until 1972, with the passage of Title IX of the Education Amendments Act. The intent was to provide more egalitarian treatment of females and males in all aspects of schooling including policies, admissions, and participation in programs (Underwood & Mead, 1995). The law gradually has improved educational equity for females, although educational discrimination can still be found (Sadker & Sadker, 1994; Sadker, Sadker, & Long, 1997). It is critical to continue to address gender equity in schools, beginning in the impressionable early childhood years. Women are entering the

CHILDREN WITH DISABILITIES   BOX 1.3

LATER LEGISLATIVE AND JUDICIAL INFLUENCES

LEGISLATION/CASE	PROVISIONS
1997, The IDEA Amendments, P.L. 105–17	• Expanded IEP team to include general education teacher and other professionals • Added provisions related to discipline and behavioral intervention • No exemption from state or district assessments • Developmental delay expanded to age 9 years • Greater access to general education curriculum and nonacademic activities • IFSP services delivered in natural settings
1998, Assistive Technology Act, P.L. 105–394, S.2432	• Rights to assistive technology and services to children with disabilities
2004, Individuals with Disabilities Education Improvement Act (IDEIA), P.L. 108–446	• Reauthorization of IDEA • Streamlined IEP Process • Strengthens emphasis on school readiness • Part C early intervention until kindergarten • Aligns with No Child Left Behind • Prevents disproportionate identification of minorities • New authority to schools for discipline • Emphasis on K-3 behavioral and academic intervention • Defines highly qualified teachers

workforce at a high rate, and nearly half of the workforce consists of women. Women need support and encouragement to ensure their success in school and to be properly prepared for success in the workforce (American Association of University Women, 1991).

Gifted and talented. Although most people agree that gifted and talented children have much to contribute to the future of society, the education of these children has been approached with ambivalence. It is commonly thought that children of high ability will be successful without assistance in their education. Governmental policy has offered meager support for the education of gifted and talented children (see Box 1.4). With the launching of Sputnik in the 1950s, a short period of interest in children of high ability occurred in reaction to public perception that the United States was falling

Law guarantees equal opportunities for girls and boys to participate in school activities and programs.

GIFTED AND TALENTED   BOX 1.4

Legislative Influences

LEGISLATION	PROVISIONS
1978, Title IX Part A, The Gifted Children Education Act	• Added services for gifted and talented children. Funding ended in 1982.
1988, Jacob K. Javits Gifted Student Education Act (ESEA)	• Added funding for education of gifted and talented children.

behind in science and math skills. It was not until the late 1970s that Americans created policy to provide services for children with talents in academics, leadership, or the arts. Unfortunately, the support was short lived, ending in 1982. The only other support specifically allocated for giftedness occurred in 1988, with the Jacob K. Javits Act, part of the Elementary and Secondary Education Act (ESEA) (Gallagher, 1994; Imbeau, 1999; Seefeldt & Barbour, 1994). Unfortunately, funding for services for gifted and talented children is still very limited. According to results of a 1990 national survey, only two cents per one hundred dollars is spent on education of school-aged children identified as gifted and talented (U.S. Department of Education, 1993).

School reform and inclusion. School reform and inclusion are inextricably intertwined from both philosophical and ethical perspectives. The primary goal of school reform is to increase the chances for each child to achieve success within the American educational system. The fundamental idea that all children, regardless of differences in socioeconomic status, family origin, ability, or other variations, deserve an opportunity for an equitable education is grounded in civil rights principles. Given that premise, school reform and the inclusive education movement have an undeniable kinship in promoting social justice for marginalized children in our nation's schools. The clear implication is that schools have an obligation not only to accept the differences of children, but also have a moral imperative to accommodate all children through differentiated instruction.

Reconceptualizing schools requires policy makers at all levels to uphold the civil rights of children and address the changing needs of families that affect their children's education. Further, educators have an obligation to ensure that accommodation is not interpreted as simplification of the curriculum. Children have a right to experience high expectations for their success and the supports necessary to achieve their individual educational goals (Baglieri & Knopf, 2004).

Many consider restructuring schools to offer greater educational access and legitimate challenges to all children to be essential to school reform. Some believe that unless schools reform toward achieving greater inclusiveness, society risks perpetuation of social inequities related to gender, race, ethnicity, socioeconomic status, and ability. Teachers may inadvertently maintain the status quo and existing disparities unless educational systems take active steps to promote educational equity (Grossman & Grossman, 1994). It has been suggested that viewing differences and disabilities of children as negative often leads to differential treatment and marginalization (Miller, 2001; Shapiro, 2000). Instead, recognizing children's differences from a more positive viewpoint as variations promotes acceptance and inclusiveness (Thomas & Loxley, 2001).

Emphasis on early years. To achieve the goal of academic excellence for all children, it is critical to begin early. In 1989, national attention focused on school reform and early childhood when President George H. W. Bush announced a set of national goals with the intent of improving the education of children by the year 2000. Most significant for early childhood education, the Goals 2000 initiative focused on the importance of the early years of a child's life toward ensuring success in school. Many previous school reform efforts concentrated on affecting outcomes through strategies aimed at secondary schools. An important anchor of the initiative was a focus on the early childhood years prior to formal school entry. The primary challenge President Bush set forth to the nation was to find effective ways to ensure that young children came to school "ready to learn." This challenge aimed school reform efforts at preventive measures and the changing needs of children and families in modern society. Emphasis was placed on the quality of life that Americans provide for children aged six years and younger. The nation was challenged to marshal resources and develop programs to ensure that all young children have access to high-quality care and educational experiences as a means of promoting better school outcomes for all children. The message to Americans was that positive outcomes for children could be achieved if children reached school age better prepared to learn in formal classroom settings.

Major research efforts were spawned, including the Carnegie Foundation reports, that helped to awaken the nation to the state of the educational system and the serious need for reform (Carnegie Task Force, 1994, 1996). Research brought to the forefront the plight of young children who are at risk of school failure. Reports enlightened the public to the inferior quality of many child-care facilities and schools in the United States.

Strong empirical evidence underscored the importance of the first three years of a child's life in determining a child's capacity to learn. In 1996, the Dana Alliance for Brain Initiatives reported that an accumulating body of evidence supported the significance of the early years. Brain research indicated that early stimulation of the senses and social experiences impact the neurological development of children and set the course of their intellectual development (Dana Alliance for Brain Initiatives, 1996). During this short window of opportunity, there are critical periods in which development of language, motor, and other areas is most efficient (Gallahue, 1995; Kuhl, 1994). Clearly, nations intending to compete in the global economy must focus significant attention on young children and the families who nurture them. Maximizing the potential of children requires societies to allocate resources in ways that will ensure all children receive proper stimulation for growth and learning.

To be effective, school reform efforts must begin before a child reaches kindergarten. Early experiences and opportunities for children to learn in home and in child-care settings are foundational to later school success. Advocates have called for high-quality child care in the United States to be available to all children who need care outside the home (Children's Defense Fund, 2005; Zigler & Finn-Stevenson, 1995). The federal commitment to early childhood education has increased noticeably over the last 20 years. This positive trend has resulted in a greater number of options for the delivery of early education and intervention services (Hemmeter, 2000). Accumulated research examining the impact of Head Start programs has consistently indicated positive results. Preschool programs yield benefits in IQ and achievement that persist beyond high school graduation. Research confirms these positive outcomes and validates assertions that preschool is "the most important grade" (Barnett & Hustedt, 2003, pp. 1, 54, 57).

However, we need to know more about specific practices that make a difference, especially for children who are seriously at risk of school failure. Consequently, simply offering more early childhood programs is not sufficient to maximize opportunities for children to succeed. For high-quality early childhood education and intervention programs, the extant research base defining effective practices in early childhood settings needs expansion to better inform educators about best practices. Validation of instructional approaches through empirical study will improve the effectiveness of early intervention efforts. Finally, it is important to know more about implementation of strategies and practices. It would be beneficial to learn from studies that determine the effects of more comprehensive implementation of practices over time. It is also critical to know the effects of various practices with children who have specific developmental or learning disabilities (Blok, Fukkink, Gebhardt, & Leseman, 2005; Hemmeter, 2000).

Sociocultural Contexts

As the cultural fabric of society becomes increasingly diverse, social patterns are growing exceedingly complex. Various social and cultural factors have combined to create intricate sociocultural contexts in schools and communities across the United States. Children's development and learning are shaped by the sociocultural contexts in which they live. These sociocultural contexts influence the lenses through which behavior and situations are interpreted (Delpit, 1995). Parents and teachers from different sociocultural contexts may vary in how they interpret the behaviors of children and how they view the developmental progress of children (Rogoff, Mistry, Goncu, & Mosier, 1993). Similarly, the sociocultural contexts influence what children learn, how they interpret their experiences and social interactions, and how they view teachers and schools (Ramsey, 1987). These culturally specific interpretations are learned early. Consequently, young children in culturally diverse early childhood settings may face conflicts between their interpretations and those of other children or teachers (Gonzalez-Mena, 2001; Rogoff, 1990). Recognizing the influence of sociocultural contexts on the learning, competencies, and achievements of children is crucial for teachers of all children (Bowman & Stott, 1994; Phillips, 1994; Ramsey, 1995). Furthermore, to help young children succeed within the complex sociocultural contexts of schools and communities, many are calling for more inclusive approaches to early childhood education (Atwater, Carta, Schwartz, & McConnell, 1994; Buysse, Wesley, & Skinner, 1999).

Intercultural competence and communication. The varied sociocultural context of communities presents a number of challenges for teaching all children in early childhood settings. One major challenge for teachers is to establish effective communication with families from various cultural and linguistic backgrounds. To achieve this goal, communication scientists recommend that teachers acquire proficiency in verbal and nonverbal communication skills. Further, communication skills must be embedded in an intercultural competence that enables a teacher to make good predictions about how his or her communications will be perceived by parents with dissimilar backgrounds (Gudykunst & Kim, 1992; Sturm, 1997). Likewise, teachers have an obligation

Learning cultural competence
begins early through interaction
with children from diverse
family backgrounds.

to prepare all children for living in a global community that requires competence in social interaction and communication with people of dissimilar backgrounds. Therefore,
children need to develop intercultural competence and adeptness in communication
skills. Teachers in inclusive classrooms can draw from research in the field of multicultural education. For success in a global society, teachers must provide opportunities for
children to acquire a broad range of social understandings, academic knowledge, and
linguistic skills.

CHANGING NEEDS OF CHILDREN AND THEIR FAMILIES

Today's early childhood teachers must be cognizant of the changing needs of children
and their families. Demographic shifts and emerging trends that affect families have
implications for inclusive classrooms and the role of parents in their children's education. It is widely acknowledged that parents are the first teachers of their children.
However, the needs of families and the ways parents are attempting to meet those needs
directly influence the amount of time and resources that parents have available for assuming their teaching role. Teachers must realize that family life today is a complex
ecology of people, relationships, and situations. A wide variety of events and conditions
affect children and families and influence the quality of their lives. Early childhood education is most effective when it reflects an understanding of the different family contexts that exist for each child.

An Ecological Perspective

Approaching early childhood education from an *ecological perspective* can help teachers to identify the various influences that make up the ecology surrounding children and their families(Odom & Wolery, 2003). Urie Bronfenbrenner proposed an ecological system model to explain the different levels of influence on children and their development within a society (see Figure 1.1). Bronfenbrenner envisioned overlapping systems exerting an influence on a child's growth and development. The model can be depicted with a child in the center surrounded by concentric circles moving outward from the child. These circles depict interacting layers of variables that impact the child's development. The inner layer, microsystem, consists of people who are in direct contact

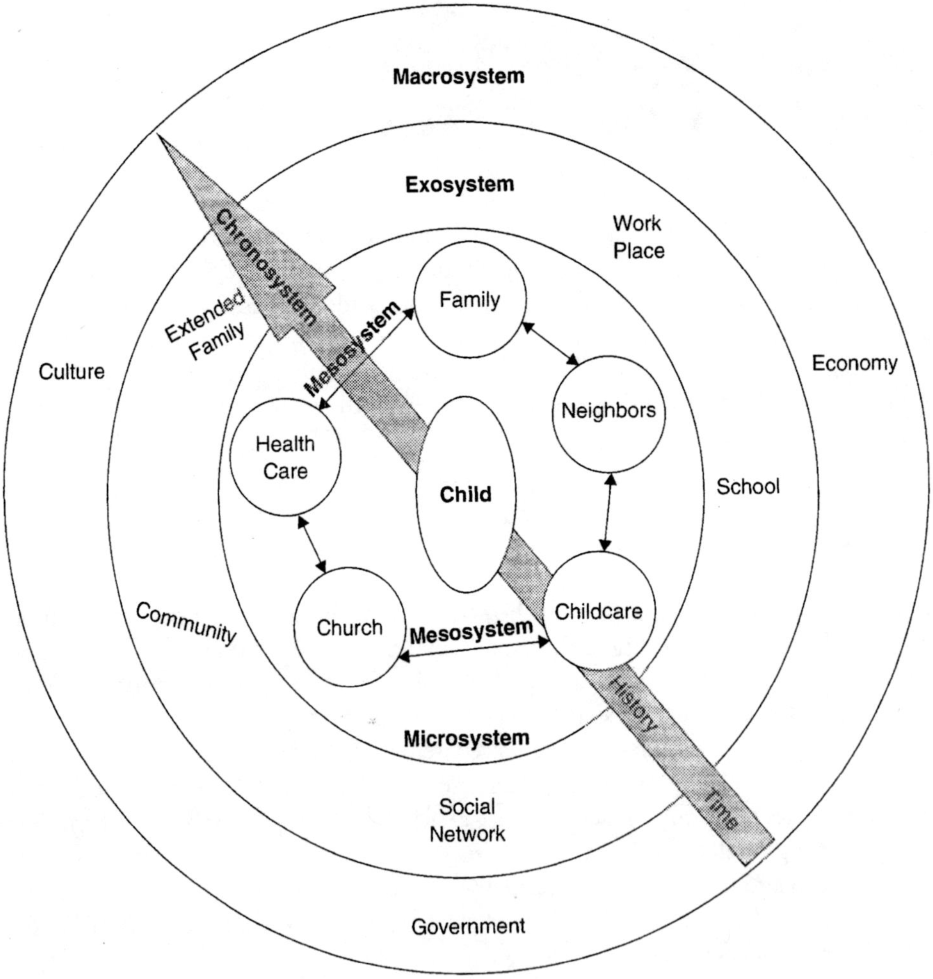

Figure 1.1   Bronfenbrenner's Ecological Theory of Development

with the child, such as family members, child-care providers, religious communities, and peers. Family, school, and neighborhood are the primary influences in the lives of the child. There are interactions among people in each group represented in the microsystem. For example, families might be influenced by people in church or their interactions with teachers. Mesosystem is the term used to describe the interactions that occur between influential groups in the microsystem nearest to the child. Next is the exosystem of larger institutions and entities that encompass the microsystem. The exosystem influences include the community, schools, and places of employment. All of these systems are supported by the macrosystem, which represents systems that exert an indirect affect on a child's development, such as culture, politics, economics, and societal institutions. Also important to the context of a child's development is the influence of time and history on the systems surrounding the child. The chronosystem refers to the interaction and influence of historical time on all support systems that influence the child during development (Bronfenbrenner, 1979, 1986; Bronfenbrenner & Morris, 1998).

Viewing the education of young children through an ecological lens helps teachers see children as individuals with various factors influencing their lives. Some influences may be shared in common with other children, whereas other influences may be specific to an individual child and family. Further, each child is unique and may react differently from other children to various influences in his or her life.

Societal Trends

Major societal trends can influence the demographic characteristics and the lives of families, as well as national policy. The following sections examine some of the overarching societal trends that have exerted a broad influence on children and families today. These influences that have led early childhood professionals toward a more inclusive approach to teaching increasingly diverse groups of young children in early childhood settings are also discussed within their historical contexts.

Advanced technology. The rapid advancement of technology has had far-reaching effects on society and has changed family life. The increasing availability of transportation has afforded mobility to a greater number of people, permitting them to engage in world travel and trade. Technology has streamlined worldwide communication, permitting almost instantaneous transmission from one end of the globe to another. Computer systems and the Internet serve as the backbone of many industries and promote world commerce. Some educators have examined the role of technology as a societal influence and a key stimulant of school reform efforts. The increasing prevalence of technology makes curricular reform necessary so society can remain competitive in the global market. However, technology has also changed the way schools teach by providing new and powerful tools to support the more advanced forms of learning that can result in superior intellectual accomplishments. Research indicates that technology can have a profound effect, but a "digital divide" exists. Some children have greater access to technology than others. Differential access is largely mitigated by poverty, with

schools serving high-poverty neighborhoods offering fewer opportunities for technological experiences, beginning in early childhood (Judge, Puckett, & Cabuk, 2004;
Means, 1994). Lessening the gap in the digital divide is important to ensure all children
have opportunities for technology use. Technology is vital for empowering all children,
especially those with special needs, so they can maximize their full potential in society
(Male, 2003).

Global interdependence. Industrialized nations have entered an era of global interdependence, as they move toward a worldwide economic system. Predictions are
that the trend toward globally competitive economies will continue into the future and
will increase the interconnections among societies. This trend has made a number of
implications apparent for teachers and the educational system in the United States.
Opportunities for employment in low-skill, minimum-wage jobs are disappearing in
high-tech industrialized nations. Inversely, the demand for a highly skilled and well-
educated workforce is increasing, as nations become more technologically advanced.
Economic promise for nations already depends heavily on the availability of a well-
prepared workforce with advanced academic skills. Expertise in communication and
literacy skills and the ability to use sophisticated problem-solving techniques are
sought-after skills in the workplace today (Berman, Minicucci, McLaughlin, Nelson, &
Woodworth, 1995; Carnegie Task Force on Learning in the Primary Grades, 1996;
Darling-Hammond, 1996; Iran-Nejad & Marsh, 1994). From the global perspective,
teaching all children means preparing them to enter a workforce that requires highly
sophisticated skills that must be gained through an advanced education of high academic quality.

The emerging global economy is also expanding the myriad of influences that affect children and families. Advanced technology has increased the mobility of the population and has made global travel commonplace. For working parents, the result may
be relocating their family multiple times during their child-rearing years. Families may
be distant from extended family members, such as grandparents, who could provide
encouragement and support to young families. The economic survival of families today is influenced not only by the economic well-being of their homeland, but also by
the economic status of other countries as well. Consequently, in a world of increasing
numbers of technologically advanced societies, it is no longer sufficient to look for influences on children and their families that exist only within the borders of individual
nations. Today's early childhood teachers are compelled to approach the challenge of
teaching all children from a broader *global perspective* (Berman et al., 1995; Darling-
Hammond, 1996; Iran-Nejad & Marsh, 1994).

Increasing diversity. The demographic composition of the United States is growingly diverse, with greater variation in culture, language, and ethnicity than ever before (Children's Defense Fund, 2005). The increasing diversity of the population has
broad implications for society and early childhood education (see Box 1.5 for definitions of diversity and cultural diversity). For society, diversity can mean greater economic prosperity and cultural enrichment, as society includes immigrant people who
bring new talents, skills, and ways of thinking (Darling-Hammond, 1996; Friend &

KEY TERMS   **BOX 1.5**

The term *diversity* is used broadly referring to the various ways young children and their families differ from one another. The term diversity is often used in conjunction with a descriptive word to specify particular characteristics of children or families. For example, *cultural diversity* is frequently used to refer to differences in heritage or cultural background.

Pope, 2005). For early childhood education, it means that traditional paradigms are changing to meet the needs of a population of children that is increasingly diverse. School-aged children suffer disparities in home language and culture compared to the school culture in which they are expected to achieve. Children of color number more than one third of the children in school, and one in ten has limited English proficiency (Kindler, 2002; National Center for Educational Statistics, 1996). Yet, teachers are overwhelmingly monolingual and majority culture (Ladson-Billings, 2001).

The impact of high immigration rates is one of the most influential trends in the United States today. The 1990 U.S. Census Bureau reported the largest wave of immigration in the history of our nation (U.S. Bureau of the Census, 1990). By the year 2020, it is projected that 46% of the school-aged population will be children of minorities (Pallas, Natriello, & McDill, 1989). Immigrants are often seeking economic improvement, greater freedom, and better futures for their children.

The increasing cultural and linguistic diversity of families are reflected in inclusive classrooms.

Some of the immigrants to the United States each year are refugees from their homelands. It is estimated that there are millions of refugees and displaced people worldwide who migrate within countries or across borders each year. The acculturation process of refugee children and families may be very different from that of willing immigrants. Whereas willing immigrants choose to leave their homeland, refugees have little choice. They are displaced due to political oppression, war, or other dire circumstances. Refugee parents often wish to preserve their homeland culture in the new country. They may be unwilling or fearful to adopt new beliefs and customs. These parents may find it difficult to transmit their values and beliefs to their children in the face of cultural conflicts experienced in the new country. Finding gainful employment can be a challenge to parents who may lack proficiency in the new language. As a result, they may have to accept menial labor for which they are overqualified. Refugee parents who were abused and maltreated in their home country may suffer from overwhelming personal problems and mental illness that further complicate their lives. Similarly, children can find adjustment in community and educational settings difficult and isolating. Children who experienced the ravages of war often emerge suffering from post-traumatic stress disorder (Pryor, 2001).

For early childhood teachers, interacting with refugee children and their parents requires tremendous sensitivity and insight. Training for these teachers should focus on ways to help children cope with the emotional trauma of violence in their past and the culture shock of being uprooted from their homes. To help refugee children learn, early childhood teachers will need to develop a broad range of strategies, including techniques to deal with stress-related disorders and to promote children's acquisition of a second language. The questions listed in Box 1.6 will help teachers reflect on the issue of diversity in the inclusive classroom.

Living in poverty. Poverty takes a high toll on children and families in the United States. Rapid escalation since 2000 resulted in nearly 37 million people suffering from poverty in 2004, affecting 13 million children. Three in five of these children live in extreme poverty, with families living on less than half of the poverty-level income. Statistics indicate that poverty rates for children are higher than rates for adults in the United States, and these statistics have soared to the highest levels in over three decades (Children's Defense Fund, 1995, 2001, 2005; DeNavas-Walt, Proctor, Mills, & U. S. Census Bureau, 2004; Olsen, 1994). Despite the wealth of the nation, children are more likely to be poor than adults. Whereas 25% of the total population in the United States lived

---

MY REFLECTION	**BOX 1.6**

- What do you already know about teaching diverse groups of young children?
- What you would like to find out about diversity?
- Are you ready to teach in inclusive classrooms?

in poverty during 2003, nearly 36% of the people living in poverty were children; the poverty rate for children under 18 years was 17.6% (DeNavas-Walt et al., 2004). The statistics for school-aged children indicates that one in five is living in poverty (Children's Defense Fund, 2001). In fact, early reports indicate children in the United States are more likely to be poor than children in Canada, Germany, and other industrialized countries in the world (Edelman, 1994).

Also characteristic of the United States is a high rate of poverty affecting children who belong to minority groups. Poverty strikes 42% of African American children and 40% of Latino children (Children's Defense Fund, 1997). In fact, the household income level for Latino families, the largest growing minority group in the United States, declined by 2.6% from 2002 to 2003 (DeNavas-Walt et al., 2004). Children in minority, single, female-headed households are particularly at risk. Approximately half of Latino and African American children in these households is living in poverty (Children's Defense Fund, 2005).

An inverse relationship exists between age and poverty. Younger children are more likely to be living in poverty conditions than older children. The typical family living in poverty in the United States usually has preschool-aged children. Six million children, nearly half of the children living in poverty in the United States, are under the age of six (American Broadcasting Corporation, 1996; Children's Defense Fund, 1997). The pervasive effects of poverty are experienced by 27% of all children under three years of age (Children's Defense Fund, 1997).

The number of families in poverty with preschool-aged children is rising. In 2003, 4.7 million U.S. families living in poverty had children under the age of 6 years living in the household. This indicates a rise from 4.3 million and 18.5% in the previous year. Society and children pay a high price when teenagers become mothers. Adolescent mothers who tend to be poorly educated are likely to subsist at the poverty level. Children being reared in families with a female householder with no father present appear to be at the highest risk of living in poverty. Nearly 53% of these children live in poverty in comparison to 9.6% of their preschool peers in married-couple families. This represents an astonishing rate of five preschool children of single mothers living in poverty to one in married households (DeNavas-Walt et al., 2004).

Teaching all children requires an understanding of the devastating effects of poverty on young children and their families. The ill effects associated with poverty remain the most pervasive of all human conditions. Poverty is the single most influential factor that can be isolated as having an effect on the outcomes for children. The effects of poverty are more significant to children's lives than their race, ethnicity, family structure, or the educational levels attained by their parents (Edelman, 1994).

Young children suffer the greatest toll from the ravages of poverty. Poverty conditions are associated with high infant mortality rates, health problems, and a slower growth and development rate of children. Predictions are that life expectancy for today's children may be less than the life span of their parents. Young children in low-income families have a greater prevalence of overweight and obesity. From 1983 to 1995, the highest increase in obesity recorded was 23% for four- to five-year-olds. Children of minorities are at the greatest risk, with percentages of increase exceeding those of White children (Children's Defense Fund, 2005).

Social and emotional consequences are also common among children living with poverty. Economically underprivileged children are at risk of becoming victims of neglect, child abuse, and suffering emotional problems. The stresses of everyday subsistence can spark conflict and domestic violence. Poverty and the resulting stress can also trigger instability among family relationships (Children's Defense Fund, 1997, 2005; Sherman, 1994).

The effects of poverty can last a lifetime impeding children's success in school and limiting their potential as future participants in the workforce (Solow, 1994). Preschool children from poor families often have less access to resources that would help to prepare them for success in school. Often their homes have fewer learning materials, and parents must rely on inferior quality child care. Once children reach school age, the neighborhood schools may offer little to ameliorate their difficult start. Schools in poverty-stricken areas are often ill-equipped, with minimal resources to use in attempts to boost the achievement of children at risk for school failure (Sherman, 1994).

Developmental disabilities or special needs. An important reason to use collaborative approaches in inclusive early childhood education is that families are often the first to suspect a problem with their children's development. It has been reported that in approximately 85% of the children identified with developmental disabilities, parents or family members were aware that the child was experiencing difficulty and were instrumental in the identification process (Lindsay & Dockrell, 2004).

Violence, neglect, and child abuse. An alarming trend in the United States is the escalating levels of violence. It is a particularly troublesome trend when that violence is aimed against the youngest members of society. Whether violence is experienced directly or tangentially, the effects are extremely detrimental to young children and their families. In 1991, the Carnegie Foundation reported that a lack of safe outdoor playgrounds and recreational facilities in violence-prone neighborhoods limits children's outdoor play activities that are critical to proper motor development (Boyer, 1991). As children reach school age, the threat of violence in the neighborhood streets makes the walk to the bus stop or schoolhouse door a frightening experience. Twelve percent of all school-aged children surveyed reported feeling afraid at times as they played outdoors. The numbers rose to 17% for children in urban areas when compared to suburban or rural scenarios. Moreover, girls reported fear in the neighborhood play settings at a higher rate compared to boys (Boyer, 1991). High levels of violence in society have renewed interest in character education and the morality of youth. These concerns have fueled the ongoing debate as to whether children's social, emotional, and moral developments fall into the arena of parenthood or early childhood education.

Children in poverty are at the greatest risk of family and neighborhood violence. They are more likely to experience a chaotic family life with unresponsive parents. Low-income neighborhoods are lacking in play environments that are safe, and harsh social environments also place children at serious risk of harm (Evans, 2004).

Homeless families. The face of homelessness has changed. Homelessness was once a condition of life suffered by a minority of single males. Today, the phenomenon of homelessness wreaks devastating affects on a growing number of single mothers with children. Thirty-eight percent of the homeless are families with children, and those children tend to be young. In New York, one in ten children in poverty housed in shelters were under the age of five years (Children's Defense Fund, 1997). Homelessness is a serious problem that inflicts health, psychological, and school-related problems. Typically, the cycle of homelessness is repeated as young mothers struggle against significant barriers, such as minimal education, substance abuse, and lack of work experience. Many of these single mothers have been victims of domestic violence (Children's Defense Fund, 1997; Koplow, 1996; Nunez, 1994, 1996).

Victims of HIV/AIDS. The number of children afflicted is rising, with acquired immune deficiency syndrome (AIDS) being the sixth leading cause of death among children aged one to four years. Brain damage, developmental delays, physical abnormalities, and mental disorders can occur in children with congenital AIDS (Centers for Disease Control and Prevention, 1992; LeRoy, Powell, & Kelker, 1994).

For many victims of human immunodeficiency virus (HIV) and AIDS, family life is permanently altered through deaths of family members and disease. Minority children are most likely to suffer the loss of their mothers (Children's Defense Fund, 1997; Working Committee on HIV Children and Families, 1996). The American Academy of Pediatrics has sounded an alarm about the crisis of children orphaned by parents dying of AIDS. A host of social and legal turmoil occurs as health care professionals and social and governmental agencies attempt to help chronically ill and dying parents plan for their children (American Academy of Pediatrics: Committee on Pediatric AIDS, 1999).

Workforce participation of mothers. In the United States, there has been an increase in the number of mothers working outside the home. In the past, it was not uncommon for mothers to join the workforce once their children reached school age. However, statistics show that these numbers are rising from 65% of mothers with school-aged children participating in the workforce in 1989 to 75% in 1992. Particularly striking, however, is the unprecedented number of mothers with younger, preschool-aged children who are now entering the workforce each year. Since 1950, when only 11.9% of mothers with children under the age of 6 years were participating in the workforce, the numbers have climbed dramatically. By 1981, the number rose to 48.9% and has continued to soar. In 1992, the figure was reported to be 58%, more than five times the number of women with preschoolers working outside the home that was reported 40 years earlier (Bureau of Labor Statistics, 1992). Another recent trend has emerged signaling change in the demographics of the workplace. Mothers of infants under one year of age, an age when children are particularly vulnerable, are entering the workforce in record numbers. Figures jumped from 31% in the mid-1980s to 54% a decade later. It was predicted that by the end of the twenty-first century, the rate of working women of childbearing age who become pregnant would reach 93%. This phenomenon was predicted to cause a swell in the numbers of mothers with infants in the workforce (Hofferth, 1992). In 2004, almost three out of four mothers were in the

COLLABORATION TIPS   BOX 1.7

Community

These ideas will help you find out about contextual factors in your community. An effective teacher for all children stays informed about the contextual factors that may influence families in the community. Effective teachers use media resources to find out about national, state, and local politics that influence policies toward the care and education of young children. Teachers talk to parents and community members to find out what the community believes is important in educating all young children.

Suggestions:
- Stay informed through television or radio news broadcasts.
- Read news magazines.
- Read local newspapers.
- Participate in community action or civic groups.
- Talk to families and community members.
- Visit the public library to find out about the historical events and policies that have influenced the community in the past.

workforce. Despite the well-documented benefits of quality care and education, access continues to be problematic, with more than three million eligible children not enrolled in Head Start programs (Children's Defense Fund, 2005).

The increased workforce participation by mothers has been precipitated by a number of factors. High divorce rates and the increasing numbers of children being reared in single-parent households are reasons often cited. However, most mothers work out of economic need. This is particularly true of single mothers whose economic needs are often acute (National Commission on Children, 1990; Women's Bureau, 1994). Nearly one fourth of all children are raised by single parents, and these households often have incomes at poverty levels and children under the age of five (National Center for Children in Poverty, 1994). These strong social trends have changed the needs of children and families.

Unfortunately, our society has few supports to address the changing needs of families who are attempting to balance work and childrearing responsibilities and the resulting stress. The increasing demand for child care is reaching crisis proportions. The lack of quality, the poor availability, and the high costs of child care jeopardize the health, development, and learning of millions of young children (Children's Defense Fund, 2005; Zigler & Finn-Stevenson, 1995). See Box 1.7 for tips on investigating contextual factors in your community.

WHAT IS INCLUSION AND INCLUSIVE EDUCATION?

Defining the Concept of Inclusion

The concept of inclusion and the construct of inclusive education have evolved over time. The meaning of these terms and the connotations each encompasses has evolved through legislative action, transformations in social thought, and societal trends.

Inclusion a dynamic construct. The concept of inclusion and inclusive education may be confusing to both novice and veteran teachers. One reason for the perplexity is that inclusion is a construct that has evolved and continues to change because of political climates and social transformations. The concept of inclusion continues to be a dynamic construct shaped by social thought, statutes, professional recommendations, and research. Further, the concept of inclusion can be viewed from different perspectives depending upon an early childhood professional's allegiance to a particular discipline or field. Consequently, professionals might attribute different facets or dimensions to this concept (Winter, 1994/95, 1999).

Early terminology. In the 1970s, the terms mainstreaming and integration were coined. These early terms referred to the placement of children who qualified for special education services into general education classrooms and child-care settings rather than segregated classrooms. However, many objected to the use of these terms because they believed a negative connotation was implied. These terms seemed to suggest that children with disabilities are not part of the mainstream of society like their typically developing peers. Consequently, many debated the issue of "belongingness." These terms implied an underlying stance that some children did not belong in the general education classrooms, but were "pushed in" based on certain criteria (Deiner, 1999; Salisbury, 1991).

Those concerned about the rights of a child with developmental delays or disabilities to experience equitable educational opportunities contend that children with disabilities are citizens and, therefore, are already members of the mainstream of society. Consequently, they argued, children with special needs possess an inherent civil right to be educated alongside their peers. The objections raised about the term mainstreaming signaled changes in social thought and soon a new term was coined: inclusion. The term inclusion was used to signify the placement of children with disabilities and special needs in child-care settings and schools they would have attended if their development had followed a typical pattern with no disability present (Rogers, 1993).

Comprehensive view of inclusion. Initially, teachers and other professionals used the terms inclusion and inclusive education in reference to the practice of placing children with disabilities and special needs in community care and general education settings with their peers who exhibited typical patterns of development. However, a more comprehensive view of inclusion began to evolve and many early childhood professionals use the terms inclusion and inclusive education in a far broader sense. Credible experts and national organizations examined demographic trends and called for educators to reconsider the conceptualization of inclusion. They recognized the increasing cultural and linguistic diversity of children in early childhood classrooms and recognized the new challenges teachers were facing. Consequently, to achieve the rights of all

Inclusive classrooms provide opportunities for all children to meet their maximum potential.

children to an equitable education, many advocated for a still broader philosophical and pedagogical approach. Experts urged teachers to adopt practices informed by a blending of theory and practice from across disciplines and fields of study to meet the needs of increasingly diverse groups of children in early childhood classrooms. These professionals argued that children with disabilities are not the only children who can benefit from early childhood settings in which teachers strive to be inclusive of all children. Other children can benefit from an inclusive approach to teaching.

Early childhood classrooms today serve a growingly diverse population of children that mirror the cultural and linguistic diversity of their neighborhoods and communities. Others point to the benefits of inclusive practices for unidentified and underserved gifted children enrolled in early childhood classrooms. Common sense dictates that classrooms in which teachers use inclusive practices, which are effective teaching strategies, offer a good learning environment for all young children. For many, a comprehensive view of inclusive education has evolved and the meaning attached to the term inclusion has expanded. Inclusion has come to mean a philosophical stance toward teaching diverse groups of children who represent a wide range of ability (see Box 1.8). Study results have recommended inclusive early childhood education as an ethical and responsible way of teaching all children (Arreaga-Mayer, Utley, Perdomo-Rivera, & Greenwood, 2003; Baca & Cervantes, 1998; Mallory, 1994; New & Mallory, 1994; Villa & Thousand, 1995).

WHAT IS INCLUSION?   BOX 1.8

"Inclusion is a commitment that *all children*, regardless of their differences, shall receive support and accommodation to ensure their success, and to preserve their right to learn among their peers." (Winter, 1999, p. 7)

Convergent Theoretical Foundation

Inclusive early childhood education has been influenced by a number of disciplines and fields of study. Traditional early childhood education, early childhood special education, multicultural education, bilingual education, study of giftedness, and gender studies are fields of study that have a bearing on the inclusive early childhood education provided to children today. These individual fields have evolved separately and have a different history.

Early childhood education. Traditional early childhood education has evolved from eclectic theoretical underpinnings. Early maturationists' ideas of Gesell and others were later influenced by Jean Piaget's cognitive constructivist theory. Maria Montessori contributed sensory learning and recognized the early childhood years as a prime learning period for children during which they are especially receptive to learning. The social cognitive theory of Albert Bandura and Lev Vygotsky's conceptualization of social constructivist cognitive theory added to the eclecticism of early childhood theory (Williams, 1999). Developmentally appropriate practices (DAP) guidelines, published by the National Association for the Education of Young Children, were developed as guidelines for practice in early childhood education and to make the eclectic theoretical base operational through application to practices (Bredekamp, 1987; Bredekamp & Copple, 1997).

Early intervention/early childhood special education. The theoretical basis for the field of special education has historically been narrow. The philosophical roots of the field were influenced by Maria Montessori's sensory approach (George, 1967; Montessori, 1912/1964). However, the most influential theory espoused in the field was that of behaviorism. B. F. Skinner, Thorndike, and others found that a child's behaviors could be changed or shaped by manipulating environmental variables and reinforcement (Alberto & Troutman, 2006; Schloss & Smith, 1994). In special education, emphasis was originally on remediation and building skills in deficit areas of development. Behaviorist theory heavily undergirded the field of special education and the practices of teachers in the field (Richarz, 1993; Safford, 1989; Widerstrom, 1986). Behaviorists' approaches have been criticized by some as incompatible with DAP (Strain & Joseph, 2004; Strain, McConnell, Carta, Fowler, & Neisworth, 1992). However, recent research indicates the potential to combine behaviorist techniques with naturalistic strategies is promising (McBride & Schwartz, 2003). Compatibility with the field of traditional early childhood education has improved with more blending of theory and practice from the fields of early intervention and special education (Odom & Wolery, 2003).

Multicultural education. The theoretical foundations for multicultural education are a composite of influences from various fields of study aimed at understanding marginalized groups of people. Its roots evolved from the civil rights movement of the 1960s and encompassed the feminist movement and the movement to afford rights to persons with disabilities. What fuels multicultural education and unites the fields involved are efforts to achieve educational equity for all children. Consequently, the field of multicultural education addresses poverty and low income, race and ethnicity, cultural and linguistic pluralism, women, and exceptionalities (which includes children who are gifted) (Sapon-Shevin, 1994/1995; Sapon-Shevin, 2001). It is a broad spectrum, drawing from many theoretical foundations that are encompassed in this wide range of fields (Banks, 1997; Grant & Sleeter, 1997). The primary theory underlying multicultural education as a field of study is social constructivism. Children acquire their knowledge of culture through experiences and interactions. Through those interactions, children socially construct their view of the world and acquire their biases (Banks, 1997).

Reconceptualization. In the 1990s, several theorists sought to reconceptualize the field of early childhood education to achieve a theoretical base that would promote more responsiveness to the increasing diversity and wide range of abilities of children in early childhood classrooms. It was thought that revamping the theoretical stance of the field would lead practitioners to improve curriculum and practices to be more culturally responsive and inclusive (Williams, 1999). Among the reconceptualization theorists, Mallory and New posited a convergent theoretical foundation for inclusive education. A convergent theoretical stance seeks commonalities across theories. The stance becomes a convergence of common tenets or principles. In contrast, eclectic theoretical stances accept multiple theories in total. The theoretical foundation for inclusive early childhood education represents a convergence of philosophical stances from across disciplines and fields of study. Mallory described a triangulated model that drew from three sets of principles:

1. *Biogenetic maturation.* The child has a level of biological capability toward learning.
2. *Developmental interactionist (constructivist).* The child learns and develops through interaction with the physical and social environment.
3. *Functional learning.* The child develops skills to achieve success in social interactions.

Mallory and New believed the diversity and complexity of inclusive early childhood classrooms warrants a set of principles derived from multiple theories of child development. This convergence of theoretical principles would become the basis for guiding the development of curriculum content and activities that meet the needs of the group as well as individuals within the class so that all children are supported in their learning (Mallory, 1994; Mallory & New, 1994).

Goals for Inclusive Early Childhood Education

Searching across fields or disciplines to seek goals related to inclusive education can lead one to find many areas of convergence. These points of intersection can be identified and stated as goals for inclusive education in early childhood. Five major goals can be used to guide an inclusive early childhood classroom:

1. Provide all children with an equitable education.
2. Enable all children to achieve success as learners.
3. Support family strengthening.
4. Build communities of learners.
5. Offer all children challenges.

Professional Advocates' Role in Defining Inclusion

A number of national professional organizations for the advocacy, care, and education of young children have voiced their support for the inclusive education movement. Equally important, professional members of these organizations have helped to conceptualization and define inclusion. Through professional debates, these organizations have refined the theory and practice recommended for inclusive early childhood education. A set of key principles is compiled from an examination of major guidelines, recommendations, and position papers published by professional organizations.

Key Principles for Inclusion

Effective early childhood practice is led by professional standards, guidelines, and recommendations. Teachers need more than a casual awareness of professional standards. Thorough knowledge of standards, guidelines, and recommendations issued by professional organizations is a prerequisite to implementation of effective strategies and practices. The following key principles have been compiled through examination of professional standards and the accumulated research base for inclusive education. Although they are not meant as a substitute for reviewing professional guidelines, these principles can remind educators what tenets are necessary to address when establishing a foundation for their inclusive classrooms:

1. View diversity as a strength.
2. Foster success of individuals within group contexts.
3. Apply recommended strategies and practices.
4. Use assessment to fuel instruction.
5. Create reciprocal partnerships with families.
6. Provide safe, challenging learning environments.
7. Emphasize prevention and early intervention.
8. Implement an integrated, active learning curriculum.

The following section provides details of the philosophical and research background for the preceding key tenets to guide effective educators in inclusive early childhood classrooms.

1. *View diversity as a strength.* Use an interdisciplinary approach that blends theory and practice. Inclusive education requires an interdisciplinary approach that blends theory and practice. The membership of an inclusive classroom is composed of unique individuals who bring strengths to the learning of all the children in the classroom. When teachers view their classrooms from a diversity perspective, they emphasize the similarities children bring to the group while prizing each child's individual contributions. Diversity becomes a strength of the group that supports each child in developing his or her individual strengths and identity (Dean, Salend, & Taylor, 1993; Derman-Sparks, 1989, 1995; York, 1991, 1992). Variety is a key element of an inclusive classroom. Providing a full palette of materials, experiences, and skill development opportunities is important so that each child can reach full potential. Teachers match individual learning styles by using a wide range of instructional practices and assessment methods. Teaching that supports the different learning styles and ability levels represented by individuals within the group helps children see how diversity can bring strength to inclusive classrooms (National Coalition of Advocates for Students NCAS, 1994; Saracho & Spodek, 1995).

2. *Foster success of individual learners within collaborative group contexts.* Inclusive education seeks to enhance the success of individual learners within collaborative group contexts. Learning through social contexts rich with communication and collaboration is the hallmark of inclusive education. For example, diverse groups of young children stimulate the language and literacy development of one another. Teachers interacting with children in the classroom results in a mutual adaptation process that promotes language acquisition (K. Au, 1993; K. H. Au, 1997; Au & Carroll, 1997; Freeman & Freeman, 1992). Learning in a diverse linguistic milieu is also important because acquiring skills toward achieving bilingualism and biliteracy have often been undervalued in schools (Cummins, 1993; Nieto, 1993, 2000). The diversity of languages present in inclusive classrooms can enhance the communicative flexibility of children, an advantage in multicultural societies (Genishi, Dyson, & Fassler, 1994). In inclusive classrooms, acquiring communicative competence, such as sign language, bilingualism, and biliteracy, is viewed a strength.

   Promoting collaboration helps children develop a sense of community with their peers. Belonging to a community of learners is good for all children and may provide additional opportunities for children with disabilities. Interaction of children can result in chances for the group to cooperate in resolving social and academic problems (Sapona & Phillips, 1993). Children who are gifted learn how to lend their strengths to team efforts so the entire community of learners will benefit from their ideas (Passow, 1994).

3. *Apply research-based recommended strategies and practices.* Use effective research-based practices to ensure success for all children. Acquire a balanced repertoire of effective strategies and practices. Match instructional support to individual children. Inclusive education requires teachers who are proficient in matching instructional support to individual children. The same strategies are not sufficient for all children. The uniqueness of individual children requires thoughtful accommodation with strategies that are recommended to improve their chances for success. Adaptations to the learning environment, materials, or learning activities can ensure a better match to children's learning styles or preferences. Children with disabilities, those who are gifted, and those who speak English as a second language are among those who will benefit from proven strategies that are individually matched to enhance their learning (Archambault et al., 1993; Arreaga-Mayer & Perdomo-Rivera, 1996; Salisbury, 1991; Salisbury et al., 1994; Tanner & Galis, 1997).

4. *Use assessment to fuel instruction.* A balanced scheme of ongoing and periodic assessment fuels instruction. Assessment is the lead and culminating activity in an effective cycle of instruction. Obtaining information about the child and his or her strengths is an important prerequisite to curriculum planning. Selection of assessment methods is critical to accurately identify each child's progress in learning the curriculum (National Coalition of Advocates for Students, 1991). Efforts to select assessments that are acceptable to families, are valid, and consider the culture and language spoken in the home help ensure the cultural relevance of the data collected on children's performance (McLean & Odom, 1993; Teachers of English to Speakers of Other Languages, Inc., 1995a, 1995b).

5. *Create reciprocal partnerships with families and professionals.* Inclusive education seeks to create true partnerships with families respecting homes as vital contexts for learning. Teachers are responsive to children, families, and the community. Diversity is considered a strength with cultures, languages, and abilities of children viewed as important assets. Teaching inclusively requires cultural responsiveness to children and families and nurturing intercultural competence and learning of children. Reciprocal partnerships are possible when communication occurs on multiple levels. Consequently, it is important to understand behaviors, nonverbal communication, and cultural interpretations specific to each family (Gonzalez-Mena, 2001; Gudykunst & Kim, 1992). Regular participation of families in classroom and school activities is associated with positive outcomes for children (Griffith, 1996; Shumow, Kang, & Vandell, 1996). Teachers in inclusive classrooms can offer families a variety of involvement opportunities so each family can choose an appropriate level of involvement (Rosenthal & Sawyers, 1996).

6. *Provide safe, accessible, challenging learning environments.* Inclusive learning environments are safe, accessible, and challenging for each child. Well-meaning adults often fail to recognize the capabilities and progress of children with disabilities (Dudley-Marling, 1993). Rather than underestimating children, especially those with disabilities, inclusive classrooms can provide children with

opportunities to acquire new skills and participate in novel experiences. While safety is foundational to each classroom, providing a level of challenge appropriately matched to individual children is central to inclusion (Baglieri & Knopf, 2004; Winter, Bell, & Dempsey, 1994). The idea of providing challenges to children extends to academic achievement. Some believe that for a classroom to be inclusive, children must have tailor-made options that include opportunities to learn high-level academic skills and higher order thinking skills (Jorgensen, 1994/1995; National Coalition of Advocates for Students, 1991, 1994).

7. *Promote success through prevention and early intervention.* Prevent problems through early identification and intervention. Inclusive education focuses on encouraging self-regulation and preventing problem behavior. From the standpoint of prevention, one might consider all early childhood classrooms as inclusive. Children with problem behavior raise concerns of parents and teachers. It has been estimated that from 14% to 20% of young children exhibit symptoms of behavioral problems (Hardman, Drew, & Egan, 1996; Hunt, Mayette, Feinberg, & Baglin, 1994). These children are at serious risk for school failure and some may warrant immediate early intervention to avert development of true behavioral disorders (Wolery & Fleming, 1992).

8. *Use an integrated, active learning curriculum.* Inclusive education curricula are integrated, meaning traditional areas of the curriculum, such as mathematics, reading and social studies, are blended into authentic contexts(Dugger-Wadsworth, 1997; Genishi, Stires, Susan, & Yung-Chan, 2001; Reisberg, 1998). Further, deficit curriculum models designed to remediate weaknesses have given way to a focus on strengths-based curricula. Based on constructivist approaches to learning, children are taught to use their strengths for learning and to build upon those strengths to achieve (Sapona & Phillips, 1993). Active learning curricula focus on how to learn for today and tomorrow, with an emphasis on learning through authentic experiences in natural contexts (Abramson, Robinson, & Ankenman, 1995; Dugger-Wadsworth, 1997; Greenwald & Hand, 1997). Using an active learning curriculum, organization of time and space provides children with natural cues for self-regulation and learning.

SUMMARY

Early childhood education is a dynamic field that continues to evolve to meet the changing needs of children and families. In recent years, significant changes in the philosophical stance and pedagogy of early childhood education have occurred in response to major societal trends. The cultural fabric of society is becoming increasingly diverse and social patterns are growing exceedingly more complex. Growing numbers of children are considered to be at risk for school failure. Inclusive education has evolved in reaction to an increasingly wide span of ability and range of experiences represented by children in early childhood settings. Changes in social thought have prompted new areas of emphasis for early childhood professionals. How the field of early childhood is defined has changed in reaction to societal trends. Early childhood education has become focused on providing a comprehensive array of services to young children who represent a diverse population. Early childhood education today involves a broad spectrum of professionals who focus on the provision of services to young children and their families. Teachers must be prepared to interface with professionals across fields to ensure that all children receive the kinds of support they need to be successful in learning.

Discussion Questions

1. Explain the influence of historical and legal occurrences, such as the Civil Rights Act of 1964, on the movement toward inclusive early childhood education.
2. Provide a rationale for using Urie Bronfenbrenner's ecological model of child development to address inclusion.
3. Discuss the major societal trends affecting families today.
4. What societal factors place children at serious risk of school failure today?
5. What are five goals teachers can strive to achieve in their inclusive classrooms?
6. Describe the key principles that help teachers implement inclusive education.
7. Why is a collaborative approach to teaching in inclusive classrooms recommended? What are the advantages of this approach for the teacher? For children? For families?
8. Define the following terms:

   a. inclusion
   b. mainstreaming
   c. zero reject
   d. least restrictive environment
   e. procedural due process
   f. intercultural competence

Inclusive Activities

1. Make a list of community agencies focusing on providing services to children and families. Check for Websites or call to find out more about each agency's mission. Pick a few agencies from your list and think about how teachers could collaborate with agency personnel to help families access services.
2. Interview a member of your local government or his or her representative. Ask about the most serious problems facing young children and families in your area. What is the city or state doing to ameliorate these problems?
3. Volunteer at a shelter for homeless families. Find out what kinds of services and resources are available for the preschool education of young children in homeless families.
4. Visit with an early interventionist who makes home visits to families with eligible children.

Ask this specialist to describe how they establish collaborative relationships with families.

5. What rights and principles does IDEA grant to children with disabilities and their families? Visit the Office of Special Education and Rehabilitative Services Website to review and summarize: http://www.ed.gov/about/offices/list/osers/index.html

6. Apply technology. As you become informed about the contextual factors in your community, you can archive what you have learned. Using technological tools will help you add information you have compiled or make changes. Try using a computer drawing software package to draw a graphic organizer illustrating the factors you have identified as influential in your area (e.g., poverty, AIDS, lack of transportation). Use lines or arrows to indicate relationships among the variables.

7. Use your computer drawing software to label concentric circles to illustrate levels of influence as suggested by Bronfenbrenner's ecological model. Your graphic organizer can help you to be a teacher researcher. You can show your graphic organizer to other teachers or persons in the community to see if they can verify the information you have amassed.

References

Abramson, S., Robinson, R., & Ankenman, K. (1995). Project work with diverse students: Adapting curriculum based on the reggio emilia approach. *Childhood Education, 71*(4), 197–202.

Alberto, P. A., & Troutman, A. C. (2006). *Applied behavior analysis for teachers* (7th ed.). Upper Saddle River, NJ: Merrill/Prentice Hall.

American Academy of Pediatrics: Committee on Pediatric AIDS. (1999). Planning for children whose parents are dying of HIV/AIDS. *Pediatrics, 103*(2), 509–511.

American Association of University Women. (1991). *Shortchanging girls, shortchanging America: A call to action.* Washington, DC: Author.

American Broadcasting Corporation. (1996). *Good morning America*: ABC News.

Archambault, F. X., Westberg, K. L., Brown, S. W., Hallmark, B. W., Zhang, W., & Emmons, C. L. (1993). Classroom practices used with gifted third and fourth grade students. *Journal for the Education of the Gifted, 16*(2), 103–119.

Arreaga-Mayer, C., & Perdomo-Rivera, C. (1996). Ecobehavioral analysis of instruction for at-risk minority students. *The Elementary School Journal, 96*(3), 245–258.

Arreaga-Mayer, C., Utley, C. A., Perdomo-Rivera, C., & Greenwood, C. R. (2003). Ecobehavioral assessment of instructional contexts in bilingual special education programs for English language learners at risk for developmental disabilities. *Focus on Autism and Other Developmental Disabilities, 18*(1), 28–40.

Atwater, J. B., Carta, J. J., Schwartz, I. S., & McConnell, S. R. (1994). Blending developmentally appropriate practice and early childhood special education: Redefining best practice to meet the needs of all children. In B. L. Mallory & R. S. New (Eds.), *Diversity and developmentally appropriate practices: Challenges for early childhood education* (pp. 185–201). New York: Teachers College Press.

Au, K. (1993). *Literacy instruction in multicultural settings.* Fort Worth, TX: Harcourt Brace College.

Au, K. H. (1997). Literacy for all students: Ten steps toward making a difference. *The Reading Teacher, 51*(3), 186–194.

Au, K. H., & Carroll, J. H. (1997). Improving literacy achievement through a constructivist approach: The KEEP demonstration classroom project. *The Elementary School Journal, 97*(3), 203–221.

Baca, L. M., & Cervantes, H. T. (1998). *The bilingual special education interface.* Upper Saddle River, NJ: Prentice Hall.

Baglieri, S., & Knopf, J. H. (2004). Normalizing difference in inclusive teaching. *Journal of Learning Disabilities, 37*(6), 525–529.

Banks, J. A. (1993). Multicultural education: Development, dimensions, and challenges. *Phi Delta Kappan, 75*(1), 22–28.

Banks, J. A. (1997). Multicultural education: Characteristics and goals. In J. A. Banks & C. A. M. Banks (Eds.), *Multicultural Education: Issues and perspectives* (3rd ed., pp. 3–31). Boston: Allyn & Bacon.

Barnett, W. S., & Hustedt, J. T. (2003). Preschool: The most important grade. *Educational Leadership*, 54–57.

Berman, P., Minicucci, C., McLaughlin, B., Nelson, B., & Woodworth, K. (1995). *School reform and student diversity: Case studies of exemplary practices for LEP students.* Santa Cruz, CA & Washington, DC: The Institute for Policy Analysis and Research, in collaboration with the National Center for Research on Cultural Diversity and Second Language Learning.

Blok, H., Fukkink, R. G., Gebhardt, E. C., & Leseman, P. P. M. (2005). The relevance of delivery mode and other programme characteristics for the effectiveness of early childhood intervention. *International Journal of Behavioral Development, 29*(1), 35–47.

Bowman, B. T., & Stott, F. M. (1994). Understanding development in a cultural context: The challenge for teachers. In B. L. Mallory & R. S. New (Eds.), *Diversity and developmentally appropriate practices: Challenges for early childhood education* (pp. 119–133). New York: Teachers College Press.

Boyer, E. L. (1991). *Ready to learn: A mandate or the nation.* Princeton, NJ: The Carnegie Foundation for the Advancement of Teaching.

Bredekamp, S. (Ed.). (1987). *Developmentally appropriate practice in early childhood programs serving children from birth through age 8.* Washington, DC: National Association for the Education of Young Children.

Bredekamp, S., & Copple, C. (Eds.). (1997). *Developmentally appropriate practice in early childhood programs* (Revised ed.). Washington, DC: National Association for the Education of Young Children.

Bronfenbrenner, U. (1979). *The ecology of human development.* Cambridge, MA: Harvard University Press.

Bronfenbrenner, U. (1986). Ecology of the family as a context for human development: Research perspectives. *Developmental Psychology, 22*(6), 723–742.

Bronfenbrenner, U., & Morris, P. A. (1998). The ecology of developmental processes. In R. M. Lerner (Ed.), *Handbook of child psychology: Vol. 1. Theoretical models of human development* (5th ed., Vol. 1, pp. 993–1028). New York: Wiley.

Bureau of Labor Statistics. (1992). *Current population survey 1981, 1986, 1992.* Washington, DC: U.S. Department of Labor.

Buysse, V., Wesley, P., & Skinner, D. (1999). Community development approaches for early intervention. *Topics in Early Childhood Special Education, 19*(4), 236–243.

Carnegie Task Force on Meeting the Needs of Young Children. (1994). *Starting points: Meeting the needs of our youngest children.* New York: Carnegie Corporation of New York.

Carnegie Task Force on Learning in the Primary Grades. (1996). *Years of promise: A comprehensive learning strategy for America's children.* New York, NY: Carnegie Corporation of New York.

Centers for Disease Control and Prevention. (1992). *HIV/AIDS surveillance.* Atlanta, GA: U.S. Department of Health and Human Services, Public Health Service.

Children's Defense Fund. (1995). *The state of America's children: Yearbook 1995.* Washington, DC: Author.

Children's Defense Fund. (1997). *The state of America's children: Yearbook 1997.* Washington, DC: Author.

Children's Defense Fund. (2001). *The state of America's children: Yearbook 2001.* Washington, DC: Author.

Children's Defense Fund. (2005). *The state of America's children: Yearbook 2005.* Washington, DC: Author.

Cummins, J. (1993). Empowerment through biliteracy. In J. V. Tinajero & A. F. Ada (Eds.), *The power of two Languages: Literacy and biliteracy for Spanish-speaking students* (pp. 9–25). New York: Macmillan/ McGraw-Hill.

Dana Alliance for Brain Initiatives. (1996). *Delivering results: A progress report on brain research.* Washington, DC: Author.

Darling-Hammond, L. (1996). The right to learn and the advancement of teaching: research, policy, and practice for democratic education. *Educational Researcher, 25*(6), 5–17.

Dean, A. V., Salend, S. J., & Taylor, L. (1993). Multicultural education: A challenge for special educators. *Teaching Exceptional Children, 26*(1), 40–43.

Deiner, P. (1999). *Resources for educating children with diverse abilities* (3rd ed.). Fort Worth, TX: Harcourt Brace College.

Delpit, L. (1995). *Other people's children: Cultural conflicts in the classrooms.* New York: The New Press.

DeNavas-Walt, C., Proctor, B. D., Mills, R. J., & U.S. Census Bureau. (2004). *Income, poverty, and health insurance coverage in the United States: 2003.* Washington, DC: U.S. Government Printing Office.

Derman-Sparks, L. (1989). *Anti-bias curriculum: Tools for empowering young children.* Washington, DC: National Association for the Education of Young Children.

Derman-Sparks, L. (1995). Developing culturally responsive caregiving practices: Acknowledge, ask, and adapt. In P. Magnione (Ed.), *A guide to culturally sensitive care* (pp. 40–63). Sacramento, CA: WestEd and California Department of Education.

Dudley-Marling, C. (1993). Challenging the children: A holistic approach to teaching students with learning problems. In A. M. Bauer & E. M. Lynch (Eds.), *Children who challenge the system* (pp. 89–115). Norwood, NJ: Ablex Publishing Corporation.

Dugger-Wadsworth, D. E. (1997). The integrated curriculum and students with disabilities. In C. H. Hart, D. C. Burts & R. Charlesworth (Eds.), (pp. 335–361). Albany: State University of New York Press.

Edelman, M. W. (1994). Introduction. In A. Sherman (Ed.), *Wasting America's future: The Children's Defense Fund report on the costs of child poverty* (pp. xiii–xxix). Washington, DC: Children's Defense Fund.

Evans, G. W. (2004). The environment of childhood poverty. *American Psychologist, 59*(2), 77–92.

Freeman, Y., & Freeman, D. (1992). *Whole language for second language learners.* Portsmouth, NH: Heinemann.

Friend, M., & Pope, K. L. (2005). Creating schools in which all students can succeed. *Kappa Delta Pi Record, 41*(2), 56–61.

Gallagher, J. (1994). *Current and historical thinking on education for gifted and talented students* (No. ED372584 EC303217). Washington, DC: Office of Educational Research and Improvement.

Gallahue, D. (1995). Transforming physical education curriculum. In S. Bredekamp & T. Rosegrant (Eds.), *Reaching potentials: Transforming early childhood curriculum and assessment* (Vol. 2). Washington, DC: National Association for the Education of Young Children.

Genishi, C., Dyson, A. H., & Fassler, R. (1994). Language and diversity in early childhood: Whose voices are appropriate? In B. L. Mallory & R. S. New (Eds.), *Diversity and developmentally appropriate practices: Challenges for early childhood education* (pp. 250–268). New York: Teachers College Press.

Genishi, C., Stires, S., and Yung-Chan, D. (2001). Writing in an integrated curriculum: prekindergarten English language learners as symbol makers. *Elementary School Journal, 101*(4), 399–417.

George, A. E. (Ed.). (1967). *Translation: The Montessori method by Maria Montessori.* Cambridge, MA: Bentley.

Gonzalez-Mena, J. (2001). *Multicultural issues in child care* (3rd ed.). Mountain View, CA: Mayfield.

Grant, C. A., & Sleeter, C. E. (1997). Race, class, gender, and disability in the classroom. In J. A. Banks & C. A. M. Banks (Eds.), *Multicultural education: Issues and perspectives* (3rd ed., pp. 61–83). Boston: Allyn & Bacon.

Greenwald, C., & Hand, J. (1997). The project approach in inclusive preschool classrooms. *Dimensions of Early Childhood, 25*(4), 35–39.

Griffith, J. (1996). Relation of parental involvement, empowerment, and school traits to student academic performance. *The Journal of Educational Research, 90*(1), 33–41.

Grossman, H., & Grossman, S. H. (1994). *Gender issues in education.* Boston: Allyn & Bacon.

Gudykunst, W., & Kim, Y. (1992). *Communicating with strangers: An approach to intercultural communication* (2nd ed.). New York: McGraw-Hill.

Hardman, M. L., Drew, C. J., & Egan, M. W. (1996). *Human exceptionality: Society, school, and family* (5th ed.). Boston: Allyn & Bacon.

Hemmeter, M. L. (2000). Classroom-based interventions: Evaluating the past and looking toward the future. *Topics in Early Childhood Special Education, 20*(1), 56–61.

Hofferth, S. L. (1992). The demand for and supply of child care in the 1990s. In A. Booth (Ed.), *Child care in the 1990s: Trends and consequences* (pp. 3–25). Hillsdale, NJ: Erlbaum.

Hunt, F. M., Mayette, C., Feinberg, E., & Baglin, C. A. (1994). Integration of behavioral consultation in an intervention setting. *Infants and Young Children, 7*(2), 62–66.

Imbeau, M. B. (1999). A century of gifted education: A reflection of who and what made a difference. *Gifted Child Today Magazine, 22*(6), 40–43.

Iran-Nejad, A., & Marsh, G. E., II. (1994). Discovering the future of education. *Education, 114*(2), 249–256.

Jorgensen, C. M. (1994/1995). Essential questions—inclusive answers. *Educational Leadership, 52*(4), 52–55.

Judge, S. L., Puckett, K., & Cabuk, B. (2004). Digital equity: New findings from the early childhood longitudinal study. *Journal of Research on Technology in Education, 36*(4), 383–396.

Kindler, A. L. (2002). *Survey of the states' limited English proficient students and available educational programs and services, 2000–2001 summary report.* Washington, DC: Department of Education, National Clearinghouse for English Language Acquisition and Language Instruction Educational Programs.

Koplow, L. (1996). Preface. In L. Koplow (Ed.), *Unsmiling faces: How preschools can heal* (pp. ix–xi). New York: Teachers College Press.

Kuhl, P. (1994). Learning and representation in speech and language. *Current Opinion in Neurobiology, 4,* 812–822.

Ladson-Billings, G. (2001). *Crossing over to Canaan: The new teachers in diverse classrooms.* San Francisco: Jossey-Bass.

LeRoy, C., Powell, T., & Kelker, P. (1994). Meeting our responsibilities in special education. *Teaching Exceptional Children, 26*(4), 37–44.

Lindsay, G., & Dockrell, J. E. (2004). Whose job is it? Parents' concerns about the needs of their children with language problems. *The Journal of Special Education, 37*(4), 225–235.

Male, M. (2003). *Technology for inclusion: Meeting the special needs of all students* (4th ed.). Boston: Allyn & Bacon.

Mallory, B. L. (1994). Inclusive policy, practice, and theory for young children with developmental differences. In B. L. Mallory & R. S. New (Eds.), *Diversity and developmentally appropriate practices: Challenges for early childhood education* (pp. 44–61). New York: Teachers College Press.

Mallory, B. L., & New, R. S. (1994). Social constructivist theory and principles of inclusion: Challenges for early childhood special education. *The Journal of Special Education, 28*(3), 322–337.

McBride, B. J., & Schwartz, I. S. (2003). Effects of teaching early interventionists to use discrete trials during ongoing classroom activities. *Topics in Early Childhood Special Education, 23*(1), 5–17.

McLean, M. E., & Odom, S. L. (1993). Practices for young children with and without disabilities: A comparison of DEC and NAEYC identified practices. *Topics in Early Childhood Education, 13*(3), 274–292.

Means, B. (1994). Introduction: Using technology to advance educational goals. In B. Means (Ed.), *Technology and education reform: The reality behind the promise* (pp. 1–21). San Francisco: Jossey-Bass.

Miller, H. M. (2001). Including "the included." *The Reading Teacher, 54*(8), 820–821.

Montessori, M. (1912/1964). *The montessori method.* New York: Schocken Books.

National Center for Children in Poverty. (1994). *Five million children.* New York: Author.

National Center for Educational Statistics. (1996). *Digest of educational statistics.* Washington, DC: Government Printing Office.

National Coalition of Advocates for Students NCAS. (1991). *The good common school: Making the vision work for all children.* Boston: Author.

National Coalition of Advocates for Students (NCAS). (1994). *Delivering on the promise: Positive practices for immigrant students.* Boston: Center for Immigrant Students, NCAS.

National Commission on Children. (1990). *Beyond the rhetoric: A new agenda for children and families.* Washington, DC: U.S. Government Printing Office.

New, R. S., & Mallory, B. L. (1994). Introduction: The ethic of inclusion. In B. L. Mallory & R. S. New (Eds.), *Diversity and developmentally appropriate practices: Challenges for early childhood education* (pp. 1–13). New York: Teachers College Press.

Nieto, S. (1993). We speak in many tongues: Language diversity and multicultural education. In J. V. Tinajero & A. F. Ada (Eds.), *The power of two languages: Literacy and biliteracy for Spanish-speaking students* (pp. 37–48). New York: Macmillan/McGraw-Hill School Publishing Company.

Nieto, S. (2000). *Affirming diversity: The sociopolitical context of multicultural education* (3rd ed.). New York: Longman.

Nunez, R. (1994). *Hopes, dreams & promise: The future of homeless children in America.* New York: Institute for Children and Poverty Homes for the Homeless, Inc.

Nunez, R. (1996). *The new poverty: Homeless families in America.* New York: Insight Books/Plenum Press.

Odom, S. L., & Wolery, M. (2003). A unified theory of practice in early intervention/early childhood special education: Evidence-based practices. *Journal of Special Education, 37*(3), 164–173.

Olsen, L. (1994). *The unfinished journey: Restructuring schools in a diverse society*. San Francisco: California Tomorrow.

Pallas, A., Natriello, G., & McDill, E. (1989). The changing nature of the disadvantaged population: Current dimensions and future trends. *Educational Researcher, 18*, 16–22.

Passow, A. H. (1994). Growing up gifted and talented: Schools, families and communities. *Gifted Education International, 10*(1), 4–9.

Phillips, C. B. (1994). The movement of African-American children through sociocultural contexts: A case of conflict resolution. In B. L. Mallory & R. S. New (Eds.), *Diversity and developmentally appropriate practices: Challenges for early childhood education* (pp. 137–154). New York: Teachers College Press.

Pryor, C. B. (2001). New immigrants and refugees in American schools: Multiple voices. *Childhood Education, 77*(5), 275–283.

Ramsey, P. G. (1987). *Teaching and learning in a diverse world: Multicultural education for young children*. New York: Teachers College Press.

Ramsey, P. G. (1995). Growing up with the contradictions of race and class. *Young Children, 50*(6), 18–22.

Reisberg, L. (1998). Facilitating inclusion with integrated curriculum: A multidisciplinary approach. *Intervention in School and Clinic, 33*(5), 272–277.

Richarz, S. (1993). Innovations in early childhood education: Models that support the integration of children of varied developmental levels. In C. Peck, S. Odom & D. Bricker (Eds.), *Integrating young children with disabilities into community programs: Ecological perspectives on research and implementation* (pp. 83–107). Baltimore: Brookes.

Rogers, J. (1993). *The inclusion revolution* (Research Bulletin No. 11). Bloomington, IN: Center for Evaluation, Development, and Research, Phi Delta Kappa.

Rogoff, B. (1990). *Apprenticeship in thinking: Cognitive development in social context*. New York: Oxford University Press.

Rogoff, B., Mistry, J., Goncu, A., & Mosier, C. (1993). Guided participation in cultural activity by toddlers and caregivers. In *Monographs of the Society for Research in Child Development* (Vol. 58).

Rosenthal, D. M., & Sawyers, J. Y. (1996). Building successful home/school partnerships: Strategies for parent support and involvement. *Childhood Education, 72*, 194–200.

Sadker, M., & Sadker, D. (1994). *Failing at fairness: How America's schools cheat girls*. New York: Scribner's.

Sadker, M., Sadker, D., & Long, L. (1997). Gender and educational equality. In J. A. Banks & C. A. M. Banks (Eds.), *Multicultural education: Issues and perspectives* (3rd ed.). Boston: Allyn & Bacon.

Safford, P. L. (1989). *Integrated teaching in early childhood: starting in the mainstream*. White Plains, NY: Longman.

Salisbury, C. (1991). Mainstreaming during the early childhood years. *Exceptional Children, 58*(2), 146–155.

Salisbury, C., Mangino, M., Petrigala, M., Rainforth, B., Syryca, S., & Palombaro, M. (1994). Innovative practices: Promoting the instructional inclusion of young children with disabilities in the primary grades. *Journal of Early Intervention, 18*(3), 311–322.

Sapona, R., & Phillips, L. (1993). Classrooms as communities of learners: Sharing responsibility for learning. In A. M. Bauer (Ed.), *Children who challenge the system* (pp. 63–87). Norwood, NJ: Ablex.

Sapon-Shevin, M. (1994/1995). Why gifted students belong in inclusive schools. *Educational Leadership, 52*(4), 64–70.

Sapon-Shevin, M. (2001). Schools fit for all. *Educational Leadership, 58*, 34–39.

Saracho, O. N., & Spodek, B. (1995). Preparing teachers for early childhood programs of linguistic and cultural diversity. In E. E. Garcia, B. McLaughlin, B. Spodek, & O. N. Saracho (Eds.), *Meeting the challenge of linguistic and cultural diversity in early childhood education* (Vol. 6, pp. 154–169). New York: Teachers College Press.

Schloss, P. J., & Smith, M. A. (1994). *Applied behavior analysis in the classroom*. Boston: Allyn & Bacon.

Seefeldt, C., & Barbour, N. (1994). *Early childhood education: An introduction* (3rd ed.). New York: Merrill/Macmillan.

Shapiro, A. (2000). *Everybody belongs: Changing negative attitudes toward classmates with disabilities* (Vol. 14). New York: Routledge.

Sherman, A. (1994). *Wasting America's future: The Children's Defense Fund report on the costs of child poverty*. Washington, DC: Children's Defense Fund.

Shumow, L., Kang, K., & Vandell, D. L. (1996). School choice, family characteristics, and home-school relations: Contributions to school achievement? *Journal of Educational Psychology, 88*(3), 451–460.

Solow, R. M. (1994). Foreword. In A. Sherman (Ed.), *Wasting America's future: The Children's Defense Fund report on the costs of child poverty* (pp. vii–ix). Washington, DC: Children's Defense Fund.

Stedman, L. C. (1997). International achievement differences: An assessment of a new perspective. *Educational Researcher, 26*(3), 4–15.

Strain, P. S., & Joseph, G. E. (2004). Engaged supervision to support recommended practices for young children in challenging behavior. *Topics in Early Childhood Special Education, 24*(1), 39–50.

Strain, P. S., McConnell, S. R., Carta, J. J., Fowler, S. A., & Neisworth, J. T. (1992). Behaviorism in early intervention. *Topics in Early Childhood Special Education, 12*(1), 121–141.

Sturm, C. (1997). Creating parent-teacher dialogue: Intercultural communication in child care. *Young Children, 52*(5), 34–38.

Tanner, C. K., & Galis, S. A. (1997). Student retention: Why is there a gap between the majority of research findings and school practice? *Psychology in the Schools, 34*(2), 107–113.

Teachers of English to Speakers of Other Languages, Inc. (TESOL). (1995a). TESOL standards ensuring access to quality educational experiences for language minority students. *Bilingual Research Journal, 19*(3 & 4), 671–674.

Teachers of English to Speakers of Other Languages, Inc. (TESOL). (1995b). TESOL statement on the role of bilingual education in the education of children in the United States. *Bilingual Research Journal, 19*(3 & 4), 661–669.

Thomas, G., & Loxley, A. (2001). *Deconstructing special education and constructing inclusion.* Philadelphia: Open University Press.

Turnbull, H. R., III. (1993). *Free appropriate public education: The law and children with disabilities* (4th ed.). Denver, CO: Love Publishing Co.

Turnbull, R., Turnbull, A., Shank, M., Smith, S., & Leal, D. (2002). *Exceptional lives: Special education in today's schools* (3rd ed.). Upper Saddle River, NJ: Merrill/ Prentice Hall.

Underwood, J. K., & Mead, J. F. (1995). *Legal aspects of special education and pupil services.* Boston: Allyn & Bacon.

U.S. Bureau of the Census. (1990). *How we're changing– demographic state of the nation.* Washington, DC: U.S. Department of Commerce, Bureau of the Census.

U.S. Department of Education. (1993). *National excellence: A case for developing America's talent.* Washington, DC: Author.

Villa, R. A., & Thousand, J. S. (1995). The rationales for creating inclusive schools. In R. A. Villa & J. S. Thousand (Eds.), *Creating an inclusive school* (pp. 28–44). Alexandria, VA: Association for Supervision and Curriculum Development.

Widerstrom, A. H. (1986). Educating young handicapped children: What can early childhood education contribute? *Childhood Education, 63*(2), 78–83.

Williams, L. R. (1999). Determining the early childhood curriculum: The evolution of goals and strategies through consonance and controversy. In C. Seefeldt (Ed.), *The early childhood curriculum: Current findings in theory and practice* (pp. 1–26). New York: Teachers College Press.

Winter, S. M. (1994/95). Diversity: A program for all children. *Childhood Education, 71*(2), 91–95.

Winter, S. M. (1999). *The early childhood inclusion model: A program for all children.* Olney, MD: Association for Childhood Education International.

Winter, S. M., Bell, M., & Dempsey, J. (1994). Creating play environments for children with special needs. *Childhood Education, 71*(1), 28–32.

Wolery, M., & Fleming, L. A. (1992). Preventing and responding to problem situations. In D. B. Bailey & M. Wolery (Eds.), *Teaching infants and preschoolers with disabilities* (2nd ed., pp. 363–406). New York: Merrill/Macmillan.

Women's Bureau. (1994). *1993 handbook on women workers: Trends and issues.* Washington, DC: U.S. Department of Labor.

Working Committee on HIV Children and Families. (1996). *Families in crisis.* New York: Federation of Protestant Welfare Agencies.

York, S. (1991). *Roots and wings: Affirming culture in early childhood programs.* St. Paul, MN: Redleaf Press.

York, S. (1992). *Developing roots and wings.* St. Paul, MN: Redleaf Press.

Zigler, E. F., & Finn-Stevenson, M. (1995). The child care crisis: Implications for the growth and development of the nation's children. *Journal of Social Issues, 51*(3), 215–217.

Chapter 2

A Professional Educator

Key Principles

- Create reciprocal partnerships with families and professionals.
- View diversity as a strength.

Objectives

After reading this chapter you will be able to:

1. List the major characteristics of proficient teachers for inclusive classrooms.
2. Discuss ways teachers can form networks with other specialists to support children and families.
3. Explain how teachers can improve their cultural competence.
4. Summarize a teacher's role as a learning facilitator.
5. Describe effective coteaching and collaborative planning processes.
6. Explain the role of the inclusive classroom teacher as an advocate for all children.
7. Discuss ways teachers promote inclusion as community liaisons.

Role as a Professional Educator

Learning Facilitator

Advocacy ← **Teachers** → Collaboration

Community Liaison

INTRODUCTION

Teaching in an inclusive classroom is complex, and the role teachers assume is multifaceted. Teachers interface with a diversity of children and families who reflect the increasing cultural and linguistic diversity of typical communities. Facilitating the social and academic learning of children who represent a wide range of abilities is a challenging endeavor. To be effective, teachers must be proficient in a broader range of skills than ever before. Moreover, the era of single teachers being responsible for a group of young children assigned to them and housed in a single classroom is rapidly being replaced. Teachers in inclusive classrooms rarely work alone. It is becoming commonplace to use team approaches to early education. This is especially true when children with disabilities are included. Today, teachers in inclusive early childhood classrooms are more likely to network with an interdisciplinary team of professionals, each of whom has specific responsibilities toward the child. This is particularly true when the child qualifies for special services under provisions of legislation that address educating children who are at risk of developmental disabilities or those with identified disabilities. This chapter examines the changing roles and different perspectives of teaching professionals, recognizing that teaching roles and responsibilities vary in different situational contexts.

CHARACTERISTICS OF EFFECTIVE TEACHERS

Who Are the Teachers in Inclusive Classrooms?

This is an important initial question to precede any discussion of inclusive education in early childhood settings. A variety of community-based settings and schools may serve as sites for inclusive education. Consequently, a number of early childhood professionals with different levels of expertise may serve in the role of "teacher." Teachers may be caregivers in child-care centers, public school personnel, or early interventionists in community agency settings. Because inclusive early childhood education is provided in a variety of community and school settings, there are no hard and fast rules regarding the kind of early childhood professional whom the children will call teacher. The preparation and experience of teachers is likely to be different, depending upon the inclusive education settings in which they are teaching. Further, the educational level of the person or persons in the teaching role might vary widely from a high school education or the equivalent to a professional with a graduate degree. For example, in community child-care facilities, a person in a caregiving role may be called teacher. An early intervention setting may have a special education professional in the teaching role. Elementary schools may assign a general early childhood teacher to the role of inclusion teacher. In some settings, the role of teacher is shared between general education and special education professionals. In other settings, bilingual specialists are part of the teaching team. Research has not yet given definitive answers regarding which arrangement might be most beneficial to children.

Legislation for children with disabilities, such as IDEA, mandates that legally binding decisions be made by a team. It is the charge of the team to determine the appropriate placement for individual children. Still, the term "teacher" must be given a broad connotation in inclusive classrooms. Nevertheless, based on the accumulated body of research on teacher effectiveness, there are some common characteristics that all expert teachers should possess. In inclusive settings where the learners are diverse, developing competence and expertise is essential to success. In the following sections, several important key areas of competence for teachers in inclusive early childhood classrooms are addressed.

THE EXPERT LEARNER ROLE

The Teacher as Learning Strategist

Research indicates that a key role of teachers in inclusive early childhood settings is that of a learning strategist who plans the curriculum and implements instruction, using a broad array of strategies gleaned from across disciplines and fields of education. In the field of bilingual special education, using an array of approaches is recommended to address the differences children have that impact their styles of learning (Baca & Cervantes,

COLLABORATION TIPS   BOX 2.1

The relationship of the special education teacher and the early childhood teacher is critical. Try these ideas to enhance collaboration:

- Divide planning and teaching tasks fairly, considering each teacher's workload of tasks.
- Share responsibility for each child in the inclusive classroom.
- Communicate honestly but always professionally.
- Each teacher should have a role in planning and evaluating curricular activities.
- Build consensus with one another to create a good fit for each teacher in organizing and managing the classroom.
- Schedule a regular time for teacher-to-teacher communication. Avoid interruptions during these conversations. Discuss what is working well and what could improve. Think aloud and problem solve together.

1998). Experts in early intervention and early childhood special education encourage teachers to provide children with a responsive physical and social environment to stimulate and provide rich learning opportunities. Using a variety of strategies for promoting children's engagement in a task is an indispensable occupation of teachers in their role as learning strategist. Responding to children's interests and bids for interaction is beneficial for all children in the inclusive classroom (Landry, Smith, Swank, Assel, & Veliet, 2001; Odom & Wolery, 2003; Wolery, 2000). Furthermore, positive teacher-child interaction that is sensitive to a child's cues has been associated with improved academic skills (Pianta, La Paro, Payne, Cox, & Bradley, 2002). For example, findings indicated that teacher actions that promote engagement of and learning in preschool children with disabilities can result in improved language outcomes (Schwartz, Carta, & Grant, 1996). Interestingly, evidence also suggested there may be a relationship between children's engagement and the strength and effectiveness of the collaborative relationship between special education and general education teachers who coteach in inclusive classrooms. The engagement of children increases when teachers have a strong relationship with each other and are able to communicate effectively (McCormick , Noonan, & Heck, 1998). Box 2.1 lists collaboration tips for the special education and the early childhood teachers.

THE LEARNING FACILITATOR ROLE

Mediating and Scaffolding Children's Learning

The importance of the teacher's role in providing prompts and cues that help mediate a child's learning process cannot be underestimated. Research has found that when parents and teachers provide a supportive scaffolding or framework, a child is able to perform at a more advanced level than the child could accomplish alone (Bodrova & Leong, 1996; Moss, 1992). The mediation of tasks by adults appears so influential in children's performance that some researchers have postulated that giftedness may be a learned phenomenon (Moss, 1992). However, little is known about how a teacher behaves in task-related interactions with children in inclusive classrooms. Previous studies of preschool and elementary inclusive classrooms have reported mixed results. Some studies reported that teachers initiate more interactions with children who have disabilities compared to typical learners (Thompson, Vitale, & Jewett, 1984). Other studies reported no difference in the number of interactions teachers initiated with children regardless of whether learning problems were present (McIntosh, Vaughn, Schumm, Haager, & Lee, 1993/1994).

Teacher-child interaction. The nature and type of the interactions between children and teachers in inclusive settings has also received some attention. Preschool teachers were affectionate toward children with disabilities and likely to offer them more assistance compared to their classmates (File, 1994; Ispa, 1981). Conversely, these teachers also were more likely to focus on behaviors of children with disabilities and to correct undesirable behaviors more frequently than those of typical learners in the classroom (Ispa, 1981). A more recent study examined the teacher-child interactions in kindergarten through second-grade inclusive classrooms at the beginning, midpoint, and end of a school year (Chow & Kasari, 1999). Comparisons were made for children across three groups: typical learners, children with disabilities, and those at risk for developmental disabilities. By the end of the school year, there were no significant differences in the amount and type of teacher-child interactions among the three groups. Even though these findings suggested that neither typical learners nor those with learning problems were given less attention in these inclusive classrooms, a serious question remains unanswered. Could some teachers have failed to recognize that some children would still benefit from additional support at the end of the year? It is possible that teachers' perceptions might influence their interactions with children. Although these studies have offered some insight, much is still unknown about the amount of interaction and the nature of interactions between teachers and children in inclusive early childhood classrooms (Chow & Kasari, 1999).

Teacher perceptions. Other studies have reported results that do suggest possible links between teachers' perceptions and their interactions with children. One Canadian study examined teacher-child interaction in third-and fourth-grade inclusive classrooms (Jordan & Stanovich, 2001). Three variables were examined to gain a better understanding of possible influences on teacher-child interaction and outcomes for children: teacher perceptions, cognitive engagement, and self-esteem. A scale was used to determine whether teachers believed children's learning outcomes were the result of characteristics of the children or whether learning outcomes could be altered with teacher intervention. Teachers who believed they were responsible for the learning of all children, including those with disabilities, interacted more frequently with all children. Moreover, findings of this study suggested that the self-concept of

Teachers provide verbal or nonverbal cues and prompts to facilitate children's learning.

children correlated with the interaction patterns they experienced with teachers. The results indicated that children assigned to teachers who believed they could make a difference in children's learning scored higher on self-concept assessments (Jordan & Stanovich, 2001).

Continuum of techniques. To be effective as a learning facilitator, teachers in inclusive classrooms use a continuum of mediation techniques. At one end of the spectrum, some children may benefit from only occasional mediation with mild prompts or cues. At the other end of the continuum, early interventionists and special educators have found that certain children require more structured mediation. In such a case, mediation is often specific information or a set of trials that are preplanned and systematically practiced with the child (Odom & Wolery, 2003). For young children, it is best to embed these interventions in their play or routines so that new learning is presented in contextually relevant circumstances (Bricker & Cripe, 1992; Horn, Lieber, Li, Sandall, & Schwartz, 2000; Losardo & Bricker, 1994).

Future research is needed to enlighten and prepare teachers for their role as mediators of all children's learning in inclusive classrooms. As mediators, teachers need better ways to gauge the amount and kind of mediation techniques that will benefit children with diverse abilities in inclusive classrooms.

THE PROBLEM SOLVER ROLE

In early childhood special education, it has long been recognized that accomplishing the inclusion of children with special needs in general early childhood classrooms is a complex undertaking. Further, when inclusion is deemed the best placement for the individual child, there can be substantial benefits for both the child with disabilities and the typically developing peers. Gains in academic achievement and social skills and abilities have been reported for children in the inclusive classroom. Because of the complexity of the issues surrounding inclusive education, teachers are usually part of an interdisciplinary team charged with a variety of tasks and decisions. It has been well-documented that team approaches to problem solving are generally preferred and appear to be more effective (O'Shea, 1999; Stainback, Stainback, & Stefanich, 1996; Villa & Thousand, 1995).

Collaborating with Families

Whereas the teacher is an active problem solver in the classroom making decisions about day-to-day classroom functioning, having a team of partners offers support for the additional responsibilities and preparation required to teach in an inclusive classroom. This is particularly true when it comes to problem solving with parents and families. The role of teachers involving families in problem-solving processes and decision making is critical to successful inclusion. This is especially true regarding the planning and implementing of accommodations and modifications for individual children. Families have valuable experience with their children, and their insights will help teachers to be more effective problem solvers (O'Shea, 1999).

Families with children who have disabilities. In addition to formal team planning processes, such as IEP planning meetings, which is required by law for children with disabilities who qualify for special services, researchers have investigated informal types of planning that involve a shared problem-solving role for teachers. In one study, collaborative partnerships involving families, teachers, and other professionals who engaged in informal planning and problem solving together were examined (Blue-Banning, Turnbull, & Pereira, 2000). Both parents and professionals perceived this strategy as beneficial for Hispanic families. The group action planning that emphasizes "person-centered" planning has been recommended as a way to ensure maximum participation of families and culturally relevant solutions for problems encountered with individual children. Results suggested that in traditional planning processes, parents perceived a disparity in power with professionals having more authority in problem solving and planning. Parents reported that the networking with professionals in this informal problem-solving method is advantageous from several standpoints. Parents say that sharing responsibilities made them feel less burdened. Further, they said group problem solving, where action steps are broken down and assigned, helped eliminate their fears about the seemingly formidable steps toward resolving problems (see Box 2.2 for one teacher's perspective on problem solving). Teachers thought Latino families

PROBLEM SOLVING **BOX 2.2**

One Teacher's Approach

This year was a constant battle with the administration to keep my assistants in the classroom instead of being pulled for lunch duty, etc. I had a problem because we had a very challenging class with very unique needs and safety issues. Pulling the assistants brought up safety concerns and decreased the time we spent on academics. When discussing the issue with the administration, I made a point to write out the concerns and issues. I tried to come up with new ideas to change the duty times before the meeting. When I went into the meeting, I always made sure they knew it was the students I was concerned about first and foremost. Usually, the administration would work with me to change things once they understood my reasons for requesting the change.

benefited from meetings where the atmosphere was one of less pressure and where the encounters with professionals were less intimidating. The opportunity for parents to be educated was also highlighted as a benefit to families. The informal networking and collaboration is highly compatible with the Latino culture in which emphasis is given to cooperation for the common good of the community (Blue-Banning, Turnbull, & Pereira, 2000).

THE CULTURALLY COMPETENT AND UNBIASED MODEL ROLE

Developing Intercultural Competence and Unbiased Inclusion

Intercultural competence is learned through participation in relationships with culturally dissimilar participants. Developing the knowledge, understanding, and communication skills that result in intercultural competence involves risk taking and the willingness to encounter and resolve cultural conflicts. It also refers to the ability to integrate knowledge and awareness gained through interactions with people of different cultural backgrounds (Gudykunst & Kim, 1992; Sturm, 1997). Modeling cultural competence is more effective when it is a school-wide effort. Creating a school environment that supports cultural and linguistic diversity also requires knowledgeable administrators who also model cultural competence and ensure that teachers are properly supported with instructional materials, translators, and other resources (see Box 2.3) (Garrett & Morgan, 2002).

The attitude of teachers toward diverse children and those with different abilities is thought to be a significant influence on educational and social outcomes for these children in inclusive classrooms. The social acceptance among children and the feelings of belongingness of individual children are significantly influenced by adults at an early age. For example, children's attitudes toward cultural diversity, gender-related behavior,

COLLABORATION TIPS   BOX 2.3

Addressing Diversity from a Teacher's Viewpoint

It is very important to make sure every child in the classroom participates. Each activity implemented in my classroom considered the diversity of my children. I had a child who spoke only Spanish. The English as A Second Language (ESL) teacher helped to make sure directions for activities were translated for the child. She also planned with me to make sure the activities we did were appropriate. I relied on the ESL teacher to translate all the information sent home to the parents as well.

and persons with disabilities are formulated very early and, once formed, are very stable (Caldera, Huston, & O'Brien, 1989; Derman-Sparks, 1993; Favazza, 1998). Although parents are the first to influence the attitudes children develop, teachers also play a role. What teachers say and do, as well as their silences, can have a major impact on the attitudes children develop toward human diversity (Favazza, 1998). Teachers' behaviors toward children are influenced by their beliefs and feelings associated with diversity and disabilities. How teachers manage their classrooms and whether they facilitate a children's social integration into their peer group is thought to be associated with attitudinal variables. When teachers model respect, tolerance, and acceptance in the classroom, they serve as strong socializing agents (see Box 2.4). Their attitude and

---

ONE TEACHER'S PERSPECTIVE   **BOX 2.4**

I have learned there are many challenges to being an inclusion teacher, but also many rewards. My students, I believe, were more accepting to their peers with special needs, and I was, too. Having the extra staff in the room also benefited my students—they were able to obtain more one-on-one attention. I learned inclusion— if done the right way—is a lot of work. I had to be flexible, yet structured. I also had to be more consistent with my discipline procedures. My students also learned that we all have different needs, and that one person's needs may be different from another's.

I believe inclusion is hard. In fact, I did not want to be part of it. It is not easy. Sometimes, I was worn out. But, when I saw how accepting my students became of the students with special needs and how much the children with special needs blossomed, it made the year worthwhile. I feel general education teachers need more special education training—if we are going to be expected to have children with special needs in our classroom. I think I would feel a lot more confident with inclusion if I had some extra training on strategies, behavior management, etc.

Modeling cultural responsiveness helps children learn understanding and cultural competence.

behaviors convey valuing of human diversity (Bacon & Schultz, 1991; Buswell & Schaffner, 1992; King, Chipman, & Cruz-Janzen, 1994; Stewart, 1990).

Identifying bias in teachers. Research has explored how to identify the attitudes of teachers and the relationship of their attitudes to behaviors of teachers and outcomes for children. It is believed that teacher attitudes about children with disabilities and the kind of placements teachers view as feasible for these children are important determinants of successful inclusion. One study reported preservice teacher's beliefs about inclusion for children with mild disabilities were almost evenly split (Garriott, Miller, & Snyder, 2003). Of the preservice teachers surveyed, slightly more, 55%, believed children with mild disabilities should be placed in general education classrooms. Conversely, 45% of more than 100 preservice teachers surveyed said that children with mild disabilities belonged in special education placements. This percentage is high, considering these views go counter to societal trends toward inclusiveness and the laws for the rights of children with disabilities. Further, these teachers reported feeling ill-prepared and believed the children would not benefit and might distract teachers and other students from learning tasks (Garriott, Miller, & Snyder, 2003). These findings are very disconcerting and may suggest attention to teacher preparation programs is seriously warranted.

Teacher education may need to be reconfigured to better prepare preservice teachers for inclusion, help alleviate misconceptions, and increase the preservice teacher's feelings of competence to accommodate diverse students. Practicing teachers have also reported concerns that they do not have sufficient training and skills to teach children with disabilities (Taylor, Richards, Goldstein, & Schilit, 1997; Vaughn, Schumm, Jallad, Slusher, & Saumell, 1996). Counter to these concerns, Staub and Peck (1994/95) have reported empirical evidence to the contrary. Research consistently refutes these common misconceptions. Children with disabilities in general education classrooms do not siphon teacher time away from other students, and achievement of students is not reduced. Further, peers do not acquire inappropriate behaviors exhibited by children with disabilities. Rather, children with disabilities appear to benefit from peer modeling of desired behaviors (Staub & Peck, 1994).

A global concern. Becoming comfortable with new roles and responsibilities are tasks early childhood teachers in industrialized countries across the globe are also confronting. As other countries extend rights to children with disabilities and include them in diverse classrooms, teachers in other countries face problems similar to those of U.S. teachers. In Australia, Tait and Purdie (2000) reported that a one-year, information-based course with some lectures covering the topic of disabilities accomplished little in changing the attitudes and perceptions of preservice teachers toward persons with disabilities. Their findings corroborated an earlier study with similar results suggesting that coursework, alone, may be insufficient to adequately prepare teachers and ensure a positive mind-set and attitudes amenable toward inclusion of children with learning problems (Hastings, Hewes, Lock, & Witting, 1996). It has been suggested that course infusion over an extended period of more than one year should be studied. Moreover, there is some evidence to suggest that greater interpersonal contact with children with disabilities as individuals may positively impact preservice teacher attitudes (Hastings et al., 1996; Jones, Wint, & Ellis, 1990; Tait & Purdie, 2000).

THE STIMULATING CREATIVITY ROLE
Encouraging the Creativity of All Children

Creativity is a construct that has no agreed upon definition. Originality, imagination, and associative fluency are aspects of creativity that have been examined in studies of preschool children (Moran, Milgram, & Fu, 1983; Moran, Milgram, Sawyers, & Fu, 1983; Moran, Sawyers, Fu, & Milgram, 1984). An accumulated body of research indicated that creativity is learned and not a characteristic imbued by one's biogenetic heritage (Baer, 1993/94). However, there apparently is a relationship between intelligence and creativity. There is evidence of a correlation between high intelligence and creativity. The relationship between these constructs seems weaker in children with lower intelligence. Some postulate that, for gifted children, the nature of the correlation may be different (Fuchs-Beauchamp, Karnes, & Johnson, 1993).

The processes of stimulating creativity and of ensuring meaningful learning for children have a kinship. While creativity may not be biologically ordained, the sensory equipment of young children and how they learn to use it to explore their world may be instrumental in their acquisition of meaningful knowledge. Creativity and problem solving appear to go hand-in-hand. In essence, some experts speculate, effective learning

Encouraging creativity and exploration helps children find exciting, new ways to learn.

is a creative process. The learner must put all the sensory information together to create understanding. This process may be neurologically akin to imagination, which gives one the ability to ponder all possibilities and solutions to a problem (Caine, 2004).

The role of the teacher is to provide all children with an experience-based curriculum rich with authentic experiences. Guiding children through project work and helping them to see the interconnections of concepts they encounter during their explorations is critical to help them develop creativity and meaningful learning. Teachers are key in assisting children to release their imaginations and actively process their experiences (Caine, 2004). Dialogue with children is important to help them move reciprocally from action to reflection, as suggested by theorist Paulo Freire (Leistyna, 2004). There are a number of implications for teachers in inclusive classrooms. High levels of teacher-child interaction, questioning, and conversations with children as they engage in learning experiences may help them develop a creative learning process. Teachers who engage their children in the arts may also increase children's capacities to entertain a full range of possibilities for problem solving and learning (Eisner, 2002). The arts allow teachers to involve children who represent a full continuum of abilities in creative expression. Success in identifying the interests and strengths of learners, even those with severe disabilities, through participation in the arts, has been reported. An array of modes of expression are available through the arts and with flexibility, children's learning differences can be accommodated. Offering all children the opportunities, with accommodations as needed, to engage in creative expression, preserves their human rights (Keifer-Boyd & Kraft, 2003). Encouraging children to engage in play activities and thematic units that integrate play and authentic learning experiences are important ways to stimulate creativity in children at all ability levels. Moreover, these strategies are highly recommended to stimulate learning in young preschoolers who are gifted (Foster, 1993).

THE CLASSROOM MANAGEMENT ROLE

Developing Effective Guidance and Classroom Management

Learning how to interact effectively. When teaching in an inclusive classroom, teachers who are sensitive to children's nonverbal cues and savvy about anticipating children's behavior are more likely to be successful in their interactions with children. Children with disabilities often exhibit expressions and behaviors that are difficult to interpret, presenting a challenge for parents, teachers, and caregivers. Difficulty interpreting a child's signals results in a dilemma regarding how to choose appropriate interaction strategies (McCollum & Bair, 1994). Investigators have reported that caregivers often appeared to have difficulty reading and interpreting the expressions and cues of children with disabilities. Misinterpretation of a child's cues can result in a lack of synchronization of the interaction between the adult and child. As a result, the caregiver experiences difficulty in responding appropriately (McCollum & McBride, 1997).

Responsive interactions. Adopting an interaction style that is sensitive, responsive, and supportive of children is a fundamental characteristic and critical skill of teachers in inclusive early childhood classrooms. Effective relationships based upon the responsiveness of teachers and children not only promote social and emotional growth, but also promote the academic learning of children. Although it is widely recognized that responsiveness is an important characteristic of teachers in early childhood classrooms, research has provided few guidelines for training teachers to be responsive and use sensitive, child-focused practices (Rimm-Kaufman, Voorhees, Snell, & La Paro, 2003).

For culturally and linguistically diverse children, the interaction between teacher and child might be especially crucial. The sensitivity of teachers to a child's expressions of affect and nonverbal cues may provide critical information to help distinguish between learning differences that might be attributable to culture or linguistic diversity of children rather than signaling developmental disabilities. Research examining teacher sensitivity and cultural responsiveness during interactions with children has been recommended. Further, it has been suggested that such investigations be conducted using ecological assessment models to capture teacher and child behaviors along with other contextual variables that surround those interactions (August & Hakuta, 1997).

Assessing teacher-child interaction. Few instruments are available to assess teacher-child interaction. Current available instruments provide an overall or global view of classroom structure and teaching practices, but do not give an in-depth view of the nature and characteristics of interaction patterns (Rimm-Kaufman et al., 2003). However, ecobehavioral assessment, an ecological observation technique, holds promise for examining specific aspects of teacher-child interaction within the context of classroom settings. The application of this assessment method has been used successfully to evaluate teacher-child interaction in bilingual education (Arreaga-Mayer, Carta, & Tapia, 1992; Arreaga-Mayer & Perdomo-Rivera, 1996) and early intervention programs (Carta, Greenwood, & Atwater, 1985; Carta, Greenwood, & Robinson, 1987). See the transition subsection under The Community Liaison Role section in this chapter for more information about ecobehavioral assessment.

Adopting Community-Building Strategies

Teachers in inclusive classrooms face unique challenges. Some authors recommend that teachers identify and use inclusive approaches, such as building a sense of community among children, to meet the demands of managing children and activities in early childhood classrooms that are increasingly diverse. Creating a classroom environment that promotes equity and inclusiveness is a fundamental responsibility of teachers in classrooms today. Teachers have the obligation to ensure that all children feel safe and nurtured. Responsiveness to children and helping all children feel welcome sets the stage for learning. Fostering a sense of belongingness and membership in a classroom community is accomplished when practices are inclusive rather than exclusionary. For example, unconditional enrollment and accepting the child's current level of development, cultural knowledge, and behavior are practices that are consistent with the philosophy of inclusion and multicultural education (Banks, 1997; Soodak et al., 2002; Soodak, 2003). Entry requirements based on academic readiness that require children to earn their way into a class or that exclude children for misbehavior are practices that separate children from settings that serve their typically developing peers. Classroom management focused on building a sense of community with realistic expectations for children is key.

Promoting friendships. Teachers who encourage cooperation and the development of friendships among children foster a sense of community in inclusive classrooms. The socialization process that occurs within social groups is very influential in helping children learn attitudes toward one another (Favazza, 1998). Children with disabilities tend to become isolated in general education classrooms and community child-care settings. Therefore, it is important for teachers to assume the role of a facilitator who keenly observes the interactions of children and seizes opportunities to help isolated children become involved. Unity among children is developed through daily rituals that bring children together, such as friendship circles, sharing a storybook reading, or enjoying other favorite group activities (Soodak, 2003). The challenge for teachers planning for a group is to select activities that are brief, engage children actively, and match the varying ability levels of children so that all may participate.

Proactive approach. The teacher's role in inclusive classrooms is to take a proactive approach to behavior. Rules are set to help children learn self-regulation of their own behavior. Teachers view their role toward behavior as supportive and educate children toward more functional behavior. Teachers eschew punitive approaches and those that exclude children, rather than teaching them how to fit into the peer group activities. Teachers place emphasis on helping children learn to engage in increasingly social cooperation (Soodak, 2003). In culturally and linguistically diverse classrooms, a proactive approach entails setting limits to preserve individual rights and to demonstrate respect for each child. The role of the teacher is to provide a model for respectful interactions that children can emulate.

THE COLLABORATION ROLE
Building a Resource Network

Collaborating with specialists. A 1986 report from the U.S. Department of Education advocated for collaboration between the fields of general education and special education in a groundbreaking move toward inclusion. The idea of professionals from different fields sharing responsibility for children with learning problems was proposed as a more effective and equitable method of educating these children (Will, 1986). For teachers, this proposal meant a huge leap from isolated teaching in solitary classrooms toward more cooperative methods of meeting children's learning needs (Hourcade & Bauwens, 2003). Such cooperation is also recommended to ensure that children in culturally and linguistically diverse classrooms are properly supported in their learning. Collaboration toward effective inclusion in diverse classrooms requires a school-wide commitment from all teachers to plan and create a positive learning climate together. When all teachers are involved in collaboration toward inclusion, there is a sense of shared responsibility for all children. As a result, it may be less likely that teachers will fall into the syndrome of viewing some children, especially those who are in the minority or differ in ability, as the sole responsibility of another teacher or specialist (Delpit, 1995; Sailor, 2002).

Collaboration is more likely to occur and meet with success if specific expectations are set. Specific roles and responsibilities must be clearly articulated to teachers and specialists. Establishing guidelines to govern interactions and planning activities is an important feature to stimulate collaboration among teachers. Providing joint preservice and inservice training for teachers and specialists fosters collaboration. Perhaps the most important strategy for promoting collaboration is designating specific times for team planning (Friend & Bursuck, 2002).

Every professional involved in teaching and providing services to children enrolled in the inclusive early childhood setting is responsible for establishing collaborative relationships with his or her colleagues. Unfortunately, it has been reported that some professionals whose caseloads of children overlap are not working together and, in fact, have never met. This lack of collaboration typifies gaps in service coordination that frequently occur in early intervention (Winton, 2000).

For early childhood special education teachers and related services professionals, services may be provided in multiple settings. Successful inclusion requires the ability

Teachers collaborate with an interdisciplinary team to meet the learning needs of children.

to collaborate and problem solve with a variety of professionals across all the learning contexts that children experience. The ability to disseminate information, communicate effectively, and to often negotiate a solution is vital to effective collaboration (Fisher, Frey, & Thousand, 2003).

Integrating therapy. The least restrictive environment (LRE) that is favored for most children is an inclusive classroom with their peers. Consequently, professionals delivering related services are usually expected to provide those services within the contexts of inclusive classrooms (Farber & Klein, 1999; National Association of State Boards of Education Study Group on Special Education, 1992). Some therapists have only been trained to provide therapy to individuals in segregated, clinical settings. They frequently express concerns about integrating services in classroom and about the relationship of therapy to instruction. They recognize a need to differentiate roles and create relationships with classroom teachers. While providing activities that might benefit all children is a good idea occasionally, the specific IEP objectives of individual children cannot be ignored.

Maintaining a therapeutic focus should be the central mission of the professional. This can be accomplished by careful planning and delineation of roles between the teacher and the therapist. Planning collaboratively can ensure that curriculum-relevant therapy is provided (Ehren, 2000). Further, there is a distinct advantage to providing therapy that is curriculum relevant. Implementation of a curriculum that is authentic and relevant may lead to more functional outcomes for children (Gallagher, Swigert, & Baum, 1998). For example, it has been recommended that speech pathologists provide educationally relevant therapy designed to facilitate a child's acquisition of the curriculum (American Speech-Language-Hearing-Association Ad Hoc Committee on the Roles and Responsibilities of the School-Based Speech-Language Pathologist, 1999). Moreover, therapists can assist teachers by suggesting modifications to curriculum and instruction or by asking teachers to reinforce or assess targeted objectives for the child (Ehren, 2000).

Interdisciplinary Team Participation

The reauthorization of IDEA in 1997 expanded participation on the IEP team (Individuals with Disabilities Education Act, Amendments of 1997, 2000). The law was amended to include a general education teacher on the interdisciplinary team when it was deemed appropriate. With increasing numbers of children in general education classrooms and community-based child-care settings, it is becoming increasingly more likely for early childhood teachers to serve on an IEP planning team. These teachers are not, however, likely to have training in special education, and their knowledge base may be very different from others serving on the team. Although child care as an inclusive placement option has been reported to be successful, child-care teachers may lack training for their role as an IEP team member (Wolery, Brashers, & Neitzel, 2002). Minimally trained staff often serve as teachers in community-based early childhood settings. The lack of special education knowledge and skills can be a problem. In child-care centers, most teachers lack training, especially in early intervention and the education of young children with special needs (Wolery et al., 2002; Wolery et al., 1994). Yet, the information about the developmental progress and learning of children is valuable to IEP team deliberations and formulation of the IEP. Equipping child care teachers with simple, effective methods of collecting and organizing information about the progress of individual children is one way to increase the child care teacher's participation on the IEP team. As a result, collaboration of the child care teacher with the team of specialists is enhanced, and the entire IEP team benefits from insights gleaned from the child care learning context (Wolery et al., 2002; Wolery et al., 1994). The role of the special education teacher on the IEP team includes evaluating educational assessment information and planning strategies, curricular modifications, and necessary accommodations to support the learner in the classroom or other educational contexts (Fisher et al., 2003).

Specialized training. Both teachers and specialists may require special training to enhance their performance as a member of an IEP planning team. The 1997 Amendments to IDEA obligated IEP teams to consider whether assistive technology devices were needed as part of the IEP of eligible children. However, no directions were provided regarding how to meet this legal mandate. Some states have developed technology training centers to provide the needed guidance and training to teachers and other professionals charged with making decisions about the kind of assistive technology that a child might benefit from and the kinds of instructional contexts the devices would need to be offered (Dissinger, 2003).

Team Planning and Coteaching Processes

Defining coteaching. Cooperative or coteaching is an instructional arrangement pairing two teachers who have distinctly different backgrounds of knowledge. In a cooperative teaching relationship, teachers blend their skills to plan and implement instruction in general education classrooms that serve a diverse group of children. Sometimes, a paraeducator joins the collaboration to assist in addressing the specific educational requirements for children with disabilities (Hourcade & Bauwens, 2003).

Effectiveness of coteaching. In inclusive early childhood education, coteaching is a recommended service delivery mode designed to provide optimal support for the inclusion of young children. The idea is that pairing a special education teacher with a general education teacher will create a complementary relationship of skills for planning and implementing instruction (see Box 2.5). Theoretically, the relationship would be ideal for ensuring proper support for a full range of children. Few studies have examined the relationship of paired teachers and whether the nature of their relationship influences the social and learning environments for children (McCormick, et al., 2001). Further, some qualitative data suggest that difficulties in coteaching relationships should be investigated as a causal factor in the termination of such pairings. A questionnaire, the Coteacher Relationship Scale, has shown promise as a tool to foster communication and evaluation of teachers and to aid supervisors in facilitation of coteaching relationships (Noonan, McCormick, & Heck, 2003).

With increased accountability of all teachers, determining accurate ways to evaluate the quality and effectiveness of cooperative teaching arrangements is vital. The key to accurate and meaningful evaluation is to decide on the important dimensions of the relationship prior to beginning the evaluation process. Decisions must be made regarding whether the process of collaboration or the outcomes for children or both of these aspects are to be evaluated. Reliable sources for data collection should be planned. Data sources might be teacher reports, parental surveys, or child assessments. Some of these data sources are objective, while others are subjective. Deciding on whether to collect objective data or subjective data under either process or outcome dimension is another critical decision. Objective data, such as how many hours the coteachers spent in collaboration, how much funding is used to support the cooperative teaching effort, or the children's assessment scores, provide verifiable measurements for use in evaluating the success of cooperative teaching. Subjective data might include surveying families to gain their opinions regarding the success of the cooperative teaching arrangement from their perspectives or that of their children (Hourcade, Parette, & Anderson, 2003; Salend, Gordon, & Lopez-Vona, 2002).

Promoting collaboration with technology. The importance of collaboration between general and special educators is well-recognized. Teaming and collaboration of these professionals, unfortunately, has been reported as limited (Hamill, Jantzen, & Bargerhuff, 1999). A variety of reasons, including lack of time, large caseloads of specialists, and itinerant arrangements of special education teachers, may present hindrances to collaboration. Other authors report a lack of collaboration at the university

---

A GENERAL EDUCATION TEACHER'S THOUGHTS   **BOX 2.5**

Having extra people in the room—special education teacher, assistants—allowed for some great innovations. For example, the special education teacher not only guided the special education students, but also gave me ideas and helped some of the students who were struggling in my class. We also team-taught, which allowed me to test my students while the rest of the class was still learning, or I could walk around and help make sure my students were grasping the concepts. The special education teacher even taught the state-mandated tutoring to my students in her classroom, while I kept her special education students in mine. This gave my students a change of pace, and I think they actually learned more from her (with her strategies) than I could have taught them.

---

level in which special education and general education teacher preparation are usually offered as separate programs (Wood, 1998). Teachers prepared in separate programs may lack the disposition and skills needed to participate in the collaborative culture of today's diverse and inclusive classrooms. Addressing the difficulty of allocating time to engage in collaborative activities requires innovative solutions. Technological tools can offer new ways to bridge the communication gap between teachers in the field and preservice teachers in preparatory programs at universities. Online discussion boards with prompts and use of threaded discussion formats have been used to increase communication and sharing of experiences between special education and early childhood majors at one university. The findings of the project suggested this method of communication shows promise as a viable model to facilitate collaboration and communication among special and general education teachers in inclusive classrooms (Geer & Hamill, 2003).

Supervising Paraprofessionals

Collaboration in inclusive early childhood settings increasingly involves paraprofessionals often as required by the IEP of children with severe disabilities. The rising numbers of paraprofessionals being assigned to inclusive classrooms are referred to by a variety of titles, such as teaching assistant, paraeducator, and teacher's aide. Qualifications and experience vary even among entry-level professionals, although most states require a minimum of a high school diploma or the equivalent. Many states do not require training for paraprofessionals (Pickett, 1996). The role of paraeducators is often poorly articulated, and their responsibilities frequently overlap with those of teachers in the inclusive classroom (Pickett, 1997). Although they have little involvement in the formulation of the IEP, paraeducators are given considerable responsibility for implementation of the IEP goals and objectives of children (Parsons & Reid, 1999). Reportedly, paraeducators engage in a wide range of instructional responsibilities, including teaching, making accommodations, and implementing behavioral interventions. Of

```
┌─────────────────────────────────────────────────────────────────┐
│         TIPS FOR SUPERVISING PARAPROFESSIONALS    BOX 2.6         │
│                  A First-Year Teacher's Approach                  │
│  One of the challenges of being a new teacher was dealing with    │
│  assistants who had been in the field longer than I had. One of   │
│  the things I did was develop a list of activities and what the   │
│  kids needed to be doing during that time, as well as what the    │
│  assistants and I should be doing. I gave the handout to them at  │
│  our first meeting before the students arrived. I went over it,   │
│  and the assistants were able to ask questions. This helped them  │
│  know exactly what I expected of them. Throughout the year, I     │
│  held biweekly meetings that allowed them to address questions    │
│  and concerns and suggest their ideas as well. I want my          │
│  assistants to know that I value their ideas, opinions, and       │
│  concerns. By taking this approach, not only did they respect me  │
│  and get things accomplished, but I also was able to benefit from │
│  new ideas and strategies that they had to offer.                 │
└─────────────────────────────────────────────────────────────────┘
```

particular concern is the independence paraprofessionals are given in relation to the minimal training and supervision they receive (Downing, Ryndak, & Clark, 2000).

Riggs (2001) surveyed paraprofessionals and found they desired training and voiced needs for specific training. Consistent with other studies, the paraprofessionals reported behavior management high on their list of priorities. Riggs recommended a three-tier system of training, including a district-wide orientation, a core of basic topics related to behavior management, communication and instruction, and training specific to the particular job assignment of the paraprofessional, such as applied behavior analysis, reading remediation, or assistive technology (Riggs, 2001).

Implications for teachers. There are a number of implications of these studies for teachers. It is becoming increasingly likely that teachers will be asked to collaborate with and supervise a paraprofessional who is limited in training. Consequently, the inclusive education teacher may need to become involved in training of the paraprofessionals. Even if district-level training is provided, classroom level training will be needed to ensure a high quality learning environment that meets the individual needs of children and the consistency of strategies and interventions required by the IEP. It is also important to learn about paraprofessionals and to gather resources from reliable sources for training (see Box 2.6).

THE INFORMED ADVOCATE ROLE

Seeking Information on Key Issues

Advocacy for quality early childhood education, particularly when children with special needs are included, is an increasingly important role for early childhood professionals. Recommendations are calling for families and advocates for children to increase their involvement in advocacy and policy at local levels. Smith (2000) predicts that local action will soon become more influential in the future of early childhood special education than federal and state government systems. She identifies two key themes that describe the historical role of federal policy in early intervention. First, federal efforts have been aimed at ensuring access to all children, including those with special needs, to community early childhood programs. Second, federal efforts have been focused on improving the quality of early childhood education through support for research, program development, and training. However, Smith points out that federal mandates are successfully implemented only when state and local efforts embrace the legislative mandates and take actions to fulfill the intent of the law (Smith, 2000).

Developing an Effective Voice

What can early childhood and early childhood special education teachers in inclusive classrooms do to ensure that services to children will be of the highest quality and matched to their individual needs? Assuming a role of advocacy at all three levels (federal, state, and local) is key. Maintaining an active membership in professional organizations allows teachers to have an active voice in policy at the national, state, and local levels (Smith, 2000). National organizations, such as the Division of Early Childhood of the Council for Exceptional Children, the National Association for the Education of Young Children, and the Association for Childhood Education International, are active in lobbying for legislation that promotes the rights and services that will benefit young children and their families.

Teachers as advocates can play an active role by staying informed about local policy making and issues that may affect children. Grassroots efforts to keep local stakeholders and policy makers informed can be very influential. Smith (2000) expresses concern about the poor range of inclusion options for preschool children. Inclusion might occur in natural community-based settings, but often these classrooms meet only minimum standards of quality. To provide higher quality, classroom settings are sometimes planned for inclusion, but the drawback with these classrooms is that they often are not typical of classrooms experienced by peers in the general community. Smith (2000) suggests that early childhood and early childhood special education professionals speak in one voice to advocate for local remedies for improving resources, training, and the quality of environments so that children with special needs can be included with their typically developing peers in natural settings within the community. More importantly, teachers as advocates can help build community awareness and shape local culture toward supporting quality care and inclusive early education for all children (Smith, 2000).

Empowering Families

A major goal for the teacher-advocate in inclusive classrooms is to use a variety of methods to empower families and increase their involvement in the education of their children. Minority families often feel vulnerable and intimidated when they must approach school personnel and officials. Yet, especially when their child has a disability, their collaboration with teachers and school professionals is critical to their children's success in school (Blue-Banning et al., 2000; Blue-Banning et al., 2004). Parents can be empowered through the formation of learning communities in which they can participate. Such learning communities allow families to join forces with teachers, related services professionals, administrators, and other local stakeholders to plan small steps toward improving early childhood education and early intervention (Winton, 2000).

THE COMMUNITY LIAISON ROLE

Identifying Community Resources

Just as all children have areas of strength, the neighborhoods and community settings in which children and families reside have strengths. Identifying the unique characteristics and strengths of the neighborhood takes some investigative effort. Teachers who take the time and expend the effort to discover specific characteristics and unique features of the neighborhood contexts are rarely disappointed. Most communities have a bright spot and people who contribute success of children in their neighborhood.

Resource people. Teachers can establish effective partnerships in the community once resource persons are identified. Resource persons can help deepen a teacher's relationship with the neighborhood and better connect the teacher to individuals as he or she builds a network for children and families. Conduct an inquiry to locate resource people, such as church leaders, neighborhood business persons, local elected leaders, and representatives (see Box 2.7 for collaboration tips).

Knowledge of Cultural Tapestry

Knowledge of the community and the rich heritage represented by its people is a critical prerequisite for teachers as liaisons. Each community is steeped in culturally ordained traditions and customs. Cultural values and preferences influence life in the neighborhood. Décor of homes, tints and hues of buildings, signs and advertisements displayed can give teachers ideas about how to create classroom environments that reflect cultural preferences and help children transition from home to school.

Understanding the cultural fabric of the social context of the neighborhood helps teachers promote the cultural competence of children. The ways people relate to one another and the patterns of interaction are influenced by culture. Beliefs about persons who are different, such as those with disabilities, evolve from cultural transmission of values and preferences.

Planning Transitions for Children

Teachers in inclusive classrooms play many roles that influence the lives of children and families. One of the most significant roles an inclusive education teacher fulfills is

COLLABORATION TIPS   BOX 2.7

Community

How Can You Find Resource Persons in the Neighborhood?

Ask parents and family members:
- Who are the respected leaders in your community?
- Who do you turn to when you need help?
- When parents are new, who can they go to for advice?
- Are there people in social agencies who are helpful?
- Are there members of active faith-based groups who can assist families?
- Who will help if you need someone to care for your child outside of school hours?
- Whom do you admire?
- Who are the role models for children?
- Who are the heroes in the community?

that of a mediator between the children and the circles of people who surround them. Similar to the theory of Urie Bronfenbrenner (Bronfenbrenner, 1979), Antonak and Livheh (1988) recognized three levels of influence in layers around a person with a disability. Closest to the individual are family and friends, with the layer just beyond being the professionals and teachers who provide services. The outermost level is the general public in the community. This is the layer where teachers can serve as key mediators to ameliorate the relationship between children with disabilities and the people in the community in which the children live (Antonak & Livneh, 1988). This concept of the teacher as a mediator between the child and the community layers of influence is relevant to keep in mind when considering the transition of children from one program of services or school to another within the community. It is also relevant because children may be receiving multiple services from different agencies within a community.

Definition and types of transitions. Transition refers to the process of changing a child from one program of services to another or a child receiving services from multiple providers simultaneously. Transitions can be viewed as "vertical" or "horizontal" in direction. Vertical transitions are those changes that are sequential across time, such as enrollment in a child-care center for early intervention with subsequent enrollment in a public school prekindergarten program as the next program of services for the child and family. Horizontal transition refers to the provision of multiple services that may be delivered at different locations to a child, such as physical therapy, occupational therapy, and child care. More research addresses vertical transitions from one program to the next rather than horizontal transition of services accessed by the family at any one given time (Rosenkoetter, Whaley, Hains, & Pierce, 2001).

Policy-guided transitions. In some cases, the role of the teacher in helping to transition children with disabilities into the community and the transition planning process is guided by governmental policy. Certain transition policies are the result of federal or state mandates that specify the requirements and parameters of planning transitions at system and individual levels. System level planning involves representatives from agencies, schools, or programs. For example, when a child will be transitioned from an early intervention program to a school district, IDEA 1997 mandates participation of representatives from each setting to conference with parents and plan the vertical transition for the child. This case exemplifies a system level transition planning effort that is precipitated by federal policy. The school district and the early intervention program are required by IDEA to collaborate with each other and the child's parents to ensure a smooth transition from one program to another.

Individual level transition planning focuses specifically on strategies for the child and the family. For instance, Part C of IDEA (1997) addresses the development of the Individualized Family Services Plan (IFSP) and requires development of a time line for the transition process. Both of these processes emphasize the individual nature of services to children and families.

Transition monitoring and evaluation. Transitions are monitored and evaluated at different levels to measure the success of the transition planning. At the systems level, the Office of Special Education Programs (OSEP) is responsible for monitoring the states' special education programs. Transition is one of the targeted cluster areas, with specified indicators and outcomes formally monitored as part of the overall evaluation of IDEA Part C implementation. Research has also been conducted to provide insight into the success of transitions and what teachers can do to improve transitions for children. Ecobehavioral assessment is a multivariate analysis technique that shows promise for evaluating the implementation of transition plans for children. Ecobehavioral assessment uses systematic, moment-to-moment observation to examine the effects of multiple contextual variables on behavior of children or teachers (Kamps, Leonard, & Greenwood, 1991). This approach has been successfully used to compare the characteristics of the classroom setting in which the child is currently enrolled to the classroom into which the child will transition. Specific attributes and conditions of classrooms can be compared. The approach takes into account the ecological contexts of the settings and the behaviors of teachers and children within those contexts. The impact of vertical transitions from preschool to kindergarten and the early grades has been studied using these techniques.

The ecobehavioral assessment approach can also evaluate children's survival skills in the new classroom to which they have been transitioned. For example, Carta, Greenwood and Robinson (1987) report that teachers have used data gathered through this methodology to plan ways to improve student engagement in tasks or to reduce the amount of time spent in transition from one activity to another during the school day (Carta & Greenwood, 1988; Carta et al., 1987). More recently, ecobehavioral assessment has also been used to examine different instructional contexts available for transitioning English language learners who are at risk of developmental disabilities. These assessments are well-suited to capturing the complexity of classroom environments, particularly child and teacher behaviors, that may impact the success of transitions for children. This type of analysis, which gathers data across multiple variables in each classroom ecology, may enlighten transition planners who must deal with decisions about individual children who are learning English as a second language. It could enable the transition planners to make better choices about the appropriateness of general education and bilingual special education programs for serving English language learners who are at risk for developmental disabilities (Arreaga-Mayer, Utley, Perdomo-Rivera, & Greenwood, 2003).

Implications for teachers. The transition planning processes have several implications for teachers in inclusion settings. Teachers must understand their roles and responsibilities regarding the transitions that are critical to the development and learning of children with special needs. Teachers will be more effective in facilitating a child's transitions if they know the federal and state policies regarding transitions and have an understanding of aspects of transitions that are not guided by policy. Further, teachers can be more supportive of families and better understand the child when they are knowledgeable about the kind and range of services provided by community agencies to the child with disabilities. Lastly, teachers can serve as change agents when they are active and informed advocates for effective policies to guide transition processes.

PREPARING FOR INCLUSIVE TEACHING

A growing number of authors are calling for professional preparation approaches that better prepare teachers for the diversity of today's classrooms. The long-standing belief that teachers with general child development education and training can teach all kinds of children has more recently been debunked. As groups of children in early childhood settings become more diverse, many contend that teachers with typical training are poorly prepared to deal with the cultural and linguistic complexity of classroom learning contexts and methods needed to facilitate the learning of all children. This is particularly true when children in a classroom speak multiple languages or low-incidence language groups, such as Tamil or Laotian. Mentoring has been suggested as one method of supporting new teachers in urban bilingual classrooms. Working with an experienced teacher can also help preservice teachers develop the ethnic literacy and teaching strategies necessary for teaching linguistically diverse children. The use of mentoring to improve the instruction of language minority children may also improve the retention of teachers in culturally diverse classrooms (Austin & Fraser-Abder, 1995; Gay & Kirkland, 2003).

Experts in the field of early childhood education, special education, bilingual education, and multicultural education, to name a few, are interested in the blending of fields from the standpoints of both theory and practice to better address the diversity of children and find effective methods for teaching all children (Arreaga-Mayer et al., 2003; Austin & Fraser-Abder, 1995; Baca & Cervantes, 1998). It is widely recognized that the attitudes and beliefs teachers hold are critical. Further, preparing teachers to use effective strategies and practices to address the diversity of children is instrumental in achieving the successful learning and inclusion of all children (O'Shea, 1999).

Multicultural Orientation

Modeling multicultural self-reflection and critical consciousness in teaching preservice teachers are effective strategies that have been recommended for developing culturally responsive teaching (Gay, 2002; Gay & Kirkland, 2003). Other initiatives have suggested requiring preservice teachers to participate in authentic multicultural experiences through a series of educational workshops. Participants would complete a self-inventory to identify areas of personal bias and measure cultural awareness. Minilectures on topics related to multicultural teaching strategies and practices would be presented. In addition to participating in multicultural mentoring, preservice teachers would plan and implement a lesson or activity with children to demonstrate their ability to apply the principles of multicultural education in an instructional setting with children. As a result of these preparatory strategies, experts believe teachers will be better prepared to create a tolerant, learning environment that would accept diversity and foster multicultural dialogue among children, families, and teachers (Pullen, 2000). Some authors contend that teachers have a moral obligation to use multicultural teaching practices. It is only in doing so that teachers will ensure high expectations for all children to learn and succeed in equitable classroom environments (Boutte, 2000; Pine & Hilliard III, 1990).

Collaborative Observation

Perhaps the wisest way to prepare teachers for the diversity of inclusive early childhood classrooms is to heed the advice of Rebecca New (1994). She urged adoption of the concept of teachers as collaborative researchers who observe and respond to the individual nuances of children. She asserted that rather than strict interpretations of the construct of developmentally appropriate practice in isolation, teachers should be prepared to think as researchers who seek truth for individual children. By collaborating with parents and viewing a child's development through the cultural lens of family, teachers may come closer to interpreting an individual child's development. Only then is it possible to match practices that have a high degree of probability for facilitating the learning of that individual child (New, 1994).

Collaboration Through Professional Involvement

Early childhood teachers interested in teaching all young children can find support for their efforts through involvement in professional organizations. Joining professional

COLLABORATION TIPS   BOX 2.8

- Join a professional organization. Many have branches for preservice teachers at colleges and universities with reduced membership rates for students.
- Read professional journals and literature.
- Start a study group to discuss articles with your colleagues.
- Bookmark Websites of your favorite organizations and visit them often for ideas and information on new legislation or changes to policies affecting your inclusive classroom.

organizations gives early childhood teachers ways to collaborate with other teachers and professionals interested in early childhood and providing inclusive early childhood education to all young children. Some organizations also attract parents and families into the membership of the organization and have literature and events to help them grow and learn in collaboration with professionals in the field. Stay informed about new developments in the field, gain support for teaching, and network with other early childhood professionals. Box 2.8 provides collaboration tips and Box 2.9 lists many professional organizations.

PROFESSIONAL ORGANIZATIONS   **BOX 2.9**

Here are a few Websites of professional organizations you can explore:

Council for Exceptional Children, Division for Early Childhood
http://www.dec-sped.org

National Association for the Education of Young Children
http://www.naeyc.org

Association for Childhood International
http://www.acei.org

Teachers of English to Speakers of Other Languages
http://www.tesol.org

National Association for Bilingual Education
http://www.nabe.org

American Association of University Women
http://www.aauw.org

SUMMARY

This chapter discussed the complex and varied role of teachers in inclusive early childhood classrooms. The roles and responsibilities of the various kinds of early childhood professionals serving in teaching roles were discussed. Responsibilities were viewed from these various interdisciplinary perspectives. Teachers serve as learning strategists who strive to improve children's learning by modeling learning strategies and facilitating children's learning processes. Teachers observe children as they solve problems, providing guidance when needed. It is essential that teachers develop cultural competence so they can be responsive to children's reception of curriculum content and learning styles. Cultural competence is invaluable in forging reciprocal relationships with families. Key characteristics of effective teachers were identified. The role of the teacher as a collaborator with specialists and other professionals was elaborated. The chapter concluded with sections on the inclusive classroom teacher as an advocate for children and families and as a community liaison. The role of the teacher assisting families to plan transitions for children from one program to another was explored.

Discussion Questions

1. What are the key characteristics that define the role of teachers in inclusive classrooms?
2. Discuss how inclusive early childhood education teachers collaborate with other teachers, professionals, and families.
3. Describe a culturally competent inclusive education teacher.
4. Describe the role of the teacher as an expert learner.
5. What types of collaboration can teachers expect, and describe their participation in these roles?
6. How can teachers prepare to serve as advocates for children?
7. Why is interaction with the community an important role for teachers?
8. What kinds of transition occur for children in early childhood settings? How can teachers partner with families to plan for smooth transitions for children?

Inclusive Activities

1. Find out whether there are nonprofit agencies in your area that train volunteers as child advocates. Are there other ways a teacher can become involved in advocacy for all children in your community?

2. Observe a teacher in an inclusive early childhood classroom. Write anecdotal notes about episodes in which the teacher is facilitating cognitive learning or problem solving.

3. Interview a teacher in an inclusive classroom about classroom management. Plan a set of questions before the interview. Ask the teacher to tell you about favorite strategies for organizing, scheduling, and keeping the classroom running smoothly.

4. Observe a coteaching team of teachers in an inclusive classroom. See if you can identify their strategies for collaboration. Talk to the teachers later face-to-face or by phone or e-mail. Ask them to verify and elaborate on the collaboration strategies you identified.

5. Shadow a related services specialist for a morning. Make a list of ways the speech therapist, occupational therapist, behavior interventionist, or other personnel interact and collaborate with families, teachers, and other professionals.

References

American Speech-Language-Hearing-Association Ad Hoc Committee on the Roles and Responsibilities of the School-Based Speech-Language Pathologist. (1999). *The guidelines for the roles and responsibilities of the school-based speech-language pathologist.* Rockville, MD: Author.

Antonak, R. F., & Livneh, H. (1988). *The measurement of attitudes toward people with disabilities: Methods, psychometrics and scales.* Springfield, IL: Thomas.

Arreaga-Mayer, C., Carta, J., & Tapia, Y. (1992). *Ecobehavioral system for the contextual recording of interactional bilingual environments: Training manual.* Kansas City: University of Kansas, Juniper Gardens Children's Project.

Arreaga-Mayer, C., & Perdomo-Rivera, C. (1996). Ecobehavioral analysis of instruction for at-risk minority students. *The Elementary School Journal, 96*(3), 245–258.

Arreaga-Mayer, C., Utley, C. A., Perdomo-Rivera, C., & Greenwood, C. R. (2003). Ecobehavioral assessment of instructional contexts in bilingual special education programs for English language learners at risk for developmental disabilities. *Focus on Autism and Other Developmental Disabilities, 18*(1), 28–40.

August, D., & Hakuta, K. (Eds.). (1997). *Improving schooling for language-minority children: A research agenda.* Washington, DC: National Academy Press.

Austin, T., & Fraser-Abder, P. (1995). Mentoring mathematics and science preservice teachers for urban bilingual classrooms. *Education and Urban Society, 28*(1), 67–89.

Baca, L. M., & Cervantes, H. T. (1998). *The bilingual special education interface.* Upper Saddle River, NJ: Merrill/Prentice Hall.

Bacon, E. H., & Schultz, J. B. (1991). A survey of mainstreaming practices. *Teacher Education and Special Education, 14,* 144–149.

Baer, J. (1993/94). Why you shouldn't trust creativity tests. *Educational Leadership, 51*(4), 80–83.

Banks, J. A. (1997). Multicultural education: Characteristics and goals. In J. A. Banks & C. A. M. Banks (Eds.), *Multicultural Education: Issues and perspectives* (3rd ed., pp. 3–31). Boston: Allyn & Bacon.

Blue-Banning, M., Summers, J. A., Frankland, H. C., Nelson, L. L., & Beegle, G. et al. (2004). Dimensions of family and professional partnerships: Constructive guidelines for collaboration. *Exceptional Children, 70*(2), 167–184.

Blue-Banning, M. J., Turnbull, A. P., & Pereira, L. (2000). Group action planning as a support strategy for hispanic families: Parent and professional perspectives. *Mental Retardation, 38*(3), 262–275.

Bodrova, E., & Leong, D. (1996). *Tools of the mind: The Vygotskian approach to early childhood education.* Upper Saddle River, NJ: Merrill/Prentice Hall.

Boutte, G. (2000). Multiculturalism: Moral and educational implications. *Dimensions of Early Childhood, 28*(3), 9–16.

Bricker, D., & Cripe, J. J. W. (1992). *An activity-based approach to early intervention.* Baltimore: Brookes.

Bronfenbrenner, U. (1979). *The ecology of human development.* Cambridge, MA: Harvard University Press.

Buswell, B., & Schaffner, B. (1992). Building friendships—An important part of schooling. *News In Print, 4*(4), 5–9.

Caine, G. (2004). Getting creativity, imagination, and learning. *Independent Schools, 63*(2).

Caldera, Y. M., Huston, A. C., & O'Brien, M. (1989). Social interactions and play patterns of parents and toddlers with feminine, masculine, and neutral toys. *Child Development, 60,* 70–76.

Carta, J. J., & Greenwood, C. R. (1988). *The validation of a classroom survival skills intervention package: Measuring short-and long-term effects on young children with handicaps.* Washington, DC: Grant funded by U.S. Department of Education.

Carta, J. J., Greenwood, C. R., & Atwater, J. B. (1985). *Ecobehavioral system for the complex assessment of preschool environments: ESCAPE* (No. ERIC [ED 288 268] [EC 200 587]). Kansas City: Juniper Gardens Children's Project, Bureau of Child Research, University of Kansas.

Carta, J. J., Greenwood, C. R., & Robinson, S. L. (1987). Application of an ecobehavioral approach to the evaluation of early intervention programs. In R. Prinz (Ed.), *Advances in behavioral assessment of children and families* (Vol. 3, pp. 123–155). Greenwich, CT: JAI Press.

Chow, V. T., & Kasari, C. (1999). Task-related interactions among teachers and exceptional, at-risk, and typical learners in inclusive classrooms. *Remedial and Special Education, 20*(4), 226–232.

Delpit, L. (1995). *Other people's children: Cultural conflicts in the classrooms.* New York: The New Press.

Derman-Sparks, L. (1993). Revisiting multicultural education: What children need to live in a diverse society. *Dimensions of Early Childhood, 21*(2), 6–10.

Dissinger, F. K. (2003). Core curriculum in assistive technology: In-service for special educators and therapists. *Journal of Special Education Technology, 18*(2), 35–45.

Downing, J., Ryndak, D. L., & Clark, D. (2000). Paraeducators in inclusive classrooms: Their own perceptions. *Remedial and Special Education, 21*(3), 171–181.

Ehren, B. J. (2000). Maintaining a therapeutic focus and sharing responsibility for student success: Keys to in-classroom speech-language services. *Language, Speech, and Hearing Services in Schools, 31*(3), 219–229.

Eisner, E. W. (2002). *The arts and the creation of mind.* New Haven, CT: Yale University Press.

Farber, J., & Klein, E. (1999). Classroom-based assessment of a collaborative intervention program with kindergarten and first-grade students. *Language, Speech, & Hearing Services in Schools, 30,* 83–91.

Favazza, P. C. (1998). Preparing for children with disabilities in early childhood classrooms. *Early Childhood Education Journal, 25*(4), 255–258.

File, N. (1994). Children's play, teacher-child interactions, and teacher beliefs in integrated early childhood programs. *Early Childhood Research Quarterly, 9,* 223–240.

Fisher, D., Frey, N., & Thousand, J. (2003). What do special educators need to know and be prepared to do for inclusive schooling to work? *Teacher Education and Special Education, 26*(1), 42–50.

Foster, S. M. (1993). Meeting the needs of gifted and talented preschoolers. *Children Today, 22*(3), 28–30.

Friend, M., & Bursuck, W. D. (2002). *Including students with special needs.* Boston: Allyn & Bacon.

Fuchs-Beauchamp, K. D., Karnes, M. B., & Johnson, L. J. (1993). Creativity and intelligence in preschoolers. *Gifted Child Quarterly, 37*(3), 113–117.

Gallagher, T., Swigert, N., & Baum, H. (1998). Collecting outcomes data in schools: Needs and challenges. *Language, Speech, and Hearing Services in Schools, 29,* 250–256.

Garrett, J. E., & Morgan, D. E. (2002). Celebrating diversity by educating all students: Elementary teacher and principal collaboration. *Education, 123*(2), 268–275.

Garriott, P., Miller, M., & Snyder, L. (2003). Preservice teachers' beliefs about inclusive education: What should teacher educators know? *Action in Teacher Education, 25*(1), 48–54.

Gay, G. (2002). Culturally responsive teaching in special education for ethnically diverse students: Setting the stage. *Qualitative Studies in Education, 15*(6), 613–629.

Gay, G., & Kirkland, K. (2003). Developing cultural critical consciousness and self-reflection in preservice teacher education. *Theory into Practice, 42*(3), 181–187.

Geer, C. H., & Hamill, L. B. (2003). Using technology to enhance collaboration between special education and general education majors. *Tech Trends, 47*(3), 26–29.

Gudykunst, W., & Kim, Y. (1992). *Communicating with strangers: An approach to intercultural communication* (2nd ed.). New York: McGraw-Hill.

Hamill, L. B., Jantzen, A. K., & Bargerhuff, M. E. (1999). Analysis of effective educator competencies in inclusive environments. *Action in Teacher Education, 21*(3), 21–37.

Hastings, R., Hewes, A., Lock, S., & Witting, A. (1996). Do special educational needs courses have any impact on student teachers' perceptions of children with severe learning difficulties? *British Journal of Special Education, 23,* 139–144.

Horn, E., Lieber, J., Li, S., Sandall, S., & Schwartz, I. (2000). Supporting young children's IEP goals in inclusive settings through embedded learning opportunities. *Topics in Early Childhood Special Education, 20*(4), 208–223.

Hourcade, J. J., & Bauwens, J. (2003). Cooperative teaching: The renewal of teachers. *The Clearing House, 74*(5), 242–247.

Hourcade, J. J., Parette, H. P., & Anderson, H. (2003). Accountability in collaboration: A framework for evaluation. *Education and Training in Developmental Disabilities, 38*(4), 398–404.

Individuals with Disabilities Education Act, Amendments of 1997, 20 U.S.C.A. §§ 1401, 1412, 1414 (2000).

Ispa, J. (1981). Social interactions among teachers, handicapped children, and nonhandicapped children in a full-inclusion preschool. *Journal of Applied Developmental Psychology, 1,* 231–250.

Jones, R. S., Wint, D., & Ellis, N. C. (1990). The social effects of stereotyped behaviour. *Journal of Mental Deficiency Research, 34,* 261–268.

Jordan, A., & Stanovich, P. (2001). Patterns of teacher-student interaction in inclusive elementary classrooms and correlates with student self-concept. *International Journal of Disability, Development and Education, 48*(1), 33–52.

Kamps, D. M., Leonard, B. R., & Greenwood, C. R. (1991). Ecobehavioral assessment of students with autism and developmental disabilities. In R. J. Prinz (Ed.), *Advances in behavioral assessment of children and families* (Vol. 5, pp. 201–237). London: Jessica Kingsley.

Keifer-Boyd, K., & Kraft, L. M. (2003). Inclusion policy in practice. *Art Education, 56*(6), 46–53.

King, E., Chipman, M., & Cruz-Janzen, M. (1994). *Educating young children in a diverse society.* Boston: Allyn & Bacon.

Landry, S. H., Smith, K. E., Swank, P. R., Assel, M. A., & Veliet, S. (2001). Does early responsive parenting have a special importance for children's development or is consistency across early childhood necessary? *Developmental Psychology, 37,* 387–403.

Leistyna, P. (2004). Presence of mind in the process of learning and knowing: A dialogue with Paulo Freire. *Teacher Education Quarterly, 31*(1), 17–29.

Losardo, A., & Bricker, D. (1994). Activity-based intervention and direct instruction: A comparison study. *American Journal on Mental Retardation, 98,* 744–765.

McCollum, J. A., & Bair, H. (1994). Research in a parent-child interaction: Guidance to developmentally appropriate practices for young children with disabilities. In B. I. Mallory & R. S. New (Ed.), *Diversity and developmentally appropriate practices: Challenges for early childhood education* (pp. 84–106). New York: Teachers College Press.

McCollum, J. A., & McBride, S. L. (1997). Ratings of parent-infant interaction: Raising questions of cultural validity. *Topics in Early Childhood Special Education, 17,* 494–519.

McCormick , L., Noonan, M. J., & Heck, R. (1998). Variables affecting engagement in inclusive preschool classrooms. *Journal of Early Intervention, 21,* 160–176.

McCormick, L., Noonan, M. J., & Ogata, V. (2001). Co-teacher relationship and program quality: Implications for preparing teachers for inclusive preschool settings. *Education and Training in Mental Retardation and Developmental Disabilities, 36*(2), 119–132.

McIntosh, R., Vaughn, S., Schumm, J., Haager, D., & Lee, O. (1993/1994). Observations of students with learning disabilities in general education classrooms. *Exceptional Children, 60*(3), 249–261.

Moran, J. D., Milgram, R. M., & Fu, V. R. (1983). Stimulus specificity in the measurement of original thinking in preschool children. *Journal of Psychology, 114,* 99–105.

Moran, J. D., Milgram, R. M., Sawyers, J. K., & Fu, V. R. (1983). Original thinking in preschool children. *Child Development, 54,* 921–926.

Moran, J. D., Sawyer, R. J., Fu, V. R., & Milgram, R. M. (1984). Predicting imaginative play in preschool children. *Gifted Child Quarterly, 28,* 92–98.

Moss, E. (1992). Early interactions and metacognitive development of gifted preschoolers. In P. S. Klein & A. J. Tannenbaum (Eds.), *To be young and gifted* (pp. 278–318). Norwood, NJ: Ablex.

National Association of State Boards of Education Study Group on Special Education. (1992). *Winners all: Call for inclusive schools.* Alexandria, VA: National Association of State Boards of Education.

New, R. S. (1994). Culture, child development, and developmentally appropriate practices: Teachers as collaborative researchers. In B. L. Mallory & R. S. New (Eds.), *Diversity and developmentally appropriate practices: Challenges for early childhood education* (pp. 65–83). New York: Teachers College Press.

Noonan, M. J., McCormick, L., & Heck, R. H. (2003). The co-teacher relationship scale: Applications for professional development. *Education and Training in Developmental Disabilities, 38*(1), 113–120.

Odom, S. L., & Wolery, M. (2003). A unified theory of practice in early intervention/early childhood special education: Evidence-based practices. *The Journal of Special Education, 37*(3), 164–173.

O'Shea, D. J. (1999). Making unvited inclusion work. *Preventing School Failure, 43*(4), 179–180.

Parsons, M. B., & Reid, D. H. (1999). Training basic teaching skills to paraeducators of students with severe disabilities: A one-day program. *Teaching Exceptional Children, 31*(4), 48–54.

Pianta, R. C., La Paro, K., Payne, C., Cox, M., & Bradley, R. (2002). The relation of kindergarten classroom environment to teacher, family, and school characteristics and child outcomes. *The Elementary School Journal, 102,* 225–238.

Pickett, A. L. (1996). *A state of the art report on paraeducators in education and related services.* New York: National Resource Center for Paraprofessionals, Center for Advanced Study in Education, City University of New York.

Pickett, A. L. (1997). *Paraeducators in school settings: Framing the issues.* Austin, TX: PRO-ED.

Pine, G. J., & Hilliard III, A. (1990). Rx for racism: Imperatives for America's schools. *Phi Delta Kappan, 71*(8), 593–600.

Pullen, P. (2000). Breaking racial stereotypes by reconstructing multicultural education. *Multicultural Education, 7*(3), 44–46.

Riggs, C. G. (2001). Ask the paraprofessionals. *Teaching Exceptional Children, 33*(3), 78–83.

Rimm-Kaufman, S. E., Voorhees, M. D., Snell, M. E., & La Paro, K. M. (2003). Improving the sensitivity and responsibility of preservice teachers toward young children with disabilities. *Topics in Early Childhood Special Education, 23*(3), 151–163.

Rosenkoetter, S., Whaley, K., Hains, A. H., & Pierce, L. (2001). The evolution of transition policy for young children with special needs and their families: past, present, and future. *Topics in Early Childhood Special Education, 21*(1), 3–15.

Sailor, W. (2002). Devolution, school/community/family partnerships, and inclusive education. In W. Sailor (Ed.), *Whole school success and inclusive education* (pp. 7–25). New York: Teachers College Press.

Salend, S. J., Gordon, J., & Lopez-Vona, K. (2002). Evaluating cooperative teaching teams. *Intervention in School & Clinic, 37*(4), 195–200.

Schwartz, I. S., Carta, J. J., & Grant, S. (1996). Examining the use of recommended language intervention practices in early childhood special education. *Topics in Early Childhood Special Education, 39,* 210–217.

Smith, B. (2000). The federal role in early childhood special education policy in the next century: The responsibilty of the individual. *Topics in Early Childhood Special Education, 20*(1), 7–13.

Soodak, L. C. (2003). Classroom management in inclusive settings. *Theory into Practice, 42*(4), 327–333.

Soodak, L. C., Erwin, E. J., Winton, P., Turnbull, A. P., Hanson, M. J., & Brault, L. (2002). Implementing inclusive early childhood education: A call for professional empowerment. *Topics in Early Childhood Special Education, 22*(2), 91–102.

Stainback, W., Stainback, S., & Stefanich, G. (1996). Learning together in inclusive classrooms. *Teaching Exceptional Children, 28*(3), 14–19.

Staub, D., & Peck, C. A. (1994). What are the outcomes for nondisabled students? *Educational Leadership, 52*(4), 36–40.

Stewart, C. (1990). Effects of practical types in preservice adapted physical education curriculum on attitudes toward disabled populations. *Journal of Teaching in Physical Education, 10,* 76–83.

Sturm, C. (1997). Creating parent-teacher dialogue: Intercultural communication in child care. *Young Children, 52*(5), 34–38.

Tait, K., & Purdie, N. (2000). Attitudes toward disability: Teacher education for inclusive environments in an Australilan university. *International Journal of Disability, Development, and Education, 47*(1), 25–38.

Taylor, R. L., Richards, S. B., Goldstein, P. A., & Schilit, J. (1997). Teacher perceptions of inclusive settings. *Teaching Exceptional Children, 29,* 50–54.

Thompson, R. H., Vitale, P. A., & Jewett, J. P. (1984). Teacher-student interaction patterns in full-inclusion classrooms. *Remedial and Special Education, 17*(5), 51–61.

Vaughn, C., Schumm, J., Jallad, B., Slusher, J., & Saumell, L. (1996). Teachers' views of inclusion. *Learning Disabilities: Research & Practice, 11*, 96–106.

Villa, R. A., & Thousand, J. S. (1995). The rationales for creating inclusive schools. In R. A. Villa & J. S. Thousand (Eds.), *Creating an inclusive school* (pp. 28–44). Alexandria, VA: Association for Supervision and Curriculum Development.

Will, M. (1986). *Educating children with learning problems: A shared responsibility.* Washington, DC: U.S. Department of Education, Office of Special Education.

Winton, P. J. (2000). Early childhood intervention personnel preparation: Backward mapping for future planning. *Topics in Early Childhood Special Education, 20*(2), 87–94.

Wolery, M. (2000). Recommended practices in child-focused interventions. In S. Sandall, M. E. McLean, & B. J. Smith (Ed.), *DEC recommended practices in early intervention/early childhood special education* (pp. 29–37). Longmont, CO: Sopris West.

Wolery, M., Brashers, M. S., & Neitzel, J. C. (2002). Ecological congruence assessment for classroom activities and routines: Identifying goals and intervention practices in childcare. *Topics in Early Childhood Special Education, 22*(3), 131–142.

Wolery, M., Martin, C. G., Schroeder, C., Huffman, K., Venn, M. L., Holcombe, A., et al. (1994). Employment of educators in preschool mainstreaming: A survey of general early educators. *Journal of Early Intervention, 18*, 64–77.

Wood, M. (1998). Whose job is it anyway? Educational roles in inclusion. *Exceptional Children, 64*(2), 181–195.

Chapter 3

Collaborating with Families and the Community

Key Principle

- Create reciprocal partnerships with families

Objectives

After reading this chapter you will be able to:

1. Discuss changing needs of families in our society.
2. Explain the ecological model of child development and the role of families within the model.
3. List the ways that cultures within the community context influence children and families.
4. Discuss how to collaborate with families to plan the curriculum and meet individual needs of children and families.
5. Conduct a parent conference and effectively communicate with families.
6. Establish a reciprocal partnership with families to increase family involvement and promote communication.

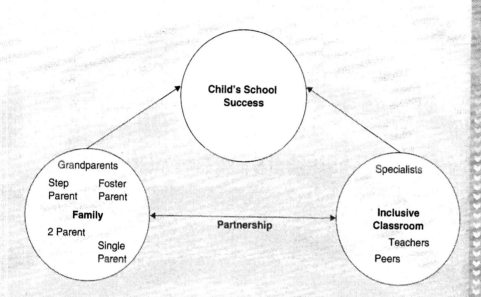

INTRODUCTION

Bridging home to inclusive classrooms requires establishing strong, collaborative partnerships with families. The diversity of communities today presents both challenges and a wealth of resources to teachers striving to help all children succeed. It is important to remember that a key goal of inclusive early childhood education is to provide high quality educational experiences for diverse groups of children who vary in ability. Ideally, these experiences occur both at school and at home through coordinated efforts of teachers and parents.

This goal cannot be achieved without responsive teaching, which means the teacher's practices take into account the rich diversity of home and community contexts that influence children and their families. Still more crucial is the responsibility of teachers to encourage families to unite with schools and form partnerships to increase the continuity between home and school. The hope is that home-school partnerships will support parents in assuming their responsibilities and encourage them to engage in high-quality interactions with their children at home.

This chapter discusses the ways teachers can interface with the rich, cultural tapestry of families who make up the fabric of typical communities today and how the communities, in turn, can support the parents. Teachers and schools are responsible for finding effective ways to bridge homes to the inclusive classrooms. Understanding how to accomplish this goal and why it is critical to establish collaborative home-school relationships is essential to achieving the goals of inclusive education. Increasing each teacher's knowledge of families' cultures is prerequisite to effectiveness in partnering with families to enhance the learning of children. The attitudes, values, and beliefs that teachers hold regarding families and the relationship of schools to homes and communities are extremely influential.

UNDERSTANDING THE CHANGING NEEDS OF FAMILIES

Responsibilities of family units have traditionally been to provide for the shelter, proper nutrition, health care, education, and other basic life components for their children. However, the capacity of families to meet these responsibilities and their resources for achieving these goals varies and changes over time. Families are influenced by a host of social, political, and economic factors that either facilitate or impede their ability to accomplish basic responsibilities, such as caring for and educating their children. Pertinent to this discussion is the widespread recognition that characteristics and needs of families, individually and as a society, will vary over time. To encourage the linkage of families and schools, it is imperative for early childhood professionals to recognize and plan for the realities that families face today.

Teachers and schools may choose to follow established models developed to guide collaboration of families and schools. However, it is vital to recognize that parental involvement models developed decades ago may not consider the full range of factors and situations that influence families currently. The extent of parental involvement that schools endorse and how early childhood teachers and administrators seek family participation gives insight about the school and its priorities (Epstein, 1995). The amount and kind of effort that education professionals expend to collaborate with families tells community members whether their participation is valued. Schools and programs endorse various roles for parents that encourage different levels of participation.

Berger (2000) identified six roles for parents that suggested participation varying in type and intensity. Although it is important to foster collaboration with families and establish productive lines of communication, teachers must be realistic about the level of participation each family can manage. Unrealistic expectations for family participation can add extra burdens to lives that might already be stressful. The key roles assumed are parents as:

1. Policy makers
2. Teachers of their own children

3. Employed resources
4. Volunteer resources
5. Temporary volunteers
6. Spectators

Some of these roles reflect minimal involvement of parents, such as the role of spectator in which the parent simply attends a meeting or as a temporary volunteer who provides occasional assistance to the school or classroom. Parents working as regular volunteers or for pay show greater levels of participation. Parents exhibit higher levels of participation when they assume more active roles in extending the curriculum at home or participating in creating policy for the school. Head Start programs exemplify the later type of participation by having Parent Advisory Councils in which parents must represent at least half the council membership (Berger, 2000).

Collaborating with All Kinds of Families

The societal definition of family has changed to include a broader range of configurations and characteristics. Families may have one or both parents present in the home or none at all. Increasing numbers of grandparents are assuming the role of primary caretakers for their young grandchildren. Families with a stepparent and a blending of stepchildren and half siblings are becoming more commonplace. Some children are residing in extended families arrangements with a number of related family members living in the same household. The extended family situation is customary in some

Contemporary families represent a variety of configurations and characteristics.

GRANDPARENT-HEADED HOUSEHOLD   BOX 3.1

Mrs. Coleman had noticed that increasing numbers of children in the Head Start center were being reared in families headed by grandparents. "Look at me Grandma!" Ezekial yelled as he jumped from the play structure into the bark chips below. His grandmother tried hard to make his life as happy as possible, but it is difficult to care for him on her limited income. "This neighborhood is not safe for children anymore," she lamented. "By the time my younger children were in high school, drugs and crime were on every street corner." Ezekial and his grandmother live in an urban neighborhood of a predominantly minority, high-poverty community. Ezekial's teenaged mother was a substance abuser who died of AIDS when he was 18 month of age. Ezekial, who is infected with HIV, lives with his grandmother who manages his health care crises as they occur and tries to provide him with a happy childhood. Grandma has health problems of her own, making the daily care of Ezekial more difficult. She feels guilty that she often doesn't feel well enough to play or read to Ezekial. "I worry about what will happen if I can't take care of Ezekial any more."

---

cultures as the natural order of family relationships. However, poverty can also precipitate the need for families, related or unrelated, to live in multiple family dwelling arrangements. Family constellations can be composed of various members who may be related by blood, marriage, or adoption. Children may also form family-type relationships with unrelated friends or life partners of adult family members. In a growing number of cases, a child's parents may be of the same gender. Family configurations may remain stable or the constitution of a child's family may vary in membership multiple times during the span of childhood. Box 3.1 demonstrates a grandparent's point of view.

Teenaged parents. Deserving particular attention in the United States is the high number of parents who are teenaged and often unmarried. Teenaged parents need strong, supportive relationships with teachers in early childhood and school settings. Children of these families are among those with the highest risks of school failure and negative outcomes in our society today. The high numbers of births to teenaged unmarried mothers accounts for about 13.1% of all births. The prognosis for teenaged parents and their children is very poor. The mothers suffer a dramatically increased likelihood of dropping out of school. More than one quarter of teenaged mothers fail to complete their high school educations. The infants born to teenaged mothers are at greater risk of low birth weight and related health problems, disabilities, and delays in development. The problems associated with teenagers giving birth continues to plague these children, resulting in high rates of academic failure and social maladjustment into adulthood (Children's Defense Fund, 1998).

It is important for teachers in inclusive settings to learn how to create good partnerships with all kinds of families. A prerequisite to establishing positive family relationships is for teachers to examine their attitudes and become aware of any prejudices

---

MY REFLECTION   **BOX 3.2**

- What kinds of families have you met?
- In what ways do you feel prepared to collaborate with all kinds of families?
- Describe how you think partnerships with families should look.
- In what ways do you believe children benefit from home-school collaboration?

---

they might be holding. Children can thrive in a variety of family configurations, provided their needs for a safe, healthy and psychologically supportive home are met. Consequently, it is critical that caregivers and teachers avoid making assumptions to the contrary based on personal biases and prejudices (see Box 3.2).

Economic and Social Pressures

Formerly popular notions of deficit-focused programs with aims to ameliorate the needs and weaknesses of poor and minority children have given way to more positive views. Emphasis is now placed on identifying the strengths of children and their families and working through those strengths to support the children's successes. Nonetheless, the impact of a family's economic security on children is undeniable. Children of low socioeconomic income status are at risk of suffering consequences attributable to discontinuity between home and school contexts. Cultural or racial minority families may find that a substantially wider gulf exists between their homes and the schools their children attend. Schools contexts are often more similar to home contexts of middle-income families and those of majority status. When cultural discontinuity between home and school is present, it may be more difficult for children and their families to adjust to school. Keeping this in mind, teachers can better determine the level of discontinuity that might exist and take steps to lessen the gap through responsiveness to each family's culture and socioeconomic circumstances (Coleman & Churchill, 1997; L. Delpit, 1995; L. D. Delpit, 1992; Meyer, Harry, & Sapon-Shevin, 1997).

Families in poverty. Family economic security is foundational to ensure that all young children enter formal school settings ready to learn. The National Center for Children in Poverty reports that among indicators for measuring school success, income is one of the most critical factors in predicting school outcomes (Knitzer, 2002). Poverty can have serious and deleterious effects on the cognitive development of children. Increasing a family's economic security can improve educational opportunities and outcomes for children (Knitzer, 2002).

Contrary to popular belief, Bowman (1994) espoused that children living in poverty and from minority group families are not at risk developmentally. Instead, they are at risk because of the mismatch of their home and school environments, which is largely ignored by schools. Further, when there is a difference between the behaviors families value and those prized by schools, children have an increased risk of school failure. Schools and child-care programs can improve the chances for young children to succeed by adopting culturally responsive practices to bridge homes to inclusive classrooms. Even when homes and schools value similar competencies, they may differ in what constitutes acceptable manifestations of desired knowledge and skills. Culturally responsive schools help support the social skill formation of children by partnering with families to encourage peer friendships and support a sense of community among children (Bowman, 1994).

Ecological Layers of Influence

Early childhood can be viewed as an ecosystem with many layers of influence, both positive and negative, that shape the growth, development, and learning of children. As introduced in Chapter 1, Urie Bronfenbrenner proposed an ecological perspective for representing the relationships and factors that influence children and their families. The family, the neighborhood, and the community exert a direct and an indirect impact on children (Bronfenbrenner, 1979; Bronfenbrenner & Morris, 1998). Effective early childhood programs seek to intervene through involvement of people and resources existing within these multiple layers of influence. Often referred to as integrated programs, these projects foster collaboration of services that exist within communities. Integrated programs are thought to be the most comprehensive approaches to improve life for children and families with the greatest likelihood of success. For example, fostering collaboration between child-care centers in public housing projects and public schools can put half-day early education programs at the public schools in reach of parents who are employed all day. One such project in Boston provided families with a greater range of early education options by linking child-care at the public housing site to early childhood programs available in the nearby public school. This linkage provided single, low-income mothers with an opportunity to work, continue their education, or receive job training while their young children received affordable early education and care seamlessly throughout the day (Lassen & Janey, 1991). Without cooperation between programs in the community, families can find it difficult to access the services available for educating and caring for their young children. Integrated programs can have tremendous community impact when these programs seek not only to improve the quality of life for children, but also to increase the potential for positive influences to be exerted by the people in the ecological system surrounding the child.

KNOWING THE COMMUNITY AND THE NEIGHBORHOOD

The community is increasingly touted as the panacea of societal ills, including difficulties in rearing and educating children. Many professionals contend that since the 1960s, the sense of community among people in neighborhoods has declined. This lack of community has been associated with the growing violence and aggression of today's youth. A popular strategy is to promote the involvement of parents and the community in educational efforts of schools and child-care centers. Communities can contribute wonderful resources to improve education, and parental support can be very beneficial in reinforcing school efforts. However, Bushnell (2001) urges caution in viewing involvement of the community as the remedy for school failure. The community is a context in which families and children live. Consequently, one must view this context pragmatically, as a complex social organization that has both positive and negative attributes (Bushnell, 2001). A neighborhood surrounding a child-care center may have strong social service agencies. However, that same area may have a high rate of substance abuse that erodes the lives of families and the community.

For teachers in inclusive classrooms, knowing the neighborhood and understanding the lives of children and families who live there, is fundamental to optimize parent involvement in schools. Teachers are more effective in establishing collaborative partnerships with families when they genuinely respect their values and choices. Showing respect when planning and scheduling events is one way of fostering collaboration. The following paragraphs are a fictional account based on facts that exemplify the importance of demonstrating respect for the neighborhood culture and customs.

At a spring faculty meeting of the Fred Sanchez Elementary School, teachers discussed ways to elicit more involvement of families in the school program. The staff suggested an orientation meeting with parents of children who would be entering kindergarten in the fall. Principal Mrs. Trevino was delighted with the idea. The neighborhood was very close-knit, so it would be easy to spread the news of this meeting through informal word of mouth and more formal mailings. Mrs. Trevino suggested that a Tuesday might be the best day to hold the event since no other meetings were scheduled on those evenings. The prekindergarten teachers remarked that a popular "novela," a Spanish-language serial program, was broadcast on television every Tuesday evening. Through conversations with parents, most of whom were teenaged single mothers, the teachers knew that the women in the neighborhood rarely missed the popular television program. The rest of the teachers agreed that a meeting scheduled opposite the novela was likely to attract low attendance. "Don't you think the parents will miss one night?" Mrs. Trevino asked. The teachers discussed the fact that watching the novela is a big, weekly social event and the young mothers have few opportunities to socialize. Each week, the mothers get together at a different home and watch the television together. As a result, the teachers were skeptical that parents would forego the novela that had taken on such prominence in the lives of the parents. Mrs. Trevino said she found it hard to believe that parents would let an hour-long television program interfere with an important meeting about their children's education, so she discounted the teachers' skepticism and scheduled the meeting for a Tuesday night. The night of the meeting came and only 11 parents, out of more than 65 expected, attended the kindergarten orientation (see Box 3.3 for a reflection on this incident).

Understanding the Cultural Heritage

Gaining an understanding of the cultural heritage, beliefs, and customs of families is prerequisite to selecting culturally responsive practices to use in the inclusive classroom. Although learning general information about cultural groups might be a good starting point, it is essential for teachers to become familiar with the culture and customs of individual families. Cultural beliefs and practices for individual families within a cultural group may vary from those of other families within a similar cultural heritage. Assuming that typical group beliefs and behaviors apply to all families could be detrimental to establishing a good working relationship with parents. Early childhood teachers need to

Families view education through the cultural lenses of their heritage.

create many opportunities to communicate with parents, formally and informally. It is through such opportunities that teachers will begin to understand the nuances of each family's cultural makeup and it affects the daily lives and roles for each family member.

Cultural incongruities. Families view school and their child's academic progress through their unique cultural filters. It is not unusual for parents to see their children differently from the way that teachers view their children. For instance, it is not infrequent for a teacher to have a difference of opinion with parents regarding whether a child has a learning disability. Families often view the child's abilities as within the normal range for the child or as a feature of the child's personality or characteristics. Families may blame conditions that exist in the home or school environment for inhibiting the progress of their child. Further, some parents may view their child's learning of a second language as a situation that impedes with their child's progress. Whereas some experts attribute the discrepancy between parent and teacher perspectives to protective tendencies of families or parental denial, other experts believe that true incongruities exist. Parents and teachers may hold different expectations for children and each may view children through dissimilar cultural perspectives (Harry, 1992).

Cultural influences and school readiness. Racial and ethnic backgrounds of families can affect parental views regarding the readiness of children for formal school settings, such as starting kindergarten. Parents from minority groups have been reported concerns about the school readiness of their children. However, minority families and less educated parents are less likely to do anything to allay their worries. On the other hand, Caucasian parents and those who are highly educated are more likely to delay kindergarten entry for their children. Researchers have speculated these differences in behavior may occur because minority families, who tend to also have low income, often have fewer choices regarding the care and education for their children. Consequently, discrepancies between minority children and their majority peers may be apparent, especially when schools serve an economically and culturally diverse population of families (Brent, May, & Kundert, 1996; Diamond, 2000).

KNOWING AVAILABLE COMMUNITY RESOURCES

Effective early childhood teachers become active members of the communities in which they teach and live. Through community involvement, teachers may become aware of potential linkages between the business community, home, and school. Early childhood teachers can play a key role in developing these relationships into viable, lasting partnerships.

School administrators and child-care center directors who are knowledgeable about their community can engage the services of skillful professionals and experts from the community for specific needs of children and families (Delaney, 2001). For example, when a child with HIV enrolls in a prekindergarten class, a health care professional could be asked to train the teachers and staff in basic procedures for handling simple health care routines and first aid treatment.

Seek Authentic Contexts in Community

The community is often a rich source of contexts for authentic learning experiences of children. Knowing the community and engaging parents in dialogue about their neighborhood can reveal the potential sites for learning that might exist near family homes. These sites might be incorporated into school experiences as field trips or they may reveal potential resource people who can visit the inclusive classroom. Other sites can be suggested to families as places they can experience with their children. With knowledge of community contexts, teachers can suggest specific ways families can expand on the school curriculum to reinforce concepts and skills being acquired by children as they visit typical community sites.

Teacher involvement in communities. Teachers in inclusive classrooms are most effective when they become involved in the community where they teach. Increasing the continuity between home and school requires knowledge of the family and the community contexts. Through community involvement, teachers can better determine ways families might be involved and measures schools can take to support families. The inverse may also be true. As families see the interest of teachers in their family and community activities, family members may be more amenable to discovering more about their child's classroom and school. This reciprocal process of discovery can result in more positive support for children. When both teachers and families have knowledge of home and school contexts, greater harmony can be established. Consequently, the probability of providing ideal support for the child's growth, development, and learning is increased.

Active participation in the neighborhood enables teachers to collaborate with families and become resource people for the community.

CREATING PARTNERSHIPS WITH FAMILIES

Philosophical orientations toward parents and families have changed over time. Professionals have moved toward greater recognition of the importance of family partnerships, family rights, and the responsibility of parents to assume a key role in their children's program of learning or intervention. Beginning in the 1970s, early childhood professionals increasingly viewed family members as part of the equation in the learning process for young children. One explanation for this change in perspective was the accumulation of a body of research studies examining the level of influence that families exert on children's school achievement. Findings of reputable studies have led researchers to conclude that families were more influential to a child's success than teachers and schools (Coleman et al., 1966; Gordon, 1979). These results have underscored the significance of building effective partnerships with families in recognition of the rights, responsibilities, and influence parents have regarding the care and education of their young children.

Promoting Family Involvement

Promoting family involvement requires positive action to meet challenges and overcome barriers that might impede family collaboration with teachers and involvement in early childhood settings. It is important to recognize the challenging conditions that might hinder the establishment of productive partnerships between teachers and families. In 1997, Coleman and Churchill reported evidence suggesting that the educational attainment of parents and the family socioeconomic level are factors that appear to influence home and school relationships. Although parents of all educational and socioeconomic levels value the concept of family involvement, parents with greater educational attainment and higher income levels exhibit more participation in school involvement opportunities. Further, these authors cautioned that evidence did not indicate that all family involvement programs are universally effective. Further, these authors suggested that there might be two major challenges to bridging home and school in early childhood. First is a lack of consensus regarding a clear definition of family involvement. The second challenge to family involvement was identified as the degree of difference existing between home and school contexts.

Defining family involvement. Regarding the challenge of defining family involvement, it has been suggested that the ambiguous definitions of family involvement might lead schools to implement activities that lack relevance for families and the classrooms. Goals for family involvement can be selected based on broad themes with relevance to specific groups of families. Some examples of overarching themes for family involvement programs included:

- Identification of family strengths
- Empowerment of parents through information
- Preparing school children along with preschool siblings (Coleman & Churchill, 1997).

Discontinuity can be viewed as a construct that represents a continuum of dissonance. The degree of difference between home and school influences the relationship established between the family and the success of the child in school and greater discontinuity widens the gap. The willingness of families and teachers to compromise and plan ways to create a smooth transition from home to school will, undoubtedly, exert a positive or negative impact on the adjustment of children to early care and educational settings.

Teachers in inclusive classrooms who desire positive outcomes for all children are committed to collaborative partnerships with families. However, when discontinuity is great, home-school relationships will require much creativity and tenacity from both parents and teachers to achieve meaningful collaboration.

Responsiveness to diverse families. According to Schine (1998), responsiveness to diverse families of today is a challenge for schools. Teachers may experience difficulty in building a relationship based on trust, a characteristic that is foundational to establishing partnerships with families. However, trust is difficult for culturally and linguistically diverse families, such as recent immigrants. When language, customs, and schools are different from those in the family's homeland, trust is difficult to achieve (Schine, 1998).

Cultural discontinuities between home and school can arise from differences in race, language, and social status of families. Power and authority are also part of the equation. Families with greater resources and higher social standing may exert more influence on schools, relationships with teachers, and school policy than marginalized families. However, when all families are given equal membership in the home-school relationship, parents can effectively serve as advocates for their children, despite lack of resources. Therefore, it is critical to value each family regardless of their social and income status and empower them to become equal partners in the relationship with teachers and schools (Lewis & Forman, 2002) (see Box 3.4).

COLLABORATION TIPS   BOX 3.4

Strategies for Promoting Involvement of Families

- Honestly examine yourself to identify areas of prejudice and bias you may hold.
- Read and study about the tenets and practices of multicultural education.
- Plan ways to find out more about your community and the beliefs people hold that may influence child-rearing practices and attitudes toward education.
- Monitor your communications and interactions with families to avoid statements that evolve from misunderstandings or stereotypical images of ethnic groups.

Families in poverty. Poverty is a significant and very pervasive condition that may present families with a host of factors that can affect the nature of their participation in a home-school partnership. Yet, most teachers come from middle-class backgrounds that are vastly different from those of children and families they serve. Often, teachers fail to understand the rationale that underlies the parenting practices of families and their opinions regarding the care and education of their young children. Teachers can better serve families when they make an effort to discover the various ways that poverty conditions affect the family unit. At the same time, teachers are cautioned to avoid the trap of thinking that poverty or minority status means children will not achieve as well as White, middle-class children in early childhood and school classrooms. Socioeconomic status or cultural and ethnic backgrounds alone do not ordain ill-fated outcomes for children and their families (L. Delpit, 1995; L. D. Delpit, 1992).

Collaboration and early intervention. Early childhood professionals are often among the first people outside the family to gain a glimpse of the child's developmental status and learning abilities. It is always best when teachers are well-prepared with a thorough knowledge of child development, so they can identify children who may benefit from early intervention. Some children may be at risk due to poverty, premature birth, family difficulties, or medical conditions. Others may begin showing evidence of patterns of development that are atypical or delayed. Teachers in early childhood classrooms have the responsibility of assisting parents in monitoring developmental and growth patterns of young children. If children are receiving regular health care, pediatricians and other health care providers might also be counted among the persons with an opportunity to monitor the developmental status of children. Teachers, however, have the advantage of seeing children on a regular basis in a variety of situations with other children and adults. Consequently, teachers have a responsibility to collect information through ongoing assessments to carefully plot the progress of young children and to keep parents informed about the performance of their child in the classroom.

Teachers in early childhood classrooms are often among the first to find consistent evidence of an atypical pattern of development or delays in a child's development. When disparities in development are detected, it is the teacher's responsibility to keep parents informed of their findings. Even though teachers must be forthright, developmental information is best communicated with sensitivity and tact. Reactions of family members may vary from cooperation and concern to hostility and indignation. For any parent, news that something may be amiss will be worrisome. For some families, the teacher's observations may mirror their own and serve to further substantiate their apprehensions. These families may readily agree with the teacher's concerns and be willing to collaborate with the teacher to seek further assessment of their child. Other families may challenge the teacher's findings and deny that any delays exist. It is extremely important for teachers to be knowledgeable regarding the possible reactions families may have and to be prepared to offer support for parents receiving possible troubling news. Relaying difficult information is never easy. Enlisting the assistance of other professionals can facilitate the conversation with parents and add to the network of persons who can lend support to the family. It may be helpful to have the director of the child-care facility or the school counselor attend the conference at which the difficult or sensitive information about the child will be communicated to the family.

Remember that observations regarding a child's development or evidence that might suggest difficulty in learning must be presented as preliminary rather than diagnostic. Teachers are obligated to inform parents that diagnoses can only be made by qualified personnel. It is important to make it clear that valid diagnoses are made by diagnosticians, school psychologists, or other licensed professionals, following administration of an appropriate diagnostic battery of assessments. Providing information regarding how to seek further assessment can be helpful to families who are faced with this difficult situation. Knowing whom to contact to initiate a referral and where those persons are located is critical information for families seeking screening for their child. When teachers can explain the referral process and give parents specific information and persons to contact, they may feel more comfortable in following through with the referral in a timely manner. Especially when families are unfamiliar with schools and other institutions, continued teacher support is necessary throughout the referral process. Keeping the lines of communication open and being ready to listen to parents' concerns may be critical to ensure they gain the information and help needed for their child.

Some families will not seek further assessment immediately. The teacher's patience and steady support may be needed, as families cope with the unpleasant news about developmental lags. Family members, friends, or others in the community may advise

Establishing reciprocal partnerships with families is critical to the success of children.

parents to wait and see if the child grows out of the behaviors or acquires the skills and abilities to catch up with the child's peers. Parents may benefit from gentle words of encouragement as they consider their options and whether they will seek the advice of professionals. Ultimatums, intimidation, or harsh predictions regarding the future of the child are ineffective strategies for inducing parents to initiate a referral. Teachers must use utmost sensitivity in understanding the perspective of the family to the largest extent possible if they are to be supportive. Passage of time may help some parents to deal with the situation. Some families may benefit from another conference scheduled several weeks after the one in which the difficult news was relayed. Teachers can continue to document the child's progress, and updates can be given to parents. Families may need additional evidence and time to ponder their options before taking the next step. The vital strategy is for teachers to listen and lend continued support as families make decisions about their child (see Box 3.5 for collaboration tips).

Families of children with disabilities. The 1997 Amendments to IDEA precipitated a paradigm shift in the interaction and roles of parents and teachers. Formerly, teachers were regarded as experts and parents were viewed as recipients of information provided. The current view is that family support and parental interaction is a major responsibility of inclusive programs. The new partnership model carries the expectation that early childhood professionals will recognize the strengths of families and respect their priorities. Unfortunately, teachers generally receive little preparation for assuming these responsibilities. Consequently, teachers who are successful in establishing effective partnerships with families often undertake the task on their own, with varying levels of administrative support. The atmosphere of the inclusive classroom and the success of implementation are influenced by the administrative support given to teachers.

COLLABORATION TIPS   BOX 3.5

Strategies for Collaboration with Families of Children with Identified Special Needs

- Help parents find training programs that prepare families to advocate for their child.
- Identify community resources and agencies that might support families and help parent make initial contacts with these agencies.
- Communicate frequently with parents. A simple greeting may initiate much needed conversation for parents who are trying to cope with difficult circumstances.
- Be patient. Families with children who are recently identified with special needs typically go through stages of denial and grief.
- Share strategies that are successful in helping the child and also encourage parents to let you know what strategies work at home.

Gaining knowledge of adult learning can help teachers become better prepared to establish partnerships with families. The principles of adult learning apply to the changes parents must make, as they reconcile their former identity with that of being a parent of a child with disabilities. Teachers can promote better partnerships by understanding the adjustments families are making as they parent the child with disabilities. Teachers can facilitate partnerships with families by recognizing parents as an invaluable source of information about their child. Families know individual and unique characteristics of their children that may not fit with textbook definitions of a disabling condition.

Family-centered approaches aim to provide care and educational services to children with disabilities in natural contexts. This means teachers and other professionals in inclusive early childhood settings form partnerships with families to better view the child in the community context. Collaboration with parents of children with disabilities or special needs requires teachers to gain an understanding of how each parent's experience varies and affects the individual family. As teachers try various strategies to better understand the uniqueness of each family, it is critical to respect the privacy of families and observe cultural boundary lines (Bodner-Johnson, 2001; Soodak et al., 2002; Wesley & Buysse, 2001).

Differences in beliefs and values can present major challenges in establishing effective parent and teacher collaboration. The level of education attained and personal experiences regarding children with disabilities are reported to influence collaborative planning of parents and teachers. When asked to prioritize the valued characteristics of children with disabilities, rankings of teachers and parents often differ. Value and belief differences are thought to explain these perceptual disparities. The implication for teachers is that one cannot assume that families hold the same priorities for their children as do teachers and schools. The priorities teachers have tend to be narrowly focused on school work and school-related behavior. In contrast, mothers viewed characteristics of their children with disabilities from a wider perspective, including home-and life-functioning of children (Reyes-Blanes, Smalley, & Swire, 2001).

Diversity and disabilities. Having a child with a disability can introduce a variety of circumstances that challenge the day-to-day functioning of any family. When the family is also a member of a minority group, mistrust may present a barrier to the formation of cohesive partnerships with schools. Disenfranchised families may have had unpleasant experiences with schools or community agencies that have lead to the mistrust of service providers. Strategies for involving families in schools and overcoming the barriers of mistrust are to use alternative routes to family involvement. For instance, some schools have formed advisory groups or councils composed of family members to empower families and to give them a voice. Community liaisons are another alternative that creates a link from home to the inclusive classroom through a neutral mediator who is familiar with families in the community (Parette & Petch-Hogan, 2000).

Other studies corroborate findings that building partnerships with families who are diverse and have a child with a disability are complex. Creating a mutually satisfying relationship between parents and teachers in such cases requires examination of fundamental issues related to home and school practices. For example, the parent of a child who is deaf or hard of hearing may want the child to speak; whereas, the teacher may be emphasizing sign language as the primary mode of communication. Identifying basic assumptions that underlie teaching practices and examining them from the parents' cultural perspectives will help to identify areas of discrepancy between home and school. Ensuring opportunities to hear and seeking to understand the voices of parents are vital toward forging more effective partnerships. Intervention strategies selected for diverse young children with disabilities are most likely to achieve desired goals when families and schools agree with both the goals targeted and the strategies used. It is expected that the beliefs of teachers and parents will sometimes collide. However, with patience and ample opportunities to communicate, home-school partnerships can begin to form and be productive (Nicholson, Evans, Tellier-Robinson, & Aviles, 2001).

Collaboration with teenaged parents. Despite notoriously poor outcomes for teenaged parents and their children, programs lag behind the growing need for such services. Teenaged parents need more intensive support in an effort to counteract the ill-effects associated with teenaged parenthood for both parents and their infants. It is wise to provide teenaged parents with excellent models of caregiving. Two components of good caregiving, good adult-child interaction and consistent care routines, are critical to increasing the chances for positive outcomes for children born to teenaged parents. Child-care providers must foster these components among both caregivers and the teenage parents of young children. Directors of child-care centers can be instrumental in guaranteeing that the care children receive is consistent and that interactions with children are of high quality. Creating this atmosphere ensures that parents have many opportunities to see modeling of good care giving techniques (see Box 3.6 for collaboration tips). Close supervision of staff and continuous staff training activities are important strategies to promote effective caregiving (DeJong & Cottrell, 1999).

Accessing and Involving the Community

Of course, families are unrivaled as a child's greatest resource. Unfortunately, changes in family structure, economics, and societal stress have left some parents and family members unable to meet all the needs of their child, especially when the child has serious health needs, developmental delays, or disabilities. Each of these families will need a level of support that fits the family's characteristics and those of their child. Collaboration of families with health care providers, related services personnel, and other professionals can help ensure a good match between community resources and family requirements for those services (American Academy of Pediatrics, Committee on Early Childhood, Adoption, and Dependent Care, 2001; Johnson & Blasco, 1997; Johnson, Kastner, & Committee/Section on Children with Disabilities, 2005). Finding available community resources and accessing those resources can be a daunting task for many families. In many communities, families must go through a tangled maze of phone calls and referral processes to get in contact with the agencies and services that might be

COLLABORATION TIPS   BOX 3.6

Strategies to Promote Collaboration with Teenaged Parents

- Adopt an open-door policy and encourage teenaged mothers and fathers to visit their children in the early childhood classroom.
- Encourage teenaged parents to play with their children while the teacher is nearby to offer encouragement and support for the interaction.
- Model simple ways to interact with infants and young children. For example, play "peek-a-boo," recite a rhyme, and help children clap to the cadence.
- Involve teenaged parents in helping gather information about their child's development. Teach them to record their child's behavior and communication.
- Give teenaged parents developmental sequence charts and show them how to compare the information they gathered about their child to milestones indicated on the charts.
- Plan for teachers to be available to chat with parents at drop-off and pick-up times. Teenaged parents need extra time with teachers to ask questions and discuss good parenting practices.

Adapted from DeJong & Cottrell, 1999.

appropriate for their child. Further, the paperwork to determine qualifications or to apply for the services can be extremely challenging, especially if the family members are illiterate or speak a native language other than English.

Among the guidelines recommended for creating family-centered programs is to focus the attention of parents on accessing community resources that are preventative in intent—specifically, those resources that are intended to address the health, safety, and education of children and families. Ensuring that family support services are within walking distance of the parents' home is another strategy for encouraging families to access support systems in the community (Swick et al., 1997).

The key to bridging the home to inclusive classrooms is to not only recognize the strengths families bring, but also recognize the support neighborhoods bring to children's learning scenarios. Early childhood teachers are more compelled to form a partnership when they recognize that parents are the experts on their own child. The knowledge parents have of their child's skills and ability is invaluable in the teacher-parent collaboration. In 1990, national attention was once again focused on the role of parents in the early education and school readiness of children. The National Education Goals Panel underscored the importance of parents as the first teachers of their children and set the goal of creating a smooth transition between home and school for all young children (National Education Goals Panel, 1997). Delaney (2001) contends that acknowledgement of the parents' role as expert on the individual characteristics and behaviors of their children is a first step toward true collaboration between teachers, schools, and families. When established from the outset, ideally prior to enrollment in a school or program, a pattern of collaboration and two-way communication between home and school becomes a critical component of inclusive education. Such collaborations benefit teachers who are trying to meet the learning needs of all children. Conversely, parents have an opportunity to benefit when teachers inform parents of typical routines and expectations in the inclusive classroom.

Dedicating space or arranging areas specifically to promote family or community relationships with child-care centers or schools is a key strategy to accomplishing collaboration. Giving these spaces a name that recognizes the cooperative goals of the endeavor is a first step to encourage partnerships to form. Names that bespeak "community" and "partnership" in the title can promote use of these spaces by teachers and community volunteers, as well as parents of children. Identifying sources of funding within the community can make greater resources available to families. Other important strategies to foster success are to hire a coordinator to run the center, to plan regular activities, and to keep the space open during evenings and weekends. In high growth areas of the community or small child-care centers and schools, space may be at a premium. In such cases, innovation is critical. Converting school buses to resource centers, dedicating space within neighborhood buildings, and cooperating with existing community centers gives schools a variety of ways to achieve community outreach and establish partnerships with parents (Johnson, 2000).

Communication approaches. Using a variety of forms of communication will help teachers develop strong lines of communication with families. Especially when families are culturally or linguistically diverse, matching the form of communication to the individual family is crucial to forming a partnership. An interpreter may be necessary to aid communication between home and school. However, the interpreter should be a professional member of the inclusive education team. This individual is carefully selected for competence in accurate translation of the language spoken in school to that of the parent. It is risky to rely on friends or other family members for interpretation since accuracy of the interpretation cannot be ensured (Parette & Petch-Hogan, 2000).

Understanding that communication is not one-way only from the teachers and schools to the parents is a significant step toward achieving partnerships. True communication involves family members and teachers in meaningful exchanges of information and ideas. Teachers can work more effectively with young children when they try to identify ways parents are successful in communicating with their children and then attempt to replicate those ways. Nuances and subtle differences in the verbal or nonverbal communication styles of parents and teachers often exist. The tone of voice used when making requests of children or facial expressions convey meaning to children. Culture can influence the kinds of communication patterns adults and children find acceptable. Teachers and parents often disagree about the best ways to communicate with children. Miscommunication is prevalent, even among people who share similar backgrounds; however, when cultural backgrounds differ, miscommunication is more likely to occur. Teachers who are aware of communication differences and try to understand the cultural differences that might underlie the communication are more likely to achieve effective partnerships with families.

Gaining intercultural competence can help teachers recognize cultural differences in communication with children and families. Improving intercultural communication skills can help teachers bridge the gap between home and school environments. Intercultural communication skills are acquired through experience in interacting and building relationships with persons of different cultural backgrounds; therefore, teachers benefit from taking the risk of initiating conversations with culturally diverse families in the communities they serve. Although these communication encounters may be awkward at times, teachers may gain insight into what will help them respect home cultures and values of families (Gudykunst & Kim, 1992; Shu-Minutoli, 1995; Sturm, 1997).

Using a variety of communication approaches to reach families and making good matches between communication modes and individual families can help extend the curriculum into home contexts. This is especially true when the curricular goal itself is to stimulate the language and communication skills of young children. Competence in language and communication requires frequent and high quality communication exchanges between children and adults. Sending home words to children's favorite songs and rhymes can encourage parents to engage in language play at home. Newsletters can help parents understand how vital language experiences are to a child's growth and development. Videotaping or digital photos of storybook readings in the classroom can help share the experience with parents and give them ideas for replicating these activities at home (Soundy, 1997). It is vital that developmentally appropriate activities suggested to parents are also relevant given the cultural context of the family (National Association for the Education of Young Children, 1996).

COLLABORATIVE PRACTICES INVOLVING FAMILIES

To achieve effective programs that promote the inclusion of all children, planning for long-term collaboration should begin in early childhood settings. Parental and family involvement that nurtures the home and school connections during a child's first school experiences sets the stage for ongoing partnerships and mutual support for each child's success throughout schooling. Schools can plan training for families that equips them with effective strategies and creates an atmosphere of support that follows children into home environments (Swick et al., 1997).

Family-Centered Practices

A critical shift in the early intervention paradigm has placed emphasis on collaboration rather than simply providing services to families. As a result, the concept of supporting families through family-centered practices has been widely embraced. Legislative action has issued mandates and professional organizations have articulated their support and recommendations for family-centered practices in early childhood. For children with special needs, the construct of family-centered practices evolved following implementation of the Individualized Family Service Plan (IFSP), mandated in 1986, for programs serving infants and toddlers with disabilities or developmental delays. Early childhood professionals expanded the application of family-centered practices to families with preschoolers following IDEA amendments addressing family support. The crux of family-centered practices is an emphasis on the family as the primary support system for children. Key strategies are strengthening families, helping them access needed resources, and encouraging family involvement in the decision-making processes regarding their child. Teachers using family-centered practices respect the diversity of families and offer flexibility in service delivery to accommodate individual families (Beckman et al., 1996; Kaczmarek, Goldstein, Florey, Carter, & Cannon, 2004; Mahoney et al., 1999; Renne, 2005).

Preparing to use family-centered strategies. Competence in specific skills can prepare teachers for collaborating with families. The skills most relevant for implementing family-centered practices include communicating effectively, taking another's perspective, and the ability to implement problem resolution processes (Kaczmarek et al., 2004). Although few families are involved in preservice education, there are early childhood professional preparation programs that involve families to provide supervised practicum experiences designed to help students acquire a skill set of family-centered practices. In one program, in addition to coursework, students participated in internships located in community-based programs serving diverse families. Parents from these programs were invited to participate in an advisory board planning experience for the students. Some family members assisted in instructing students or presenting information on topics related to family-centered practices. Students reported that interactions with families influenced their attitudes and job decisions. Students' evaluations revealed family interactions had a positive effect on their skill development and commitment toward using family-centered practices (Mandell & Murray, 2004).

Implementation in preschools. Whereas family-centered practices for infants and toddlers are often implemented in the home, preschoolers are usually served in child-care centers or school programs. The Head Start program is a model that pioneered the provision of comprehensive support to families. A more recent model involved training parents of older children with disabilities to serve as family consultants (FC) for families with younger children. While program staff provide support to families, the FCs were trained to augment that support with face-to-face meetings, phone calls, and home visits. The role of the FC was to encourage families to participate in planning, IEP meetings, and other interactions in the educational setting. Through building relationships with families, the FC became influential in helping families navigate the system and make decisions about their children's education. Initial skepticism of school personnel eventually gave way to acceptance of the role of the FC. The school expanded the FC role to include work in classrooms and helping with field trips so the FCs could become more familiar with the children (Kaczmarek et al., 2004).

Involving Families in Program Planning and Evaluation

Considering the current prevalent view that family-school partnerships are valuable, involving families in various aspects of program planning and evaluation is a logical step. Swick et al. (1997) emphasized the importance of involving families in program evaluation to refine the activities and methods used by early childhood programs. With the realization that parents are valuable resources to programs, teachers can connect with families through meaningful dialogue that results in true partnerships (Benham, 2001).

Perceptions of families are particularly important in evaluating the effectiveness of inclusive programs. Families can assist professionals in identifying problem areas that might create barriers to the inclusion of all children. Involving families in periodic focus group sessions is reported as one successful method of gaining information and opinions of parents regarding their children's experiences in the inclusive classroom. Panels composed of teachers, parents, and professional staff can exchange observations and ideas to enlighten all stakeholders about the issues and concerns associated with providing quality care and education to children in inclusive classrooms. Parents are concerned whether the environment of classrooms provides sufficient accessibility to their children. Of special concern to families are the attitudinal barriers to inclusion, meaning the existence of unfavorable attitudes of teachers and classmates toward children with disabilities. Families also report concerns about whether teachers have sufficient training to adapt the curriculum and use practices that sufficiently accommodate children with special needs to ensure each child's success. Providing forums for parents and family members to express their

---

LIFE WITH JENNY   BOX 3.7

"I was planning to return to work after the baby was born," explained Mrs. McDonald. "I had an ideal pregnancy and worked up to my delivery date. Soon after Jenny was born, the diagnosis of cerebral palsy was made. My husband and I were devastated! I still planned on returning to work as I had an excellent career that I wanted to continue to pursue. We are just another middle-income family with two children and our family really needs both incomes to make ends meet. Toward the end of my maternity leave, I began to panic. I could find no one qualified to care for my child, and I was growing depressed from the isolation of caring for Jenny by myself. I desperately needed help and the pediatrician suggested a local advocacy organization. Through the organization, I was able to get some of the help I needed but it hasn't been easy. Jenny is now 3 years old; she is enrolled in an early intervention program, and we are meeting today to discuss the IFSP. I'm hoping we can address some of the problems our family is having as we continue to adjust to the care and health needs of Jenny. The orthopedic surgeon tells us that Jenny will need surgery in the next six months to correct problems that reduce her mobility. I don't know how we will be able to cope with Jenny's care during her recovery and the surgeon tells us to expect more surgeries after this one. I worry about our older son, too. His childhood is different from his peers and he seems to resent the attention we must pay to Jenny."

MY REFLECTION   BOX 3.8

1. Discuss what kinds of changes occur in the lives of families who have children with disabilities or special health care needs.

2. What are some of the issues that the individualized family service plan (IFSP) team might discuss?

3. What kinds of agencies and organizations could provide services to this family?

4. How can the team find solutions that will help Jenny's family more effectively cope?

5. If you were a team member, how would you involve the family in the IFSP process?

views helps teachers and administrators better understand the realities families face (see Box 3.7 for one parent's view and Box 3.8 for the teacher's reflection regarding the parent's view). Further, these opportunities give teachers insight into how parents perceive the inclusive classroom and the teaching practices aimed at helping their children be successful. Such knowledge can result in policies that are mindful of families and respect the preferences and the goals families have set for their children. Administrators can consider family values in planning for the allocation of resources to better support the program and individual children in inclusive classrooms (Pivik, McComas, & LaFlamme, 2002).

Trust and confidentiality. The Family Educational Rights and Privacy Act is a federal mandate that ensures the right of confidentiality to all families. IDEA specifically ensures these and other rights to families of children with disabilities. It is important to remind parents and family members that you will honor their right to privacy and treat all communications as confidential. Legally, teachers are obligated to adhere to the intent of each of these mandates. Maintaining the confidence of parents is a crucial foundation in developing trusting relationships with families.

Gaining the trust of parents is critical to the effective implementation of inclusive programs. When teachers use family-centered practices (those that respect families and their culture), trusting relationships are possible. Through a trusting partnership, families are empowered as valuable contributors to the inclusive classroom (Soodak et al., 2002).

Parent conferences. Although only families with children who qualify for special services are legally entitled to the IFSP or IEP processes, all children deserve to be treated as individuals. Teachers can work toward the goal of serving all children by involving family members in planning. Parent conferences can be a critical element in the planning process if teachers recognize parent conferencing as an opportunity to involve families as knowledgeable allies and partners. Time during conferences can be devoted to identifying each child's strengths and interests. Together, families and teachers can plan ways to accommodate the child's individual style of learning, both at home and school. Teachers in inclusive early childhood settings can use regularly scheduled parent conferences for conveying information about a child's progress and for planning with families to ensure the provision of future opportunities for the child to succeed. Parent conferences are most productive when teachers foster two-way communications in which families are made to feel comfortable in asking questions and offering information about their children.

Allotting sufficient time for conferences can make a large difference in the quality of communications that occur between parents and teachers. Often, teachers plan enough time for giving parents a quick report on the child's progress but allow insufficient time for listening to parents. Conferences can be invaluable when families are invited to ask questions and voice their concerns. More importantly, conferences can be highly productive when teachers elicit ideas from parents and plan with them to better meet the learning needs of children. Allowing for a generous span of time with each family provides an opportunity for teachers to gain insight into the values and child-rearing practices parents endorse. Further, families and teachers need time together to discuss ways to bridge any differences that they discover between home and school goals and practices. When substantial differences exist, it may take more than one meeting to formulate strategies that are mutually acceptable to both teachers and parents.

Linguistic differences between families and teachers may create a gap in communication that could complicate a resolution or even obscure the recognition that different views are held. One strategy for bridging the communication gap is the use of parents as liaisons who are either community volunteers or hired into the position. Harry (1992) suggests that parent liaisons are effective in establishing more personal relationships with parents (see Box 3.9). When children with disabilities are present, the parent liaison can help apprise those families of the assessment and planning processes necessary for properly serving these children.

When interacting with families, there is still no substitute for teachers who are sensitive and responsive to the concerns of parents. Yet, the policies of the program and the larger system are influential in setting the stage for effective family and teacher interactions. Parent conferences and support for other family interactions need support from

IKUFUMI'S FAMILY   BOX 3.9

Ikufumi and his family are recent immigrants to this country. No teacher in the school spoke the family's home language, so a community member was engaged as an interpreter to translate newsletters and other communiqués. Informal communication between the teacher and Ikufumi's parents at arrival and departure times for the exchange of information was of limited effectiveness. To compensate, Mr. Walker, the teacher, scheduled parent conferences at more frequent intervals for the family. Mr. Walker arranged for the interpreter to facilitate the communication at these meetings.

directors of child-care centers and administrators of school programs. When family and school partnerships are viewed as critical to children's successes, facility-level supports, such as paid time for conferences, appropriate spaces that afford confidentiality to conversations, and follow-up with other school or community professionals, is needed to ensure effectiveness of the partnerships. Box 3.10 details parent conference tips for before, during, and after the conference.

PARENT CONFERENCE TIPS — BOX 3.10

Before

- Send home a questionnaire asking about goals and concerns parents have for their child.
- Know school policies and procedures for parent conferences.
- Ask parents for convenient dates and times for meeting. Try to offer morning, afternoon, and evening options to accommodate family work and care schedules.
- Gain background information regarding the cultural heritage of families in your class.
- Schedule generous spans of time for each family to avoid rushing or interrupting conversations prematurely.

Day of Conference

- Make the conference area welcoming and comfortable. Have pamphlets for parents available and perhaps a light snack.
- Post a sign on the door and take other steps to minimize interruptions.
- Provide adult-sized chairs and tablets for writing notes.
- Show examples of the child's progress.
- Give parents ample time to discuss their goals and priorities for their child.
- Incorporate family suggestions and emphasize ways to work together to enhance the progress of children.
- Plan the next contact with parents and schedule phone calls before the next face-to-face conference, if necessary.
- Conclude by summarizing suggestions or concerns and any agreed upon plans to ensure clarity for all.
- End on a positive note, and remember to thank parents for attending the conference.

After

- Follow up by sending parents any information promised.
- Mark follow-up meetings or phone calls on calendar.
- Contact other professionals for consultation, if needed.
- Plan ways to implement family priorities and act upon their concerns.

SUMMARY

The purpose of this chapter was to prepare teachers for establishing mutually beneficial, collaborative partnerships with families and the community. Issues surrounding families and educational settings for young children were explored. Way in which to gain the perspectives of parents and family members regarding their children's education was discussed. The chapter drew implications from research and suggested practical applications for teachers to improve their relationships with families and the community. Understanding the lives of families is critical for bridging home and school environments for children. Teachers in inclusive classrooms should seek to gain insight into the home context and develop culturally competent ways to communicate with families. Sensitivity to the lives and challenges faced by all kinds of families in today's inclusive classrooms is necessary to establish effective partnerships with families. Creating partnerships with parents requires offering many opportunities for families to participate in classrooms and schools. Teachers need to be responsive to families, respect their priorities, and identify the strengths that families bring to the partnership. Offering a variety of ways for parents to become involved in their child's education allows families to select levels of involvement that match their time and responsibilities.

Discussion Questions

1. What are some of the social and economic challenges that families face?
2. Discuss ways teachers can be responsive to the priorities and goals of families who have children with disabilities or special learning needs.
3. Summarize the key strategies for communicating with all kinds of families.
4. What are some of the ways families are changing in their characteristics?
5. Identify some of the challenges that families face in today's world.
6. Describe the role of teachers in creating a partnership with parents.
7. Discuss strategies for promoting the involvement of families in providing good early care and educational experiences for children.
8. How can teachers be prepared to work with families of children with special needs?
9. How can teachers become responsive to culturally and linguistically diverse families?

Inclusive Activities

1. Visit different places in the neighborhood surrounding a school in your community. Learn more about the library, churches, playgrounds, recreational facilities, markets, and community service providers. What transportation systems serve the families in the neighborhood?

2. Interview a member of the community who comes from a different cultural heritage from your own. Ask about family traditions, beliefs, and values.

3. Talk with a teacher who has a child with special needs in the classroom. Ask about the challenges and teaching strategies used to enhance the child's learning.

4. Read more about families of different family configurations to gain insight into their daily lives and child-rearing practices.

5. Find out about the values and culture of the community. Talk to parents with different cultural backgrounds.

6. Gain a parent's perspective on collaboration. Talk to several parents who have children in school. Ask them what they think are effective strategies for achieving productive conferences between parents and teachers.

References

American Academy of Pediatrics, Committee on Early Childhood, Adoption, & and Dependent Care. (2001). The pediatrician's role in family support programs. *Pediatrics, 107*, 195–197.

Beckman, P. J., Newcomb, S., Frank, N., Brown, L., Stepanek, J., & Barnwell, D. (1996). Preparing personnel to work with families. In D. Bricker & A. H. Widerstrom (Eds.), *Preparing personnel to work with infants and young children and their families: A team approach*. Baltimore: Brookes.

Benham, V. (2001). Early childhood advisors expand view of learning. *Scholastic Early Childhood Today, 16*(1), 8–9.

Berger, E. H. (2000). *Parents as partners in education: Families and schools working together*. Upper Saddle River, NJ: Merrill/Prentice Hall.

Bodner-Johnson, B. (2001). Parents as adult learners in family-centered early education. *American Annals of the Deaf, 146*(3), 263–269.

Bowman, B. T. (1994). The challenge of diversity. *Phi Delta Kappan, 76*(3), 218–224.

Brent, D., May, D. C., & Kundert, D. K. (1996). The incidence of delayed school entry: A twelve-year review. *Early Education and Development, 7*, 121–135.

Bronfenbrenner, U. (1979). *The ecology of human development*. Cambridge, MA: Harvard University Press.

Bronfenbrenner, U., & Morris, P. A. (1998). The ecology of developmental processes. In R. M. Lerner (Ed.), *Handbook of child psychology: Vol. 1. theoretical models of human development* (5th ed., Vol. 1, pp. 993–1028). New York: Wiley.

Bushnell, M. (2001). This bed of roses has thorns: Cultural assumptions and community in an elementary school. *Anthropology & Education Quarterly, 32*(2), 139–166.

Children's Defense Fund. (1998). *The state of America's children: Yearbook 1998*. Washington DC: Author.

Coleman, J. S., Campbell, E. Q., Hobson, C. J., McPartland, J., Mood, A., Weinfeld, F. D., et al. (1966). *Equality of educational opportunity*. Washington, DC: U.S. Government Printing Office.

Coleman, M., & Churchill, S. (1997). Challenges to family involvement. *Childhood Education, 73*(3), 144–148.

DeJong, L., & Cottrell, B. H. (1999). Designing infant child care programs to meet the needs of children born to teenaged parents. *Young Children, 54*(1), 37–45.

Delaney, E. M. (2001). The administrator's role in making inclusion work. *Young Children, 56*(5), 66–70.

Delpit, L. (1995). *Other people's children: Cultural conflicts in the classrooms*. New York: The New Press.

Delpit, L. D. (1992). Education in a multicultural society: Our future's greatest challenge. *Journal of Negro Education, 61*(3), 237–249.

Diamond, K. E., Reagan, Amy J., Bandyk, Jennifer E. (2000). Parents' conceptions of kindergarten readiness: Relationships with race, ethnicity, and development. *The Journal of Educational Research, 94*(2), 93–100.

Epstein, J. L. (1995). School/family/community partnerships: Caring for the children we share. *Phi Delta Kappan, 76*(9), 701–712.

Gordon, I. J. (1979). The effects of parent involvement in schools. In R. S. Brandt (Ed.), *Partners: Parents and schools.* Alexandria, VA: Association for Supervision and Curriculum Development.

Gudykunst, W., & Kim, Y. (1992). *Communicating with strangers: An approach to intercultural communication* (2nd ed.). New York: McGraw-Hill.

Harry, B. (1992). *Cultural diversity, families, and the special education system.* New York: Teachers College Press.

Johnson, C. P., & Blasco, P. A. (1997). Community resources for children with special health care needs. *Pediatric Annals, 26,* 679–686.

Johnson, C. P., Kastner, T. A., & Committee/Section on Children with Disabilities. (2005). Helping families raise children with special health care needs at home. *Pediatrics, 115*(2), 507–511.

Johnson, V. R. (2000). The family center: Making room for parents. *Principal, 80*(1), 26–31.

Kaczmarek, L. A., Goldstein, H., Florey, J. D., Carter, A., & Cannon, S. (2004). Supporting families: A preschool model. *Topics in Early Childhood Education, 24*(4), 213–226.

Knitzer, J. (2002). Children's readiness for school: Toward a strategic policy framework. *News & Issues, 12*(3), 1.

Lassen, M. M., & Janey, C. B. (1991). Public school, public housing: A collaboration for education. *Equity and Choice, 7,* 3–12.

Lewis, A., & Forman, T. A. (2002). Contestation or collaboration? A comparative study of home-school relations. *Anthropology & Education Quarterly, 33*(1), 60–89.

Mahoney, G., Kaiser, A. P., Girolametto, L., MacDonald, J., Robinson, C., Safford, P., et al. (1999). Parent education in early intervention: A call for a renewed focus. *Topics in Early Childhood Special Education, 19*(3), 131–140.

Mandell, C. J., & Murray, M. M. (2004). Innovative family-centered practices in personnel preparation. *Teacher Education and Special Education, 28*(1), 74–77.

Meyer, L. H., Harry, B., & Sapon-Shevin, M. (1997). School inclusion and multicultural issues in special education. In J. A. Banks & C. A. M. Banks (Eds.), *Multicultural Education: Issues and Perspectives* (3rd ed., pp. 334–360). Boston: Allyn & Bacon.

National Association for the Education of Young Children. (1996). NAEYC position statement: Responding to linguistic and cultural diversity—Recommendations for effective early childhood education. *Young Children, 51*(2), 4–12.

National Education Goals Panel. (1997). *Getting a good start in school.* Washington, DC: National Education Goals Panel.

Nicholson, K., Evans, J. F., Tellier-Robinson, D., & Aviles, L. (2001). Allowing the voices of parents to help shape teaching and learning. *The Educational Forum, 65*(2), 176–185.

Parette, H. P., & Petch-Hogan, B. (2000). Approaching families. *Teaching Exceptional Children, 33*(2), 4–10.

Pivik, J., McComas, J., & LaFlamme, M. (2002). Barriers and facilitators to inclusive education. *Exceptional Children, 69*(1), 99–107.

Renne, D. (2005). Teaching family-centered practices on-line and on-campus. *Journal of Special Education Technology, 20*(3), 74–76.

Reyes-Blanes, M. E., Smalley, S. Y., & Swire, M. (2001). Are we playing the same tune? Mothers and teachers prioritize characteristics of children with disabilities. *Preventing School Failure, 46*(1), 24–30.

Schine, J. (1998). Families as partners. *Schools in the Middle, 8*(3), 20–22.

Shu-Minutoli, K. (1995). Family support: Diversity, disability, and delivery. In E. E. Garcia & B. McLaughlin (Eds.), *Meeting the challenge of linguistic and cultural diversity in early childhood education* (Vol. 6, pp. 125–140). New York: Teachers College Press.

Soodak, L. C., Erwin, E. J., Winton, P., Brotherson, M. J., Turnbull, A. P., Brault, L., et al. (2002). Implementing inclusive early childhood education: A call for professional empowerment. *Topics in Early Childhood Special Education, 22*(2), 91–102.

Soundy, C. S. (1997). Nuturing literacy with infants and toddlers in group settings. *Childhood Education, 73*(3), 149–153.

Sturm, C. (1997). Creating parent-teacher dialogue: Intercultural communication in child care. *Young Children, 52*(5), 34–38.

Swick, K. J., Grafwallner, R., Cockey, M., Roach, J., Davidson, S., Mayor, M., et al. (1997). On board early: Building strong family-school relations. *Early Childhood Education Journal, 24*(4), 269–273.

Wesley, P., & Buysse, V. (2001). Communities of practice: Expanding professional roles to promote reflection and shared inquiry. *Topics in Early Childhood Special Education, 21*(2), 114–123.

Chapter 4

Diversity and Inclusive Classrooms

Key Principle

- View Diversity as a Strength

Objectives

After reading this chapter, you will be able to:

1. Discuss the characteristics of children who might enroll in early childhood classrooms located in diverse communities.
2. Compare and contrast typical classrooms in child care, preschool, and early primary grades.
3. Outline the referral and diagnostic processes involved when a child is experiencing difficulty in school.
4. Explain the importance of early detection and early intervention strategies.
5. Discuss the early identification and intervention of children with various developmental conditions and disabilities.
6. Summarize characteristics that may help teachers identify children who are gifted.

The Children in Your Class

Developmental patterns

Linguistic diversity

Economic levels

Range of experiences

Cultural diversity

Gifted and talented

Gender characteristics

Special needs

INTRODUCTION

Typical classrooms are becoming increasingly diverse and inclusive of children who represent a full continuum of development. Consequently, most teachers will work with children who have a wide range of ability levels. Moreover, typical classrooms are microcosms of communities that are increasingly multicultural and linguistically diverse. Technological advances and industrialization have led to increased mobility of families and parents who participate in the workforce of a global economy. Children in inclusive classrooms will most likely reflect the cultural richness of the community where the school is located. Early childhood teachers are faced with the challenge of promoting the acquisition of knowledge and mediating the learning processes of children at various levels across a wide span of ability. They need to place emphasis on individual learners while helping children function in a learning community with their peers. Teachers facilitate the unique learning styles of children, identify their strengths, and encourage their curiosity and interests. When teachers aim their teaching toward their perception of the middle level of ability in their classrooms, it is unlikely that the learning needs of children at the margins will be met. Both the teacher's commitment toward teaching inclusively and the skill in using an array of evidence-based practices are required if all children are to have the best possible opportunity for educational success.

Case examples in this chapter present views of typical classrooms in various early childhood settings, including child care and elementary school scenarios. Children and the effects of their various traits on achievement and success in school are portrayed. Typical patterns of growth and development are also described. Expected behaviors and acquisition of skills for typical learners are contrasted with atypical patterns of learning and development. Emphasis is placed on helping teachers to identify children who are at risk of school failure and those who may benefit from additional services to facilitate their learning so that their chances for future success in school increases. A critical emphasis in inclusive early childhood classrooms is to prevent small areas of difficulty from growing into more serious problems or delays that further impede learning through carefully planned interventions that are implemented early in a child's education. Box 4.1 lists children's major developmental milestones to observe in the typical classroom.

CHILDREN REPRESENTING A FULL CONTINUUM OF DEVELOPMENT

Teachers may feel a twinge of apprehension when they are assigned to teach an inclusive classroom. Special education teachers may have concerns about meeting IEP goals and objectives in an integrated setting. General education teachers may wonder how to support the growth and development of children with disabilities. However, most of the children served in inclusive classrooms will probably attain developmental milestones and demonstrate usual patterns of development within their average age range. These patterns of typical development and milestones marking specific achievements, such as saying a child's first words, crawling, walking, and recognizing colors, have been established through the accumulation of large bodies of research in child development. Keep in mind, however, that much of what we know about child development has been drawn from studies conducted in the United States with children who were of majority status and with middle- to upper-income levels. Fewer studies are available to enlighten us about the development of children of color, of different cultures, or living in different countries of the world. Recent studies are emerging to elaborate our understanding of cultural differences and the role these play in child development worldwide. However, it is vital to recognize that the full realm of child development research is yet to be uncovered regarding the cultural and linguistic diversity of children across the globe (Berk, 1994; Trawick-Smith, 1997).

Research in fields of medicine, child development, psychology, and other disciplines has helped to define typical development. Research has provided enlightenment regarding the significance of the early years of a child's development in revealing

TYPICAL CLASSROOM CHARACTERISTICS OF CHILDREN'S MAJOR DEVELOPMENTAL MILESTONES   BOX 4.1

DEVELOPMENTAL DOMAIN	3-4 YEARS OLD	5-6 YEARS OLD	7-9 YEARS OLD
Language	• Mastered most sounds • Speaks in sentences • Recites simple rhymes • Listens to stories	• Tells story from pictures in a book • Asks about meaning of words • Speaks fluently and engages in conversations	• Learn to read around age 7 • Can express thoughts in writing • Elaborates writing to explain concepts
Cognitive	• Counts to 5 • Follows 2-part directions • Understands concepts "in", "on", and "under" • Sorts objects into simple categories	• Compares sizes and weights • Lengthening attention span • Asks "why" questions	• Can focus attention and complete most age-appropriate tasks • Explains, uses logic, and acquires academic concepts
Social/Emotional	• Developing trust and independence • Learning to play with peers	• Identifies emotions • Selects playmates usually of same gender • Follows simple rules of game	• Beginning to see another's perspective • Better definition of self • Better self-control and respects rights of others • Peers increasingly important
Motor	• Catches large ball • Hops on both feet • Draws a circle • Cuts paper with scissors	• Bounces and catches ball • Hops on 1 foot • Cuts on a line • Prints first name • Reproduces letters	• Skips alternating feet • Rides 2-wheel bike • Writes letters and words from left to right • Cuts interior piece from paper

that children are in a period of rapid mental and physical development at that time. The period from birth to age 10 is a fertile period in brain development when neural synapse creation brings windows of opportunity. It is a critical time because some of the windows of opportunity are short-lived and close before a child enters kindergarten. For example, the syntactic aspects of language development appear to be largely completed by age six. Syntactic knowledge means children have acquired the ability to comprehend the rules for words into phrases and sentences. Children develop an understanding of grammatical acceptability, and they can transform sentences from one sentence type to another to convey a message. Understanding the syntax of a language also means that children can combine words to create an almost infinite number of new sentences to communicate with others. This complex language skill is acquired early, and the window of opportunity closes approximately at age 5 to 6, when children typically enter school. Around age 10, the brain begins a process of pruning the synapses that have not proven useful to the child. A child's experiences during the early childhood years largely determine whether a synapse is preserved or eliminated (Nash, 1997).

Children at the Margins

Noncategorical approaches. In 1990, the language changes of reauthorization amendments, the Individuals with Disabilities Education Act (P.L. 101-476), signaled a philosophical turn. Referring to children by categories of disabilities or "labels" had clearly fallen out of favor. Instead, "child-first" language was favored and emphasis was placed on the child rather than disabling conditions that represented only certain characteristics of the child. Early childhood professionals begin to favor noncategorical approaches to inclusion, that is, focusing on the strengths of a child rather than the child's areas of deficit.

Categorical programs assume that children fit the labels or categories applied to them. The result of a categorical approach can be the marginalization of certain children and segmentation of services. There are several detrimental outcomes that have been associated with categorical orientations toward educating children. One of those outcomes is the overidentification of children in to special programs. Disproportionate numbers of children whose families live in poverty and those who represent racial or ethnic minorities are diagnosed as eligible for special education services (Wang, Reynolds, & Walberg, 1994/1995). There are also concerns about children who have high achievement and ability. The Goals 2000 Summit emphasized the need to focus attention on high-achieving children as well as those at the low performing end of the continuum (U.S. Department of Education, 1993). However, even children with high ability can feel stigmatized and suffer isolation from peers when their differences are highlighted by separate programs (Sapon-Shevin, 1994/1995, 2001). Inclusive education has come to be viewed as the preferred method of responsively meeting the learning needs of diverse groups of children with a wide span of ability (Carnegie Task Force on Learning in the Primary Grades, 1996).

Inclusion service delivery mode. Including children with disabilities in general early childhood classrooms is no longer unusual. By the late 1990s, the trend toward inclusion of school-aged children with identified disabilities was clear. Of the 6.5 million children identified with disabilities that interfered with their education, over 75% were included in general education classrooms. By the beginning of the next century, the inclusive education trend was overwhelming. In 2001, the Department of Education reported that in a single decade, the number of children with disabilities participating in general educational classrooms had more than tripled (U.S. Department of Education, 2001a).

Children Served Under IDEA

Rates of children served under the IDEA mandate has continued to rise from implementation in the early 1990s to the present. More children are identified earlier and receive service sooner compared to previous years. Family incomes have risen, and the educational levels of parents have increased. The racial and ethnic composition of children with disabilities has become more diverse in tandem with the rest of society (U.S. Department of Education, 2001b).

Infants and toddlers. Increasing numbers of infants and toddlers who qualify for services under IDEA, Part C, are receiving early intervention at home and in community-based settings. Partly due to the effective Child Find procedures delineated in IDEA, there

Early intervention for developmental delays can reduce gaps between children with special needs and their peers.

was a 40% increase in the number of infants and toddlers served from 1994 to 2000 (U.S. Department of Education, 2001b). The year 2000 figures represented the largest single-year increase; 53% of these children were aged 2 to 3 years old, and many were deemed at risk of developmental delays. Under the law, children are considered at risk when it is estimated that early intervention services are necessary to avert the substantial delays that they are likely to suffer without the targeted early intervention. In 2000, some states reported a majority of the infants and toddlers who qualified for Part C services were considered at risk of substantial developmental delays. More than 75% of Part C infants and toddlers in California and 54% in Hawaii were reported as at risk. For 68% of the cases, early intervention occured in natural home environments, compared to 14% in special programs and 28% in community service-provider or child-care programs (U.S. Department of Education, 2001b).

Preschoolers. As of the census of 2000, 5% of the total population of children aged 3 to 5 years were eligible and received services under the provisions of IDEA, Part B. There was a 31.7% increase in qualifying children from the 1992–1993 school year to the 2000–2001 school year. Fifty-two percent of the preschoolers served in the 2000–2001 school year had speech and language impairments, and this disability category was most prominent among the older preschool children. Younger preschool-aged children were more likely to gain eligibility for services that addressed developmental delays. Racial and ethnic differences were apparent in preschool intervention services; children who were White were overrepresented in Part B early intervention, whereas Latino children were underrepresented. There were also differences reported in the types of settings where children received services. Community early childhood settings were the most frequent placements reported for American Indian, White, and Black preschoolers. Placements for Latino and Asian/Pacific Islander children were more likely to be in early childhood special education classrooms (U.S. Department of Education, 2001b). These differences are significant because children served in naturally inclusive community settings may have opportunities to reap the social and possible academic benefits associated with inclusive education in natural environments. Children who are placed in early childhood special education classrooms will probably experience fewer opportunities for natural social interactions and learning experiences with peers who are typical learners.

School-aged. The percentage of school-aged (6 to 17 years) children with disabilities served under IDEA is 11.5% of the total enrollment. Four disability types accounted for 87.7% of all children served: specific learning disabilities, speech or language impairments, mental retardation, and emotional disturbances. Half of the school-aged children receiving services under IDEA have been identified with specific learning disabilities. Several categories have shown significant growth over the last decade. Other health impairments, autism, and developmental delays are categories that continue to grow. Moreover, there appear to be overrepresentations and underrepresentations based on race and ethnicity (U.S. Department of Education, 2001b).

CULTURAL AND LINGUISTIC DIVERSITY

Diversity and the Child Development Research Base

When making decisions regarding whether a child's development is typical, it is important to understand the origins of the research base in child development and to recognize the shortcomings inherent in earlier child development research methodology. Much of the accumulated research on the development of children was conducted with middle class, Anglo-American children as subjects. Children of color were underrepresented in studies, and earlier researchers were less likely to view their development through multicultural lenses (McLoyd, 1990; Spencer, 1990; Trawick-Smith, 1997). Yet, there is research illustrating how culture influences behaviors and patterns of interaction. Children are influenced by the customs and values of their culture group. Play, communication styles, interactions with others, and preferred ways of learning can differ in children from various cultures (Frost, Wortham, & Reifel, 2001; Ramsey, 1987). Consequently, more recent research has begun to place greater emphasis than has been given to including children of non-European heritage and those with different socioeconomic backgrounds in child development studies. This trend is providing early childhood professionals with more reliable information about typical development in light of various differences that may be attributable to culture or "culturally adaptive" behaviors. The latter term refers to the ways that children learn, use language, or behave because these behaviors are encouraged or valued by their family, community, or peers. Children of different cultures often learn to act in ways that allow them to fit more comfortably into the mainstream culture (McLoyd, 1990; Trawick-Smith & Lisi, 1994). Consequently, children may interact with children and adults in their home and neighborhood environments very differently from the way they interact in school. Effective teachers recognize that children process cross-cultural experiences and seek adjustments to reconcile differences in customs and social interaction patterns. Supporting children's efforts to understand their home culture and also function in other cultural milieus that are different from their own is a critical teaching strategy when providing an inclusive education for children.

Increasing Diversity

The cultural and linguistic diversity in U.S. classrooms is rapidly increasing. Children in minority groups are now the majority in school in a number of states, including the highly populated states of Texas and California (U.S. Department of Education, 1996). Twenty-five percent of the children in California schools have limited English proficiency (California Department of Education, 1997). The Federal Interagency Forum on Child and Family Statistics reported in 1998 that children with racial or ethnic minority backgrounds constitute approximately one third of the school-aged population in the United States (Sapon-Shevin, 2001). Projections indicate that nearly half of the population in the United States in the year 2050 will be a minority; nearly one quarter of the total population is predicted to be Latino, more than double the figures reported in the 1995 Census (Day, 1996).

DESCRIPTION OF TYPICAL CLASSROOMS

Typical early childhood classrooms are inclusive of all kinds of children. This means teachers are serving increasingly diverse groups of children. Children's personal and family characteristics vary, and their abilities represent a wide range of variation. Today, teachers can usually expect their classrooms to mirror a pluralistic society that is both multicultural and multilingual. Children in the early childhood classroom usually represent multiple racial and ethnic groups, with the Latino population being the fastest growing ethnic group in America. Consequently, most classrooms show enrollment of increasing numbers of Latino children from Mexico, Puerto Rico, Central America, and various countries in South America. Teachers also teach children from Asia, Eastern Europe, Africa, the Middle East, and many other countries from across the globe. In addition to Anglo-American first names, such as Jason, Amy, and Michael, teachers have Ahmad and Basimah from the Middle East, Famida from India, Ulan from Africa, and Guan-yin from China. Joaquin's grandparents emigrated from Mexico, and Maria Adelina recently arrived from Guatemala. Cultural backgrounds of children are varied and influenced by many factors, including whether their immigration was forced or by choice and how recently their families emigrated from their countries of origin. Most classrooms represent a mix of recent immigrants and second- or third-generation immigrants at different stages of acculturation. Although the majority of children speak English, some are learning English as a second language. Their first language and the language their families speak at home are Arabic, Farsi, Mandarin, and other native tongues.

Children in typical classrooms also constitute a wide range of abilities. Generally, early childhood classrooms will include two to three children diagnosed with attention deficit hyperactivity disorder (ADHD). Children with social and emotional problems are increasingly identified and served in typical classrooms. Sometimes the behavioral problems of children are short-lived, as they adjust to the divorce of their parents, moving to a new city, or other disruptions in their daily lives. However, increasing numbers of children suffer from abuse or neglect and their problems are pervasive and long term. Children who learn easily and advance rapidly represent the higher end of the continuum of ability in the typical classroom. There may even be a child who is intellectually gifted or possesses special talents in music or the arts, or excels in physical prowess. The continuum of ability in the typical classroom also includes children who have identified disabilities and special needs. It could be David, who exhibited autistic tendencies and was recently diagnosed with Asperger's syndrome, or Rosa, a child with moderate cerebral palsy. Children in classrooms today are diverse in their cultures, languages, and ability. Because most classrooms are inclusive, teacher education and staff development have begun to broaden the scope to imbue teachers with a greater range of skills and strategies for teaching all kinds of children. The following section describes the kinds of classrooms one typically sees when visiting child-care centers and schools today.

Preschool

Ms. Thompson teaches 3- and 4-year-olds at a neighborhood preschool. About 40% of the children in her class are Caucasian of various European heritage backgrounds. Children whose backgrounds are ethnic minorities constitute 53%, and the remaining children are of mixed racial and ethnic background. Ms. Thompson greets each child as they arrive and helps them with their coats and backpacks. This is a relaxed beginning to the day, where children are not rushed, and there are opportunities to exchange a few words with family members. Children proceed to the interest center of their choice, as long as there is still a clothespin to clip on their shirts; each center has a designated number of clothespins indicating how many children can play in the center at a time to prevent overcrowding. The children are playing in the interest centers in small groups or pairs. Juan, Eluterio, and Jaime, who all speak Spanish at home, are building in the block center with Li, who speaks Mandarin at home. The children are communicating with one another in English most of the time. Occasionally, they use a few words in their home language. Ms. Thompson is always available if children need help in communicating with one another, but, usually, they are capable of making themselves understood through a combination of verbal and nonverbal communication attempts. Ms. Thompson works with Delia, a child who has cerebral palsy, and her friend, Allison, in the art area. Both children are experimenting with finger paint. Ms. Thompson encourages Delia to try different patterns of motion using her fist or hand since she needs practice in developing her fine motor skills. Her parents hope she will have better control and be able to hold a pencil to draw and write. Allison is a good model for Delia. Allison loves to make sweeping movements across the page and glides her fingertips in the slippery red, blue, and violet paint. She chatters happily to Allison and stops sometimes to help her make a new pattern with her hands. Depti runs through the block center and knocks over the stack of blocks Danny and Li have built. They hardly have time to react before Depti is off to the water play area, splashing water on the children playing with measuring containers there. Depti speaks some English, but communication is still difficult for her, being a recent immigrant from Bangladesh. Ms. Thompson follows in Depti's path, helping children to rectify the damage and continue their play. She is watchful and keeps anecdotal records to help determine whether Depti's behavior is a matter of adjustment, lack of communication, or a problem with attention. She is trying to establish communication with Depti's parents to gain more insight. She may enlist the assistance of special services personnel at the nearby elementary school for advice about what strategies to use in helping Depti become better integrated into her new setting.

This preschool provides children with a relaxed atmosphere and a number of interesting areas for play together with friends. Children intermingle fairly easily with others who are different from themselves. There are some conflicts as children learn to share and take turns. Sometimes, Ms. Thompson has to help children by facilitating communication barriers or promoting social skills. Children spend much of their time in informal interactions and play both indoors and outside on the playground. They are getting used to sharing a common schedule and school routines. Ms. Thompson understands this is not an easy task for some children who are in a group setting for the first time. She is alert to difficulties children might have when the preschool setting is very different from their homes and customs are unlike those of the child's home country or culture. Ms. Thompson is very patient and always ready to assist a child who is having a rough day. She knows most children will become familiar with the classroom activities and usual routines by the end of the year.

In preschool, the pace is unhurried, and children have large blocks of time to play in indoor interest centers and outdoors on the playground. Also, children begin to anticipate clean-up times, meals, snacks, and rest times between play and center times. Ms. Thompson spends much of her time interacting with children and facilitating their interactions with one another. She teaches children good health care habits and how to get along with their peers. Ms. Thompson reads in the library corner or other quiet spots in the room each day. She knows that 3- and 4-year-olds will have a better experience when they are read to individually or in a small group. Children are beginning to be introduced to some activities in large groups, such as music with movement and large motor games. Centers are filled with activities that introduce children to early academic experiences, such as things to count, nature and science corners to explore, and dramatic play for creating realistic and fanciful play themes.

Kindergarten

The kindergarten classroom closely resembles the preschool setting. Interest centers are arranged throughout the room. Like the preschool, the library area is clearly delineated, and writing materials are available in each center area. Children assemble on a large rug at the beginning of the day and often join together to share a story or play an alphabet game sometime during the day. Group times are for planning times, such as when field trips are discussed or the next day's learning center activity is selected. Children practice language and observational skills by discussing the weather or marking the calendar with symbols for weather changes, birthdays, and other events.

Children enrolled in Mrs. Chung's class came to kindergarten with a wide span of experiences. Some children, like Quon and Wen, have had many experiences in the world beyond their home. Others, like Saidi, have barely ventured beyond their own doorstep. Much like preschool, some children are entering a group educational setting for the first time. Miguel needed support and patience as he learned to adjust to school routines and activities. David, with prior preschool experience, found it easy to settle into routines. However, some of these children may still find it difficult to adjust to routines and establish friendships in another new setting. The kindergarten at Lawndale Elementary has a state-mandated curriculum, standards for performance, and assessments. Mrs. Goldman is obligated to help children meet these standards so they can achieve promotion to first grade at the end of the year. It is a challenge that requires careful assessment and planning throughout the year. Most of the children will succeed, but every year, there are several who experience difficulty. Some children in Mrs. Chung's class have been read to by parents, preschool teachers, and librarians for thousands of hours by the time they reach kindergarten. Others have had few book experiences and do not yet understand simple conventions, such as how to hold a book, to distinguish a word from a sentence, and to identify the progression of reading from left to right across the page.

Elevated standards have emerged as accountability requirements continue to rise. The expectation in most states is for all children to begin formal reading instruction in kindergarten. The challenge for teachers in kindergarten is to ensure all children, regardless of their developmental level and experiences, achieve the standards for literacy established by the school district.

The Primary Grades

Most of the children in Mr. Garcia's first-grade classroom attended kindergarten last year. However, for some children, this is their initial year of formal education because attendance is not mandatory in the state until age 6. Guan-yin and Aziz were cared for by grandparents and extended family members during their preschool years. Neither has experienced formal reading and literacy instruction. Victor is beginning to use invented spellings of words in his response journal, whereas Kevin writes complete sentences with most words spelled correctly. Mercedes, who has cerebral palsy, is included in the classroom. She works alongside her peers with a paraeducator who assists with her instruction. The schedule for this first grade is highly structured to fit with those of other first-grade classrooms in the school. Specialized classes, such as physical education and art/music/movement, are rotated across the week. Related services for children who qualify are also planned into the complex schedule. For instance, children who require speech therapy are scheduled for sessions with the speech pathologist several times a week. With increased accountability, Mr. Garcia is required to use state adopted curricula and textbooks and is accountable for the results of his instruction. The classroom is arranged with desks grouped into pods of 4, with children seated facing one another. Although no learning centers are present, there is a library corner for reading, equipped with books and a variety of writing materials for journaling.

IDENTIFICATION OF CHILDREN NEEDING SPECIAL SERVICES
Importance of Early Identification

As mentioned earlier in this chapter, the majority of children in preschool and primary classrooms will demonstrate developmental patterns that fall well within the range of social, cognitive, language, and physical development that is considered typical for their age. However, some children's development may be at the margins of what is expected of children their age. Some children may be precocious and may later be identified as gifted. Others will evidence more worrisome patterns of development, indicating they may be at risk of developmental delays or other problem behavior that will require careful monitoring. Watching for children who are functioning outside the usual developmental range is a critical aspect of inclusive education. School failure is "catastrophic" (Whitehurst & Lonigan, 2001). Children at greatest risk are children of poverty, those whose primary language is not English, children of color, and those with language or developmental disabilities (Rosenkoetter & Barton, 2002; Snow, Burns, & Griffin, 1998). It is critical to provide these young children with access to intensive emergent literacy and problem-solving experiences in home and child care contexts prior to the introduction of formal reading instruction. Further, it is vital for caregivers to screen children for develomental delays and, when necessary, assist families in gaining access to early intervention services for their children to prevent school failure (Sandall, McLean, & Smith, 2000).

Increased emphasis on early identification and intervention is critical to ensure the best outcomes possible for all children. There is reason to believe that children who would benefit from special services are being identified and served earlier than in previous years. Results of two longitudinal studies launched by the Office of Special Education Programs can be compared. Results of an examination of a cohort of students in the late 1980s, The National Longitudinal Transition Study (NLTS) completed in 1993, can now be compared to the National Longitudinal Transition Study-2 (NLTS2), a replication study launched in 2000. Of interest to professionals in early childhood is the data revealing that children in the second cohort were first identified 8 months earlier (5.9 years old) than children in the original study, whose average age was 6.6 years upon identification. Consequently, children in the more recent study were more likely to receive services substantially earlier, thereby increasing the benefits derived from these services and the likelihood of achieving better outcomes overall (U.S. Department of Education, 2001b).

Goals for Early Identification

A prominent goal of inclusive early childhood education is to identify children who may need extra support. Providing early intervention, when it is warranted, can prevent problem conditions from worsening, may stimulate development overall, or improve skills and abilities in certain developmental domains. When intervention is carefully matched to the child's individual needs, it is possible to avert subsequent placement in special education or to, at least, improve a child's chances for success in school. A substantial research base has accumulated through years of early intervention research, and findings indicate that early identification and intervention are critical for children with disabilities. Early identification of children with special needs and the provision of immediate, intensive intervention can improve a child's current functioning. Equally important, early identification and intervention can improve the prognosis for children and allow them to have improved outcomes (Casto & Matropieri, 1986; Guralnick, 1997). Further, children who receive special services early and achieve greater success in functioning and learning are also more likely to gain lifelong benefits (Lazar & Darlington, 1979, 1982; Schweinhart, Barnes, & Weikart, 1993).

Early Detection and Referral

Identification of children who may benefit from early intervention is an important role for teachers in inclusive classrooms. The children most likely to be identified early are those with obvious medical conditions, physical disabilities, or syndromes with clearly discernable symptomology. For example, children with Down syndrome or cerebral palsy are very likely to be detected at birth or shortly after birth due to the organic basis for these conditions and apparent symptomology. In contrast, children with developmental or learning disabilities are difficult to identify in their early years because these children do not readily exhibit overt markers or symptoms of their conditions (O'Brien, Rice, & Roy, 1996). Frequently, these children are well into their elementary school years before their disabilities are identified. A 1987 multisite study of a large sample of over 1,500 elementary school children receiving special education services reported that less than one third of these children were identified before they entered kindergarten; only 16% of the children in the sample had their disability detected prior to the age of three years (Palfry, Singer, Walker, & Butler, 1987). These findings have prompted research to determine the precursors of eligibility that may be evident before age 3. A study of children from the National Institute of Child Health and Development, Study of Early Child Care, examined early detection and referral by pediatricians and health care professionals compared to children detected through screening assessments. Interestingly, the study concluded that pediatricians, who are usually among the first outside the family to have contact with young children, had difficulty detecting potential delays and disabilities. The implication of the study is that these key professionals may benefit from training on risk factors to help them more accurately identify children in need of early intervention services (La Paro, Olsen, & Pianta, 2002; Scott, Singaraju, Kilgo, Kregel, & Lazzari, 1993).

The Identification Process

Skills for teachers. Professionals in early childhood classrooms have always been on the front lines in identifying children who are likely to benefit from early intervention. In early childhood settings, children may be entering group care and educational settings outside their homes for the first time. Consequently, early childhood teachers are often among the first professionals in a child's life to detect a problem in an area of the child's development and learning. Developing a keen ability to identify children who may benefit from early intervention is one of the most important skills that teachers in inclusive classrooms can acquire. Teachers with experience are often familiar with the usual developmental patterns of children. Frequently, experienced teachers recognize that a child's behavior or development may be moving beyond the range of typical development. Although experience is gained over time, there are ways that all teachers and prospective teachers can actively seek to enhance their early identification skills. Consider the following suggested strategies for self-improvement:

- Participate in preservice or inservice staff development seminars and workshops geared toward early identification.
- Enroll in college or university courses that address early identification and inclusive education topics, such as children with disabilities or special needs, culturally and linguistically diverse children, giftedness, teaching strategies and techniques, partnership and communication with families, and assessment.
- Study child development from a multicultural perspective.
- Become an astute observer of children and learn various ways to document your observations.
- Acquire more skill and improve your comfort zone in establishing strong lines of two-way communications with parents and families so that information about children's growth and development can be shared.
- Join professional organizations, such as the Division for Early Childhood (DEC) of the Council for Exceptional Children (CEC). This organization and its publications will keep you well-informed about the latest research on how to teach children with special needs. Information about changes in legislation affecting teachers and educational settings is also disseminated through CEC.

Extra support for learning. Just as teachers are often among the first to suspect problems that may interfere with learning, they are also in a position to provide the first intervention to children who experience difficulty learning. The teacher is usually the person who initiates informal attempts toward improving a child's progress in development and learning. Informal intervention can be as simple as:

- Repeating activities with a child (e.g., reading a story, playing a learning game, performing an addition problem).
- Guiding a child through an activity that other children are doing independently.
- Increasing support through physical or verbal prompts.
- Structuring the activity differently by adding a longer time frame, eliminating some of the items to pare down the size of task.

It is important to keep records and document the extra support you provide to certain children and the result of your strategies. For some children, additional support from the teacher may be sufficient for improving their learning. If the child continues to have difficulty, the family and teacher may seek help of professionals through the formal referral and diagnostic processes (see Box 4.2 for collaboration tips with the diagnostician).

Role of professionals. It is imperative to remember that the terms "identification" or "detection" are different from the term "diagnosis." Only qualified professionals are capable of diagnosing disabling conditions. Qualified professionals are those with training, professional licenses, and earned credentials in diagnostic processes and test administration that can diagnosis a disabling condition. Similarly, only physicians who have earned

Some children benefit from increased support and guidance during learning activities.

COLLABORATION TIPS   BOX 4.2

With the Diagnostician, A Teachers's View

Throughout the year, I collaborated with the diagnostician. The diagnostician is very knowledgeable and was always able to answer my questions and concerns about the various disabilities exhibited in my classroom. When I received a new student, we would work together to gather as much information as possible about the student, so he or she could be evaluated. I filled out inventories and observations for the diagnostician, and I learned information from her that she gathered from the previous testing and schools. My students also reach the age where re-evaluations were necessary at the end of the school year. I would gather a whole packet of information and confer with the diagnostician about the child. Frequently, the diagnostician would test the child and come to me afterward for some additional information, such as, "he did not answer this, can he do that?" My relationship with the diagnostician is very helpful, and working well with her has made things run smoothly and efficiently. I gained new insight to the children with disabilities in my classroom, as well as new strategies and ideas.

proper credentials and licenses can diagnose health and medical conditions of children that may require special treatment and accommodations in educational settings. The term identification is used in this book to refer to the processes of observing behaviors or symptoms and seeking verification through various levels of assessment. The assessment process often begins with simple screenings and may proceed through to more formal standardized measures, such as intelligence tests or achievement batteries.

Findings of one study implied that even professionals may benefit from additional training regarding referral and diagnosis of young children with developmental delays (Shevell, Majnemer, Rosenbaum, & Abrahamowicz, 2001). In the study, comprehensive diagnostic evaluations by specialty clinics, such as developmental pediatric or pediatric neurology clinics, yielded different outcomes than those of referring physicians who requested a confirmatory diagnostic evaluation. In one third of the cases, the delay sub-type diagnosis of the clinical evaluation was different from the subtype suspected by the referring physician (Shevell et al., 2001).

Understanding the Referral Processes

Prereferral intervention. This process has been adopted and implemented in some states since the mid-1980s. According to some authors, the intent of the prereferral intervention is to reduce the need for labeling and categorization of children (Buck, Polloway, Smith-Thomas, & Cook, 2003; Carter & Sugai, 1989). Other authors report the intent is focused on the desire of schools to address the diverse learning needs and behavioral problems of children in inclusive classrooms (Chalfant & Pysh, 1989).

Team approaches are often used to decide on prereferral intervention strategies. The teams base the strategies on strengths of the child and generate interventions that general education teachers can implement (Fuchs et al., 1990). Prereferral is a process that permits immediate assistance to the teacher and may help eliminate problem behaviors before these behaviors become a well-established pattern (Lane & Wehby, 2002).

In a recent survey study, teachers expected that they would receive intervention strategies and the support of knowledgeable professionals in implementing the recommended strategy (Lane, Mahdavi, & Borthwick-Duffy, 2003). They also felt some obligation to inform the parents of their concerns as part of the prereferral process. When the problem was severe, teachers were less likely to welcome support. Teacher's experience and the grade level they taught did not predict their desire for implementation support. The findings of this study suggest that prereferral teams may be more successful when the following steps are taken when designing an intervention:

- Consider the severity problem and the strength of the teacher's desire for help.
- Demonstrate the intervention and provide in-classroom, follow-up support.
- Provide consultation to address behavioral concerns (Lane et al., 2003).

If the child requires further diagnosis, the formal assessment and diagnostic processes can be initiated. If a child is found eligible for services under the law, teachers may be asked to participate in the team process to develop the individualized education program. The participation of early childhood professionals in developing the individualized family service plan (IFSP) is discussed in this chapter. For families of older children, the development of an individualized education program (IEP) may be necessary. In Chapter 5, the participation of teachers and other related services personnel with families to develop the IEP is described.

CHARACTERISTICS OF CHILDREN NEEDING SPECIAL SERVICES

Most children who are found eligible for special services through the referral and diagnostic processes are children with high-incidence disabilities. This term refers to a variety of conditions that are generally mild and do not require children to be educated in segregated settings. You are very likely to serve these children in inclusive classrooms where they can learn alongside their peers. For some children, accommodations may be necessary to ensure their success. You may need to modify the usual curriculum, provide extra support, or adapt the environment or equipment to accommodate the learning needs of individual children. Of the school-aged children who are eligible for services under IDEA, approximately 88% are diagnosed with high-incidence conditions. These conditions include learning disabilities, speech and language problems, mild mental retardation, and emotional disturbances. The remaining children qualified for services due to low-incidence disabilities that occur less frequently. These conditions include children with autism spectrum disorders, sensory impairments, physical impairments, illness and health conditions, and multiple disabilities (U.S. Department of Education, 2001b). Serving children with low-incidence disabilities in your inclusive classroom requires careful planning and team effort. Often related services are required to maximize their potential for success in school.

A Strength-Based Approach

The following sections provide teachers with some key facts and information about children with high- and low-incidence disabilities. However, it is essential to take a strength-based approach to teaching in inclusive classrooms. Identifying the strengths children bring to their learning is a critical prerequisite to facilitating their success. Inclusive classrooms that focus on the strengths of children are more likely to offer legitimate challenges matched to individuals that will propel them toward meeting their fullest potential. All children, even those with serious disabilities, deserve challenges that are based upon their individual strengths (Jorgensen, 1994/1995). It is not sufficient to offer children opportunities to only acquire functional living skills. Every child, regardless of disabilities, has the right to develop higher order cognitive skills (National Coalition of Advocates for Students, 1991).

In the following sections, it is important to understand that the characteristics discussed will not apply to all children diagnosed with the condition. There is considerable variation among children with the same diagnosis and it is essential to recognize the unique strengths and abilities of each child.

CHILDREN WITH COGNITIVE AND LEARNING DISABILITIES
Children with Cognitive Delays and Mental Retardation

Definition and characteristics. Children with cognitive delays and mental retardation are characterized by general intellectual functioning that is significantly below average, with an IQ measuring approximately 70 or lower. Severity of the condition can vary in individuals from mild and moderate to severe or profound conditions. In addition to a slower learning rate than their peers, children with this condition have some degree of difficulty with adaptive functioning or the ability to cope with the ordinary routines and usual tasks of everyday living. Adaptive functioning difficulties may also be evident in communication, social, and living skills that may later interfere with the individual's acceptance in society and the ability to live independently. Although the IQ score of children with mental retardation tends to be stable, some children can improve their adaptive functioning with training. Whereas some children have physical characteristics or facial features associated with mental retardation, such as Down syndrome or fetal alcohol syndrome, most children do not have features that distinguish them from other children (American Psychiatric Association, 2000).

Prevalence. Approximately 1% of the population has mental retardation, with more than three fourths of these individuals diagnosed with a mild form of the condition. Boys are one and one-half times more likely to have this condition than girls. A variety of biological and psychosocial factors are thought to be possible causes for this condition including heredity, prenatal and perinatal problems, and environmental factors, such as lead poisoning. In approximately 40% of cases, the etiology that predisposed the child to this condition is never identified. Comorbidity of other mental disorders, such as depression and attention deficit hyperactivity disorder, is common (American Psychiatric Association, 2000).

Early identification and intervention. Some children with mental retardation in your classroom may already be identified. For instance, children with Down syndrome are usually identified at birth. In these cases, families may already have an IFSP and a team of specialists with whom you may be asked to collaborate. Children with cognitive delays or mild mental retardation may not yet be identified. Observing children's play activities may provide some clues to children's mental and social functioning. Children with mental retardation may play differently in that their activities may be less sophisticated than those of their peers. For example, studies reported that children with Down syndrome engage in more repetitive play with objects than their peers (Frost et al., 2001; Hughes, 1998). Communication problems may tend to isolate these children from the social play activities of other children.

Early intervention for children who may have cognitive delays or mental retardation includes providing plentiful opportunities to play in "real" play situations with their peers (Bailey & McWilliam, 1990). Consequently, inclusive classrooms are ideal for offering these children a wealth of play opportunities. Teachers can encourage all children to participate in play and other activities and provide extra support to those who need it, when necessary, to ensure their successful interaction with peers.

Children with Learning Disabilities

Definition and characteristics. Recognizing that individuals who have problems in learning represent a wide spectrum, some authors use the term "learning differences" rather than "disorder" or "disability" (Koller & Goldberg, 2002). Children with learning differences exhibit a marked discrepancy between their intellectual development, as measured by an IQ test, and academic acquisition of reading, mathematical, or written expression skills, as measured by achievement tests. Children with learning differences are at high risk of school failure and account for approximately 40% of the adolescents who drop out of school. Associated conditions include problems in social skills and poor self-esteem. Delayed language development and developmental coordination disorders are commonly found among children with learning disabilities.

Causes of learning disabilities are thought to vary from genetic predisposition to neurological or medical conditions, such as lead poisoning, fragile X syndrome, or fetal alcohol syndrome. Cognitive processing difficulties may arise from impairments of basic learning abilities in perceptual, linguistic processing, or memory systems (American Psychiatric Association, 2000).

Prevalence. The prevalence of specific learning disabilities is estimated to be between 2% and 10% of the general population. Of children enrolled in public school, it is believed that 5% have specific learning disabilities (American Psychiatric Association, 2000). Whereas 3.3% of preschoolers served under IDEA in 2000–2001 were diagnosed with learning disabilities, half of all school-aged children were given this diagnosis (U.S. Department of Education, 2001b).

Early identification and intervention. Ophthalmologists are frequently consulted when children with normal motivation have reading problems. Teachers may notice a child has difficulty decoding words and comprehension of text. Parents often believe a visual problem exists, yet visual screening might rule out visual problems as a cause. An audiologist may administer hearing screenings to address a child's difficulty with sound-symbol relationships. Teachers and parents may observe a child being rejected by peers and having difficulty understanding subtle social cues and nuances of others speech and body language. Psychiatrists may be consulted when children have social and interpersonal relationship difficulties (Koller & Goldberg, 2002).

Children with Challenging Behavior

Definition and characteristics. In early childhood, Wolery and Fleming (1992) described children with "problem behavior" as those whose behaviors warranted close monitoring or were cause for concern by teachers and families. It is important to be aware that gender appears to have a relationship with behavior of children. Boys are reportedly four times more likely to be identified with behavioral problems than girls. Moreover, boys tend to exibit the externaled types of behavioral problems, such as aggression, disobedience, and antisocial behavior. Girls are more likely to internalize their behavior problems, resulting in withdrawal, anxiety, and fearfulness (Cullinan, Epstein, & Kauffman, 1984; Cullinan, Epstein, & Sabornie, 1992).

Emotional and behavioral disorders can encompass a variety of problems including impulsivity, antisocial tendencies, aggression, and social withdrawal. Social relationships and functioning are generally affected, and academic failure is highly associated with maladaptive behaviors (Gable, Hendrickson, Tonelson, & Van Acker, 2002). Two major categories of disorders can arise by middle school in at-risk children who fail to receive intervention: conduct and oppositional defiant disorders. Conduct disorder is typified by consistent patterns of rule violation and infringement on the rights of others. Hostility and disobedience toward authority figures and refusals to comply with requests are behaviors associated with oppositional defiant disorders (American Psychiatric Association, 2000).

Pediatric bipolar disorder (PBD) is a mood disorder that is a chronic and recurrent condition with serious repercussions for children and their families. Children with BPD are more likely to suffer problems with peer and family relationships and poor school performance, ultimately resulting in increased school dropout rates. BPD is difficult to diagnose in children and depression can manifest as anger or irritability, making it difficult to distinguish. BPD can manifest as manic periods of at least one week of abnormally elevated mood. Mixed bipolar episodes are also possible with manic periods and depressive periods. Children with BPD often show symptoms of other problems such as attention deficit hyperactivity disorder, conduct disorder, and anxiety disorders. Psychotrophic medications are often used to treat children with pediatric BPD (Danielyan & Kowatch, 2005). Although the number of drug options has increased, it is often difficult to match the medication to patients because drugs have different effects on individual children. Consequently, it can be a roller coaster of ups and downs that create turmoil and stress for the entire family (Kluger & Song, 2002).

Prevalence. The incidence of children who have behavioral disorders or those considered at risk of developing problem behavior is reported to be on the rise (Feil & Becker, 1993; LaRocque, Brown, & Johnson, 2001; Sinclair, Del'Homme, & Gonzalez, 1993). Overall, prevalence rates are estimated at 1% to 10% for children with conduct disorders and 2% to 16% of children having oppositional defiant disorder (American Psychiatric Association, 2000). Studies have reported that up to one quarter of children in community samples evidence symptoms of oppositional defiant disorder as early as age 2 (Fox, Dunlap, & Powell, 2002; Webster-Stratton, 1997). Reports estimate that approximately 3% of children suffer from depression (Abrams, Theberge, & Karan, 2005).

Early detection and intervention. Behavioral problems in children can be detected as early as age 2 through screening. Families begin to notice behavioral problems early; however, often professionals consulted by parents are unprepared to recognize or to help parents deal with the problem behavior of children (LaRocque et al., 2001). Studies reported that behaviors that are problematic or engender concern are exhibited by 6% to 10% of children enrolled in Head Start programs (Forness, Kavale, MacMillan, Asarnow, & Duncan, 1996; Sinclair et al., 1993). Most children with serious emotional and behavioral problems are not identified until elementary school, with approximately 17% identified at age 9 and fewer than 50% receiving services at age 12 (Del'Homme, Kasari, Forness, & Bagley, 1996).

When delay in identification occurs, valuable time is lost. The problem behaviors are usually well-established in the child's behavioral repertoire and very intensive treatment will be needed. Early detection is an important goal because prevention is a less expensive alternative compared to remediation. Further, the prognosis for positive outcomes and long-term success is greater when intervention is initiated early. Equipping teachers and other professionals with screening tools is critical. Becoming familiar with diagnostic manuals, such as the *Diagnostic and Statistical Manual of Mental Disorders* (DSM-IV-TR) published by the American Psychiatric Association (2000) is also essential for early detection. This manual describes early behaviors that warrant careful attention of parents and teachers (LaRocque et al., 2001).

There are a number of factors to consider when early identification efforts are initiated. Homelessness increases the risk of children developing behavioral disorders; 65% of homeless children in Los Angeles suffered from behavioral problems or depression (Zima, Wells, & Freeman, 1994). Culture and ethnicity of children must be considered to avoid bias and over- or underidentification of children from diverse backgrounds (Forness et al., 2000; Serna, Forness, & Nielsen, 1998).

Families begin to notice behavioral problems in children early although treatment often occurs later.

Mood disorders, such as depression and PBD, are difficult to diagnosis in children, especially when they have difficulty remembering and verbalizing information. Families can be crucial in making the diagnosis and providing information that helps distinguish these disorders from others that have similar symptoms. Families may notice changes in appetite, sleep patterns, or vague physical complaints. In school, children may have poor attendance, refuse to do assignments, or have conflicts with others. Individualized treatment, which may include medication, family therapy, and education, is used to reduce the periods of depression. Children can learn coping skills to help manage stress that might trigger a depressive episode. During childhood, there are no apparent gender differences in the occurrence of a major depressive disorder (MDD) in children (Emslie & Mayes, 1999).

Another approach to treatment is using an ecological systems approach (Bronfenbrenner & Morris, 1998). This model can be used to help design interventions for children with depression by examining influences on children's behavior at different societal levels. Perhaps the family, at the microsystem level, needs support to reduce sources of stress in the child's life that prolong depressive episodes. The divorce of parents or incarceration of a parent may exert an economic hardship as well as an emotional toll on the family. By examining possible influences at various levels in the child's world, a team of professionals, including the classroom teacher, can plan to aim intervention at targeted areas in which influence may be strongest and most likely to exert a positive effect (Abrams et al., 2005).

Children with Attention Deficit Hyperactivity Disorder

Definition and characteristics. Children with this disorder show persistent patterns of three primary symptoms that distinguish this condition: inattention, impulsivity, and hyperactivity. These symptoms are manifested by the child before the age of 7 (American Psychiatric Association, 2000; Schirduan, Case, & Faryniarz, 2002). There are three subtypes of ADHD:

1. Attention deficit/hyperactivity, combined type
2. Attention deficit/hyperactivity, predominantly inattentive type
3. Attention deficit/hyperactivity, predominantly hyperactive-impulsive type (American Psychiatric Association, 2000).

Prevalence. This disorder is one of the most prevalent of childhood disorders, with 1.35 to 2.25 million children diagnosed. Estimates are that 3%–7% of school-aged children suffer from some form of this disorder (American Psychiatric Association, 2000; Schirduan et al., 2002).

Early identification and intervention. As toddlers, teachers and parents may notice a child engaging in extreme motor activity. However, it is easy to dismiss these symptoms because toddlers are rather active. Most children are diagnosed when they reach school age. In elementary school, it becomes more apparent that the behaviors are pronounced when compared to peers. Further, these symptoms begin to interfere with a child's functioning in the school environment (American Psychiatric Association,

INCLUSIVE STORY: CAMERON BOX 4.3

A Teacher's View

Cameron is a 4-year-old boy with severe attention deficit hyperactivity disorder (ADHD). When he is not on his medication, he not only is very impulsive and hyperactive, but also is aggressive toward other children. Cameron is destructive to furnishings, toys, and materials in the classroom. Most of the time he is on his medication, but if his mother runs out, he may go a couple of days without it. During that time, we have to keep him very occupied. We give him extra tasks, such as helping the teacher pass out materials or feeding the class pets. If he is not occupied, he can be seen running around, crawling under the tables, and taking things away from other children. Cameron will hit, punch, or kick other children so fast that it is hard to catch him. Most of the time, he is on some level of medication that helps to reduce his aggressiveness and hyperactivity. Cameron is still very impulsive and has a hard time sitting still for long. He usually can't stay seated to complete his work. I have allowed him to stand while he works, and he seems to be able to stay on task longer that way. Cameron will also impulsively take something from another student. I am working on teaching him some beginning strategies to help him manage his own behavior. Cameron is a very intelligent boy who, when he is paying attention and on task, is ahead of most children in the class academically. Unfortunately, his ADHD sometimes gets in the way of his learning. Other students do not really like to interact with Cameron because of his aggressiveness. Sometimes a child will play with him until Cameron does something to hurt the child or is aggressive. As he learns more self-management strategies, hopefully Cameron will overcome some of the symptoms.

2000). Teachers should be aware that ADHD and learning disorders frequently co-occur. Further, these children had more significant problems than children with learning disabilities alone (Mayes, Calhoun, & Crowell, 2000). For preschool children, teachers should watch for children who cannot develop friendships and have difficulty in socializing with peers. Immediate early intervention is imperative for children who are chronically inattentive, impulsive, and rarely complete tasks. Behavioral intervention may also reduce the need for medication in some children (Boyajian, DuPaul, Handler, Eckert, & McGoey, 2001; Brim & Whitaker, 2000; Flood & Wilder, 2002). A preschool teacher's view of a student with ADHD is detailed in Box 4.3. When children reach the primary grades, teachers should be alert for children who are not achieving well academically. The frustration children feel because of school failures can lead to low self-esteem. Children with ADHD who experience school failure are at risk of developing oppositional defiant disorder, which is considered a prelude to the more serious conduct disorder. A child's perception of self as an academic failure is very influential in precipitating behavioral disorders (Pisecco, Wristers, Swank, Silva, & Baker, 2001).

CHILDREN WITH PHYSICAL CHALLENGES
Children with Developmental Coordination Disorders

Characteristics. Some children have difficulty with physical motor tasks that interfere with their achievement in school and their daily life-functioning. Children with a developmental coordination disorder evidence significant delays in the development of motor coordination that is not associated with medical conditions, such as cerebral palsy or muscular dystrophy. Children with this disorder may have mental retardation; however, the motor delay exhibited is greater than expected for that condition. Children with a developmental coordination disorder do not meet the criteria for a pervasive developmental disorder because the delay is in only one developmental area, motor coordination. Their lack of coordination impedes their general life-skill functioning and academic performance.

Prevalence. It is important for early childhood teachers to know about this disorder because it is estimated to affect a rather high percentage of children, as high as 6%, in the 5 to 11 years of age range. For some children, the condition improves by adolescence, although for others it is a lifelong disability.

Early identification. Teachers and parents should be alert to motor characteristics that are delayed compared to children's same-age peers. Parents may be the first to notice a child who has difficulty holding eating utensils, running, or buttoning clothing. Teachers may notice children who are clumsy compared to their peers and fail to meet usual milestones in motor development. In preschool, children with a developmental coordination disorder lack self-care routines, such as zipping pants after toileting and putting on coats and outerwear. Kindergartners may have difficulty manipulating puzzles, constructing with blocks, and playing pitch and catch with balls. Children in the early grades may still exhibit a tendency to drop items, whereas their peers rarely spill or drop items. They experience difficulty in producing legible handwriting, playing ball games and other sports, or engaging in outdoor activities (American Psychiatric Association, 2000). See Boxes 4.4 through 4.6 for characteristics and collaboration tips for this disorder.

DEVELOPMENTAL COORDINATION DISORDER   BOX 4.4

- Clumsiness
- Poor in sports and outdoor games
- Difficulty in dressing (e.g., buttoning, zipping, tying)
- Illegible printing and handwriting
- Fails to meet developmental milestones in gross and fine motor development

COLLABORATION TIPS   BOX 4.5

With the Occupational or Physical Therapist

Depending on the students in the classroom, the occupational therapist (OT) and physical (PT) may visit once a week or even less than that. I worked with them to implement various techniques and strategies into my daily routine. Our collaboration enhanced the students' programs. From strategies such as having students write with broken crayons to including daily gross motor activities, the ideas from the OT/PT helped to enhance my program.

Children with Communication Disorders

Definition and characteristics. There are several types of communication disorders that children may exhibit. Children with expressive language disorders experience difficulty expressing their thoughts and feelings. They may have a limited vocabulary, difficulty remembering words, or problems formulating sentences. Children with mixed receptive-expressive disorders have difficulty expressing themselves and understanding the speech and language communication of others. Children with phonological disorders have difficulty with speech production appropriate for their age and dialect. The impairment of sound production interferes with a child's functioning, either academically or socially. Stuttering is another serious communication disorder. Children with stuttering have a disruption of normal fluency and time patterns that make speech understandable to others. Difficulty in communicating leads to stress and anxiety, as well as low self-esteem. Speech problems can be associated with other conditions, such as mental retardation, hearing impairments, or cerebral palsy. It is

COLLABORATION TIPS   BOX 4.6

Adaptive Physical Education

A weekly motor lab was set up in collaboration with the adaptive physical education teacher. The students loved having her come in, and I also enjoyed the ideas and feedback on various activities I did with the students. One of her jobs was to evaluate the 5- or 6-year-olds before the end of the school year. The evaluation helped place the children in the appropriate physical education setting for the next school year. Having extra feedback, support, and ideas helped me plan for various gross motor activities to hone specific skills the children needed to practice.

common for children with expressive language disorders to also have a phonological disorder. Heredity may be a factor in communication disorders. It is also thought that an underlying neurological processing of language causes communication disorders.

Prevalence. Of the children under 3 years of age, 10% to 15% have language delays. Among school-aged children, 3% to 7% of children have language disorders, primarily the expressive language type (American Psychiatric Association, 2000). Of children served under IDEA, 55% of the children are identified with speech or language impairments, and nearly 19% of school-aged children are diagnosed with language problems (U.S. Department of Education, 2001b).

Early identification and intervention. A serious consideration for identification and referral of children with possible language disorders is the native and secondary language of the child. Care must be taken in assessing children formally and informally to ensure proper consideration for the linguistic diversity of the child. Assessments that are culture and language fair should be selected. Equally important, administrators of assessments should be trained in assessing bilingual children. It is imperative to consider the language proficiency of children in both their primary and secondary languages. Language dominance is an extremely important factor in expression of language. A child may be highly expressive in the native language but less proficient in conveying her message in the secondary language (Salend & Salinas, 2003). Teachers should watch for children with phonological problems in preschool because difficulty in this area is highly associated with difficulty in learning to read (Gersten & Geva, 2003).

CHILDREN WITH LOW-INCIDENCE CONDITIONS

Children with low-incidence conditions are also included in inclusive education classrooms. Teachers will serve fewer of these children overall. It is estimated that approximately 6% of children will have low-incidence conditions. However, it is still important to have some basic understandings about the importance of identification and early intervention with children whose disabilities or conditions are less common.

Children with Pervasive Developmental Disorders

Definition and characteristics. Children with pervasive developmental disorders include children with autism, Rett's disorder, childhood disintegrative disorder, and Asperger's syndrome. These disorders are characterized by developmental impairments in key areas that particularly affect communication and social interaction. Stereotypical behaviors are often present, as well as mental retardation. Children with these disorders have narrowly focused interests and lack interest in developing relationships with others (American Psychiatric Association, 2000).

Prevalence. Less than 3% of preschoolers served under IDEA are diagnosed with autism spectrum disorders, and the number drops to 1.4% for school-aged children (U.S. Department of Education, 2001b).

Early identification and intervention. Children with autism spectrum disorders are often identified in early childhood when a lack of interest in social relationships and perseverative and stereotypical behaviors set children apart from peers. Behavioral interventions have historically been used to help these children develop communication and functional skills (Cohen, 1999). Augmentative forms of communication are often taught to children to increase their options for successful communication (Ogletree & Harn, 2001; Ziring, Brazdziunas, Cooley, Kastner, & Al, 1998). It is important to monitor the functioning skills and abilities of children with autism to increase their independence (Schwartz, Boulware, McBride, & Sandall, 2001). See Boxes 4.7 through 4.9 for a teacher's view and collaboration tips for children with low-incidence conditions.

Children with Sensory Impairments

Definition and characteristics. The two major sensory impairments are hearing and visual. Visual problems can include inherited conditions, corneal scarring, vitamin A deficiency color blindness, retinopathy of prematurity, optic nerve hypoplasia, and other conditions that cause blindness or low vision (Hatton, 2001). Children with hearing impairments have difficulty with communication and social interactions. Children with visual impairments also exhibit difficulty in social interaction and play (D'Allura, 2002).

A CHILD WHO HAS AUTISM, A TEACHER'S VIEW   BOX 4.7

From the day I met five-year-old Austin, I knew he was smart, but that he was also going to be a handful. He needs a picture schedule system on a daily basis to let him know ahead of time what is next. If something in the schedule changes, Austin throws a tantrum. He can't handle changes well, so I make sure to let him know if something is going to be different. Austin has a hard time eating. He wants to eat the same thing all the time—peanut butter and jelly sandwich and chips. If I try to feed him something different, he throws a fit. When it comes to academics, he is ahead of his peers in reading. It used to be rote (memorization of the words), but now he can read without much help from me. He is also an excellent speller and can write words. Even though Austin is strong in certain academic areas, his speech and language skills are delayed. He spontaneously says a sentence or two here and there, but most of the time just uses 3- to 4-word phrases. Socially, Austin is lagging. He is exhibiting some parallel play, but very little interaction with other children—except when he is intentionally poking them to get their reaction. Austin does not seem to be concerned about what other students think of his actions. For example, he often picks his nose or tries to pull down his pants during large group activities. Austin is also fascinated with patterns. He lines objects up in rows, and he fixes things that are messy. One day he got a drink of water while walking in line, and now he has to get water every day while in line.

COLLABORATION TIPS   BOX 4.8

TEACHER COLLABORATION WITH A BEHAVIOR INTERVENTIONIST

A child I had last year returned for the next school year. I knew the child had some behavior problems that needed to be resolved; however, I had tried practically everything I knew already. Collaborating with the interventionist gave me plenty of new ideas and she actually came in to give me suggestions and coach me through some of the behavior problems. From time to time after the initial contact, we would exchange e-mail, and she was there to answer any other questions or concerns I had along the way.

Prevalence. Approximately 1.4% of preschool children served under IDEA are deaf or hard of hearing. Children with visual impairments number about 0.6% of the preschoolers that are served (U.S. Department of Education, 2001b).

Early identification and intervention. Sensory impairments of children impact their entire family. Families with children who are deaf or hard of hearing experience difficulties in establishing relationships with their children. Communication is difficult and frustrating for both the parents and their children. Parents may not know the communication mode of the child. Children who are deaf are less responsive in communicative situations, even when families have a common communication mode. Support for families is needed and children will need assistance in forming friendships (Jackson & Turnbull, 2004). Children who are deaf or hard of hearing are now often identified

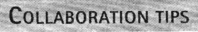

COLLABORATION TIPS   BOX 4.9

TEACHER COLLABORATION WITH A SPEECH PATHOLOGIST

The speech pathologist can't be in the room every second of the day to help the students with their language. Collaborating with her not only gave me new and fun ideas to try, but also benefited the students. Since improving and fostering speech and language was important for my students all day long—and not just twice a week, I worked with the speech pathologist throughout the year to provide my students with additional opportunities for speech and language development during each day. She gave me ideas and strategies that I could use throughout the day—without her having to be there. She also was aware of my themes and tailored her lessons to my themes.

Having a child with a sensory impairment impacts the entire family. Improving communication with the child can enhance family relationships.

during infancy because of improved technology and screening methods. The advantage of early detection is the ability to increase the chances for improving language acquisition and avoiding emotional and social difficulties (Curnock, 1993). Children with visual impairments may need scaffolding to encourage social interaction with peers (D'Allura, 2002). These children may also benefit from behavioral intervention to address the stereotypical rocking that is common among young children with visual impairments (McHugh & Lieberman, 2003).

Children with Sensory Integration Disorders

Some children are thought to have sensory integration problems that interfere with their language development and learning processes (Ayres, 1972; 1979). Children with cerebral palsy, pervasive developmental disorder, autism, mental retardation, language disorders, and learning disabilities are among those suspected as having sensory integration problems. Sensory integration is described as the ability to process sensory information in the central nervous system. Processing involves the brain receiving stimuli from the senses, interpreting that information, and responding to it. Sensory integration therapy, often provided by an occupational therapist, tries to improve the processing of sensory information by the brain. Speech therapists may also use sensory integration (SI) therapy to improve language and speech development. In this case, SI aims at brain-stem level sensory processing thought to provide a foundation for higher cognitive functioning and auditory processing related to language. The results of research studies to establish the effectiveness of SI therapy are controversial.

Consequently, it is recommended that if sensory integration therapy is implemented, the progress of children should be monitored to determine usefulness of this therapy for individuals (Griffer, 1999).

Other Health Impairments

Approximately 2.2% of preschoolers have health impairment of various types that may interfere with their learning (U.S. Department of Education, 2001b). Congenital conditions, such as muscular dystrophy, affect the learning and functioning of young children (Eeg-Olofsson, 1999). HIV/AIDS is an epidemic affecting large numbers of children during their early childhood years. Congenital AIDS can result in mental retardation, brain damage, and a host of developmental and medical problems (Centers for Disease Control and Prevention, 1992; LeRoy, Powell, & Kelker, 1994).

Children Who Are Gifted and Talented

Children who are considered gifted or talented are often thought to be at one extreme of the continuum. It is commonly believed that these children will achieve favorably under ordinary circumstances and require minimal attention to their learning needs. However, some researchers dispute an undifferentiated approach to gifted and talented children. Betts and Neihart (1988) proposed that giftedness can be manifested in different ways within the personalities of children. These researchers identified six profiles of giftedness to help teachers and parents support the behavioral and emotional needs of gifted children at home and school. The profile types are as follows:

1. *Type I: The Successful.* Approximately 90% of gifted children learn well and behave appropriately. They learn what is required to gain attention and to succeed. However, these children tend to become bored with school and may underachieve as adults.

2. *Type II: The Challenging.* Often unrecognized, these highly creative children win friendships with their appeal and sense of humor. However, they challenge authority figures and may be disruptive in school.

3. *Type III: The Underground.* These children deny their talents to gain peer acceptance and a sense of belongingness.

4. *Type IV: The Dropout.* Anger, withdrawal, depression, and defensiveness are present in gifted children who find that school does not meet their learning needs.

5. *Type V: The Double-Labeled.* These gifted children are rarely identified because they also have physical, emotional, or learning disabilities. Difficulty with assignments or incomplete work may be evident. They may not manifest behaviors that typically identify children as gifted.

Gifted and talented children also need support as well as appropriate levels of challenge to succeed.

6. *Type VI: The Autonomous Learner.* Frequently, these children are not identified early. Parents, however, may notice at home their desire to learn for the sake of learning. They are respected by peers and adults and tend to have a high self-esteem. These children are self-directed and goal-oriented learners (Betts & Neihart, 1988).

SUMMARY

This chapter discussed the full spectrum of children served in inclusive early childhood classrooms. The cultural and linguistic diversity of children was recognized as increasingly typical of early childhood settings. A discussion summarized the important ways that cultural diversity affects children's learning. The wide range of ability levels present in most early childhood classrooms was discussed, with emphasis on the importance of early identification and early intervention of children who are at risk and those with identified disabilities. Information was presented on IDEA and how eligible children are served under this mandate. The importance of identifying children's individual strengths was emphasized as a critical approach to help all children reach their maximum potential. This chapter also illustrated various typical classroom settings for children in the early childhood age range.

Discussion Questions

1. List the major characteristics of children with language disorders. How can you identify children who may need further diagnosis?
2. What skills must teachers acquire to collaborate with others in the early identification process?
3. What are the characteristics of children with cognitive and learning disabilities?
4. How can a teacher identify children with attention deficit hyperactivity disorders?
5. What behaviors might indicate a child is gifted?
6. How do teachers observe children to discern their patterns of growth and development?
7. How do characteristics such as gender, economic levels of families, and culture interact with children's developmental patterns?
8. Describe your first impressions of the typical child-care, preschool, and early primary classrooms. How are these classrooms similar? How are these classrooms different?
9. How can teachers prepare for early intervention and in identifying children who may have special learning needs?

Inclusive Activities

1. Explore Websites of school districts in your community to see whether schools, agencies, or teachers can actively participate in efforts to provide early screening and early intervention for children at risk of school failures.

2. Make a list of agencies and organizations in your area that provide services to children with disabilities. These organizations can serve as resources for you and the families of children you teach.

3. Contact one of the agencies you found in your area and try to arrange a visit with an adult who has a disability or a family member of a child with a disability. Ask that person to explain what life is like for someone with a disability and listen to his or her experiences.

4. Form a group with 4 to 5 of your classmates and plan a simulation to experience what it might be like to have a disability. Demonstrate your simulation in class so others might gain insights from the experience. For example, try a typical early childhood activity, such as an art activity or block building. However, use a blindfold to simulate blindness or use only one hand to simulate a physical disability.

References

Abrams, K., Theberge, S. K., & Karan, O. C. (2005). Children and adolescents who are depressed: An ecological approach. *Professional School Counseling, 8*(3), 284–292.

American Psychiatric Association. (2000). *Diagnostic and statistical manual of mental disorders DSM-IV-TR* (4th, revised ed.). Washington, DC: American Psychiatric Association.

Ayres, A. J. (1972). *Sensory integration and learning disorders.* Los Angeles: Western Psychological Services.

Ayres, A. J. (1979). *Sensory integration and the child.* Los Angeles: Western Psychological Services.

Bailey, D. B., & McWilliams, R. A. (1990). Normalizing early intervention. *Topics in Early Childhood Special Education, 10*(2), 33–47.

Berk, L. E. (1994). *Child development* (3rd ed.). Needham Heights, MA: Allyn & Bacon.

Betts, G., & Neihart, M. (1988). Profiles of the gifted and talented. *Gifted Child Quarterly, 32*(2), 248–253.

Boyajian, A. E., DuPaul, G. J., Handler, M. W., Eckert, T. L., & McGoey, K. E. (2001). The use of classroom-based brief functional analyses with preschoolers at-risk for attention deficit hyperactivitiy disorder. *The School Psychology Review, 30*(2), 278–293.

Brim, S. A., & Whitaker, D. P. (2000). Motivation and students with attention deficit hyperactivity disorder. *Preventing School Failure, 44*(2), 57–60.

Bronfenbrenner, U., & Morris, P. A. (1998). The ecology of developmental processes. In R. M. Lerner (Ed.), *Handbook of child psychology: Theoretical models of human development* (5th ed., Vol. 1, pp. 993–1028). New York: Wiley.

Buck, G. H., Polloway, E. A., Smith-Thomas, A., & Cook, K. W. (2003). Prereferral intervention processes: A survey of state practices. *Exceptional Children, 69*(3), 349–360.

California Department of Education. (1997). *Language census report for California public schools.* Sacramento, CA: Author.

Carnegie Task Force on Learning in the Primary Grades. (1996). *Years of promise: A comprehensive learning strategy for America's children.* New York: Carnegie Corp.

Carter, J., & Sugai, G. (1989). Survey on prereferral practices: Responses from state departments of education. *Exceptional Children, 55*, 298–302.

Casto, G., & Matropieri, M. A. (1986). The efficacy of early intervention programs: A meta-analysis. *Exceptional Children, 52*, 417–424.

Centers for Disease Control and Prevention. (1992). *HIV/AIDS surveillance.* Atlanta, GA: U.S. Department of Health and Human Services, Public Health Service.

Chalfant, J. C., & Pysh, M. V. (1989). Teacher assistance teams: Five descriptive studies on 96 teams. *Remedial and Special Education, 10*, 49–58.

Cohen, S. (1999). Zeroing in on autism in young children. *The Journal of Association for Persons with Severe Handicaps, 24*(3), 209–212.

Cullinan, D., Epstein, M. H., & Kauffman, J. M. (1984). Teachers' ratings of students behaviors: What constitutes behavior disorders in schools? *Behavioral Disorders, 10*, 9–19.

Cullinan, D., Epstein, M. H., & Sabornie, E. J. (1992). Selected characteristics of a national sample of seriously emotionally disturbed adolescents. *Behavioral Disorders, 17*, 273–280.

Curnock, D. A. (1993). Identifying hearing impairment in infants and young children: Universal screening at birth comes a step closer. *BMJ, 307*(13), 1225–1226.

D'Allura, T. (2002). Enhancing the social interaction skills of preschoolers with visual impairements. *Journal of Visual Impairment & Blindness, 96*(8), 576–584.

Danielyan, A., & Kowatch, R. A. (2005). Management options for bipolar disorder in children and adolescents. *Pediatric Drugs, 7*(5), 277–294.

Day, J. C. (1996). *Population projections of the United States by age, sex, race, and Hispanic origin.* Washington, DC: U.S. Government Printing Office.

Del'Homme, M., Kasari, C., Forness, S., & Bagley, R. (1996). Prereferral intervention and students at-risk for emotional or behavioral disorders. *Education and Treatment of Children, 19*, 272–285.

Eeg-Olofsson, K. E. (1999). Congenital muscular dystrophy care of children and families. *Scandanavian Journal of Rehabilitation and Medicine, Supp 39*, 53–57.

Emslie, G. J., & Mayes, T. L. (1999). Depression in children and adolescents: A guide to diagnosis and treatment. *CNS Drugs, 11*(3), 181–189.

Feil, E. G., & Becker, W. C. (1993). Investigation of multiple-gated screening system for preschool behavior problems. *Behavioral Disorders, 19*, 44–53.

Flood, W. A., & Wilder, D. A. (2002). Antecedent assessment and assessment-based treatment of off-task behavior in a child diagnosed with attention deficit hyperactivity disorder (ADHD). *Education and Treatment of Children, 25*(3), 331–338.

Forness, S., R., Serna, L. A., Nielson, E., Lambros, K., Hale, M., & Karvale, K. A. (2000). A model for early detection and primary prevention of emotional or behavioral disorders. *Education and Treatment of Children, 23*(3), 325–345.

Forness, S. R., Kavale, K. A., MacMillan, D. L., Asarnow, J. R., & Duncan, B. B. (1996). Early detection and prevention of emotional or behavioral disorders: Developmental aspects of systems of care. *Behavioral Disorders, 21*, 226–240.

Fox, L., Dunlap, G., & Powell, D. (2002). Young children with challenging behavior: Issues and considerations for behavior support. *Journal of Positive Behavior Interventions, 4*(4), 208–217.

Frost, J. L., Wortham, S., & Reifel, S. (Eds.). (2001). *Play and child development.* Upper Saddle River, NJ: Merrill/Prentice Hall.

Fuchs, D., Fuchs, L., Gilman, S., Reeder, P., Bahr, M., & Fernstrom, P., et al. (1990). Prereferral intervention through teacher consultation: Mainstream assistance teams. *Academic Therapy, 25*, 262–276.

Gable, R. A., Hendrickson, J. M., Tonelson, S. W., & Van Acker, R. (2002). Integrating academic and non-academic instruction for students with emotional/behavioral disorders. *Education and Treatment of Children, 25*(3), 459–475.

Gersten, R., & Geva, E. (2003). Teaching reading to early language learners. *Educational Leadership, 60*(7), 44–49.

Griffer, M. R. (1999). Is sensory integration a different way of analyzing challenging behavior?: A critical review of the evidence. *Language, Speech, & Hearing Services in Schools, 30*(4), 393–400.

Guralnick, M. J. (1997). *The effectiveness of early intervention.* Baltimore: Brookes.

Hatton, D. D. (2001). Model registry of early childhood visual impairment: First year results. *Journal of Visual Impairment & Blindness, 95*(7), 418–433.

Hughes, F. P. (1998). Play in special populations. In O. N. Saracho & B. Spodek (Eds.), *Multiple perspectives on play in early childhood education.* Albany: State University of New York Press.

Jackson, C. W., & Turnbull, A. (2004). Impact of deafness on family life: A review of literature. *Topics in Early Childhood Special Education, 24*(1), 15–29.

Jorgensen, C. M. (1994/1995). Essential questions—inclusive answers. *Educational Leadership, 52*(4), 52–55.

Kluger, J., & Song, S. (2002, August 19). Young and bipolar. *Time, 40, 49, 51.*

Koller, H. P., & Goldberg, K. B. (2002). Spotting learning differences. *Review of Ophthalmology,* 90–93.

La Paro, K. M., Olsen, K., & Pianta, R. C. (2002). Special education eligibility: developmental precursors over the first three years of life. *Exceptional Children, 69*(1), 55–66.

Lane, K. L., Mahdavi, J. N., & Borthwick-Duffy, S. (2003). Teacher perceptions of the prereferral intervention process: A call for assistance with school-based interventions. *Preventing School Failure, 47*(4), 148–155.

Lane, K. L., & Wehby, J. (2002). Addressing antisocial behavior in the schools: A call for action. *Academic Exchange Quarterly, 6,* 4–9.

LaRocque, M., Brown, S. E., & Johnson, K. L. (2001). Functional behavioral assessments and intervention plans in early intervention settings. *Infants and Young Children, 13*(3), 59–68.

Lazar, I., & Darlington, R. (1979). *Lasting effects after preschool* (No. OHDS 79-30179). Washington, DC: Administration for Children, Youth and Families, Office of Human Development Services.

Lazar, I., & Darlington, R. (1982). *Lasting effects of early education: A report from the Consortium for Longitudinal Studies* (Vol. 47).

LeRoy, C., Powell, T., & Kelker, P. (1994). Meeting our responsibilities in special education. *Teaching Exceptional Children, 26*(4), 37–44.

Mayes, S. D., Calhoun, S., & Crowell, E. W. (2000). Learning disabilities and ADHD: Overlapping spectrum disorders. *Journal of Learning Disabilities, 33*(5), 417–424.

McHugh, E., & Lieberman, L. (2003). The impact of developmental factors on stereotypic rocking of children with visual impairments. *Journal of Visual Impairment & Blindness, 97*(8), 453–474.

McLoyd, V. C. (1990). Minority children: Introduction to the special issue. *Child Development, 61,* 263–266.

Nash, J. M. (1997, February 3, 1997). Fertile minds. *Time,* 48–56.

National Coalition of Advocates for Students. (1991). *The good common school: Making the vision work for all children.* Boston: Author.

O'Brien, M., Rice, M., & Roy, C. (1996). Defining eligibility criteria for preventative early intervention in an NICU population. *Journal for Early Intervention, 20,* 283–293.

Ogletree, B. T., & Harn, W. E. (2001). Augmentative and alternative communication for persons with

Autism: History, issues, and unanswered questions. *Focus on Autism and Other Developmental Disabilities, 16*(3), 138–140.

Palfry, J. S., Singer, J. D., Walker, D. K., & Butler, J. A. (1987). Early identification of children's special needs: A study in five metropolitan communities. *The Journal of Pediatrics, 111,* 651–659.

Pisecco, S., Wristers, K., Swank, P., Silva, P., & Baker, D. B. (2001). The effect of academic self-concept on ADHD and antisocial behaviors in early adolescence. *Journal of Learning Disabilities, 34*(5), 450–461.

Ramsey, P. G. (1987). *Teaching and learning in a diverse world: Multicultural education for young children.* New York: Teachers College Press.

Rosenkoetter, S., & Barton, L. R. (2002). Bridges to literacy: Early routines that promote later school success. *Zero to Three, 22,* 33–38.

Salend, S. J., & Salinas, A. (2003). Language differences or learning difficulties: The work of the multidisciplinary team. *Teaching Exceptional Children, 35*(4), 36–43.

Sandall, S., McLean, M. E., & Smith, B. J. (2000). *DEC recommended practices in early intervention/early childhood special education.* Longmont, CO & Denver, CO: Sopris West and the Division for Early Childhood, Council for Exceptional Children.

Sapon-Shevin, M. (1994/1995). Why gifted students belong in inclusive schools. *Educational Leadership, 52*(4), 64–70.

Sapon-Shevin, M. (2001). Schools fit for all. *Educational Leadership, 58,* 34–39.

Schirduan, V., Case, K., & Faryniarz, J. (2002). How ADHD students are smart. *The Educational Forum, 66*(4), 324–328.

Schwartz, I. S., Boulware, G. L., McBride, B. J., & Sandall, S. (2001). Functional assessment strategies for young children with Autism. *Focus on Autism and Other Developmental Disabilities, 16*(4), 222–227.

Schweinhart, L. J., Barnes, H. V., & Weikart, D. P. (1993). *Significant benefits: The high/scope perry preschool study through age 27* (Monograph No. 10). Ypsilanti, MI: High/Scope Educational Research Foundation.

Scott, F. G., Singaraju, S., Kilgo, J. L., Kregel, J., & Lazzari, A. (1993). A survey of pediatricians on early identification and early intervention services. *Journal of Early Intervention, 17,* 129–138.

Serna, L. A., Forness, S. R., & Nielsen, E. (1998). Intervention versus affirmation: Proposed solutions to the problem of disproportionate minority representation in special education. *Journal of Special Education, 82,* 48–52.

Shevell, M. I., Majnemer, A., Rosenbaum, P., & Abrahamowicz, M. (2001). Profile of referrals for early childhood developmental delay to ambulatory subspecialty clinics. *Journal of Child Neurology, 16*(9), 645–650.

Sinclair, E., Del'Homme, M., & Gonzalez, M. (1993). Systematic screening for preschool behavioral disorders. *Behavior Disorders, 18,* 177–188.

Snow, C., Burns, M. S., & Griffin, P. (Eds.). (1998). *Preventing reading difficulties in young children.* Washington, DC: National Academy Press.

Spencer, M. B. (1990). Development of minority children: An introduction. *Child Development, 61,* 267–269.

Trawick-Smith, J., & Lisi, P. (1994). Infusing multicultural perspectives in an early childhood development course: Effects on the knowledge and attitudes of inservice teachers. *Journal of Early Childhood Teacher Education, 15,* 8–12.

Trawick-Smith, J. W. (1997). *Early childhood development: A multicultural perspective.* Upper Saddle River, NJ: Merrill/Prentice Hall.

U.S. Department of Education. (1993). *National excellence: A case for developing America's talent.* Washington, DC: Author.

U.S. Department of Education. (1996). *Digest of education statistics, 1996.* Washington, DC: U.S. Government Printing Office.

U.S. Department of Education. (2001a). Twenty-five years of educating children with disabilities: The good news and the work ahead. Washington DC: American Youth Forum and Center on Education Policy.

U.S. Department of Education. (2001b). *Twenty-fourth annual report to Congress on the implementation of the Individuals with Disabilities Education Act.* Washington, DC: Author.

Wang, M. C., Reynolds, M. C., & Walberg, H. J. (1994/1995). Serving students at the margins. *Educational Leadership, 52*(4), 12–16.

Webster-Stratton, C. (1997). Early intervention for families of preschool children with conduct problems.

In M. J. Guralnick (Ed.), *The effectiveness of early intervention* (pp. 429–453). Baltimore: Brookes.

Whitehurst, G. J., & Lonigan, C. J. (2001). Emergent literacy: Development from prereaders to readers. In Susan B. Neuman & D. K. Dickinson (Ed.), *Handbook of Early Literacy Research* (pp. 11–29). New York: Guilford Press.

Wolery, M., & Fleming, L. A. (1992). Preventing and responding to problem situations. In D. B. Bailey & M. Wolery (Eds.), *Teaching infants and preschoolers with disabilities* (2nd ed., pp. 363–406). New York: Merrill/Macmillan.

Zima, B. T., Wells, K. B., & Freeman, H. E. (1994). Emotional and behavioral problems and severe academic delays among sheltered homeless children in Los Angeles County. *American Journal of Public Health, 84*(2), 260–264.

Ziring, P. R., Brazdziunas, D., Cooley, W. C., Kastner, T. A., Kummer, M. E., Gonzalez de Pijem, L., et al. (1998). Auditory integration training and facilitated communication for autism. *Pediatrics, 102*(2), 431–433.

PART II

Creating a Classroom for All Children

Chapter 5

Planning Differentiated Curriculum and Instruction

Key Principle

Implement an integrated, active learning curriculum

Objectives

After reading this chapter you will be able to:

1. Explain the theoretical foundations and practices that are the basis for curriculum development in inclusive early childhood classrooms.

2. Prepare accommodations for individual learners that are matched to a child's strengths.

3. State several ways to collaborate with families to plan the curriculum.

4. Summarize planning of an individualized education program (IEP) or individualized family services plan (IFSP) for children with disabilities or special needs.

5. Provide a rationale for providing differentiated instruction in inclusive early childhood classrooms.

6. Articulate the importance of professional standards and guidelines for practice to promote evidence-based practices in inclusive early childhood classrooms.

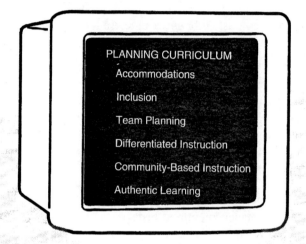

PLANNING CURRICULUM
Accommodations
Inclusion
Team Planning
Differentiated Instruction
Community-Based Instruction
Authentic Learning

INTRODUCTION

Selecting flexible curricula and using evidence-based practices to deliver instruction are of major importance for inclusive early childhood teachers. This chapter discusses the critical need for teachers to gain skill in preparing and using curricular plans that differentiate instruction for all children and provide appropriate levels of support to accommodate individual children. Accommodating individuals is also necessary to promote educational equity for all children. This chapter also addresses effective methods of engaging in collaborative planning with teachers, related services professionals, and families to ensure stimulation of learning in both home and school contexts. Guidelines and recommendations for using evidence-based practices are specified and their importance is discussed.

DIFFERENTIATED INSTRUCTION IN INCLUSIVE CLASSROOMS

Differentiated curriculum and instruction is a comprehensive approach to teaching, whereby teachers seek to motivate all children to reach their full learning potential. The goal is to provide a learning environment that is equitable, democratic, and motivating to all children (Broderick, Mehta-Parekh, & Reid, 2005; Tomlinson, 2001; Tomlinson & Edison, 2003). This is accomplished by offering children a variety of options for learning that respects their diversity. Teachers offer children choices in content, pace of learning, and assessment methods. Differentiating these features in the learning cycle creates a more inclusive environment customized to accommodate individuals (Tomlinson & Edison, 2003).

Differentiation and Range of Ability

All learners benefit from differentiation. Children with a high ability are better included when curriculum modifications allow them to learn beyond the standard levels that are typically available for their children of their age. Providing a differentiated challenge for gifted children requires the teacher to have sufficient command of the subject matter, planning time, resources, and administrative support. Further, teachers must have good classroom management and pedagogical skills to deal with multiple tasks occurring simultaneously in the classroom (VanTassel-Baska & Stambaugh, 2005). Children with disabilities also benefit from differentiated curriculum that challenges them to attain higher levels of thinking. This is important because often expectations are low for children with disabilities and, consequently, their motivation may also be lowered from the lack of challenge. When instruction is primarily teacher-initiated and controlled, children tend to become inattentive or disruptive. Unfortunately, these behaviors can interfere with memory and learning (Gallagher, 2004).

Motivation and Culture

Differentiated instruction recognizes that motivation, a common phenomenon across cultures, is fundamental for stimulation of learning processes. As such, seeking ways to motivate the individual learner becomes a prime responsibility of teachers (Ginsberg, 2005; Tomlinson & Allan, 2000). It is the teacher's role to make learning relevant for each child so that a personal connection to the curriculum content can be constructed through the child's individual learning process (Tomlinson & Edison, 2003). With differentiated instruction, teachers view the curriculum from an interdisciplinary lens, providing culturally responsive instruction to children (Ginsberg, 2005). For learners, differentiated approaches to curriculum and instruction offer daily opportunities to acquire knowledge in ways that are responsive and matched to their individual strengths and learning goals. Moreover, children learn in heterogeneous environments that are respectful, as well as accessible. Differentiation creates inclusive classrooms where each child is safe, valued, and challenged (George, 2005; Thomas & Loxley, 2001; Tomlinson, 2001, 2005).

Individual and Group Perspectives

Differentiated instruction is a concept that has been defined in various ways. Tomlinson (2004) defines differentiated instruction from the perspective of the individual child. From the child's standpoint, instruction is differentiated if it achieves a match between the child's interests, learning preferences, and appropriate level of challenge (Tomlinson, 2004). From this perspective, differentiated instruction is compatible with obligations to accommodate individual children with any adaptation or modification of curriculum, instruction, or the learning environment necessary to support the child's learning. A variety of terms are used to describe inclusive teaching: accommodation, adaptation, modification, responsive, and differentiated. Although the preferred terminology may change, the fundamental responsibility of teachers is to ensure a good fit between the curriculum and the children with their diverse strengths and needs (Hoover & Patton, 2005). To accomplish this goal, certain children may benefit from teaching practices, such as embedding explicit strategies or providing assistive technology to meet their learning goals.

One can also view the notion of differentiated instruction from a group perspective. When differentiated instruction is implemented, a true community of learners is formed, with all learners individually accommodated and able to contribute to and participate in the group's learning process. The role of teachers is to ensure that both individual and group learning goals are met. Teachers implementing differentiated instruction maintain high expectations for all children and offer individually appropriate levels of support to ensure each child's success (Friend & Pope, 2005; Hoover & Patton, 2005; Tomlinson, 2004).

The concept of universal design has influenced curriculum planning for diverse groups of children enrolled in inclusive classrooms. Teachers using universal design principles seek to provide equal access to the curriculum by building flexibility into instruction and offering all learners options. With a range of options and choices for learners already built into the scheme of curriculum and instruction, instructional planning by teachers is more efficient, and fewer accommodations are necessary for individual children (Friend & Pope, 2005).

Roles and Responsibilities

Teachers have many responsibilities in the complex role of planning for differentiated instruction. Ensuring instruction that is effective for the group and for individual children requires teachers to apply child development knowledge and have proficiency in organizing time and resources for instruction (Tomlinson, 2004). When children are diverse in ability, the role of the teacher is to weave the optimal combination of curricular content and teaching strategies to support each child's success in learning. In inclusive classrooms, it is a constant process of adjusting the level of facilitation individual children need, based upon ongoing assessment of their learning. Key ingredients to this process are teacher knowledge of the subject matter underlying the curriculum content and assessment information on the child's prior knowledge, skills, and task performance. Assessment is essential for determining a child's content knowledge and metacognitive skills so that teachers can offer proper support for the child's constructivist learning process (Karp & Voltz, 2000).

Whereas the teacher and planning teams assume numerous responsibilities in providing differentiated instruction, there are several good arguments for encouraging learners (even those who are very young) to assume some responsibility for the differentiation of their own learning opportunities. Children progress toward greater independence and self-understanding in their learning processes. Encouraging them to voice their expectations, learning goals, and desired levels of support can foster their independence and self-efficacy as learners. Moreover, allowing children to play a role in differentiated instruction creates a community of learners in which individuals contribute their uniqueness to the shared learning of all (Tomlinson, 2004).

Assess-to-Inform Differentiation

Assessment is a critical component of differentiated instruction as an essential set of tools to help teachers create the match between children and variables in the learning situation. Assessment informs planning for differentiated instruction so that the level of support teachers provide is individually appropriate, so children can learn alongside their peers (Friend & Pope, 2005; Tomlinson, 2004). Assessment in differentiated instruction is an ongoing, formative process with flexibility to address achievement and motivation of diverse groups of young children (Tomlinson, 2005).

BLENDING THEORY AND PRACTICE

To teach inclusively in early childhood education, a professional must become adept at blending the theories and practices of various disciplines and fields. Professionals across fields have entered into discussions and debates to arrive at common platforms and unite a pedagogical stance for inclusion's theories and best practices. Most notable among these debates was an ongoing dialogue spanning several years between the fields of early childhood education (ECE) and early childhood special education (ECSE). Each of these fields evolved separately from different theoretical stances. Early childhood education is an eclectic foundation of theory and practice that is considerably influenced by developmental interactionist or constructivist theoretical bases. In contrast, ECSE was highly influenced by behaviorist roots in special education. Blending theory and practice across these fields to achieve inclusion has required commitment, study, and dialogue by professionals in both fields.

Professional Dialogues

In 1987, the National Association for the Education of Young Children (NAEYC) published a set of guidelines for accepted practices for early childhood education

Assessment leads and informs curricular planning to ensure a good match for each child.

professionals. The developmentally appropriate practice (DAP) (Bredekamp, 1987) guidelines were embraced by ECE teachers across the field. However, when they compared them with early childhood special education practices, some ECSE professionals criticized the usefulness of the guidelines for serving children with special needs in inclusive early childhood settings (Safford, 1989). An evaluative period ensued causing each field to challenge their traditions and consider new methodologies. Amidst the serious debates about the value of DAP for children with special needs in inclusive early childhood classrooms, each field articulated their positions and clarified their theoretical and pedagogical stances. The crux of the debate centered upon whether DAP alone was sufficient to propel learning of all children (Carta, Atwater, Schwartz, & McConnell, 1993; Carta, Schwartz, Atwater, & McConnell, 1991; Johnson & Johnson, 1992; Johnson & Johnson, 1993; McLean & Odom, 1993; Wolery, Strain, & Bailey, Jr., 1992). Professionals lacked a research basis for providing definitive answers to questions raised in the dialogues. A positive outcome of the controversy and the debates that followed has been increased research to identify best practices that help all children learn. Moreover, this process of evaluation has led to greater consensus regarding inclusion and achieving the goal of educational equity and success for all children. The research basis to inform practice in early childhood settings providing early intervention services has burgeoned. Many credible studies now exist, expanding an accumulated research base. Recommendations for identifying effective, evidence-based practices have been compiled and disseminated (Odom & Wolery, 2003).

Professional Standards and Guidelines

Professional organizations, such as the Council for Exceptional Children, NAEYC, and the Association for Childhood Education International have published the positions and rejoinders for members and others interested in inclusion. Organizations have led efforts to promote teaching more inclusively in early childhood education. Top researchers and theorists have sought to provide practitioners with guidelines, position papers, and other tools to assist them in their efforts to teach all children effectively.

Effective teachers of all young children are aware of standards, guidelines, and recommendations issued by professional organizations. More importantly, these teachers become knowledgeable about the implications of these guidelines and use these documents as tools to improve their teaching. The following are some of the major guidelines and sets of recommendations that teachers in inclusive early childhood classrooms should review and use to guide their professional development and practice:

- *The Good Common School: Making the Vision Work for All Children* (National Coalition of Advocates for Students, 1991). This coalition originated during the 1960s civil rights movement. This publication lists 10 entitlements of all children regarding educational opportunity. The document highlights the right to learn in an integrated setting that is responsive to individual differences.
- *Developmentally Appropriate Practice in Early Childhood Programs* (Bredekamp, 1987; Bredekamp & Copple, 1997). Revised in 1997, these landmark documents articulated best practices for early childhood educators. The concepts of developmentally appropriate practices that are also age appropriate and individually appropriate were introduced in these guidelines.
- *DEC Position on Inclusion* (Division for Early Childhood Council for Exceptional Children, 1993a).
- *DEC Position on Early Intervention Services for Children Birth to Age Eight* (Division for Early Childhood of the Council for Exceptional Children, 1993b).
- *DEC Recommended Practices: Indicators of Quality in Programs for Infants and Young Children with Special Needs and Their Families* (Division for Early Childhood Council for Exceptional Children, 1993c).
- *Infants and Toddlers with Special Needs and Their Families* (Sexton, Snyder, Sharpton, & Stricklin, 1993). The 1993 position papers and sets of recommendations clarified practices in ECSE and served as a prelude to consensus building between the fields of ECE and ECSE.
- *Teachers of English to Speakers of Other Languages (TESOL) Standards and Statement of Rights* (Teachers of English to Speakers of Other Languages, 1995a, 1995b). These documents endorsed the right of culturally and linguistically diverse children to participate in an integrated program with their peers.
- *Personnel Standards for Early Education and Early Intervention: Guidelines for Licensure in Early Childhood Special Education* (Division for Early Childhood Council for Exceptional Children, National Association for the Education of

Young Children, & Association of Teacher Educators, 1995). This landmark document represented consensus of three major professional organizations and signaled a unified stance for defining roles of teachers and appropriate practices for inclusive early childhood settings. These guidelines call for culturally competent professionals to serve diverse children and families.

- *Guidelines for Preparation of Early Childhood Professionals* (National Association for the Education of Young Children, 1995, 1996). Position statements were issued by NAEYC in 1996, endorsing the prior 1995 consensus document.

- *DEC Recommended Practices in Early Intervention/Early Childhood Special Education* (Sandall, McLean, & Smith, 2000). This document is a revised and improved version of the earlier document by the same name.

COLLABORATIVE PLANNING FOR INCLUSION

Potential Obstacles

Increasing accountability and pressures. National reports indicated that implementing strategies that recommend inclusion benefit all children. Unfortunately, teachers have insufficient time to engage in quality instructional and curricular planning during typical school days. Yet, teachers report they are expected to cover more curricular content, teach larger classes, and ensure student achievement meets rising performance standards (Joint Committee on Teacher Planning for Students with Disabilities, 1995). When children with disabilities are included in federally funded programs, such as services provided under the Individuals with Disabilities Education Improvement Act (IDEIA, 2004) Part C and Section 619 of Part B, accountability can be daunting. Teachers are held accountable for demonstrating the effectiveness of their program using more rigorous assessment and evaluation models than previously required. Teachers are required to target specific outcomes and select assessment measures that will generate data proving the effectiveness of the program (Harbin, Rous, & Mclean, 2005). Consequently, planning time for teachers has never been more necessary. Teachers are obligated to plan curricular activities that are effective, and, further, they are required to demonstrate the success of the curriculum with more precision than previously required.

Lack of resources and resource specialists. Teachers in general early childhood education and community-based child-care settings have few opportunities to engage in curriculum planning in collaboration with other teachers or specialists, such as speech therapists, special education teachers, behavior interventionists, occupational therapists, or other professionals. Further, general education teachers have limited opportunities to receive training from these specialists that would allow them to implement specialized strategies or curricula more effectively (Joint Committee on Teacher Planning for Students with Disabilities, 1995; Schloss, 1992; Wolery et al., 1994). When professional development opportunities are offered to advance the technical skills of

Professional organizations keep teachers informed regarding curricular standards and methods of planning.

general education teachers, collaboration may be enhanced. It is likely that through training, teachers and specialists will be able to span the gap between their fields through the development of common understandings of key concepts and methodology. Further, they may feel more comfortable collaborating when professional development training introduces general education teachers to terminology used in the specific fields of specialists.

Systematic Planning

A number of systems for planning have been devised that may prove useful for inclusive classrooms. Systematic planning methods seek to streamline planning and make the process more efficient. Moreover, the principles that underlie the planning systems can help ensure that teachers address recommended practices and use evidence-based methods, resulting in more effective and powerful instruction for inclusive early childhood classrooms. Systematic approaches can benefit planning by helping teachers remain focused on critical aspects of differentiated instruction purported to have the greatest chance of improving children's success in school. The next sections review curriculum planning systems that can be useful in providing a framework to guide curriculum planning teams in inclusive classrooms.

The SMART planning system. In 1997, SMART planning was introduced as a five-point streamlined system to guide teachers through the process of planning differentiated curriculum and instruction for inclusive early childhood classrooms. The system was based on a cross-disciplinary review of professional literature to ensure considering the ability and the cultural, linguistic, and demographic diversity of inclusive classrooms. The resulting system establishes a focus on five critical aspects of planning for inclusion suggested by research. Practically, the intent of the system was to help teachers design more powerful instruction given the constraints of time, lack of resources, and the pressures teachers face. The acronym SMART helps teachers remember to incorporate five key foci into planning.

Select. Making good choices regarding the curricular activities and materials is critical to inclusion. Teachers can collaborate with families in the selection process to ensure a good fit between children and the curriculum. A developmentally appropriate curriculum that affords some flexibility in choices of teaching strategies and content is preferable to permit accommodation for individuals.

Match. In addition to considering cultural background, strengths and learning preferences are critical to ensure each child's success in learning. Particularly important is making a good match between the teaching strategies used to facilitate learning and the individual child.

Adapt. Although planning should focus on working through a child's strengths, some accommodation for disabilities may be necessary. Multidisciplinary teams in collaboration with families can decide on the least intrusive adaptations needed to facilitate an individual child's learning. Carefully planned accommodations, such as assistive technology, can increase a child's chances for social acceptance and academic achievement in classrooms with their peers.

Relevant. The long- and short-term significances of the curriculum content and the skills taught are considerations for planning. Teaching functional curricula within authentic community-based contexts can help children integrate new concepts and skills into real life. Collaborating with families to plan and evaluate curricula can improve the cultural relevance of the classroom activities.

Test. Assessment before, during, and after differentiated instruction is the hallmark of effective planning in inclusive classrooms. Assessing-to-inform instructional planning helps children meet their individual learning goals. Planning for the success of each child requires that assessment must lead curricular planning. Embedded assessment is also critical so teachers can make adjustments during the learning activities, based on the child's performance. Evaluation of the outcomes of differentiated instruction using culturally and linguistically fair methods is critical to promoting steady progress of children (Winter, 1997).

Using the SMART planning system, the questions in Box 5.1 can be used as a quick reference to ensure all criteria established by the system have been meet by curricular activities planned for inclusive early childhood classrooms.

CREDE principles. In 1998, The Center for Research on Education Diversity and Excellence (CREDE) published a set of key principles focused on the education of

---

THE SMART PLANNING SYSTEM   BOX 5.1

Select

    1. Are the curricular activities and materials flexible to promote learning of children who are diverse in ability, language, culture, and socioeconomic levels?

    2. Is a constructivist perspective at the heart of the learning activities (i.e., active learning, authentic, child centered)?

    3. Do the curricular activities allow teachers to accommodate individual children?

    4. Do the curricular activities afford opportunities for social interaction and cooperation?

    5. Are the curricular activities culturally responsive and are there activities for families?

Match

    6. Are the individual learning goals of children matched to the activities?

    7. Do learning activities match the different learning styles and preferences of children?

Adapt

    8. Are activities easy to adapt, if necessary, to accommodate individual children?

    9. Can each child be successful with the least intrusive adaptation possible?

Relevant

    10. Are curricular activities pertinent to the goals of children now and in the future?

    11. Are learning activities authentic to enhance the transfer of skills and concepts to real-life situations?

    12. Can teachers embed activities into natural routines of the classroom and home contexts?

Test

    13. Does assessment inform planning of the activities and evaluation of outcomes for individual children?

    14. Is authentic assessment embedded into activities?

    15. Are assessments culturally and linguistically fair?

---

children with special needs who are English language learners. These guidelines suggest planning new learning activities based upon familiar experiences and previous learning. In social learning experiences, it was recommended that teachers facilitate opportunities for thinking, problem solving, and verbalization within these contexts (Tharp, 1998).

    Curriculum differentiation factors. In 2005, Hoover and Patton proposed six curricular factors to consider when planning differentiated instruction for English language learners with special needs. These researchers proposed differentiation not only to address variations in language, but also to consider authentic ways to use language in the classroom. Consideration of cultural values and learning styles of children is crucial to differentiation. Assessing to determine each child's background of prior knowledge, concepts, and skills is fundamental in challenging all children to develop higher order thinking skills (Hoover & Patton, 2005).

Curriculum compacting. When children who are gifted or high achieving are included in early childhood classrooms, adjustments to the curriculum may be necessary to offer an appropriate level of challenge to these children. Based on earlier work of Renzulli, this procedure plans for a streamlined version of curricular content for children who can progress at an accelerated pace. By eliminating repetition and adding more challenging enrichment activities, teachers can engage children who are gifted in curricular activities customized for their ability level (Kennedy, 1995; Reis & Purcell, 1993; Reis & Renzulli, 1992; Reis, Westberg, Kulikowich, & Purcell, 1998; Renzulli, 1977; Renzulli & Reis, 1986).

Planning matrix. Based on Gardner's multiple intelligences theory (Gardner, 1983; Gardner, 1995) crossed with five levels of cognitive problems, a group of researchers devised a planning matrix with a number of purposes. It can be used to plan noncompetitive, authentic learning activities that challenge children who are gifted and talented. The same matrix is useful for gathering assessment data to inform planning and evaluate outcomes of instruction. The tool helps teachers plan for learning experiences at different levels of challenge and encourages children to engage in creative problem-solving processes. The matrix has proven useful in differentiating instruction for children of both genders in culturally diverse classrooms (Maker, Nielson, & Rogers, 1994).

Pyramid planning systems. This type of system was designed to facilitate collaborative planning for classrooms including children who are diverse in ability. Teaching teams can plan for differentiation and assessment of content across the curriculum. A three-level graphic organizer in the shape of a pyramid helps teachers plan to offer different levels of complexity using the same curriculum. Concepts and skills at the base of the pyramid represent curricular content that all children will learn. Moving upward, the smaller, middle layer represents content that some children will acquire. The smallest peak layer of the pyramid lists enrichment-level content with advanced challenges. Collaborative teams can use the pyramid as a useful planning tool (Schumm, Vaughn, & Harris, 1997).

Taxonomies. Traditionally used to address a full range of cognitive levels, taxonomies continue to be simple, useful tools for differentiating curriculum and instruction. The widely used Bloom's taxonomy is hierarchical system structured to help teachers consider different levels of cognitive thought from simple to complex (Bloom, 1956). A taxonomy can be used to develop questions at various levels of difficulty, a technique purported to scaffold language and concept development of English language learners (Herrell & Jordan, 2004). Bloom's taxonomy can also be used as a thinking frame to plan thematic curriculum units for groups of children who vary in cognitive ability (Joint Committee on Teacher Planning for Students with Disabilities,

1995). Barrett's taxonomy (Barrett, 1972), aimed at articulating levels of reading comprehension from literal to inferential is another taxonomy based on Bloom's scheme that is useful for differentiated planning (Eanes, 1997). Taxonomies, such as Bloom's and Barrett's, are useful for stimulating children to develop higher levels of cognitive thought and can be useful for children who are gifted (Renzulli, 1986).

Universal design for learning. An approach to curricular planning for diverse groups of learners that is gaining wide acceptance is to use principles based upon the concept of universal design. The idea of universal design emerged from the field of architecture in response to ADA legislation. The approach addressed the adaptations and integration of assistive technology needed for persons with disabilities into an overall design that accommodates all people. It is gaining in popularity and is applied widely to ensure that environments and merchandise are designed for all consumers (Mace, 1998). This concept was applied to education and learning by the Center for Applied Special Technology as universal design for learning (UDL)(Hitchcock, Meyer, Rose, & Jackson, 2002). The elements of universal design have been applied to both assessment of children's achievement and the design of differentiated curriculum and instruction with positive results (Friend & Pope, 2005). Application of universal design to curriculum content and materials ensures that all children, including those with disabilities, will have access to learning opportunities alongside their typically developing peers. Using universal design principles in designing curriculum helps planning teams adapt and modify curriculum more efficiently so all children have better access to curricular content and materials. Curriculum based on universal design is flexible and provides built-in alternatives, rather than relying on teachers to add on modifications. Consequently, customization is streamlined and it is less time-consuming, a benefit to busy teachers with little planning time. Using universal design techniques from the start can reduce the need for assistive technology to support the learning of children with certain disabilities (Acrey, Johnstone, & Milligan, 2005).

The goal is to ensure accessibility of the curriculum and learning materials on a daily basis for all children in the inclusive classroom. Teachers using this approach use constructs for planning curricular content or assessments so that curricular content is relevant and all information presented is related to the larger construct. Nonbiased materials that are accessible to all children are used. Materials are readable, easy to understand, and amenable to accommodations that might still be needed for certain children to gain access (Acrey et al., 2005; Council for Exceptional Children, 1999).

Selecting Curricula and Approaches

Compare curriculum to children's strengths. For children with disabilities, the match of the curriculum and instructional strategies to their individual strengths and characteristics can impact their successful performance of tasks (Cole, Dale, Mills, & Jenkins, 1993; Cole, Mills, Dale, & Jenkins, 1991; Scruggs & Mastropieri, 1993). Some experts believe the selection of the curriculum and practices that best match a child's characteristics can facilitate a child's participation and largely determines the extent of integration a child with disabilities can achieve in inclusive classrooms (Bricker, 1995). Evidence-based best practices have been established for the field of early childhood education (Bredekamp & Copple, 1997) and the field of early intervention/early childhood education (Odom & Wolery, 2003). However, unless the best practices that teachers select are matched to the child's specific cultural and learning characteristics, the child may not achieve success in learning. Consequently, the emphasis of inclusive education is to match the curriculum and strategies to individual children (Carta, 1994; Scruggs & Mastropieri, 1993).

Flexibility. An important goal of inclusive education is selecting a curriculum model that affords flexibility to meet the needs of the children as a group, as well as meeting the needs of individuals. Teachers are obligated to make whatever accommodations are reasonable and necessary to allow a child with disabilities to participate in activities with their peers (Deiner, 1999; Grubb, 1993; Surr, 1992; Underwood & Mead, 1995). However, inclusive classrooms are complex, with culturally and linguistically diverse children and children with a full range of ability. Consequently, the curriculum and instructional approaches selected must be useful for children speaking languages other than English and must be useful, given different communication modes that children might use. Children will also span a wide range of ability and may include children who are gifted and talented. Selecting a flexible curriculum model will enable teachers to accommodate all children without jeopardizing the curriculum's integrity or using multiple curricula, a tactic that would increase complications in planning (National Association of State Boards of Education Study Group on Special Education, 1992).

Team Planning of Curriculum and Approaches

Formal and informal collaboration. Multidisciplinary teams of teachers and professionals are responsible, by law, for planning the IEP for children with disabilities. The IEP specifies the goals and objectives targeted for accomplishment. Further, the team plans the time line and approaches to help the child achieve the stated goals. For other children in the class, however, there is no legal mandate governing their program with similar specificity. Yet, ideally, all the children in the inclusive classroom deserve the most effective curriculum and methods available. Consequently, in selecting the curriculum and instructional approaches for an inclusive classroom, the teacher is wise to use an informal team approach. Invitations to other teachers to help plan will also help to gain new perspectives. Specialists who work with certain children in the class can contribute ideas to the teacher's curriculum planning periodically. Since inclusive early childhood classrooms may necessitate sharing teaching responsibilities with others, it is important to choose flexible curricula. Teachers in inclusive classrooms may coteach with a special education teacher, tutor individual children, or teach alternately with another teacher or specialist (Roach, 1995; Salisbury, 1991; Salisbury et al., 1994). The latest reauthorization of IDEA (IDEIA 2004) now recognizes that children without disabilities might gain some tangential benefits from related services personnel who provide their services in the inclusive classroom setting (Harbin et al., 2005).

Involving families. Families are vital in selecting the curriculum and strategies that teachers use. Seeking input from families prior to selection is essential to gain the best match between the curriculum and the characteristics of individual children. Box 5.2 details a unit schedule and collaboration tips for parents, and Box 5.3 provides a classroom activity example.

COLLABORATION TIPS   BOX 5.2

This is given to parents at the beginning of the year. If they have ideas, materials during the year, this gives them an opportunity to participate in their children's education.

Unit Schedule

August	Welcome to School, Gingerbread man
	All About Me
September	My Family/Friends/Me
	5 Senses
October	Fall/Apples
	Community Helpers
	Spiders
	Pumpkins/Squash
November	Fall Leaves
	Autumn Weather
	Thanksgiving
	Food/Nutrition
December	Seasons
	Snow, Snowmen
January	Winter/Weather
	Bears/Hibernation
	Space
	Rocks/Fossils
February	Dinosaurs
	Friendship/Patriotism/Rodeo
	Rodeo/Cowboys
	Texas
March	Spring
	Plants/Seeds
	Eggs/Birds
April	Farm
	Insects
	Ponds
	Land Animals (wild, tame)
May	Ocean Life
	Summer Vacation/Transportation
June	What Will 1st Grade Be Like?

LITERACY ACTIVITY EXAMPLE   **BOX 5.3**

Students have the opportunity to walk around the room and write words they find that begin with the letters below.

Today I found these words:

j _____

k _____

y _____

v _____

w _____

z _____

Multidisciplinary teams of teachers and specialists collaborate to plan curricular activities that challenge all children.

Planning Curriculum with Families

True partnerships between families and schools can result in curricula that are better matched to children and more likely to prepare all children for life in our diverse world. Families, when viewed as equally responsible as schools, are natural contributors to ensure the authenticity of the curriculum used to educate all children toward academic and life success. Mutually supportive partnerships can be achieved when teachers and schools move beyond the goal of providing a "web of support" for families (Winter, 1999) and recognize the contributions that families can make are also supportive of schools.

Promoting multicultural values and cultural competence is best accomplished by sharing that responsibility with families. Rather than unidirectional methods in which information flows primarily from school to home, establishing two-way support and communication is essential to ensure opportunities for true collaboration. Together, teachers and families can identify challenges to offering classrooms with opportunities for all children to develop prodiversity attitudes and competencies. Joint home-school efforts increase the likelihood of children acquiring the competence to enhance their chances for successful interactions within a diverse sociocultural context. Teachers can examine their teaching practices, methods of grouping children, and ways of involving parents to ensure cultural responsiveness. Similarly, families can evaluate their home interactions and relationships in terms of multicultural learning. Teachers and families can work together to learn more about ways to provide home and school environments

COLLABORATION TIPS*   BOX 5.4

Working with Your Child at Home

Dear Parents:

I have compiled a packet of ideas, activities and flash cards for you to use with your child at home. In our weekly newsletter, you will see the concepts and letters your child will be working on at school. This packet provides you with the tools to work on those same key concepts at home.

Letters

Please make sure you only introduce the letters we have already introduced at school—check our weekly newsletter to see what letter we'll be introducing or reviewing. When teaching your children letters:

1. Hold up lowercase and capital letter flash cards—one at a time.
2. Say the letter and then give the sound.
3. Have your child repeat the letter and sound.
4. When your child is familiar with the letters, you can hold the flash cards up and have the child tell you the letter and sound.
5. You can also ask your child what words start with the letter.
6. Put several letters on the table and have your child pick out the letter you say.
7. Write the letter as you say the name and sound. Have your child repeat.

Writing Name

Use the enclosed sentence strip and D'Nealian letter guide to write your child's name.

1. Have the child trace the letters with his or her finger.
2. Have the child trace the letters with a pencil.
3. Set the name in front of the child, and have him or her use it to try to copy his or her name.
4. You can use the single-letter flash cards and start with one letter at a time first.

* See Appendix A for the full text.

---

that nurture prodiversity attitudes and culturally competent interaction skills among children. Planning together can ensure that multicultural learning experiences are available to children in both contexts (Banks, 1993; Edwards, Fear, & Gallegos, 1995; Swick, Boutte, & Van Scoy, 1995/96). Boxes 5.4 and 5.5 contain collaboration tips for involving parents in the home-school context.

COLLABORATION TIPS   BOX 5.5

Prekindergarten Newsletter

Dear Parents,

We just finished up a week of bunny fun. It's hard to believe we only have about 6 weeks left of school. Here's a schedule of the themes coming up:

April 21–24—Ponds

April 28–May 2—Dinosaurs
May 5–9—Zoo

May 12–16—Circus

May 19–23—Ocean

May 27–June 2—Summer Fun

If you have anything at home related to these themes that you'd like to donate to the class, we'd appreciate it (arts and crafts, etc.). Feel free to continue to contact me at any time with any questions/comments you have about your child's education.

Thank you!

Jenny Smith
Teacher

Ways to gain family involvement in planning. Welcome nights and open houses in the fall are an ideal time to invite families to give their ideas and input to curriculum planning for their children. These invitations can be reiterated during subsequent parent conferences with individual families. Eliciting ideas and suggestions from family members helps teachers determine what curricular content families endorse. Further, teachers can learn about the goals that families have for their children, so that school goals can be bridged to priorities for families. Box 5.6 lists collaboration tips to strengthen home-school communications, and Box 5.7 details a parents training lesson.

Planning Learning Activities for Families

As part of the usual weekly planning routines, teachers can devise home activities that are extensions of instructional activities children have experienced in the classroom. When children are exposed to concepts in both home and school contexts, chances to acquire these concepts are increased. Children benefit from having multiple opportunities to gain specific pieces of information to cement concepts and elaborate their understanding of concepts. Giving families ideas for involving children in the practice of newly introduced skills can reinforce these skills and help children generalize them to different settings. Home activities that are carefully matched to the concepts and skills being introduced by teachers in classrooms immerse children more intensively into the curricula across two influential contexts in their lives—home and school. Teachers acknowledge the value of these experiences for stimulating children's learning when they send carefully planned activities home for parents to try.

Teachers can also recognize the contributions families make on their own toward the education of their children. Families are interested in creating rich learning experiences for their children at home. However, some parents lack confidence in their ability to teach their own children. Teachers can alleviate their fears by making parents

COLLABORATION TIPS   **BOX 5.6**

Ideas for Home-School Communication

- Greet parents warmly at arrival and departure times to set the stage for more in-depth conversations at another time.
- Set aside time for longer conversations with parents when issues arise.
- Keep parents informed of curricular goals and how you plan to address goals and objectives in the classroom.
- Give parents opportunities to react to your instructional planning, and be open to amend plans based on objections or suggestions of families.

COLLABORATION TIPS   BOX 5.7

Parent Training Lesson Plan

We want Deborah to learn her colors. We will start off learning red, and then move on to yellow. We will use discrete trial training. Discrete trial training is when a teacher presents one concept to the child, the child responds with an answer, and then the child is reinforced with either a treat or verbal praise. This pattern is repeated for a specific number of times.

Objectives:

- Learn color red.
- Learn color yellow.

Directions:

Work with Deborah every evening. Please complete 2 sets of 10 trials per evening. After the first set of 10, please allow Deborah to take a short break to watch television—or do something that she enjoys. After the break, please complete the second set of 10 trials. Follow these simple steps:

1. Trial #1:

   1. Put out the red apple.
   2. Say, *Show me red.*
   3. Take Deborah's hand, shape it so the index finger is extended, and point to the red apple.
   4. Say, *Yes! That's red. Great job!*
   5. Give reinforcer and note the data sheet.
   6. Repeat trial 9 more times. It may take a number of times of you taking her finger and placing it on the color before she does it independently.

2. Take a break! Make sure you let Deborah spend a few minutes doing something she enjoys.

3. Trial # 2

   1. Put out the red apple.
   2. Say, *Show me red.*
   3. If she points to it, go to step 4. If not, take Deborah's hand, shape it so the index finger is extended, and point to the red apple.
   4. Say, *Yes! That's red. Great job!*
   5. Give reinforcer and note the data sheet.
   6. Repeat trial 9 more times.

4. You are finished for tonight! Thank you!

NOTE: Once Deborah is able to correctly point to red 10 times, add in another color for her to choose from, such as a yellow banana. If Deborah points to the wrong color, direct her finger to the right color and praise/reinforce her. To make sure she knows red, cover up the two fruits and move them around—so the red is not always staying in the same place.

DATA SHEET: Please mark on the data sheet after every trial—20 times per evening. Put **P** if Deborah needed you to physically prompt her. Mark **I** if Deborah was able to point to the correct color on her own—independently.

REMEMBER:

- If Deborah independently points to the color, reinforce her immediately with food and praise.
- If Deborah does not point to right answer, take Deborah's hand, shape it so the index finger is extended, and point to the correct fruit. Then, immediately provide reinforcement.

aware of the many ways they might already extend children's learning at home. Helping families become aware of the importance of simple activities, such as counting flatware for setting the dinner table or reciting nursery rhymes during daily commutes, builds parents' confidences in their ability to be the first teacher of their child. These family efforts can be recognized when teachers talk to parents during conferences or during informal conversations at daily arrival and departure times. Ask parents to write down a few of the activities they do that relate to learning simple mathematical understandings. Parents can record times they counted, pointed out sizes or shapes of things as they played with children, or engaged in household activities or care routines with their children (Anderson & Smith, 1999).

ACCOMMODATING INDIVIDUAL LEARNERS

Each child brings unique skills and abilities to the early childhood setting. Diversity of cultures, languages, personalities, and abilities creates a complex social environment that is rich with opportunity to learn. Ensuring accessibility of the learning environment and equity of opportunity for learning experiences are foundational to early childhood education that is inclusive. Consequently, the careful application of strategies and practices that help children take advantage of the benefits of inclusive settings is important. The goal of inclusive classrooms is to foster a collaborative learning community in the classroom where children cooperate and talk together to learn. Yet, all children are unique individuals who will approach learning in different ways and from various cultural perspectives. Preserving an atmosphere of collaboration where children have many opportunities to communicate ideas and share activities, while matching accommodations so each child can participate, is the task of the teacher in inclusive classrooms.

Promoting Equity and Equality of Opportunity

The increasing diversity of inclusive early childhood classrooms has led to calls for culturally sensitive pedagogy that is responsive to the culture, customs, and values of children and their families (Gay, 2000; Ladson-Billings, 1994, 1997, 2001). A major goal of the multicultural education movement has been to provide sound, culturally sensitive curricular content that is delivered using culturally responsive teaching practices. The primary objective was to improve the academic performance of minority children and those living in low-income families (Banks, 2000). Achieving this objective is also necessary to address the continuing problem of the disproportionate identification of English language learners (ELLs) for special education services. Teachers are more likely to over-or underidentify ELLs as requiring special education compared to children who speak English. Adaptations of the curriculum are often necessary to ensure that ELLs, especially those with learning or behavioral problems, access the curricular content. Providing a differentiated curriculum for these children is paramount to their success in school (Gonzalez, Brusca-Vega, & Yawkey, 1997; Hoover & Patton, 2005).

Collaboration to Accommodate Individual Children

The primary goal of inclusive education is to enhance the opportunity for all children to succeed. Achieving this goal requires collaboration of professionals and families to identify the best methods and techniques for accommodating individual children. Parents of children with disabilities and special needs, like parents of children with typical development, want to plan for the future of their children. They have hopes and dreams for their children and they seek the best support for helping their children achieve those goals. Parents and families can be involved in every step from identification of children who may be eligible for special services to the formation of the IFSP or IEP to meet the needs of individual children and their families (Lindsay & Dockrell, 2004).

Individualized Family Service Plan/Individualized Education Plan Collaboration. When a child qualifies for special services as specified in the Individuals with Disabilities Education Act (IDEA), the collaboration of professionals with those families proceeds within the parameters established by federal mandate. As discussed in Chapter 1, IDEA ensures the right of children with disabilities, aged 6 through 21 years, to receive a free and appropriate education. Part B of IDEA allows states to choose whether to provide services to qualifying children aged 3 to 5 years. Similarly, states can provide services to infants and toddlers under Part C of IDEA.

Pertinent to this discussion regarding families, IDEA also provides for the involvement of parents in the educational planning and decision-making processes. The law specifies that it is the right of families to participate and to decide on what their roles

---

INDIVIDUALIZED FAMILY SERVICES PLAN   BOX 5.8

Summary

- Name of family services coordinator
- Child's current developmental levels
- Family priorities for child
- Resources of family
- Outcomes targeted for child
- Procedures for attaining targeted outcomes
- Time line and criteria for evaluating outcomes
- Description of services
- Plan for transition to next early childhood setting

---

will be in the decision-making processes regarding their children. Parents have the right to determine which decisions they want to make and which ones will be deferred to others. Families and early childhood professionals collaborate to plan an IEP for children 3 years and older or an IFSP for families with qualifying children less than 3 years of age (Deiner, 1999; Turnbull, 2002). Boxes 5.8 and 5.9 list the major areas of an IFSP and IEP, respectively.

Some argue that collaboration with families during the execution of an IFSP or IEP process is often inhibited or fails to occur. This happens when teachers and other professionals use practices that virtually disqualify the involvement of parents from the process. For example, if teams of teachers and professionals prepare materials or draft the plan prior to the IFSP/IEP meeting without allowing parents to become familiar

---

INDIVIDUALIZED EDUCATION PROGRAM   BOX 5.9

Summary

- Current level of educational performance
- Goals and objectives
- Criteria for evaluation
- Services and supplemental aids
- Participation in general education
- Modifications
- Description of services
- Transition plan

with those items, parents cannot fully participate in the process. When professionals use educational jargon and fail to ask parents questions to gain their perspectives, observations, and opinions, the risk of parents feeling disenfranchised is high (Valle & Aponte, 2002). Communication that is genuine without patronization is critical to promote collaboration that is mutually satisfying for families and professionals.

Teachers play a critical role toward ensuring that the rights of children and families are preserved and the intent of the law is upheld. One of the major obligations of schools and teachers is to encourage participation of families in the IFSP or IEP planning processes. To ensure opportunity, schools may provide some families with transportation to scheduled decision-making process meetings. When families with children who have disabilities speak a language other than English, interpreters will be needed to ensure maximum participation and understanding during the IFSP or IEP processes (Parette & Petch-Hogan, 2000).

When interpreters are used in an IFSP or IEP process, additional qualifications beyond proficiency in both languages of home and school are needed. Training in cross-cultural interpretation and familiarity with early intervention systems are critical to ensure effective communication with parents during the processes. Cross-cultural interpretation means the interpreter has competence in not only interpreting the verbalizations of parents, but also interpreting their nonverbal communications, such as pauses, silences, facial expressions, and other body movements that may be culturally ordained. Families should also be given an opportunity for choice in selecting an interpreter for their children's IFSP or IEP. The family's right to privacy and the confidentiality of information must be ensured during the IFSP or IEP meeting. For many cultural groups, including most Asian families, having a child with a disability is considered to be a private matter that is not discussed in public with others outside the family (Hyun & Fowler, 1995).

Planning outcomes for families in the IFSP also requires sensitivity to family practices that may be influenced by culture. Care routines, sleeping and eating patterns may be different in diverse households and unfamiliar to teachers and caregivers of other cultures. Consequently, teachers should informally interview families to better understand their parenting practices and to plan for realistic and attainable outcomes that will be valued by the family (Hyun & Fowler, 1995).

Planning Transitions

Collaboration with family members and specialists is critical to help children with disabilities make a smooth transition from one placement to another. Often in early childhood, the child is transitioning from a child-care or preschool program to kindergarten or first grade. Transition planning is especially crucial when children are moving from a preschool special education program to an inclusive setting with typically developing peers (Fox, Dunlap, & Cushing, 2002). Research findings suggest that identifying differences in various aspects of the physical and social environments of school or child-care settings can provide valuable information to help multidisciplinary teams plan for smooth transitions of children to other early childhood settings. Ecobehavioral analysis techniques can help compile an accurate portrait of the physical characteristics, teacher interactions, and child interactions that typically occur in each classroom setting. Transition planning teams can use ecobehavioral data to compare one classroom to another to detect major differences. Plans can then be devised to help acquaint the children and their families with schedules, conditions, demands, and other features of the new inclusive classroom setting (Greenwood & Carta, 1987; Greenwood, Carta, Kamps, Terry, & Delquadri, 1994; Greenwood & Rieth, 1994). For culturally and linguistically diverse children, ecobehavioral analysis data has also been used to create smooth transitions. The ability to view the classroom from multiple dimensions simultaneously gives teachers and transition planning teams detailed information to help children communicate in the new setting (Arreaga-Mayer, Carta, & Tapia, 1992; Arreaga-Mayer & Perdomo-Rivera, 1996; Arreaga-Mayer, Utley, Perdomo-Rivera, & Greenwood, 2003).

DIFFERENTIATING LEARNING EXPERIENCES

Differentiated Curriculum and Instruction

Many features of early childhood classrooms create a solid platform for inclusive education. The contructivist-based curricula traditionally used in the field of Early Childhood Education are compatible with differentiated approaches needed to include all children, especially individuals with special needs. It is critical for teachers to plan the type of accommodations for each child and match the intensity of the intervention strategy to the needs of the child. To plan for differentiation of instruction, teachers must become proficient in using a variety of adaptations and strategies (Baker & Zigmond, 1990; Leister, 1993; Schumm & Vaughn, 1991). Yet, studies indicate that teachers are reluctant to change their teaching styles and they tend to make few adaptations for individual children in their inclusive classrooms. When differentiation is not planned and children are involved in undifferentiated whole-group instruction, children with learning disabilities assume passive roles in the inclusive classroom (Baker & Zigmond, 1990; McIntosh, Vaughn, Schumm, Haager, & Lee, 1993/1994).

The importance of accommodation through differentiated instructional methods cannot be understated. When instruction is differentiated, teachers only lose inconsequential amounts of instructional time, even when children with severe disabilities are present (Hollowood, Salisbury, Rainforth, & Palombaro, 1995). Regular professional development training and professional support may be necessary to ensure that teachers are successful in planning for the success of each child. Teachers must be trained beyond simple familiarity with strategies. Teachers must achieve true proficiency in implementing instructional strategies and adaptations (Fuchs, Fuchs, Hamlett, Phillips, & Karns, 1995; Salisbury et al., 1994).

Planning Community-Based and Authentic Learning Experiences

Teachers can intertwine academic curricula and functional curricula in their inclusive classroom. Functional curricula help children develop concepts and skills necessary for

LESSON PLAN   BOX 5.10

Ms. Smith's Preschool Program for Children with Disabilities
Lesson Plans for 3/28

Objectives

1. To learn about various helpers in our community and transportation through songs, books and extension activities, then create various crafts resembling items (medical bags, etc.) of community helpers and vehicles.
2. Introduce letter j.
3. Continue practicing writing names or tracing.

Morning warm-up (gross motor)/circle time

- "Good Morning" song, "Number Rock," Calendar and "Days of Week' song
- Focus activity: "Wheels on the Bus" song

Children follow teacher with hand motions and singing. Then, I talk about the various community helpers and transportation we have already talked about and introduce the mail carrier. "Do you ever help your parents check the mail box? How does the mail get there? A person called a mailman or mailwoman delivers the mail to your box. Can you tell me what this is? (I hold up a stamp). You need this to send a letter. We pay for stamps. Have you ever received a letter or package in the mail? It's exciting, isn't it?

I then read the "Jolly Postman" book. I have to summarize parts because it is too long. I really like this book because we can take letters out of envelopes and read them. It's very hands-on, and the kids have fun.

Extension/fine motor activities

1. Mailboxes: Children paint pretend mailboxes (cardboard boxes) blue. Once dry, we help them attach a flag, and then they can make pretend letters to go in it.
2. Stamps and envelopes: Children use a variety of used stamps to decorate their envelopes. They must also either write or trace their names in the upper left side.
3. Mail bags: Children lace together two pieces of construction paper to create their very own mail bags, then decorate.
4. Letter J practice. Children practice writing the letter j with teacher's help. I first have them come up with words and items that start with j. Then we draw it in the sky with our fingers. Some children will be able to trace and then write the letter on their own, while others may just have to trace.

Centers

One of my centers is a play dough activity to practice the letter j. I have a laminated piece of construction paper with the capital and lower case j on it. Children cover up the letters with play dough.

The dramatic play center includes dress-up (police, fire, doctor, mail carrier), and chairs arranged to resemble a car with a cardboard steering wheel.

LESSON EVALUATION   BOX 5.11

I think my lesson had all the common features, but arranged differently. My circle time is relatively short to keep the children's short attention spans. I extend on the circle time lesson as the children complete their extension activities.

During the lesson, I showed the children various items related to our Community Helper theme. They also really enjoyed the songs. I had no trouble obtaining the children's attention and focus with the "Wheels on the Bus" song and hand motions.

During an extension activity to make mailboxes, I asked the children about checking their own mailboxes. Each child said his or her parents allowed him or her to get the mail. We also had several children who just celebrated birthdays. So, I asked if they received any cards or packages in the mail-creating connections.

Being a preschool program for children with disabilities class, we follow the same schedule on a daily basis. My lessons always follow the same patterns, so the children know exactly where to focus their attention and what is going to happen next.

I think my lesson focused on the application, analysis and synthesis areas, along with plain knowledge and comprehension of Bloom's taxonomy. Students gained knowledge and comprehension of concepts during circle time, and then explored the theme more during the extension activities.

The main form of assessment that I used was observation. I also worked on individual IEP goals during my lessons, and documented progress.

Next time, I might include a role-playing activity where the children can pretend to be mail carriers and deliver mail, as well as learn how to create and send mail.

---

living productively. Community-based instruction has proven successful at all levels, including the early childhood age range (Field, LeRoy, & Rivera, 1994; Helmke, Havekost, Patton, & Polloway, 1994; Notari-Syverson & Shuster, 1995). Providing learning experiences in authentic contexts helps children apply their academic skills and generalize their concepts to real-life situations (Beck, Broers, Hogue, Shipstead, & Knowlton, 1994; Notari-Syverson & Shuster, 1995). Community-based or community-referenced instruction adds authenticity to the early childhood curriculum by adding functional life-skill activities. Box 5.10 displays a lesson plan for community-referenced instruction, and Box 5.11 details the lesson's evaluation. Planning field trips or activities in community settings on-site helps children apply their functional knowledge and skills (Beck et al., 1994; Udvari-Solner & Thousand, 1995).

Language and Literacy in the Differentiated Curriculum

While it is beyond the scope of this book to detail each curricular area, the importance of language and literacy skills for children in inclusive classrooms bears some discussion. Hence, the following sections summarize how teachers can address language and literacy in the differentiated curriculum of an inclusive early childhood classroom.

In early childhood, language and literacy development occur rapidly. By age 3, typical children have acquired all the fundamental language skills needed for communication. Around the age of 6, most children have begun to unlock the codes for reading and writing. Accordingly, language acquisition and literacy development constitute major areas of emphasis in the differentiated curriculum. In inclusive classrooms, language is viewed as a broad construct. As such, strategies for enhancing language development include those aimed at promoting both receptive and expressive language abilities of children. Recognition is given to the various ways children might communicate. Consequently, sign language and use of different alternatives or supplements with oral language are facilitated. Facilitating a child's ability to understand or gain meaning from the communication of others is a major goal. Likewise, fostering a child's expression of thoughts and ideas through a mode of communication that is appropriate for each child is also a critical aim of this category of strategies.

Important for inclusive education. The extant research base clearly indicates that acquisition of language and literacy skills are vital to later reading, writing, and overall academic success. Literacy begins at birth as infants experiment with oral language capabilities (Clay, 1977; Hiebert, 1981). Receptive and expressive language continue to develop throughout childhood as a major component of a child's literacy development. The term "emergent literacy" is used to denote the continuum of literacy development for children beginning at birth and continuing through adulthood (Teale & Sulzby, 1987). Rather than viewing components of language and literacy development as isolated steps or skills, the notion of emergent literacy represents cognizance of the interrelatedness of skills and abilities and the multidimensional characteristics of language and literacy development (Ricard & Snow, 1990; Roth, Speece, & Cooper, 2002). To bring national attention to young children's critical need for rich literacy environments and to articulate the key strategies recommended as best practices, two professional organizations issued a joint position statement.

The International Reading Association (IRA) and the National Association for the Education of Young Children (NAEYC) collaboratively took a stance in recognition of the early years, birth through age eight, as the most critical time in a child's life for literacy development (1998). The position paper has served as a guide for early childhood teachers in selecting reading and writing practices to use in a variety of settings including public schools, child-care centers, preschools, and family child-care homes. The intent of these organizations was also to inform community and family members including parents, grandparents, and older siblings who may interact with young children in literacy activities. Consequently, the position statement identified developmentally appropriate practices that teachers can use to stimulate language and literacy development of children in preschool through the primary grades. The professional collaboration that resulted in the position paper merged research-based knowledge from the fields of reading and early childhood education. Further, the collaboration of these organizations and fields signified an important step toward a unified stance for early language and emergent literacy teaching standards.

Another advancement for inclusive classrooms is the fact that the position statement addressed the literacy development of children from diverse backgrounds and those at risk of school failure. IRA and NAEYC advised teachers to set challenging but achievable goals for all children, and recommended adapting activities or instruction to help ensure each child's success (International Reading Association & National Association for the Education of Young Children, 1998).

In the following section, important principles and practices for promoting language and literacy development in inclusive early childhood settings are presented with the research basis that justifies the use of these practices.

The cognitive and language relationship. Although the exact nature of the relationship is still not fully understood, the existence of a kinship between cognition and language is recognized by theorists. According to Vygotsky, language is a powerful mental tool that contributes to our thinking processes and propels our learning (Vygotsky, 1978). Language allows children to share their activities, problem solve together, and create new ideas (Bodrova & Leong, 1996). Further, Vygotskian theory holds that adults who are actively involved in children's learning provide scaffolding, that is, use various strategies, cues, and physical assists to help children perform at a higher level than they could do independently. The underlying social constructivist theory articulated by Vygotsky (1978), Rogoff (1990), and others has provided the foundation for the sociocognitive model of literacy development. The sociocognitive model assumes that reading comprehension depends upon the skills and abilities gained during the development of receptive and expressive skills associated with oral language. Some of the oral language skills children acquire are contextualized, meaning these abilities are highly dependent upon the context of settings for background information. Other oral language skills are decontextualized, meaning that children must use linguistic cues, such as syntax, to construct the meaning of language. Undergirded by the sociocognitive model, a key principle of inclusive education is to emphasize language and communication development and actively assist all children in using their acquired language skills as a bridge to literacy (Dickinson & Smith, 1994).

Oral language connections to literacy. The sociocognitive model explains story understanding and, then reading comprehension as the result of a child's ability to draw upon oral language skills to derive meaning from discourse (Dickinson & Snow, 1987; Dickinson & Tabors, 1991). Consequently, oral language skills have been found to be closely related to literacy development (Dickinson & Smith, 1994; Dickinson &

Teachers and family members are language models who help children develop literacy through practical uses of reading and writing.

Snow, 1987; Dickinson & Tabors, 1991). There is research evidence that suggests that different component skills that develop as oral language is acquired appear to have a relationship to specific reading skills and abilities. For example, abundant research indicates that phonological awareness contributes to a child's ability to learn to read (Speece, Roth, Cooper, & de la Paz, 1999; Vellutino & Scanlon, 2001). Yet, more research is needed to clarify the exact nature of the relationship between oral language and how language skills influence the process and acquisition of learning to read (Dickinson, McCabe, & Sprague, 2003; Roth et al., 2002).

Key language and literacy practices. To enhance language and literacy learning of all children, teachers in inclusive classrooms promote the development and use of oral language and literacy skills. Offering abundant and varied opportunities for children to develop language and emergent literacy skills is critical to their development as a learner. Studies of effective teaching practices to promote language acquisition and literacy skills reveal that exemplary kindergarten and primary grade teachers actively involve children in a full spectrum of language and literacy-oriented experiences and tasks. Further, they immerse children in intensive activities so children can gain the most exposure to skill development opportunities. Children in classrooms of effective teachers are highly productive and have many opportunities to learn through different modes (Pressley, Rankin, & Yokoi, 1996; Wharton-McDonald, Pressley, & Mis'retta, 1996).

Model language and literacy use. Family members and teachers are important models to help children value reading and writing in their lives. Children who are learning English as a second language (ESL) or those who are becoming bilingual (acquiring two languages simultaneously) benefit from accurate models in both languages. There are many misconceptions about children's language learning. Dispelling commonly held myths, research suggests that young children do not acquire language more easily and quickly than adults (Hakuta, 1986). Consequently, children acquiring a second language should not be overlooked. Teachers should ensure a rich language environment for children, with models in both the child's languages as the ideal situation. It is important to recognize the difficulties children face in acquiring a second language and to avoid pressuring children to acquire the second language quickly. Valuing the home culture and accepting a child's communication attempts provides a supportive school environment (Soto, 1991).

Provide a context for language and literacy activities. Evidence suggests that most children in inclusive early childhood classrooms acquire language and literacy skills best when opportunities for learning are presented within contexts that are meaningful and relevant to each child. Once popular in bilingual education and special education, rigid, compensatory approaches to language development have fallen out of favor. These deficit-focused approaches treated language acquisition from a remedial perspective. Vocabulary and grammatical development was introduced didactically, with emphasis on repetition of grammatical patterns and vocabulary words in isolation (Soto, 1991). Research has continued to substantiate the benefits of promoting language and communication opportunities more naturally within typically occurring classroom activities and experiences.

For children with special communication and language needs, inclusive classrooms offer rich contexts for language that bring meaning to words and real communicative intent to verbalizations. These advantages are thought to increase a child's motivation for communicating and opportunities to participate in communication events (Fey, 1986). However, children with expressive language problems may need strategies aimed at increasing their ability to initiate and maintain social interactions with their peers. Furthermore, being aware of the interplay among factors that influence communication, specifically language, culture, and disability, is critical to selecting teaching strategies. When the child's first language is not the predominant language of other children in the classroom, support for communication among children can increase the success of social interactions and verbal interchanges.

Provide a literacy-rich environment. Calls for print-rich and literacy-rich classroom environments have been widespread. Recent research indicates that the community-at-large should be alerted to the influence of neighborhood surroundings on the literacy of young children. The use of print and contexts for literacy that are available in a child's neighborhood can facilitate or limit opportunities to value literacy and benefit from early exposure to print (Newman & Celano, 2001).

Involve families in literacy activities. The best way to help children is to ensure a strong connection between home modeling and school use of language and literacy. It would be difficult to separate the contributions to a child's early language and

Collaborative Planning: One Teacher's Perspective on IEP Planning Team

As part of the team, it was my role to monitor and implement the goals and objectives, as well as collaborate with the parents and other staff to create new ones. One of the most important things I do is work with the parents when implementing and creating objectives. Sometimes they may have better ways to do the task or may need help with something. Before a meeting, I make sure to fill out as much of the paperwork as possible beforehand. I also make sure to visit with the other team members and parents to work on the goals. When I go into the meeting, I like to have everything ready to go. During the meeting, I may chair it or just give my input. I also make sure to have a progress report ready and am prepared to discuss the child's current competencies with the committee.

literacy development made by home and school contexts. The two contexts work in tandem to influence the opportunities children have for acquiring language and literacy skills and abilities. See Box 5.12 for collaboration tips for IEP planning. The ideal would be to have rich contributions to language and literacy development from literate models in both home and school contexts (Dickenson & Tabors, 1991; Dickinson & Tabors, 2001).

SUMMARY

This chapter discussed how professionals across disciplines and fields have evaluated theory and accepted practice. The result has been a convergence of theory and blending of evidence-based practice to form the theoretical and pedagogical foundations for inclusive early childhood education. Involving parents and families in planning is critical to a child's success in an inclusive early childhood program. The processes of developing an IFSP or IEP for young children was summarized. Teachers can build relationships with other teachers and professionals that will also contribute to the quality of the curriculum used and the strategies implemented in their classroom. Various systems to aid teachers in planning were introduced in designing differentiated curriculum and instruction. A section on language and literacy in the differentiated curriculum was included to illustrate integration of these key domains across the curriculum.

Discussion Questions

1. Why is it important to know how to collaborate with other professionals and specialists to plan the curriculum in an inclusive early childhood classroom?
2. What are some of the barriers you may have to overcome to plan a differentiated curriculum?
3. Why should you become knowledgeable about professional standards and guidelines? How can these documents be used in planning for inclusion?
4. Explain how to communicate with families about curriculum and instructional practices. How can you involve parents in your curricular planning?
5. How can authentic learning experiences in community-based settings enrich the curriculum for children in inclusive classrooms?
6. Can you articulate procedures for activities to parents or assistants?

Inclusive Activities

1. Find sample lesson plans on Websites or activities you have prepared for demonstration teaching. Use the SMART planning system guidelines to evaluate these lessons. What changes would you make to improve the activities and bring them into accordance with the SMART guidelines?

2. Compose a newsletter for families to go with a unit of study or set of lesson plans you have designed in your practice teaching classroom or an inclusive classroom you have observed.

3. Show one of your unit plans or lessons to parents and ask for their opinions. In particular, ask whether the activities are acceptable to the family in light of their culture, customs, and beliefs.

4. Ask parents of a child with disabilities to evaluate a lesson plan. Ask whether the activities in the plan are a good match for the strengths and learning goals of their child.

5. Form a planning team with 4-5 students. Assume different roles: general education teacher, special education teacher, parent, and speech therapist. Role-play and plan a lesson for young children from these perspectives.

6. Observe an inclusive classroom serving children with a wide range of abilities. Plan a lesson and ask a few of your classmates to evaluate the lesson. If possible, ask the teacher in the classroom where you observed to evaluate your lesson plan.

References

Acrey, C., Johnstone, C., & Milligan, C. (2005). Using universal design to unlock the potential for academic achievement of at-risk learners. *Teaching Exceptional Children, 38*(2), 22–31.

Anderson, A. L. H., & Smith, A. B. (1999). Community building with parents. *Kappa Delta Pi Record, 35*(4), 158–161.

Arreaga-Mayer, C., Carta, J., & Tapia, Y. (1992). *Ecobehavioral system for the contextual recording of interactional bilingual environments: Training manual.* Kansas City: University of Kansas, Juniper Gardens Children's Project.

Arreaga-Mayer, C., & Perdomo-Rivera, C. (1996). Ecobehavioral analysis of instruction for at-risk minority students. *The Elementary School Journal, 96*(3), 245–258.

Arreaga-Mayer, C., Utley, C. A., Perdomo-Rivera, C., & Greenwood, C. R. (2003). Ecobehavioral assessment of instructional contexts in bilingual special education programs for English language learners at risk for developmental disabilities. *Focus on Autism and Other Developmental Disabilities, 18*(1), 28–40.

Baker, J., & Zigmond, N. (1990). Are regular education classes equipped to accommodate students with learning disabilities? *Exceptional Children, 56*(6), 515–526.

Banks, C. A. M. (1993). Parents and teachers: Partners in school reform. In J. A. Banks, & C. A. M. Banks (Eds.), *Multicultural education: Issues and perspectives* (3rd ed.). Boston: Allyn & Bacon.

Banks, J. A. (2000). Series foreword. In G. Gay (Ed.), *Culturally responsive teaching: Theory, research, and practice*. New York: Teacher's College Press.

Barrett, T. C. (1972). Taxonomy of reading comprehension. In *Reading 360 Monograph*. Lexington, MA: Ginn.

Beck, J., Broers, J., Hogue, E., Shipstead, J., & Knowlton, E. (1994). Strategies for functional community-based instruction and inclusion for children with mental retardation. *Teaching Exceptional Children, 26*(2), 44–48.

Bloom, B. C. (1956). *Taxonomy of educational objectives: Cognitive domain*. New York: David McKay.

Bodrova, E., & Leong, D. (1996). *Tools of the mind: The Vygotskian approach to early childhood education*. Upper Saddle River, NJ: Merrill/Prentice Hall.

Bredekamp, S. (Ed.). (1987). *Developmentally appropriate practice in early childhood programs serving children from birth through age 8*. Washington, DC: National Association for the Education of Young Children.

Bredekamp, S., & Copple, C. (Eds.). (1997). *Developmentally appropriate practice in early childhood programs* (Rev. ed.). Washington, DC: National Association for the Education of Young Children.

Bricker, D. (1995). The challenge of inclusion. *Journal of Early Intervention, 19*(3), 179–194.

Broderick, A., Mehta-Parekh, H., & Reid, D. K. (2005). Differentiating instruction for disabled students in inclusive classrooms. *Theory Into Practice, 44*(3), 194–202.

Carta, J., Atwater, J., Schwartz, I., & McConnell, S. (1993). Developmentally appropriate practices and early childhood special education: A reaction to Johnson and McChesney Johnson. *Topics in Early Childhood Special Education, 13*(3), 243–354.

Carta, J., Schwartz, I., Atwater, J., & McConnell, S. (1991). Developmentally appropriate practice: Appraising its usefulness for young children with disabilities. *Topics in Early Childhood Special Education, 11*(1), 1–20.

Carta, J. J. (1994). Developmentally appropriate practices: Shifting the emphasis to individual appropriateness. *Journal of Early Intervention, 18*(4), 342–343.

Clay, M. H. (1977). *Reading: The patterning of complex behavior*. Exeter: NH: Heinemann.

Cole, K., Dale, P., Mills, P., & Jenkins, J. (1993). Interaction between early intervention curricula and student characteristics. *Exceptional Children, 60*(1), 17–28.

Cole, K., Mills, P., Dale, P., & Jenkins, J. (1991). Effects of preschool integration for children with disabilities. *Exceptional Children, 58*(1), 36–45.

Council for Exceptional Children. (1999). *Universal design; Research connections: Ensuring access to the General Education Curriculum*. Retrieved January 21, 2006, from http://ericec.org/osep/recon5/rc5sec1.html.

Deiner, P. (1999). *Resources for educating children with diverse abilities* (3rd ed.). Fort Worth, TX: Harcourt Brace.

Dickinson, D., & Tabors, P. O. (Eds.). (2001). *Beginning literacy with language: Young children at home and school*. Baltimore: Brookes.

Dickinson, D. K., McCabe, A., & Sprague, K. (2003). Teacher rating of oral language and literacy (TROLL): Individualizing early literacy instruction with a standards-based rating tool. *The Reading Teacher, 56*(6), 554–564.

Dickinson, D. K., & Smith, M. W. (1994). Long-term effects of preschool teachers' book readings on low-income children's vocabulary and story comprehension. *Reading Research Quarterly, 29*(2), 105–120.

Dickinson, D. K., & Snow, C. E. (1987). Interrelationships among prereading and oral language skills in kindergartners from two social classes. *Early Childhood Research Quarterly, 2*, 1–26.

Dickinson, D. K., & Tabors, P. O. (1991). Early literacy: Linkage between home, school, and literacy achievement at age five. *Journal of Research in Childhood Education, 6*(1), 30–46.

Division for Early Childhood Council for Exceptional Children. (1993a). *DEC Position on inclusion.* Pittsburgh, PA: Author.

Division for Early Childhood Council for Exceptional Children. (1993b). *DEC position on early intervention services for children birth to age eight.* Pittsburgh, PA: Author.

Division for Early Childhood Council for Exceptional Children. (1993c). *DEC recommended practices: Indicators of quality in programs for infants and young children with special needs and their families.* Reston, VA: Author.

Division for Early Childhood Council for Exceptional Children, National Association for the Education of Young Children, & Association of Teacher Educators. (1995). *Personnel standards for early education and early intervention: Guidelines for licensure in early childhood special education.* Pittsburgh, PA: Division for Early Childhood Council for Exceptional Children.

Eanes, R. (1997). *Content area literacy: Teaching for today and tomorrow.* Albany, NY: Delmar Publishers.

Edwards, P. A., Fear, K. L., & Gallegos, M. A. (1995). Role of parents in responding to issues of linguistic and cultural diversity. In E. E. Garcia & B. McLaughlin (Eds.), *Meeting the challenge of linguistic and cultural diversity in early childhood education* (Vol. 6, pp. 141–153). New York: Teachers College Press.

Fey, M. E. (1986). *Language intervention with young children.* Boston: Allyn & Bacon.

Field, S., LeRoy, B., & Rivera, S. (1994). Meeting functional curriculum needs in middle school general education classrooms. *Teaching Exceptional Children, 26*(2), 40–43.

Fox, L., Dunlap, G., & Cushing, L. (2002). Early intervention, positive behavior support, and transition to school. *Journal of Emotional and Behavioral Disorders, 10,* 149–157.

Friend, M., & Pope, K. L. (2005). Creating schools in which all students can succeed. *Kappa Delta Pi Record, 41*(2), 56–61.

Fuchs, L., Fuchs, D., Hamlett, C., Phillips, N., & Karns, K. (1995). General educator's specialized adaptation for students with learning disabilities. *Exceptional Children, 61*(5), 440–459.

Gallagher, J. (2004). The importance of constructivism and constructivist pedagogy for disability students in education. *Disability Studies Quarterly, 24*(2), 1–15.

Gardner, H. (1983). *Frames of mind: The theory of multiple intelligences.* New York: Basic Books.

Gardner, H. (1995). Reflections on multiple intelligences: Myth and messages. *Phi Delta Kappan, 77,* 200–209.

Gay, G. (2000). *Culturally responsive teaching: Theory, research, and practice.* New York: Teacher's College Press.

George, P. (2005). A rationale for differentiating instruction in the regular classroom. *Theory Into Practice, 44*(3), 185–193.

Ginsberg, M. B. (2005). Cultural diversity, motivation, and differentiation. *Theory Into Practice, 44*(3), 218–225.

Gonzalez, V., Brusca-Vega, R., & Yawkey, T. (1997). *Assessment and instruction of culturally and linguistically diverse students with or at-risk of learning problems: From research to practice.* Boston: Allyn & Bacon.

Greenwood, C., & Carta, J. (1987). An ecobehavioral interaction analysis of instruction within special education. *Focus on Exceptional Children, 19,* 1–12.

Greenwood, C., Carta, J., Kamps, D., Terry, B., & Delquadri, J. (1994). Development and validation of standard classroom observation systems for school practitioners: Ecobehavioral assessment systems software (EBASS). *Exceptional Children, 61*(2), 197–210.

Greenwood, C., & Rieth, H. (1994). Current dimensions of technology-based assessment in special education. *Exceptional Children, 61*(2), 105–113.

Grubb, B. (1993). The Americans with Disabilities Act and learning disabilities. *LDA Newsbriefs, 28*(4), 3–4.

Hakuta, K. (1986). *Mirror of language: The debate of bilingualism.* New York: Basic.

Harbin, G., Rous, B., & Mclean, M. (2005). Issues in designing state accountability systems. *Journal of Early Intervention, 27*(3), 137–164.

Helmke, L., Havekost, D., Patton, J., & Polloway, E. (1994). Life skills programming: Development of a high school science course. *Teaching exceptional Children, 26*(2), 49–53.

Herrell, A., & Jordan, M. (2004). *Fifty strategies for teaching English language learners* (2nd ed.). Upper Saddle River, NJ: Merrill/Prentice Hall.

Hiebert, E. H. (1981). Developmental patterns and interrelationship of pre-school children's print awareness. *Reading Research Quarterly, 16,* 236–260.

Hitchcock, C., Meyer, A., Rose, D., & Jackson, R. (2002). Providing new access to the general curriculum:

Universal design for learning. *Teaching Exceptional Children, 35*(2), 8–17.

Hollowood, T., Salisbury, C., Rainforth, B., & Palombaro, M. (1995). Use of instructional time in classrooms serving students with and without severe disabilities. *Exceptional Children, 61*(3), 242–252.

Hoover, J. J., & Patton, J. R. (2005). Differentiating curriculum and instruction for English-language learners with special needs. *Intervention in School & Clinic, 40*(4), 231–235.

Hyun, J. K., & Fowler, S. A. (1995). Respect, cultural sensitivity, and communication. *Teaching Exceptional Children,* 25–28.

International Reading Association, & National Association for the Education of Young Children. (1998). Learning to read and write: Developmentally appropriate practices for young children. *Young Children, 53*(4), 30–46.

Johnson, J. E., & Johnson, K. M. (1992). Clarifying the developmental perspective in response to Carta, Schwartz, Atwater, and McConnell. *Topics in Early Childhood Special Education, 12*(4), 439–457.

Johnson, K. M., & Johnson, J. E. (1993). Rejoinder to Carta, Atwater, Schwartz, and Mcconnell. *Topics in Early Childhood Special Education, 13*(3), 255–257.

Joint Committee on Teacher Planning for Students with Disabilities. (1995). *Planning for academic diversity in America's classrooms: Windows on reality, research, change, and practice.* Lawrence, KS: The University of Kansas Center for Research on Learning.

Karp, K. S., & Voltz, D. L. (2000). Weaving mathematical instructional strategies into inclusive settings. *Intervention in School and Clinic, 35*(4), 206–215.

Kennedy, D. M. (1995). Plain talk about creating a gifted-friendly classroom. *Roeper Review, 17*(4), 232–234.

Ladson-Billings, G. (1994). *The dreamkeepers: Successful teachers of African-American children.* San Francisco: Jossey-Bass.

Ladson-Billings, G. (1997). What we can learn from multicultural education research. In *Education 1997/1998* (pp. 181–184). Guilford, CT: Dushkin/McGraw-Hill.

Ladson-Billings, G. (2001). *Crossing over to Canaan: The new teachers in diverse classrooms.* San Francisco: Jossey-Bass.

Leister, C. (1993). Innovative teaching in the 1990's: Technology competencies needed by teachers of pre-school age children with severe disabilities. *Reading Improvement, 30,* 134–139.

Lindsay, G., & Dockrell, J. E. (2004). Whose job is it? Parents' concerns about the needs of their children with language problems. *The Journal of Special Education, 37*(4), 225–235.

Mace, R. (1998). *A perspective on universal design: Edited excerpt.* Retrieved January 21, 2006, from http://www.adaptenv.org/index.php?option=Resource&articleid=156&topicid=28

Maker, C., Nielson, A., & Rogers, J. (1994). Giftedness, diversity, and problem-solving. *Teaching Exceptional Children, 27*(1), 4–18.

McIntosh, R., Vaughn, S., Schumm, J., Haager, D., & Lee, O. (1993/1994). Observations of students with learning disabilities in general education classrooms. *Exceptional Children, 60*(3), 249–261.

McLean, M. E., & Odom, S. L. (1993). Practices for young children with and without disabilities: A comparison of DEC and NAEYC identified practices. *Topics in Early Childhood Education, 13*(3), 274–292.

National Association for the Education of Young Children. (1995). *Guidelines for preparation of early childhood professionals.* Washington, DC: Author.

National Association for the Education of Young Children. (1996). *Guidelines for preparation of early childhood professionals.* Washington, DC: Author.

National Association of State Boards of Education Study Group on Special Education. (1992). *Winners all: Call for inclusive schools.* Alexandria, VA: National Association of State Boards of Education.

National Coalition of Advocates for Students. (1991). *The good common school: Making the vision work for all children.* Boston, MA: Author.

Newman, S., & Celano, D. (2001). Access to print in low-income and middle-income communities: An ecological study of four neighborhoods. *Reading Research Quarterly, 36,* 8–26.

Notari-Syverson, A., & Shuster, S. (1995). Putting real-life skills into IEP/IFSPs for infants and young children. *Teaching Exceptional Children, 27*(2), 29–32.

Odom, S. L., & Wolery, M. (2003). A unified theory of practice in early intervention/early childhood special education: Evidence-based practices. *The Journal of Special Education, 37*(3), 164–173.

Parette, H. P., & Petch-Hogan, B. (2000). Approaching families. *Teaching Exceptional Children, 33*(2), 4–10.

Pressley, M. C., Rankin, J., & Yokoi, Y. (1996). A survey of instructional practices of primary teachers nominated as effective in promoting literacy. *Elementary School Journal, 96*(4), 363–384.

Reis, S. M., & Purcell, J. H. (1993). An analysis of content elimination and strategies used by elementary classroom teachers and the curriculum compacting process. *Journal for the Education of the Gifted, 16*, 147–170.

Reis, S. M., & Renzulli, J. S. (1992). Using curriculum compacting to challenge the above-average. *Educational Leadership, 50*, 51–57.

Reis, S. M., Westberg, K. L., Kulikowich, J. M., & Purcell, J. H. (1998). Curriculum compacting and achievement test scores: What does the research say? Gifted Child Quarterly, *42*(2), 123–129.

Renzulli, J. S. (1977). *The enrichment triad model: A guide for developing defensible programs for gifted and talented.* Mansfield Center, CT: Creative Learning Press.

Renzulli, J. S. (Ed.). (1986). *Systems and models for developing programs for the gifted and talented.* Mansfield Center: Creative Learning.

Renzulli, J. S., & Reis, S. M. (1986). The enrichment triad/revolving door model: A schoolwide plan for the development of creative productivity. In J. S. Renzulli (Ed.), *Systems and models for developing programs for the gifted and talented* (pp. 216–266). Mansfield Center, CT: Creative Learning.

Ricard, R., & Snow, C. (1990). Language skills in and out of context: Evidence of children's picture descriptions. *Journal of Developmental Psychology, 4*, 251–266.

Roach, V. (1995). Supporting inclusion: Beyond the rhetoric. *Phi Delta Kappan, 77*(4), 295–299.

Rogoff, B. (1990). *Apprenticeship in thinking: Cognitive development in social context.* New York: Oxford University Press.

Roth, F. P., Speece, D. L., & Cooper, D. H. (2002). A longitudinal analysis of the connection between oral language and early reading. *The Journal of Educational Research, 95*(5), 259–272.

Safford, P. L. (1989). *Integrated teaching in early childhood: starting in the mainstream.* White Plains, NY: Longman.

Salisbury, C. (1991). Mainstreaming during the early childhood years. *Exceptional Children, 58*(2), 146–155.

Salisbury, C., Mangino, M., Petrigala, M., Rainforth, B., Syryca, S., & Palombaro, M. (1994). Innovative

practices: Promoting the instructional inclusion of young children with disabilities in the primary grades. *Journal of Early Intervention, 18*(3), 311–322.

Sandall, S., McLean, M. E., & Smith, B. J. (2000). *DEC recommended practices in early intervention/early childhood special education.* Longmont, CO & Denver, CO: Sopris West and the Division for Early Childhood, Council for Exceptional Children.

Schloss, P. J. (1992). Mainstreaming revisited. *Elementary School Journal, 92*(3), 233–244.

Schumm, J., & Vaughn, S. (1991). Making adaptations for mainstreamed students: General classroom teachers' perspectives. *Remedial and Special Education, 12*(4), 15–24.

Schumm, J. S., Vaughn, S., & Harris, J. (1997). Pyramid power for collaborative planning. *Teaching Exceptional Children, 29*(6), 62–66.

Scruggs, T., & Mastropieri, M. (1993). Current approaches to science education: Implications for mainstream instruction of students with disabilities. *Remedial and Special Education, 14*(1), 15–24.

Sexton, D., Snyder, P., Sharpton, W. R., & Stricklin, S. (1993). Infants and toddlers with special needs and their families. *Childhood Education, 69*(5), 278–286.

Soto, L. D. (1991). Understanding bilingual/bicultural young children. *Young Children, 42*(2), 30–36.

Speece, D. L., Roth, F. P., Cooper, D. H., & de la Paz, S. (1999). The relevance of oral language skills to early literacy: A multivariate analysis. *Applied Psycholinguistics, 20*(2), 167–190.

Surr, J. (1992). Early childhood programs and the Americans with Disabilities Act (ADA). *Young Children, 47*(5), 18–21.

Swick, K., Boutte, G., & Van Scoy, I. (1995/96). Families and schools: Building multicultural values together. *Childhood Education, 75*–79.

Teachers of English to Speakers of Other Languages. (1995a). TESOL standards ensuring access to quality educational experiences for language minority students. *Bilingual Research Journal, 19*(3 & 4), 671–674.

Teachers of English to Speakers of Other Languages. (1995b). TESOL statement on the role of bilingual education in the education of children in the United States. *Bilingual Research Journal, 19*(3 &4), 661–669.

Teale, W., & Sulzby, E. (1987). Literacy acquisition in early childhood. In D. Wagner (Ed.), *The future of literacy in a changing world* (Vol. 1, pp. 120–129). New York: Pergamon.

Tharp, R. (1998). *From at-risk to excellence: Research, theory, and principles for practice (Research Report 1).* Santa Cruz, CA: Center for Research on Education, Diversity, and Excellence.

Thomas, G., & Loxley, A. (2001). *Deconstructing special education and constructing inclusion.* Philadelphia: Open University Press.

Tomlinson, C. A. (2001). Differentiated instruction in the regular classroom: What does it mean? How does it look? *Understanding Our Gifted, 14*(1), 3–6.

Tomlinson, C. A. (2004). Sharing responsibility for differentiating instruction. *Roeper Review, 26*(4), 188–189.

Tomlinson, C. A. (2005). Grading and differentiation: Paradox or good practice? *Theory Into Practice, 44*(3), 262–269.

Tomlinson, C. A., & Allan, S. D. (2000). *Leadership for differentiating schools and classrooms.* Alexandria, VA: Association for Supervision and Curriculum Development.

Tomlinson, C. A., & Edison, C. C. (2003). *Differentiation in practice: A resource guide for differentiating curriculum, Grades 5–9.* Alexandria, VA: Association for Supervision & Curriculum Development.

Turnbull, R. (2002). *Exceptional lives: Special education in today's schools* (3rd ed.). Upper Saddle River, NJ: Merrill/Prentice Hall.

Udvari-Solner, A., & Thousand, J. (1995). Promising practices that foster inclusive education. In R. A. Villa & J. S. Thousand (Eds.), *Creating an inclusive school* (pp. 87–109). Alexandria, VA: Association for Supervision and Curriculum Development.

Underwood, J. K., & Mead, J. F. (1995). *Legal aspects of special education and pupil services.* Boston: Allyn & Bacon.

Valle, J. W., & Aponte, E. (2002). IDEA and collaboration: A Bakhtinian perspective on parent and professional discourse. *Journal of Learning Disabilities, 35*(5), 469–479.

VanTassel-Baska, J., & Stambaugh, T. (2005). Challenges and possibilities for serving gifted learners in the regular classroom. *Theory Into Practice, 44*(3), 211–217.

Vellutino, F. R., & Scanlon, D. M. (2001). Emergent literacy skills, early instruction, and individual differences as determinants of difficulties in learning to read: The case for early intervention. In S. Neuman & D. Dickinson (Eds.), *Handbook of early literacy research* (pp. 295–321). New York: Guilford Press.

Vygotsky, L. (1978). *Mind in society: The development of higher psychological functions.* Cambridge, MA: Harvard University Press.

Wharton-McDonald, R., Pressley, M., & Mis'retta, J. (1996). *Outstanding literary instruction in first grade: Teaching practices and student achievement.* Albany, NY: National Reading Research Center.

Winter, S. M. (1997). "SMART" planning for inclusion. *Childhood Education, 73*(4), 212–218.

Winter, S. M. (1999). *The early childhood inclusion model: A program for all children.* Olney, MD: Association for Childhood Education International.

Wolery, M., Huffman, K., Holcombe, A., Martin, C. G., Schroeder, C., & Venn, M. L. (1994). Preschool mainstreaming: Perceptions of barriers and benefits by faculty in general early childhood education. *Teacher Education and Special Education, 17*(1), 1–9.

Wolery, M., Strain, P. S., & Bailey, Jr., D. B. (1992). Reaching potentials of children with special needs. In S. Bredekamp & T. Rosegrant (Eds.), *Reaching potentials: Appropriate curriculum and assessment for young children* (Vol. 1, pp. 92–111). Washington, DC: National Association for the Education of Young Children.

Chapter 6

Creating a Positive Social and Emotional Climate

Key Principle

- Emphasize prevention and early intervention

Objectives

After reading this chapter, you will be able to:

1. Describe a positive, personalized learning environment for children.
2. Discuss ways to promote social and emotional development of children.
3. Explain how cultural competence is developed.
4. Understand how to prevent problem behavior in children.
5. Describe how to identify children with potential behavior problems.

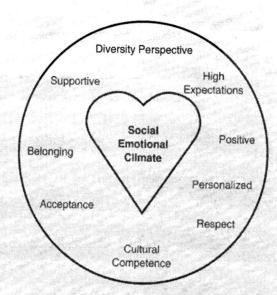

Diversity Perspective

Supportive

High Expectations

Belonging

Social Emotional Climate

Positive

Personalized

Acceptance

Respect

Cultural Competence

INTRODUCTION

Emphasis in this chapter is placed on ways to ensure that all children are provided with positive support for their social and emotional development. Teachers can make a difference in the lives of children by developing close, interactive relationships that instill trust and security. Creating a classroom climate that fosters prosocial behavior and builds self-esteem can prevent problem behavior from arising. This chapter also discusses collaborative efforts in communities and schools toward improving early detection of problem behavior and the provision of high quality care and learning environments for preschool children.

SUPPORTING CHILDREN'S SOCIAL/EMOTIONAL DEVELOPMENT

Relationship to Success in School

The critical relationship between the social and emotional domains of children's development and their success in school is gaining more prominence and a higher priority among issues considered by prestigious national organizations and top governmental officials. The U.S. Surgeon General and major national organizations have issued reports emphasizing the critical need for children's mental health and social development to be given the highest priority. Further, the issues of maltreatment and abuse have risen to the apex of national concern. The U.S. Surgeon General, Dr. Richard Carmona, has announced a focus on child abuse prevention and has emphasized the role of families in young children's emotional and social development. Calls have been issued for emphasis on early detection of children at risk for emotional and behavioral problems and intervention during the toddler and preschool years (National Advisory Mental Health Council Workgroup on Child and Adolescent Mental Health Intervention Development and Deployment, 2001; Shonkoff & Phillips, 2000; U.S. Department of Health and Human Services, 2005a, 2005b).

Success in school, from the academic perspective, has gained considerable attention in recent years. The trend toward greater accountability for the academic progress of children in school has gained the focus of the media. Although the No Child Left Behind Act (2002) has stirred up much controversy regarding academic accountability, this legislation has also focused attention on the need to support and enhance the social and emotional development of children. Moreover, early intervention for children with problem behaviors received a boost from The Good Start Initiative. The latter legislation underscored the benefits of preventing behavioral problems through quality intervention strategies aimed early, before patterns of problem behavior become well-entrenched and more difficult to change (Hester et al., 2004).

The current definition of school readiness encompasses age-appropriate attainment of fundamental social and emotional skills. For example, the ability to cooperate with others and demonstrate a level of self-control appropriate for the age of the young child are considered key elements of the concept of school readiness. These social skills are thought to be equally important to academic skills in determining success as a child enters school (Nelson, 2005).

Risk Factors

A key strategy for improving child outcomes is to reduce the number of risk factors that might negatively influence a child's growth and development. Even when the child has attended preschool and the home environment has been enriched, children with risk factors still perform below peers without risk factors (Nelson, 2005). Consequently, an initial step in determining the status of children's social and emotional well-being is to collecting information about the "social address" variables that may exert an influence on children's behavior and learning. Family demographics, such as a low socioeconomic status, ethnic minority status, and speaking English as a second language, are all family variables with capacity to influence the developmental trajectory of children (Lan & Lanthier, 2003). Regrettably, one in every six children live in poverty, and the statistics for younger children are more bleak; two in five children from birth to kindergarten suffer the disadvantages of an impoverished family life (National Center for Children in Poverty, 2002). Because social address risk factors are so influential in the academic, social, and behavioral outcomes of children, there have been calls for renewed emphasis on ensuring that each family is offered needed financial and social support to enhance their child-rearing and parenting skills (Fox, Dunlap, & Powell, 2002; Nelson, 2005; Shonkoff & Phillips, 2000).

Poverty and behavior. Poverty is a powerful determinant of a child's development, cognitive and behavioral in particular, and his or her achievement in school. Further, studies have reported that maternal characteristics, such as depression and the ability to cope, are associated with the presence of behavioral problems in children. Clearly, young children born into impoverishment suffer a much higher risk of psychological problems. Children in poor families are at serious risk of developing psychiatric disorders later in their childhood or adult life (Carnegie Task Force on Learning in the Primary Grades, 1996; Carnegie Task Force on Meeting the Needs of Young Children, 1994; Duncan, Yeung, Brooks-Gunn, & Smith, 1998; Duncan & Klebanov, 1994).

Home influence on behavior. The young child's home environment is a major influence on child outcomes and behavior. Homes that promote school success in children are ones that offer high levels of cognitive stimulation and provide children with many opportunities to acquire good social skills through interaction with others. Teachers can help families understand the importance of providing a variety of experiences that will facilitate learning social skills (Nelson, 2005). Play, for example, is fundamental to developing good social skills and has been linked to a higher motivation to learn. Positive experiences in playing with peers at home is mirrored in play at school. Conversely, it appears that difficulty in play situations and aggressive behaviors exhibited during play in the home setting are also reflected in peer play at school (Fantuzzo & McWayne, 2002).

Concepts of risk and resiliency. Children who experience poverty, illness, violence, abuse, and other risk conditions are not necessarily doomed to failure. There is evidence suggesting some children develop protective factors that increase their resilience and act as a buffer, shielding them from harmful effects of early disadvantages and deprivation. Promoting resiliency is another endeavor in which collaboration of teachers and other professionals with families can yield important advantages for children. Families can have characteristics that have a positive effect on promoting resiliency in children. When family conditions help a child develop resiliency, the home environment is laying the foundations for success despite the odds stacked against the child (Rak & Patterson, 1996). Children whose personality characteristics include having an amicable temperament and possessing good cognitive ability are likely to handle stress well. Children who live with both parents and have formed a strong attachment relationship with a significant parent or adult in their life are also more likely to be resilient in the face of adversity. In preschool and elementary school settings, children who form good relationships with teachers and their peers tend to exhibit effective coping and re-silience that compensates for the presence of various risk factors (Fox et al., 2002; Shonkoff & Phillips, 2000).

Addressing the whole child. It is critical to identify vulnerable children early to help avert future abuse and maltreatment and to increase the likelihood of positive out-comes for severely at-risk children. Child-centered approaches that involve partner-ships among community agencies and schools have been recommended as an effective approach to address problems in child development. The Head Start program exempli-fies a model designed to build a system of support around our nation's most vulnera-ble children. Such system approaches involving family, community, and schools can be effective in assessing and supporting the social and emotional development of vulner-able young children. Key people in the child's life can contribute information that reveal the social and emotional development of a child within the context of the child's overall development. Further, persons close to the child will be cognizant of the cul-tural and community contexts supporting the child's growth and learning. Partnering with community agencies that work with vulnerable children can increase the rele-vance of the assessment from the community context. Agencies with a history of work in children's mental health can help compare an individual child's assessment in light of known risk factors for children in the neighborhood or community. It is critical to use reliable measurements that yield sound data and are sensitive to the culture and language of the child. Partnerships among major contributors to the child's develop-ment formed during the assessment process can continue into the intervention phase. The major contributors in the child's life are often effective collaborators committed to enhance the learning of that child (Fantuzzo, McWayne, & Bulotsky, 2003).

Teachers in inclusive classrooms can encourage parents to take part in the informal or formal social and emotional assessments of their children. As a resource person for families, teachers can encourage families to access the community resources available to help determine services that might be beneficial to their children and family. It is also critical for schools to marshal collaborative efforts to support families of young chil-dren enrolled. Therefore, teachers can encourage administrators to assume a leadership role in the formation of community agency and school partnerships. Such encourage-ment by early childhood teachers is vital advocacy work toward improving early iden-tification and intervention.

ESTABLISHING A POSITIVE ATMOSPHERE FOR LEARNING

Accumulated research indicates that an effective classroom climate for enhancing learn-ing and fostering good social and emotional support has the following characteristics:

- Reasonable and clearly articulated expectations
- High rates of engagement and success
- Modeling, feedback, and role-playing to teach appropriate behavior
- Recognition for prosocial and positive behavior

- Nurturant and supportive teachers
- Consistency and predictability in routines
- Culturally responsive and competent teachers (Hester et al., 2004)

Providing a Personalized Learning Environment

It is critical to take steps early to ensure all children development competence and feelings of success. Planning for children to experience positive socioemotional learning environments that are geared for their individual strengths and needs is vital to promote their development. Once negative school experiences begin to occur, it may be very difficult to reverse the downward spiral and long-term ill effects children are likely to suffer. Studies of adolescents indicated that youths who experience failure in school and are at-risk of dropping out have developed personal risk factors that perpetuate their failure. Low self-esteem is one of the key factors thought to contribute to lack of motivation in school. Once children believe there is no way to exert control over their circumstances, they feel isolated from peers and teachers. Unfortunately, these feelings of separation and vulnerability are difficult to reverse and often contribute to the likelihood that children will continue to be unsuccessful in academic work and peer relationships in school (Lan & Lanthier, 2003).

Conveying High Expectations to All Children

Attitudes of teachers are critical to the success of children in an inclusive early childhood classroom. Beliefs about the capability of individual children to learn successfully

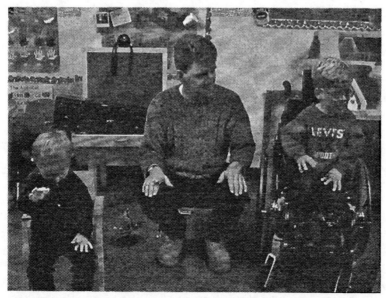

Holding high expectations for all helps children gain confidence.

strongly influence the message sent to children. Teachers who believe all children can learn to convey high expectations and support children in their efforts to meet those expectations. Moreover, teachers who see diversity of ability in their classrooms as a challenge and a moral commitment are instrumental in supporting one another. Collaborating to lend support and encourage learning together is extremely important. Teachers who hold high expectations for all children and accept the challenge of guiding each child to success are likely to attain high-quality classroom instruction. Further, teachers who support one another and encourage each other to hold high expectations for children are likely to increase their confidence level of their teaching abilities. Having confidence as a teacher is related to instilling confidence in children. Teaching children to be active, rather than passive, learners who can successfully solve problems independently leads children to success and to set higher expectations for themselves (Prater, 2003; Weiner, 2003).

Recognizing the Strengths of Each Child

Identifying the strengths and abilities of children and helping them to work toward those strengths is a key tenet of inclusion (Winter, 1999). Unfortunately, when young children are poor and belong to a minority group, it has been reported that teachers perceive these children as less competent than their peers. The strengths and abilities of children from low-income families tend to be overlooked, and they are often set apart from other children in class (Delpit, 1995). When a child's behavior is a challenge, teachers may overlook the child's areas of strengths and fail to develop a warm and supportive relationship with the child. It is critical for teachers to learn to recognize children's strengths and accurately judge their abilities even when their behaviors are challenging or their social and emotional development appears immature (Espinosa & Laffey, 2003).

Teacher-child relationship. Establishing a close, supportive relationship with an adult, such as a teacher, can improve the chances for a child to build resiliency and develop effective coping skills (Benard, 1993; Bronfenbrenner, 1979, 1986). Failure to establish a positive relationship with teachers can place vulnerable children at greater risk. A seminal research study conducted in the 1970s was among the first to describe the various ways that teachers set apart children from low-socioeconomic backgrounds during their early years of school from kindergarten through second grade. Patterns of treatment by teachers affected seating arrangements, grouping, and level of teachers' behavioral control (Rist, 2000). Undoubtedly, teacher perceptions of a child's behavior shapes the teacher's treatment of the child and the expectations held for the child's performance (Pianta, 1994, 1999). There is evidence that as early as the child-care setting, children can be treated differently based on the opinions teachers form about their abilities and behavior. When teachers find a child's behavior challenging, they attempt to exert more control. Under a more restrictive learning environment, children lose their freedom to explore and independently initiate activities of their own choosing (Howes & Smith, 1995).

Promote coping skills. Various related service personnel are involved in helping teachers and families foster good social and emotional skills of young children.

Psychologists and school counselors are well-recognized as consultants to parents and teachers regarding children's behavior. However, other related services providers also have an interest in certain aspects of growth and development that might influence children's behavior. For example, collaboration with an occupational therapist (OT) can help teachers and parents promote the development of good coping skills in children. The ability to adapt to the environment and experiences are influenced by the nature of the relationships children form with family members, caregivers, and teachers. Occupational therapists play a supportive role in coaching families' and teachers' interactions with children to promote optimal growth and development. The OT evaluates the home and school contexts and suggests ways to improve the atmosphere and resources needed to improve children's behavior, social interaction, and emotional development. Collaboration with an OT is extremely important to help teachers and parents understand children with behavioral problems and developmental delays. For example, an OT can evaluate whether children's responses signal the need for behavioral intervention or whether the origin of the reaction arises from sensory defensiveness or difficulty adapting to the environment. An OT can help modify discrepant behavior to achieve more consistency between the children's responses and the behaviors that are culturally valued by the family and acceptable in the classroom setting (Hanft & Anzalone, 2001).

Encouraging Social Interaction and Cooperation

Learning how to interact successfully with peers is a vital aspect of social development in the early years of a child's life. Understanding more about peer experience and the formation of friendships in inclusive settings is important, so that all children can enjoy a sense of belonging and membership—a basic tenet of inclusion.

IDENTIFYING AND PREVENTING PROBLEM BEHAVIOR
Early Identification of Problem Behavior

Research is abundantly clear regarding the critical role of early detection and intervention in preventing behavioral problems in children. There is no substitute for prevention to ameliorate social and behavioral outcomes for children. The preponderance of evidence indicates that behavioral patterns of children are established early in life. Once behavioral patterns are established, these habits are difficult to change. The trajectory for a child's social and emotional outcomes is set, and it is unlikely behaviors will improve as the child gains in age. In fact, problem behavior in the early years is a prelude to the more serious antisocial and mental health disorders in later years (Hester et al., 2004; Webster-Stratton & Reid, 2003). Estimates indicated that a staggering 50% of children who exhibited serious behavioral problems during their preschool years will experience unfavorable social and emotional outcomes by adolescence. Problems, such as drug abuse, school dropouts, criminal activity, and social rejection by

Small group activities increase participation and social interaction.

peers, might be averted with prompt identification and treatment of problem behavior during a child's preschool years (Campbell, 1994).

The common misconception that young children will outgrow their problem behaviors often results in delays in children receiving interventions. The reluctance of teachers and parents to identify and label children puts them at greater risk of establishing behavioral patterns that will be difficult to change later. By the time children are diagnosed and receive intervention for emotional/behavioral disorders (EBD), they are typically in the late elementary grades (Hester, Baltodano, Gable, Tonelson, & Hendrickson, 2003). Box 6.1 details a teacher's collaboration tips for a parent conference to discuss behavior problems.

Preventing Occurrences of Problem Behavior

Corroborating an earlier survey of teachers in inclusive classrooms (Joint Committee on Teacher Planning for Students with Disabilities, 1995), early childhood teachers have reported again that children with problem behavior are their greatest concern (Conroy, Davis, Fox, & Brown, 2002). When there are several children in the classroom who have difficulty self-regulating, listening, and following directions, whole-group activities may be difficult. Small-group activities that afford more possibilities for active participation and social interaction may be preferable. Box 6.2 demonstrates a sticker chart that is used as a behavior management strategy. Another alternative is allowing some work to be completed individually using computer technology. Offering opportunities to meet objectives using computers may help children at risk of problem

COLLABORATION TIPS*   BOX 6.1

I. Identifying Information

- **Class:** Preschool program for children with disabilities (PPCD)
- **Child:** A child with ADHD and mild cerebral palsy on left side of body. The child is bright and very close to being academically where his peers are, but has some behavior problems. The child has a hard time spending time in the general education classroom.
- **Parents:** The child's mother was in attendance at the conference. She is a working mom who is involved in the child's education. She is very willing to collaborate with me and tries to make sure to help the child at home.
- **Conference Manager:** The PPCD teacher
- **Time:** This conference was held four weeks after school started.

II. Rationale of Conference

- **Purpose/Intent:** I held this conference to discuss the child's behavior. I would like to discuss with mom the results of the behavior interventionist's visit. I want to tell her and show her some of the ideas the interventionist had, as well as talk about holding an admission, review, and dismissal meeting to reduce the child's time in general education kindergarten. I believe these measures will help to reduce and hopefully eliminate some of the behavior problems. (Unplanned: We also ended up discussing some recent problems mom has had and a new behavior management system she implemented at home that seems to be helping.)
- **Type:** Planned.
- **Initiation:** I initiated the conference.

III. Preconference Preparation

- I prepared a folder of work samples, as well as my notes on his behavior. I was prepared to show the mother examples of the strategies suggested by the interventionist: a picture schedule system, first/then cards, and the reward system. I also provided mother a copy of the behavior interventionist's report.

* See Appendix B, Parent Conference I, for the full text.

behavior to achieve both academic and behavioral goals in the inclusive classroom. Use of computers for children with difficulty regulating their behavior provides an alternative to whole-group instruction in early elementary grades by offering a more structured setting for acquiring skills. The computer environment is highly responsive and

BEHAVIOR MANAGEMENT   BOX 6.2

JOSE'S STICKER CHART

	MONDAY	TUESDAY	WEDNESDAY	THURSDAY	FRIDAY
Math					
Writing					
Literacy Centers					
Lunch					
Specials					
Quiet time					
Theme					

stimulating for children who can benefit from engagement in an individual activity pe-riodically. Whereas the child may gain in academic skills using the computer, teacher-child interaction should be planned so the relationship can continue to be supportive of the child's social and emotional development (Espinosa & Laffey, 2003).

Functional Behavioral Assessment

In accordance with IDEA (1997), teachers are required to implement specific measures for children who exhibit problem behavior. Positive behavioral support (PBS), also known as function-based intervention, informed by functional behavioral assessment (FBA) is required to fully comply with the law (Barnhill, 2005; Burke, Hagan-Burke, & Sugai, 2003; Gable et al., 2003). These proactive approaches are an application of behaviorist theory and methodology. The purpose of an FBA is to determine why a problem behavior is occurring so the planning team can design intervention strategies to stop or decrease the unwanted behaviors (Barnhill, 2005). Aiming an FBA at three levels can provide an efficient, yet comprehensive approach to preventing challenging behavior. School-wide approaches are the first level of prevention, whereby common behavior problems are identified. A midlevel assessment aims at children with behav-iors that are mild to moderately challenging. The third level refers to an FBA that plans interventions for children whose behavior is most serious and resistant to prior inter-vention efforts. This systematic way of applying an FBA efficiently prevents problems and reserves very intensive assessment for only the most resistant problem behavior (Scott & Caron, 2005).

Children may need productive time to work, individually.

Conducting an FBA. Rather than a single method, an FBA is a collection of assessment procedures designed to gather data about a child's behaviors and the circumstances surrounding the occurrence of these behaviors. An FBA helps teachers determine antecedent events that occur before the behavior and the consequences of the child's actions. These procedures also help to establish what purpose or function the behavior may serve. The child's behavior may be to gain attention or a desired item. In other cases, the child may wish to avoid a situation or want to provide sensory stimulation. It is also necessary to collect information about what reinforces or rewards the behaviors, making it more likely that these behaviors will be maintained (Barnhill, 2005; Gable et al., 2003).

Teachers and families can collaborate with other specialists in a team effort to describe the problem behavior as an initial step in the FBA process. Families have valuable information on how the child behaves at home and the strategies used in managing the child's challenging behavior. Collaborating with families can help inform the prereferral process and establish a strong partnership to support intervention later (Salend & Sylvestre, 2005). Baseline data are then collected to inform the team using both indirect and direct methods. Indirect methods are a quick way of gathering information from family and school records, assessments, and health reports. Direct methods are more time-consuming and may include observations organized to gather detailed information about the child's actions and the functions the child's behaviors may serve. Often, the reasons for the child's behaviors take little time to detect (Barnhill, 2005; Gable et al., 2003). An ABC observation, often conducted by a school counselor, provides information describing the antecedents, the behaviors, and the consequences of the behaviors of concern to the team. Adding a fourth area for teacher reflections to the ABC observation method can help teachers think about the cultural influences that might influence children's behavior (McKinney, Campbell-Whately, & Kea, 2005). A more involved method, experimental functional analysis, can be conducted as a final way of verifying the effects of variables suggested by prior direct or indirect methods. In experimental functional analysis, teachers or other team members manipulate identified variables systematically to determine their effects on problem behaviors. For example, teachers might change a task, move the location of activities, or modify learning materials to see if these changes might affect the behavior. These FBA procedures gather helpful information so the teacher and planning team can design effective behavioral intervention plans (BIPs) customized for individual children (Barnhill, 2005; Pindiprolu, Lignugaris/Kraft, Rule, Peterson, & Slocum, 2005).

Benefits of an FBA. The advantages of function-based approaches for children with severe disabilities and behavior disorders is substantiated by research. Less is known about the effectiveness of FBAs with children who have learning disabilities. However, such studies are beginning to show evidence of the advantages in identifying and improving behaviors of children with learning disabilities as well (Burke et al., 2003). Planning interventions without an FBA is inefficient and may strengthen the behavior by inadvertently providing reinforcement that prolongs the behavior. In contrast to trial and error methods, the FBA procedures help teachers design a BIP that is more likely to be effective in reducing the problem behavior (Barnhill, 2005). As others have reported, an FBA has the advantage of helping teachers view the child separate from the problem behavior that may be disruptive or annoying in the classroom. Further, using an FBA to identify behavior can lead to providing intervention earlier, when it will be most effective in preventing more serious behavioral disorders (Gable et al., 2003).

Positive Behavioral Supports

Positive behavioral support (PBS) consists of individualized intervention strategies focused on prevention of problem behavior. PBS strategies are evidence-based because they result from the functional behavioral assessment. Since PBS is designed for individual children based on their needs, PBS is considered a child-centered approach to intervention (Dunlap et al., 2003). An effective PBS method for children with pervasive developmental disorders, Asperger's syndrome, and autism is the technique of introducing social stories (see Box 6.3 for a sample). Children with autism spectrum disorders have difficulty in social situations with their peers. Based on information gathered in the FBA, teachers can write social stories that illustrate how children can behave in specific social situations, such as in the cafeteria or on the playground. Adding picture cues is a good idea because many children with autism rely on visual information. The social story method of PBS has proven effective in helping children with autism participate in social situations that occur in school and the community (Crozier & Sileo, 2005).

In addition to being useful in early childhood classrooms and schools, PBS has proven effective in home contexts. Increasing numbers of research studies have reported

BEHAVIOR MANAGEMENT   BOX 6.3

Social Stories

After attaching pictures above the text, the teacher and child read these together many times a day. Social stories can be written for all kinds of behaviors and social situations.

PABLO IS QUIET IN KINDERGARTEN

When Ms. Garcia is speaking, Pablo is quiet.

When Pablo sits on the carpet, Pablo is quiet.

Quiet means Pablo is not talking.

PABLO DOES HIS WORK

When Ms. Garcia asks Pablo to sit at the table,

Pablo says yes.

Pablo then stands up and goes to the table.

Pablo sits down at the table.

Pablo does his work.

After Pablo finishes his work, Pablo gets a reward.

---

that families can learn to implement PBS successfully in home and in community contexts. These findings are important to help improve family life for households including children with severe disabilities, such as children with autism. A PBS can help families establish routines that allow the family to function more smoothly with less disruptive behaviors, causing less stress for family members (Buschbacher, Fox, & Clarke, 2004).

Benefits of a PBS. Providing positive behavioral support has been reported to benefit all children, including those who are diverse (Jones & Jones, 2001; Lewis & Sugai,

Effective classroom management encourages positive behavior in the classroom.

1999). Consequently, there is reason to believe that implementation of PBS in inclusive classrooms may be beneficial in preventing problem behavior. Evidence suggests PBS improves the behavior of children with developmental disabilities, but little is known about the effects of this approach with children who are at risk of behavioral disorders. However, a review of 20 years of published studies did reveal several clear trends. Prevention-focused approaches have largely replaced punishment-oriented behavioral interventions of the past. Emphasis is now on providing individual support to increase desirable behaviors and replace problem behaviors with more acceptable behaviors. Positive behavioral interventions are being successfully implemented in less restrictive environments, such as homes and community early childhood settings. Another trend identified is that few initiatives are aimed at early identification of children who are at risk of developing behavioral disorders. This is unfortunate because the outcomes for children who receive early intervention are much better than those for whom intervention is delayed. Also unfortunate is the finding that revealed only a few studies have focused on children age 2 and younger (Conroy, Dunlap, & Clarke, 2005).

Intervention in classrooms. Teachers can collaborate with families to plan and implement intervention strategies designed to give children with mood disorders support. One simple intervention is to plan the daily schedule to include more opportunities for children to participate in physical activities and exercise throughout the day. Expression of feelings through creative and artistic outlets is another avenue for healing children with depressive disorders. Some children may simply lack a sufficient vocabulary of "feeling" words to describe their emotions. Increasing the child's vocabulary with such words may promote effective communication and enhance the development of friendships and other social relationships. Planning for children to

Partnerships with families results in more effective Positive Behavioral Support (PBS) for children.

experience daily success helps break the negative cycle of depression. Helping children set attainable goals and supporting children to ensure the achievement of tasks toward those goals can improve a child's self-esteem. Collaborating with parents, teachers can encourage healthy nutrition and the avoidance of caffeine and sugar consumption that might contribute to a child's fatigue and mood fluctuations (Abrams, Theberge, & Karan, 2005).

Developing an Effective Classroom Management Style

It is vital for caregivers and teachers to develop skill in managing the classroom and facilitating positive behavior in the classroom. Research indicates that ineffectual classroom management exacerbates problem behavior in children (National Institute of Child Health and Human Development, 1998; Webster-Stratton, 1997). In inclusive classrooms, teachers are best prepared to guide children's social development and collaborate with diverse parents when they are confident in using a wide range of strategies. Having a full palette of techniques and methods at their disposal gives teachers many options for helping children in the classroom and for parents to support their children's social and emotional development at home.

Guidance methods. Teachers who acquire an authoritative style of classroom management, using a variety of child guidance techniques, provide a sound foundation of support for most children on a daily basis (Kostelnik, Whiren, Soderman, Stein, & Gregory, 2002; Marion, 2003). Child guidance methods of facilitating children's social and behavioral learning in early childhood have been widely recommended by child development experts as foundational to effective classroom management (Bredekamp, 1987; Bredekamp & Copple, 1997).

Teaching and guiding social development and behavior in the inclusive classroom, however, also requires flexibility to meet individual needs within the social ecology of the group. Consequently, teachers prepared by being competent in using methods that have proven effective in supporting the development of children with challenging behavior or severe problems will be most effective in managing their inclusive classrooms.

National organizations in both general early childhood education and early childhood special education have reached a consensus. These organizations recommend the use of child guidance and positive support techniques as fundamental for promoting the children's behavior and social development of all children. However, they also agree on the need for teachers to use other techniques to address the individual social and behavioral goals for certain children (Division for Early Childhood Council for Exceptional Children, 1993; Division for Early Childhood Council for Exceptional Children, National Association for the Education of Young Children, & Association of Teacher Educators, 1995; Division for Early Childhood of the Council for Exceptional Children, 1993).

Behaviorist methods. Applied behavior analysis, also referred to as behavior modification or direct instruction, is an effective method of efficiently managing the behavior of children. When ethically used, applied behavior analysis methods can be used to shape, change, or eliminate targeted behaviors of children (Alberto & Troutman, 2006; Becker & Carnine, 1981; Miltenberger, 1997; Schloss & Smith, 1994). The field of special education has historically used applied behavior analysis to improve problem behavior exhibited by children with challenging behavior. For individuals with developmental disabilities, behavior modification is a popular set of tools used to teach children functional behaviors for improving living skills and reducing behaviors that can impede classroom learning (Becker & Carnine, 1981; Rusch, Rose, & Greenwood, 1988). Children with developmental disabilities in inclusive classrooms can demonstrate a number of behaviors that interfere with the learning and socialization processes of themselves and others (see Box 6.4 for a collaboration tips form). Problem behavior, such as aggression, destructiveness, and self-injurious behavior, can disrupt learning in inclusive classrooms and jeopardize the inclusion of individual children. However, research indicates these behaviors can often be reduced, controlled, or extinguished through careful and consistent use of behavior modification techniques (Barrett, 1986; Rusch et al., 1988).

Collaborating with families. Establishing a family-centered philosophy to address children with challenging behavior is a positive approach that is likely to bring greater consistency to implementing strategies and helping families access resources in the community. Consistency is vital to the success of early intervention strategies to prevent or change problem behaviors exhibited by young children. Continuity across home and school contexts requires coordination of efforts and a commitment to achieve the consistency needed to achieve positive results. Early intervention occurring within a collaborative relationship with the family allows teachers and other professionals to inform, guide, and support the family as the primary context of influence on the

COLLABORATION TIPS

BOX 6.4

FALL CONFERENCE FORM
Kindergarten

Name___Ben X

1. Strengths:
   Knowing letters, numbers, colors, always able to answer questions asked, rhyming

2. Things to work on:
   Behavior, concepts about print

3. Kinder checklist:
   Not all areas will be marked the first nine weeks.

4. Kinder observation survey results:

child's behavior and social development. Families of children with significant risk factors or those with disabilities already function within daily stresses and difficult circumstances. When teachers and other professionals form partnerships with families, they can provide support that may relieve some of the helplessness and stress these families experience in dealing with their children's problem behavior.

Family-centered partnerships between parents and teachers and other professionals can be instrumental in helping parents access community resources that offer support for families of children with problem behavior. Families are often served by a number of different federal or governmental programs, and each program has policies and procedures through which they must navigate to obtain access to needed services. Parents can become frustrated by the complexities of differing eligibility criteria and services offered by each agency (Fox et al., 2002; Hester et al., 2004). Thus, teachers who are informed about services and agencies in the community that provide help for children with challenging behavior can be a valuable resource for families.

Families and teachers working together is the most effective strategy for helping children develop self-regulation, positive self-esteem, and other desired aspects of social and emotional development. Teachers can help parents gain more effective parenting styles and better behavioral management techniques. Behavior modification techniques, derived from behaviorist theory and practice, have long been used with

COLLABORATION TIPS*   BOX 6.5

I. Identifying Information

- **Class:** Preschool Program for Children with Disabilities (PPCD)
- **Child:** A five-year-old child with ADHD and processing problems. The child, for the most part, behaves well in my class. He has on occasion, been a little impulsive or hyperactive due to switching medications. His main issue is processing. He often stares off into space and is behind academically.
- **Parents:** The child's father was in attendance at the conference. He is a working dad who is very involved in his child's education. He is very willing to collaborate with me and make sure to match what is being done at school is done at home. Also, our school speech pathologist who provides speech for the child, the school's occupational therapist, and the child's private speech pathologist were present.
- **Conference Manager:** The PPCD teacher and the school speech pathologist
- **Time:** This conference was held six weeks after school started from 2:30 to 3:30 PM.

II. Rationale of Conference

- **Purpose/Intent:** This conference was held as per a request from the child's father. He had several topics that he wanted to discuss. First, he wanted to request another admission, review, and dismissal meeting (ARD) to change some of the child's goals. He also wanted to have a discussion on what some more appropriate goals would be. Last, he wanted the private speech pathologist to meet the school's, so they could maybe compare notes and collaborate their efforts.
- **Type:** Planned pre-ARD conference. The conference went as planned.

* See Appendix B, Parent Conference II, for the full text.

children who have problem behaviors to shape better behavioral pattern and habits. Behavior modification techniques have proven effective for children even when their behavioral problems are severe. Limited research is available describing results of the use of behavior modification by parents with typical children. One study, however, suggests parents can successfully use behavior modification with professionals to help develop and monitor the program (see Box 6.5 for an example). Parents must be willing and have family circumstances that permit consistency in following the programmatic regime. The effect can be a more harmonious family life and the prevention of negative behavioral patterns in the child (Glickling, 2001).

Behavior and health. Further, there are findings that suggest behavior modification may be useful when parents and professionals use these techniques as part of an overall scheme toward reversing the alarming trend of obesity in preschool children. Interestingly, early obesity and poor eating habits may have a relationship to poor parenting and behavioral management skills in parents and caregivers. Several studies have suggested that lack of adequate parenting skills among mothers in low-income families contributes to poor behavioral support for young children. Low-income parents frequently misinterpret a young child's crying as hunger and offer food to soothe the child. Parental perception of overweight differed from indications of growth chart data, and parents used food to regulate children's behavior (Baughcum, Burklow, Deeks, Powers, & Whitaker, 1998; Jain et al., 2001).

Lack of skills in parenting commonly results in parents using food to elicit or reinforce desired behavior of their children. Poor parenting skills can also lead to dictating food choices and overcontrolling eating situations. The result of using food to control children's behavior can undermine a child's natural cues that signal hunger and satiation (Satter, 1986, 1995). Helping parents acquire some basic skills in the use of behavioral modification techniques as part of an authoritative style of parenting may help families support children's social and emotional development and help break the cycle of early obesity in some families. Collaborating with health care professionals, such as a school nurse, teachers and families can use behavior modification interventions to improve eating habits of children (Drohan, 2003).

Using a Continuum of Interventions and Mediation Techniques

Differentiated approach for diversity. The diversity of children in inclusive classrooms necessitates a differentiated approach planned for individual children within the classroom group. Teachers can plan different levels of positive support for children matched to their needs and the activity in which the child will engage. Vigilant observation of children and their interactions with others can guide teachers in selecting the intervention techniques and appropriate level of intensity. Teachers can also plan with families to match the intensity of the intervention to the individual children and their families. Minimal intervention may be needed for some behaviors, whereas other behavioral patterns that are chronic or severe may require increased consistency and intensity of strategies to precipitate improvement (Fox et al., 2002; Hester et al., 2004). See Box 6.6 for collaboration tips in meeting with the behavior interventionist.

Collaboration of teachers. It is common for children, even those without disabilities, to receive educational services in several different settings or classrooms throughout the day. Specialists provide art, music, physical education, and other special subjects to children in settings designed and equipped for these activities. Children with disabilities may move to other settings on campus for related services by physical therapists, speech pathologists, occupational therapists, and other professionals.

Interventions may require adjustment when applied in various settings. As discussed in Chapter 7, an ecology of physical and social variables can influence a child's

COLLABORATION TIPS   BOX 6.6

MEETING WITH THE BEHAVIOR INTERVENTIONIST

January								
6	7	8	9	10	11-12	13-17	20	21
Holiday	No data	7:45 AM: not happy 8:30 AM: cried during circle time 8:45 AM: calmed and participating	No date	9:45 AM: did not want to participate in adaptive P.E.	Weekend	No data	Holiday	9:45 AM: did not want to participate in OT/PT activities

January						February		
25-26	27	28	29	30	31	1-2	3	4
Weekend	No data	9 AM: throwing supplies on floor/not following directions	Not following directions/ throwing items	Not keeping hands and feet to himself— a class rule	No data	Weekend	Pushing others 9 AM: had a hard time staying on task	Not keeping hands to himself

February								
10	11	12	13	14	15-16-17	18	19	20
Off task not following directions	8:30 AM: Circle time, kept getting up, off task 9:45 AM: would not come in from playground	off task, inattention, could not keep hands off others	8 AM: talking back to adults 8:30 AM: kicked teacher 9:30 AM: kicked another child	Holiday	weekend/ holiday	8 AM: not keeping hands off others	asking to go home– not good	8 AM: playing pretend guns 8:30 AM: not following directions, not keeping hands to himself

behavior. Consequently, a behavioral intervention designed for one classroom or setting may not transition smoothly to another setting. Collaboration of teachers can help ensure that the positive and full effects of a behavioral intervention will occur in all settings the child experiences. When the home settings are also considered by extending the collaboration to include the family, the maximum benefit of the intervention strategies may be felt, and greater continuity is achieved across both home and school contexts.

Multiple levels. To increase the likelihood of successful intervention, strategies are best aimed at multiple levels or aspects of the classroom ecology. The following are key strategies suggested for multiple levels of the classroom context:

- Endorse school-wide behavioral expectations
- Initiate high quality programs
- Provide predictable, stable environments
- Promote social interaction
- Facilitate verbal and nonverbal communication
- Acknowledge positive behavior (Hester et al., 2004).

CREATING A CLIMATE OF RESPECT AND ACCEPTANCE

Acquiring Cultural Competence

The first step in providing children with an inclusive classroom in which respect and acceptance are foundational is to acquire cultural competence. With increasing numbers of multiethnic inclusive education classrooms, cultural competence is now considered an essential skill for teachers so they can foster similar abilities in the children they teach. A climate of respect and acceptance mediated by a culturally competent teacher is essential for preventing inappropriate or disruptive behavior. Within this safe environment, children can gain self-awareness, recognize their own ethnocentrism, and learn to resolve conflicts that might arise (Weinstein, Tomlinson-Clarke, & Curran, 2004). The goal of inclusive classrooms is to create a climate in which children develop self-regulation rather than reliance on external control from authority figures. Achieving this goal means teachers must emphasize social constructivist approaches and minimize use of behaviorist methods (Ladson-Billings, 1994; Weinstein et al., 2004).

Defining the construct. Interestingly, despite calls for teachers to gain cultural competence, definitions vary and there are no universally accepted standards for measuring this construct. Furthermore, studies to better define the construct and to explore culturally competent practices and attitudes of children's teachers and caregivers are very limited (Obegi & Ritblatt, 2005). Box 6.7 lists some collaboration tips for cultural competence.

Importance of cultural responsiveness. With increasing diversity among families served in early childhood settings, the need for teachers to acquire cultural competence has never been more urgent. Cross-cultural variations can exist between the methods teachers use and those families employ in caregiving and educating young children. Yet,

COLLABORATION TIPS

BOX 6.7

- Recognize cultural competence as a lifelong pursuit and actively seek experiences that will help you acquire cultural sensitivity.
- Interact with people from diverse racial and ethnic backgrounds.
- Become aware of and acknowledge your own biases and stereotypes.
- Listen to others and respect their viewpoints.
- Actively learn about the culture and customs of others through conversations, attending cultural events in the community, and reading literature and newspaper articles.

congruence across contexts is optimal to foster a sense of belonging and personal security for all children (Delpit, 1995; Garcia, McLaughlin, Spodek, & Saracho, 1995; Obegi & Ritblatt, 2005). Teachers who make an effort to understand the customs and child-rearing practices of families are more likely to treat each child with respect and offer activities that are culturally relevant. Cultural competence enables teachers to collaborate with parents to bring greater continuity to practices that support children's social and emotional development at both home and school.

Research findings suggest there are a number of potential benefits when teachers gain cultural competence. Teachers who are aware of their own biases and have learned

Culturally competent teachers are responsive to families and offer greater continuity to support children's social and emotional development at school.

about the cultures of others are more inclined to plan their curriculum based on tenets of multicultural education. These teachers use culturally responsive teaching strategies and provide children with curricular activities relevant for their cultural background (Derman-Sparks, 1995; Gonzalez-Mena, 2001; Phillips, 1995). Another key benefit of teachers acquiring cultural competence is the ability to better understand minority children's behavioral responses that might be different from those of children in the majority culture (Gay, 2000; Howard, 1999). Teachers who understand culturally oriented behaviors of children are better mediators of cultural conflicts that arise in the inclusive classroom. Guidance provided by the teacher to help resolve conflicts gives children a good model for developing their own cultural competence (Sheets, 1996; Sheets & Gay, 1996; Weinstein et al., 2004).

Enhancing collaboration. Teachers can improve their collaboration with diverse children and their families by developing skill in communicating and interacting effectively with people of cultural backgrounds that are different from their own. Characteristics of teachers, such as years of experience in the field, ethnicity, and motherhood, bear little or no influence on the cultural competence demonstrated through interactions with children in the classroom. However, several studies do suggest the best way to gain proficiency in culturally responsive communication and interaction with families is to receive training on diversity promotion and responsive practices. Formal education, through college courses in child development or early childhood education, seems to be the most effective way to learn skills and attitudes related to cultural competence (Honig & Hirallal, 1998; Obegi & Ritblatt, 2005). However, professional development through inservice training and coaching are two methods also recommended to reach teachers who are not enrolled in colleges or universities (Obegi & Ritblatt, 2005). The goals of the training must be to increase self-awareness, improve communication skills, and help teachers learn to interact with others in effective, culturally sensitive ways.

SUMMARY

This chapter discussed how to provide a positive social and emotional climate for children's learning and development. There are a number of significant risk factors, such as poverty, child abuse, and health problems that impact a child's mental health. Moreover, social and emotional problems can reduce a child's chances for success in school. Ways to personalize the learning environment and convey high expectations to all children were discussed as key influences in the school environment. Emphasis was placed on how to identify and prevent problem behaviors. Early identification of problem behavior is critical. Early intervention can prevent the development of behavior disorders. The concepts of a functional behavioral assessment and positive behavioral supports were introduced and detailed information on implementation was provided. The chapter ended with a discussion of the role of cultural competence for teachers and children in the inclusive early childhood classroom.

Discussion Questions

1. List three reasons cultural competence is imperative for teachers and children.

2. What are the most important ways to collaborate with families to provide a good home and school environment for children's social and emotional growth and development?

3. What are key strategies for identifying children who might have potential behavioral problems?

4. What can teachers do in their inclusive classrooms to prevent problem behaviors from occurring?

5. In what ways do you feel confident in preventing behavior problems in the classroom?

6. How can you distinguish between a potential behavior problem and serious behavioral disorders?

7. What do you know about communicating with parents and families about their children's problem behaviors?

8. With whom might you collaborate to ensure a positive social and emotional atmosphere in your classroom?

9. Describe a functional behavioral assessment and summarize how it can be accomplished.

10. Define positive behavioral support and discuss the major advantages of using PBS.

Inclusive Activities

1. Observe an inclusive early childhood classroom for a morning. Select one child at a time and follow the child's activities for at least 10 minutes. Write anecdotal descriptions of the child's behaviors and social interactions with peers and teachers during the time period you are observing. Describe behaviors objectively without interjecting your own opinions. Pretend to be a photo journalist and simply narrate what you observe.

2. Find journal articles to read more about children with problem behaviors and the effects of home and school variables on children's behavior and actions.

3. Locate the Barnhill (2005) journal article for detailed information on how to implement an FBA and PBS.

4. Observe a child in an inclusive classroom for at least two hours. Watch for patterns of behavior that may recur repeatedly through the observation period. How did the teacher interact with the child? What strategies would you use to guide the child's behavior?

5. Talk to a teacher and ask for strategies and favorite tips for establishing a positive classroom atmosphere.

References

Abrams, K., Theberge, S. K., & Karan, O. C. (2005). Children and adolescents who are depressed: An ecological approach. *Professional School Counseling, 8*(3), 284–292.

Alberto, P. A., & Troutman, A. C. (2006). *Applied behavior analysis for teachers* (7th ed.). Upper Saddle River, NJ: Merrill/Prentice Hall.

Barnhill, G. A. (2005). Functional behavioral assessments in schools. *Intervention in School and Clinic, 40*(3), 131–143.

Barrett, R. P. (1986). *Severe behavior disorders in the mentally retarded: Nondrug approaches to treatment.* New York: Plenum Press.

Baughcum, A. E., Burklow, K. A., Deeks, C. M., Powers, S. W., & Whitaker, R. C. (1998). Maternal feeding practices and childhood obesity. *Archives of Pediatric and Adolescent Medicine, 152,* 1010–1014.

Becker, W. C., & Carnine, D. C. (1981). Direct instruction: A behavior theory model for comprehensive educational intervention with the disadvantaged. In S. W. Bijou & R. Ruiz (Eds.), *Behavior modification: Contributions to education* (pp. 145–210). Hillsdale, NJ: Erlbaum.

Benard, B. (1993). Fostering resiliency in kids. *Educational Leadership, 51*(3), 44–48.

Bredekamp, S. (Ed.). (1987). *Developmentally appropriate practice in early childhood programs serving children from birth through age 8.* Washington, DC: National Association for the Education of Young Children.

Bredekamp, S., & Copple, C. (Eds.). (1997). *Developmentally appropriate practice in early childhood programs* (Revised ed.). Washington, DC: National Association for the Education of Young Children.

Bronfenbrenner, U. (1979). *The ecology of human development.* Cambridge, MA: Harvard University Press.

Bronfenbrenner, U. (1986). Ecology of the family as a context for human development: Research perspectives. *Developmental Psychology, 22*(6), 723–742.

Burke, M. D., Hagan-Burke, S., & Sugai, G. (2003). The efficacy of function-based interventions for students with learning disabilities who exhibit escape-maintained problem behaviors: Preliminary results from a single-case experiment. *Learning Disability Quarterly, 26*(1), 15–25.

Buschbacher, P., Fox, L., & Clarke, S. (2004). Recapturing desired family routines: A parent-professional behavioral collaboration. *Research & Practice for Persons with Severe Disabilities, 29*(1), 25–39.

Campbell, S. B. (1994). Behavior problems in preschool children: A review of recent research. *Journal of Child Psychology and Psychiatry, 36*(1), 113–149.

Carnegie Task Force on Learning in the Primary Grades. (1996). *Years of promise: A comprehensive learning strategy for America's children.* New York, NY: Carnegie Corporation of New York.

Carnegie Task Force on Meeting the Needs of Young Children. (1994). *Starting points: Meeting the needs of our youngest children.* New York: Carnegie Corporation of New York.

Conroy, M. A., Davis, C. A., Fox, J. J., & Brown, W. H. (2002). Functional assessment of behavior and effective supports for young children with challenging behavior. *Assessment for Effective Instruction, 27,* 35–47.

Conroy, M. A., Dunlap, G., & Clarke, S. (2005). A descriptive analysis of positive behavioral intervention research with young children with challenging behavior. *Topics in Early Childhood Special Education, 25*(3), 157–166.

Crozier, S., & Sileo, N. M. (2005). Encouraging positive behavior with social stories: An intervention for children with autism spectrum disorders. *Teaching Exceptional Children, 37*(6), 26–31.

Delpit, L. (1995). *Other people's children: Cultural conflicts in the classrooms.* New York: The New Press.

Derman-Sparks, L. (1995). Developing culturally responsive caregiving practices: Acknowledge, ask, and adapt. In P. Magnione (Ed.), *A guide to culturally sensitive care* (pp. 40–63). Sacramento, CA: WestEd and California Department of Education.

Division for Early Childhood Council for Exceptional Children. (1993). *DEC recommended practices: Indicators of quality in programs for infants and young children with special needs and their families.* Reston, VA: Author.

Division for Early Childhood Council for Exceptional Children, National Association for the Education of Young Children, & Association of Teacher Educators. (1995). *Personnel standards for early education and early intervention: Guidelines for licensure in early childhood special education.* Pittsburgh, PA: Division for Early Childhood Council for Exceptional Children.

Division for Early Childhood of the Council for Exceptional Children. (1993). *DEC position on early intervention services for children birth to age eight.* Pittsburgh, PA: Author.

Drohan, S. H. (2003). Managing early childhood obesity in the primary care setting: A behavior modification approach. *Pediatric Nursing, 28*(6), 599–610.

Duncan, G. J., Yeung, W. J., Brooks-Gunn, J., & Smith, J. R. (1998). How much does childhood poverty affect the life chances of children? *American Sociological Review, 63*(3), 406–423.

Duncan, J. B., & Klebanov, P. K. (1994). Economic deprivation and early childhood development. *Child Development, 65*(2), 296–318.

Dunlap, G., Conroy, M., Kern, L., DuPaul, G., Van Brakle, J., & Strain, P. (2003). *Research synthesis on effective intervention procedures: Executive summary.* Tampa, FL: University of South Florida, Center for Evidence-based Practice: Young Children with Challenging Behavior.

Espinosa, L. M., & Laffey, J. M. (2003). Urban primary teacher perceptions of children with challenging behaviors. *Journal of Children & Poverty, 9*(2), 135–156.

Fantuzzo, J., & McWayne, C. (2002). The relationship between peer-play interactions in the family context and dimensions of school readiness for low income preschool children. *Journal of Educational Psychology, 94*(1), 79–87.

Fantuzzo, J., McWayne, C., & Bulotsky, R. (2003). Forging strategic partnerships to advance mental health science and practice for vulnerable children. *The School Psychology Review, 32*(1), 17–37.

Fox, L., Dunlap, G., & Powell, D. (2002). Young children with challenging behavior: Issues and considerations for behavior support. *Journal of Positive Behavior Interventions, 4*(4), 208–217.

Gable, R. A., Butler, C. J., Walker-Bolton, I., Tonelson, S. W., Quinn, M. M., & Fox, J. L. (2003). Safe and effective schooling for all students: Putting into practice the disciplinary provisions of the 1997 IDEA. *Preventing School Failure, 47*(2), 74–78.

Garcia, E. E., McLaughlin, B., Spodek, B., & Saracho, O. N. (Eds.). (1995). *Meeting the challenge of linguistic and cultural diversity in early childhood education* (Vol. 6). New York: Teachers College Press.

Gay, G. (2000). *Culturally responsive teaching: Theory, research, and practice.* New York: Teacher's College Press.

Glickling, E. E. (2001). From a dawdling to a doing daughter. *Education, 95*(4), 381–385.

Gonzalez-Mena, J. (2001). *Multicultural issues in child care* (3rd ed.). Mountain View, CA: Mayfield.

Hanft, B. E., & Anzalone, M. (2001). Issues in professional development: Preparing and supporting occupational therapists in early childhood. *Infants and Young Children, 13*(4), 67–78.

Hester, P. P., Baltodano, H. M., Gable, R. A., Tonelson, S. W., & Hendrickson, J. M. (2003). Early intervention with children at risk of emotional/behavioral disorders: A critical examination of research methodology and practices. *Education and Treatment of Children, 26*(4), 362–381.

Hester, P. P., Baltodano, H. M., Hendrickson, J. M., Tonelson, S. W., Conroy, M. A., & Gable, R. A. (2004). Lessons learned from research on early intervention: What teachers can do to prevent behavior problems in schools. *Preventing School Failure, 49*(1), 5–10.

Honig, A. S., & Hirallal, A. (1998). Which counts more for excellence in childcare staff: Years in service, education level or ECE coursework? *Early Childhood Development and Care, 145*, 31–46.

Howard, G. R. (1999). *We can't teach what we don't know: White teachers, multiracial schools.* New York: Teacher's College Press.

Howes, C., & Smith, E. (1995). Relations among child care quality, teacher behavior, children's play activities, emotional security, and cognitive activity in child care. *Early Childhood Research Quarterly, 10*(4), 381–404.

Jain, A., Sherman, S. N., Chamberlin, L. A., Carter, Y., Powers, S. W., & Whitaker, R. C. (2001). Why don't low income mothers worry about their preschoolers being overweight? *Pediatrics, 107*, 1138–1146.

Joint Committee on Teacher Planning for Students with Disabilities. (1995). *Planning for academic diversity in America's classrooms: Windows on reality, research, change, and practice.* Lawrence, KS: The University of Kansas Center for Research on Learning.

Jones, V. F., & Jones, L. S. (2001). *Comprehensive classroom management: Creating communities of support and solving problems.* Needham, MA: Allyn & Bacon.

Kostelnik, M. J., Whiren, A. P., Soderman, A. K., Stein, L. C., & Gregory, K. (2002). *Guiding children's social development: Theory to practice* (4th ed.). Albany, NY: Delmar Thomson Learning.

Ladson-Billings, G. (1994). *The dreamkeepers: Successful teachers of African-American children.* San Francisco: Jossey-Bass.

Lan, W., & Lanthier, R. (2003). Changes in students' academic performance and perceptions of school and self before dropping out of schools. *Journal of Education for Students Placed at Risk, 8*(3), 309–332.

Lewis, T. J., & Sugai, G. (1999). Effective behavior support: A systems approach to proactive school wide management. *Focus on Exceptional Children, 31*(6), 1–24.

Marion, M. (2003). *Guidance of young children* (6th ed.). Upper Saddle River, NJ: Merrill/Prentice Hall.

McKinney, S. E., Campbell-Whately, G. D., & Kea, C. D. (2005). Managing student behavior in urban classrooms: The role of teacher ABC assessments. *The Clearing House, 79*(1), 16–20.

Miltenberger, R. G. (1997). *Behavior modification: Principles and Procedures.* Pacific Grove: Brooks/Cole.

National Advisory Mental Health Council Workgroup on Child and Adolescent Mental Health Intervention Development and Deployment. (2001). *Blueprint for change: Research on child and adolescent mental health.* Bethesda, MD: National Institute of Mental Health.

National Center for Children in Poverty. (2002). *Child poverty fact sheet: Low-income children in the United States: A brief demographic profile.* NY: Center for Children in Poverty, Mailman School of Public Health, Columbia University.

National Institute of Child Health and Human Development. (1998). Early child care and self-control, compliance, and problem behavior at twenty-four and thirty-six months. *Child Development, 69*(4), 1145–1170.

Nelson, R. F. (2005). The impact of ready environments on achievement in kindergarten. *Journal of Research in Childhood Education, 19*(3), 215–221.

Obegi, A. D., & Ritblatt, S. N. (2005). Cultural competence in infant/toddler caregivers: Application of a tridimensional model. *Journal of Research in Childhood Education, 19*(3), 199–213.

Phillips, C. B. (1995). Culture: A process that empowers. In P. Magnione (Ed.), *A guide to culturally sensitive care* (pp. 2–9). Sacramento, CA: WestEd and California Department of Education.

Pianta, R. C. (1994). Patterns of relationships between children and kindergarten teachers. *Journal of School Psychology, 32*(1), 15–31.

Pianta, R. C. (1999). *Enhancing relationships between children and teachers.* Washington, DC: American Psychological Association.

Pindiprolu, S. S., Lignugaris/Kraft, B., Rule, S., Peterson, S., & Slocum, T. (2005). Scoring rubric for assessing students' performance on functional behavior assessment cases. *Teacher Education and Special Education, 28*(2), 79–91.

Prater, M. A. (2003). She will succeed! Strategies for success in inclusive classrooms. *Teaching Exceptional Children, 35*(5), 58–64.

Rak, C. F. & Patterson, L. E. (1996). Promoting resilience in at-risk children. *Journal of Counseling & Development, 74*(4), 368–373.

Rist, R. (2000). Students social class and teacher expectations: The self-fulfilling prophecy in ghetto education. *Harvard Educational Review, 70,* 266–301.

Rusch, F. R., Rose, T., & Greenwood, C. R. (1988). *Introduction to behavior analysis in special education.* Upper Saddle River, NJ: Prentice Hall.

Salend, S. J., & Sylvestre, S. (2005). Understanding and addressing oppositional and defiant classroom behaviors. *Teaching Exceptional Children, 37*(6), 32–39.

Satter, E. M. (1986). The feeding relationship. *Journal of American Dietetic Association, 86,* 352–356.

Satter, E. M. (1995). Feeding dynamics: Helping children eat well. *Journal of Pediatric Health Care, 9,* 178–184.

Schloss, P. J., & Smith, M. A. (1994). *Applied behavior analysis in the classroom.* Boston: Allyn & Bacon.

Scott, T. M., & Caron, D. B. (2005). Conceptualizing functional behavior assessment as prevention practice within positive behavior support systems. *Preventing School Failure, 50*(1), 13–20.

Sheets, R. H. (1996). Urban classroom conflict: Student-teacher perception: Ethnic integrity, solidarity, and resistance. *Urban Review, 28*(2), 15–21.

Sheets, R. H., & Gay, G. (1996). Student perceptions of disciplinary conflict in ethnically diverse classrooms. *NASSP Bulletin, 80*(580), 84–94.

Shonkoff, J. P., & Phillips, D. A. (Eds.). (2000). *From neurons to neighborhoods: The science of early childhood development.* Washington, DC: National Academy Press.

U.S. Department of Health and Human Services. (2005a). *Making prevention of child maltreatment a national priority: Implementing innovations of a public health approach.* Retrieved July 7, 2005, from http://www.surgeongeneral.gov/healthychild/workshop.html

U.S. Department of Health and Human Services. (2005b). *U. S. Surgeon General issues second "Healthy Dozen List"—Toddlers.* Retrieved July 7, 2005, May 19, 2005, from http://www.surgeongeneral.gov/pressreleases/sg05192005.html

Webster-Stratton, C. (1997). Early intervention for families of preschool children with conduct problems. In M. J. Guralnick (Ed.), *The effectiveness of early intervention* (pp. 429–453). Baltimore, MD: Brookes.

Webster-Stratton, C., & Reid, M. J. (2003). Treating conduct problems and strengthening social and emotional competence in young children: The dina dinosaur treatment program. *Journal of Emotional and Behavioral Disorders, 11*(3), 130–143.

Weiner, H. M. (2003). Effective inclusion: Professional development in the context of the classroom. *Teaching Exceptional Children, 35*(6), 12–18.

Weinstein, C. S., Tomlinson-Clarke, S., & Curran, M. (2004). Toward a conception of culturally responsive classroom management. *Journal of Teacher Education, 55*(1), 25–38.

Winter, S. M. (1999). *The early childhood inclusion model: A program for all children.* Olney, MD: Association for Childhood Education International.

Chapter 7

Designing the Inclusive Physical Environment

Key Principle

- Provide safe, challenging learning environments

Objectives

After reading this chapter you will be able to:

1. Summarize research findings regarding the environmental effects that might have an impact on learning.
2. Interpret research on environmental factors and apply the information.
3. Evaluate the physical learning environment for promotions of learning.
4. Use continuums to plan for flexible learning environments adaptable for individual learners.
5. Collaborate with families and other professionals to create optimal learning environments for all children.

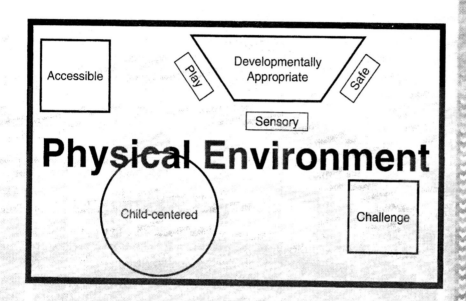

INTRODUCTION

It is critical to avoid underestimating the influence of the environment in an inclusive early childhood classroom. The designs of both indoor and outdoor spaces for learning and play can influence the type and variety of learning experiences available to children. The diversity of children and their abilities necessitates carefully designed physical environments that support the learning of the wide range of children typically found in inclusive classrooms of child-care centers and schools. The chapter begins with a look at the theoretical underpinnings that suggest the importance of considering environmental variables when planning and maintaining environments to support children's learning. A review of the findings of environmental research follows, providing a basis for planning inclusive environments. This chapter also examines what research has revealed about the influence of different environmental variables on children in a classroom setting. The implications of research for the design of indoor and outdoor learning environments will be suggested. This chapter details how to plan for safety and accessibility for all children in an inclusive classroom. Issues related to cultural diversity and planning culturally relevant and comfortable learning spaces are discussed. The chapter ends with attention devoted to the integration of technology into learning environments of inclusive classrooms.

THE ROLE OF THE PHYSICAL ENVIRONMENT IN LEARNING

How important is the physical environment in promoting the growth, development, and learning of young children? Those who study and educate children have pondered that question for many centuries, and it is a topic of continuing concern. The question recalls the longstanding nature vs. nurture theories, and arguments are still unresolved as to how much influence one can attributed to inborn, inherited characteristics as opposed to environmental factors and the role these variables play in shaping behavior and learning.

Historical and Theoretical Perspectives on Environments

Historically, theorists have contemplated the role of environmental contexts in the growth, development, and learning of children. John Amos Comenius (1592–1670) was one of the first theorists who recommended a sensory approach to teaching. He recognized that children learned through exploring and manipulating concrete objects and materials, using their senses as a primary medium of learning (Keating, 1967). Later, Marie Montessori (1870–1952) noticed the importance of sensory stimulation in teaching children with developmental disabilities (George, 1967). The theory of environmentalism was hypothesized by John Locke (1632–1704) who postulated that children entered life as a tabla rasa or blank slate. He believed the intellectual development of children was primarily the result of the environmental contexts in which they were raised rather than individual characteristics of children (Nidditch, 1975). Early theorists, such as Jean Jacques Rousseau (1712–1778), advanced the notion that children learn best in natural outdoor environments. According to this theory, allowing children to play in natural settings encouraged children to learn through free exploration, and afforded many opportunities for children to satisfy their curiosity (Boyd, 1962). Later theorists, such as Friedrich Wilhelm Froebel (1782–1852) and Maria Montessori, introduced the idea of preparing the environment with materials designed specifically to stimulate learning. Both Froebel and Montessori added specially constructed toys and learning materials to the learning environment. Montessori, in particular, expected children to interact with the prepared materials in prescribed ways (Dyck, 2002).

Other environmentalists began to see the influence of the social components of learning contexts in tandem with physical aspects of the environment. Johann Heinrich Pestalozzi (1746–1827) envisioned the role of adults as colearners and mediators of the physical environment to promote children's learning (DeGuimps, 1890). In a broader view, Robert Owen (1771–1858) recognized the role of society as an influence in creating environmental conditions that shaped children's belief systems, values, and learning (Bamford, 1844). Constructivist theories of Jean Piaget (1896–1980) and Lev Vygotsky (1896–1934) recognized the physical and social aspects of the learning environment for supporting the learning of children. Piaget focused on the child's actions upon the environment and explained children's development as a result of their interactions with the physical and social aspects of their contexts. Piaget believed in the existence of a relationship between a child's playful interactions with the environment and cognitive development. He posited that children construct knowledge through interaction with the environment, which, in turn, advances cognitive development (Piaget, 1952, 1962). Vygotsky's ideas emphasized the social influences in a child's environment that stimulate and possibly advance the development of children beyond what they could learn independently. He introduced the concept of zone of proximal development as a way to explain how children can perform at a higher level when assisted by a more expert learner (Vygotsky, 1978, 1986).

The field of special education has been profoundly influenced by behaviorist theory and the behavior modification movement that evolved during the late nineteenth and early twentieth centuries. Ivan P. Pavlov, Edward L. Thorndike, John B. Watson, and B. F. Skinner are the major contributors to the theory that environmental events control human behavior. Applied behavioral analysis methods are widely used in special education to help children with severe behavior problems learn and acquire skills (Richarz, 1993; Safford, 1989; Schloss & Smith, 1994; Widerstrom, 1986).

Attributing some level of influence to the physical environment and the social interaction of people within the environmental contexts of children is, therefore, not a new idea. However, modern research and technology have given us methods to explore the influences of environment in systematic ways. As a result, we are uncovering more scientific facts and information about the factors that might influence children's development and learning. As this emerging body of knowledge grows and matures, implications for school environments (inclusive classrooms, in particular) can be derived.

Goals and Challenges for Inclusive Classrooms

The goal of inclusive early childhood classrooms is to create a physical environment that supports the growth, development, and learning of a heterogeneous and culturally diverse group of children who vary widely in ability. Embracing the diversity of the children and endeavoring to create a physical arrangement that allows all children to work toward their strengths is the thrust of inclusive classrooms. This goal differs considerably from approaches that expect conformity and participation in whole-group instruction. Proponents of inclusive approaches favor learning environments that support the diversity children bring to the group and promote equity of children at the margins (Wang, Reynolds, & Walberg, 1994/1995). The idea of inclusive learning environments is to provide a variety of challenging learning opportunities that draw children into social-group arrangements for learning to maximize the power of social thinking and problem solving.

Another important tenet of inclusion is to make accommodation for individual children, when necessary, to accomplish the goal of fostering each child's participation in learning activities with their peers. Inclusion cannot be achieved by simply placing all children in the same physical environment. Besides being safe and accessible, it is crucial for the physical environment to support a tolerant, accepting learning community to which all children have membership. To accomplish that goal, the environment must also bring all children into different groupings of peers and teachers throughout the day, giving all children full access to learning experiences. Promoting full participation and equity of opportunity for all, regardless of gender, culture, primary language, or ability is a core challenge for inclusive classrooms. However, it is a fundamental principle that permits children to learn through collaboration with one another and interaction with their teachers, specialists, and teaching assistants. Planning the physical environment of the inclusive classroom to support a full range of learning opportunities sets the stage for individual children to meet challenges and achieve success in school.

Significance of Environments for Learning

The environment for an inclusive classroom is different from traditional settings for special education, which typically were segregated from mainstream classrooms (Lucas & Thomas, 1990). Inclusion is practiced in those general education classroom settings and the effects of those settings on children with special needs is still limited. However, for some time, there have been experts who have expressed concerns about the amount of decoration often found in general early childhood classrooms. Teachers of young children have been criticized for their tendency to use bright colors and hang a variety of decorations that seem aimed more at amusement rather than learning (Katz & Chard, 1989). It is true that research has not yet revealed definitive answers to all the questions that have arisen about the potential effects of environmental elements on children's learning. Should the environment provide a high level of stimulus or is a low stimulus better? Should colors be bright or more neutral? Teachers in the field of special education often opt for less stimuli and fewer distracts. Although research on school environments per se is still limited, it is vital for teachers to be aware of studies that do exist and may provide some preliminary guidance in planning the physical environments of inclusive early childhood settings. Early studies of school environments have suggested that younger children may be more sensitive to environmental variables than older children and adults. Young children appear to be particularly vulnerable to both positive aspects and harmful effects of learning environments (Weinstein & Weinstein, 1979). Research by early environmentalists suggests young children are less adept at filtering out detrimental stimuli and adapting to environmental stressors. With age and experience, children gain in their proficiency in dealing with adverse influences, such as noise, crowding, and uncomfortable temperatures (Altman & Wohlwill, 1978).

Cultural geography, urban planning, and, more recently, the newer field of environmental psychology, have entertained questions about the environmental contexts of

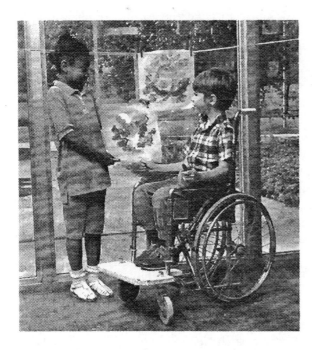

Young children appear particularly sensitive to characteristics of early learning environments.

children. Research has been conducted regarding the possible effects of environmental variables on children and their development and learning. The effects of poor urban environments on the development of children was found to place children at risk (Horm, 2003). However, studies of school environments have been limited. Yet, some experts argue that research on environmental variables that might exert an influence on children in school settings, homes, and neighborhoods deserve greater attention and can inform educational policy and instructional practices (Ellis, 2002, 2004). The link between poverty and environment certainly deserves exploration. It is clear that children who live and attend school in impoverished neighborhoods are at a higher risk of educational and behavioral problems (Fujiura & Yamaki, 2000; Magnuson, Meyers, Ruhm, & Waldfogel, 2004; Wright, Diener, & Kay, 2000). Moreover, it has been reported that ecological variables can have either adverse or positive effects on children's behavior and learning (Greenwood & Carta, 1987; Heller, 1990). However, limited information is available regarding how to identify potentially influential variables in classrooms and better understand the effects that environmental factors might have on individual children.

The Physical State of Schools

Emerging research on school environments suggests the safety of school environments should not be assumed. Moreover, the effects of environmental variables, both present and absent, can have a dramatic impact on children's learning. Studies suggest a link between school performance and the state of the school infrastructure. Evidence of achievement score improvements in schools where conditions of school buildings were renovated have been analyzed, and have shown a relationship between school infrastructure and the academic success of children (Berner, 1993; Harter, 1999). Maureen Edwards at Georgetown University studied the relationship between the physical condition of schools in Washington, DC, and the achievement of children attending those schools. Controlling for socioeconomic status and other variables, Edwards' "Schoolhouse in the Red" research findings indicated that the achievement scores of children in schools that were in poor physical condition lagged nearly 11% behind their peers in excellent schools (Dyck, 2002; Hansen, 1993). Dismal physical environments are associated with poor school attendance and may undermine the self-worth of children, resulting in apathy. Widespread decay of schools is reported, with schools having unhealthful conditions and inadequate space and supplies to serve children enrolled (Piccigallo, 1989). Old adages proliferating the idea that children can learn despite the characteristics of the learning environment have been called into question (Hayes, 1986).

It is well-documented that the quality of the child-care system in the United States is poor and few meet quality standards on basic quality indicators (Blau & Mocan, 2002; NICHD Early Child Care Research Network, 1999). The substandard quality of child care has led to calls for serious change to occur. Some authors recommend that the ultimate goal is merging the child-care system with the public school educational systems (Brauner, Gordic, & Zigler, 2004). In all likelihood, parents would favor such a move. A 1991 Carnegie Foundation report stated families clearly indicated a preference for serving preschoolers in public school settings (Boyer, 1991). Many Head Start centers already coexist within public school campuses and increasingly, public schools are offering programs for four-year-olds. However, embedding early care in public schools raises issues about the quality of physical environments available in some public school settings. Legitimate concerns about the state of disrepair of many urban schools have caused others to wonder whether moving child care to public school campuses, alone, would solve the problem or further aggravate the situation. Without comprehensive renovations, some contend that decaying school environments may further imperil the health and learning of children (Piccigallo, 1989). As more early childhood classrooms become inclusive, serving increasing numbers of health-fragile children and those with special needs, the quality of the school environment becomes an issue of concern. The architectural design of many elementary schools, especially of older ones, is also problematic for inclusive programs serving young children. Older schools were often built with hard elements and architectural features designed for use by older children and adults, such as steep staircases, hard flooring, and clustered bathroom facilities. Inclusive programs serving young children, especially those with fragile health and physical challenges, will certainly encounter challenges when housed in aging public school buildings already in need of renovation.

THE LEARNING ENVIRONMENT AS A COMPLEX ECOLOGY

Some experts propose that schools and classroom learning environments can be viewed as ecologies or habitats for children. With such a conceptualization, the classroom environment is seen as an interactive system of factors that can influence children's growth, behavior, and learning (Weinstein, 1979). Initial thoughts about environment usually invoke a list of all the physical features that compose the area. Certainly, features such as lighting, color, temperature, space, and density, are aspects of the environment that might have an influence on children's behavior. However, the ecology of a classroom learning environment is composed of more than physical factors. While physical variables may be very influential, physical features alone are not likely to exert an independent influence. Rather, some environmental scientists hypothesize that physical features interact with other variables, such as social factors, in an intricate interplay that sets the stage for learning to occur.

A host of variables compose the complex ecology of an inclusive classroom. These factors can be organized into three major categories of environmental features found to interact with one another:

1. Characteristics of children: personal attributes of individuals and the group
2. Physical environment: features of the classroom or playground
3. Climate of classroom: the social and organizational aspects of the classroom

Children's characteristics, attitudes, culture, and beliefs influence their reaction to the physical environment of the classroom.

Children bring personal characteristics to the learning environment that interact with other environmental features. Children's ages, gender, and other genetically inherited characteristics and traits affect their classroom interactions. Other characteristics are socially transmitted to children by family and community heritage. As a result, the culturally acquired characteristics, attitudes, and beliefs of children also influence the way they react to stimuli in the environment. The environment itself has physical features that influence learning and social interactions of children. Room size, density or crowding, overall design, light, and temperature are among the variables that create the classroom setting. The third category of variables thought to interplay in the ecology of the classroom subsume the social and organizational factors present in the environment. The management and discipline techniques a teacher employs, the rules set in place, and the routines and schedules adhered to in the classroom will interface with children's characteristics and the physical environment to influence children's behavior and learning. The curricula selected for use and the teaching practices adopted by the teacher and the school are also critical components of the overall classroom climate that compose the ecology of the classroom in which children are expected to encounter experiences for learning. The interplay of these three sets of variables can exert an impact on two key influences on children's learning. One is the attitudes children develop about learning:

- Are children curious?
- Do children want to learn?
- What is their satisfaction with the school and teacher?

The second key influence relates to how children approach learning:

- What kinds of behaviors do children develop for learning?
- Do children participate in learning activities?
- Are children engaged in the learning process long enough to be successful?

Rather than viewing the physical environment of the classroom as simply an architectural structure, teachers and other professionals who collaborate to educate children can view the inclusive classroom as a habitat for children. Although controlling all the variables in the classroom is virtually impossible, understanding the factors at play is critical to facilitate the learning of all children. Controlling some of the variables is a realistic goal and research suggests that sometimes even minor changes to the physical environment can have dramatic effects on behavior, learning, and social interactions (Gifford, 1997; Weinstein & Weinstein, 1979). Along with physical and social aspects, cultural factors are also identifiable components in the learning contexts of children (Taylor & Gousie, 1988). Recognition of the existence of cultural nuances that influence learning is an essential understanding for teachers. The transmission of culturally ordained customs, behaviors, and patterns of learning occur in classrooms and deserve recognition by teachers.

There are several implications of viewing the classroom as an ecology or learning habitat for children. Certainly if teachers understand that their physical classroom environment is an interactive system of variables as research suggests (Weinstein & Weinstein, 1979), then monitoring the classroom is also viewed differently. The classroom environment can no longer be considered as an independent system completely separate and apart from the social systems in operation within the classroom. Evaluating the interactions of systems and the effects of individual variables is necessary. Also essential is monitoring and evaluating the effects of variables on individual children. Because of the increasing diversity of children in inclusive classrooms, it is crucial to evaluate the extent of support for learning and socializing that the physical environment lends to each child, given their personal constellation of characteristics. Because some variables change daily or even from moment to moment in a classroom, remaining vigilant is important to maintain an optimal learning environment for children.

Teachers can collaborate with others to help monitor and maintain a supportive physical environment for all children. Asking parents and family members to help monitor the classroom and also their child's reaction to it can help. Letting parents know that their observations about the classroom are welcome is one strategy for involving them in the ongoing task of monitoring the physical classroom environment. Asking colleagues on the teaching team to help monitor the classroom ecology is often a good source of information. Having open communication with colleagues about environmental variables and ways to control them can provide teachers with helpful advice and tips. Offering to visit each other's classrooms from time to time to give an objective opinion is another good idea. Professionals who work with children in the inclusive classroom can also be a good source of ideas and information. An occupational therapist may view the classroom differently than a classroom teacher. Speech therapists may evaluate aspects of the room that promote language acquisition or they might be more attuned to the acoustical aspects of the classroom. Involving other professionals in monitoring the physical environment can bring new perspectives and different lenses for viewing the inclusive classroom.

The ecology of an inclusive early childhood classroom is exceedingly complex. The physical features of the classroom are sometimes reconfigured to accommodate wheelchairs and other apparatus for children with poor mobility. The social-organizational structure of the classroom must adapt to schedules of various specialists providing auxiliary services to qualifying children with special needs. The personal characteristics of children in inclusive classrooms vary, with some behavioral characteristics of children exhibited as a manifestation of a particular medical condition, disability, or syndrome. The intricate complexity of the inclusive classroom makes it even more critical for teachers to know about the variables at play and ways to plan for optimal learning environments.

Designing Child-Centered Environments

The concept of learning environments designed specifically for children is widely embraced and has relevance for inclusive classrooms. Physical environments help shape the course of children's development. Children learn about their world through observing and acting upon their physical environment (Odom & Wolery, 2003). Child-sized furniture and specially prepared materials can stimulate interest and help children develop concentration and motivation for learning. For all children, the desired outcome is to provide children with a learning context that supports concentration and promotes full engagement in tasks so that learning can occur (Rathunde, 2001). Young children develop and learn when their physical environment provides materials and toys that are contingently responsive to their play and actions (Landry, Smith, Swank, Assel, & Veliet, 2001).

Children's preferences. Keeping children's preferences in mind can result in room layouts, furnishings, and decor that are child centered and provide more inclusive environments for learning. Unmistakably, even very young children have preferences for different kinds of environmental stimuli. Children discriminate among environmental variables of their learning environment and can indicate their preferences. Cohen and Trostle (1990) examined the preferences of kindergarten and first-grade children regarding six indoor and outdoor environmental stimuli variables: size, shape, complexity, color, texture, and lighting.

These researchers found age-related and sex-related differences in the preferences of children. Results of the study suggested older children have stronger preferences for indoor and outdoor environments that have more intense lighting and bolder color schemes with features that are more varied and complex. In contrast, younger children preferred the large-sized features of environments and more subtle colors and lighting.

Role of collaboration. Collaboration is key to ensuring child-centered physical environments for inclusive classrooms. Teachers, school administrators, parents, and community members all play a role in providing safe, attractive learning environments

A well-organized classroom with comfortable furnishings motivates children to learn.

for children. Establishing good lines of communication among all stakeholders is fundamental to ensure well-designed play and learning spaces for children. All partners need to be informed and brought into discussions about what is required to create school infrastructure and maintain buildings once they are built or improved.

Administrators of inclusive programs can be influential in several ways. An important role of school principals, child-care center directors, and administrators of Head Start programs is to inform the community of the importance of healthy, safe school environments in promoting the learning and achievement of children. Administrators have an obligation to communicate to parents and the community about the costs of building and maintaining safe indoor and outdoor spaces for children. Administrators help set an example for parents and the community to follow by providing appealing and well-maintained learning environments for all children. Teachers can help administrators monitor the school environment and bring areas needing improvement to the attention of the administrator (Crampton, Thompson, & Vesely, 2004).

The places where children live and attend school can be influential far beyond childhood (Chawla, 1992). Children, especially those who are poor or those with disabilities, have less choice and access regarding the environments (Ellis, 2004).

THE CLASSROOM GEOGRAPHY MATCH

Achieving synchrony among environmental variables, children's preferences, teachers' practices, and family culture and values creates a match between the classroom geography and people in the learning environment. Making changes to optimize the learning environment of the inclusive classroom may be easier and more effective than trying to make accommodations for individual children. Environmental accommodations seem very fitting for early childhood settings in which the emphasis is on prevention of problems and early intervention to avert a fuller manifestation of serious disorders from emerging. Changes to the environment may impart benefits for all children without the need to single out individual children from the group as other interventions or services might require. Environmental restructuring may be particularly advantageous for children at risk for developmental problems who will gain benefits that might allay problems that are more serious. However, to ensure a good geographical fit between the classroom layout and children, teachers need to exercise flexibility and have a willingness to change the room arrangement (see Figure 7.1 for a sample classroom layout). Consideration for the interplay of a number of variables in the classroom ecology is also necessary.

Geography and Teaching Practices

In addition to individual characteristics, preferences, and needs of children, it is essential to bear in mind the styles of teaching and types of practices teachers will adopt and use in the inclusive classroom. Furthermore, in an inclusive classroom, it is also essential to consider the instructional styles of all professionals, including support personnel and

Figure 7.1   Planned Areas for Small Group Cooperation in an Inclusive Classroom

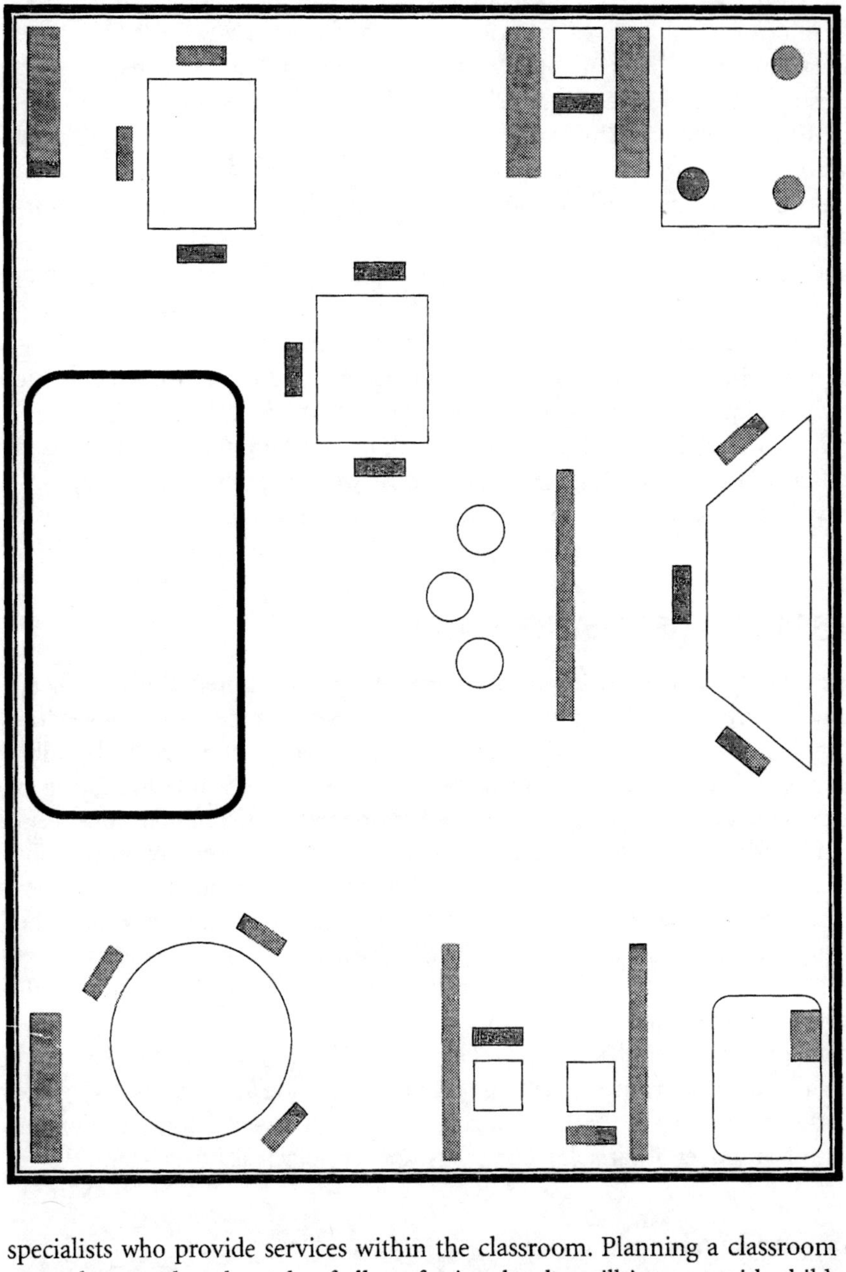

specialists who provide services within the classroom. Planning a classroom environment that matches the style of all professionals who will interact with children in the classroom will necessitate honest communication and may require compromise. Further, a geographical match can occur only when teachers are cautious in planning the restructuring of the classroom spaces to meet curricular aims and goals of the group and individual children enrolled in the inclusive classroom (Lucas & Thomas, 1990).

Classroom viewed from a distance to show small group spaces, large meeting area and individual areas.

If it is true that the geography of the classroom is most effective when matched to the teaching practices and aims of the teacher, then the converse may also be true. That is, it is conceivable that when classroom geography is ill-matched to support certain teaching practices, teachers may be discouraged from implementing these teaching practices, despite their beliefs about the benefits of these strategies for children in their inclusive classrooms. Whereas additional research may determine the truth of this statement, at least one study suggests that a disparity can exist between the kind of practices teachers believe will be beneficial to children in their inclusive classrooms and the practices that they actually implement. Even though this difference in perception and reality might be explained by a need for more training as the authors of the study suggested (Schumm, Vaughn, Gordon, & Rothlein, 1994), it also seems possible that geographical features of the classrooms will present barriers or obstacles that might hinder implementation. An examination aimed at better understanding the role of geographical features of classroom arrangements and the use of teaching practices thought to facilitate inclusion seems in order. To what extent do environmental variables and classroom layout influence the teaching practices used? Which, if any, environmental variables exert an influence on teaching practices selected by teachers? Research investigations designed to examine the nature of the interaction between the environment and teaching practices might help ascertain the true nature of the relationship between environmental variables and teaching practices.

A collaborative atmosphere among teachers, specialists, and administrators can facilitate a good match between the classroom geography and teaching practices. In the social-organizational realm of the classroom's ecology, the kind of moral support offered to teachers by their administrators is a critical factor in matching the geography of the classroom to teaching practices. Moral support from other teachers can also influence how well best practices are implemented in the classroom (Nelson, 2000). Viewing the match of teaching practices and the classroom layout from the lens of another may help teachers select arrangements more objectively. The ability to put children's needs first before the preferences of teachers may be encouraged when objective views of others are drawn into the decision-making process.

There is a dearth of research to enlighten us on the effects of selecting classroom layouts, and we have little substantiation to judge how much of the decision is based upon predilections of teachers or their interpersonal needs. However, it is possible that teacher preferences are significant influences on the choices they make as they plan their classroom environment and that some of these selections evolve from the teacher's own interpersonal needs and comfort levels. One study of preservice teachers found a relationship between teachers who had a high need for control and the environmental arrangements that placed teachers in positions of control (Feitler, Weiner, & Blumberg, 1970). If there is a tendency for teachers to choose arrangements they believe will afford more control, it could be cause for concern. Other studies suggested that when teachers provide a highly structured environment, passivity is increased, challenge is reduced, and children have few opportunities to develop critical thinking skills and independence in learning (Desouza & Sivewright, 1993; Dreeben & Gamoran, 1986; Greenwood, Delquadri, & Hall, 1984). Motivation of children to learn also appears to erode in highly structured classrooms (Deci & Ryan, 1985). Of course, all of these findings are adverse to the goals of inclusive education classrooms and are

Children have opportunities to practice cooperation in small group areas of the classroom.

BOX 7.1

detrimental to children's chances for success in school. Additional research may help to enlighten us on the effects of teacher preferences on the environmental geography of the classroom. Through further examination, it may be possible to delineate interpersonal and intrapersonal influences in the teachers' environmental decisions and to better understand to what extent the classroom environment might reflect teachers', preferences rather than children's.

Creating an inclusive room with different kinds of spaces may enable teachers and specialists to use a variety of teaching strategies and techniques effectively. Areas arranged for small groups will lend support to cooperative learning activities. An area for large-group meetings can also be used for motor development or exercise. Devoting some spaces in the classroom to individual or pair work allows for independent work, tutoring, or individual therapy sessions (see Box 7.1).

Effects of geography on children. Studies suggest that geographical layouts of classroom interiors do exert an influence on children, their behavior, and their learning. Arrangements of furniture in the classroom, the amount of space, and the location of the teacher's desk can have an impact on learning. Classrooms where children are arranged in groups are likely to have greater interaction but also a higher level of noise. If a quieter room is desired, arranging the room with designated physically separate activity areas that accommodate up to three children at a time can reduce noise levels in the classroom. When teacher's desks were located in the periphery rather than centrally located, teachers had to move throughout the room to supervise children. These rooms are reported to promote child engagement and quiet participation in tasks (Lucas & Thomas, 1990; Weinstein, 1979). When teacher interaction is distributed across the classroom, children benefit. On the other hand, when teacher-child interaction is restricted in an action zone, an area where the teacher remains much of the time, some children are likely to be excluded (Delefes & Jackson, 1972). For example, children who are deaf or hard of hearing (Saur, Popp, & Isaacs, 1984), children who are withdrawn, or those easily distracted might miss important information unless they remain within the action zone of the classroom (Lucas & Thomas, 1990).

Cultural considerations for planning of learning environments is necessary to ensure the best fit for diverse groups of children. Research is limited to enlighten teachers regarding the variables to consider and ways to match the geography of the classroom to the diversity of the classroom; however, current studies suggested that cultural variations do exist. For example, African American children have been reported to favor learning environments that afford plenty of physical activity, rather than geographical arrangements that support more sedentary learning activities (Hale, 1994).

The clear implication of action zone research is for teachers to avoid creating geographical areas in the classroom where most of the teacher-child interaction occurs. By arranging the geography of the room, teachers can encourage free movement throughout the classroom for both teachers and children. Rather than limiting themselves to a few instructional areas, teachers can self-monitor to ensure they are providing full coverage of the room for supervision purposes. Another implication for instruction is that monitoring the position of children with special needs or who have difficulty in learning in relation to the instructional activities is essential, particularly when those activities will be led by the teacher. Furthermore, when the dynamics of the class change, such as when membership of the class changes, teachers will need to reevaluate the classroom layout to ensure a good fit for newly enrolled children along with existing members of the group.

Environmental accommodations designed to match the geography of the classroom layout to children and teachers can optimize the learning opportunities for all children. A good match can mean equitable learning opportunities for all and can better ensure that children with special needs will be integrated more transparently into the inclusive classroom.

Developing Environmental Consciousness and Competence

Whereas most educators would agree that learning environments have potential to exert a positive influence on the development and learning of children, there is also the potential to inhibit or impede learning. Teachers who know little about environmental variables and their possible effects may fail to recognize potential impediments to children's learning. Their inability to mediate the learning environment and failure to control detrimental factors in the classroom can lead to a mismatch between the classroom environment and individual learners.

Some studies suggested that teachers who question their environment may eventually take steps to change their classroom. Teachers who recognize that there are qualities of the classroom they dislike, even if they have no idea how to change these features, are beginning to develop a consciousness of their surroundings. Unfortunately, environmental consciousness alone does not necessarily result in action to change the physical environment. Awareness of environmental variables is passive and an insufficient reason to transform the classroom environment. Transformation begins when teachers actively manipulate the classroom variables in an effort to improve the atmosphere for learning. However, it is rare for teachers to receive proper training to enhance their environmental consciousness and gain skills that increase their competence in arranging the learning environment to promote the comfort, welfare, and learning of young children. Moreover, few tools to help teachers evaluate their classroom spaces are currently available. Teachers need help identifying characteristics that are flexible and can be adjusted to improve the use of space in the classroom (Martin, 2002). What can teachers gain from becoming more environmentally conscious and attempting to improve the ecology of their classroom? Some authors believe teachers have positive feelings regarding their competence when they exert some level of control over their classroom environment. Successfully conquering environmental challenges in the classroom affords teachers a sense of independence and empowerment that may boost their confidence and lift their spirits (Trancik & Evans, 1995). Satisfaction with the improved classroom environment appears related to the willingness of teachers to continue their teaching career (Johnson, 1990). Further, it has been posited that beneficial effects of comfortable, well-designed classroom environments may also indirectly influence the attitudes of teachers and children and result in improved children's behavior and achievement (Lackney, 1994; Moore & Lackney, 1993).

USING CONTINUUMS TO DESIGN INCLUSIVE CLASSROOMS

A key goal of inclusive classrooms is to ensure that the learning environment accommodates the learning styles, strengths, and needs of individual children. The collaborative teaching team mediating the classroom environment is responsible for making decisions about how to provide an accommodative learning environment for the children as a group and as individuals. The team makes judgments from their different discipline perspectives about the variables and features to manipulate or change to create the best the learning environment for the children in their inclusive classroom. In fact, environmental changes are often simpler to accomplish than traditional special intervention strategies and have shown promising results (Wheldall, 1988).

BOX 7.2

PRESCOTT'S SEVEN DIMENSIONS OF CHILD-CARE ENVIRONMENTS

1. Softness/hardness
2. Open/closed
3. Simple/complex
4. Intrusion/seclusion
5. High mobility/low mobility
6. Risk/safety
7. Large Group/individual

Prescott's Dimensions

The idea of using continuums to evaluate the physical and social aspects of early childhood environments was first introduced by Elizabeth Prescott in the late 1960s. While using an ecological approach to study the quality of child-care environments, Prescott and her associates noticed the multidimensional character of child-care environments. These investigators identified seven dimensions (listed in Box 7.2) that are typically present in early childhood environments and conceptualized these dimensions as continuums (Jones, 1977; Prescott, 1984).

The work of Prescott (1984) and others has implications for contemporary inclusive education classrooms that have exceedingly complex physical and social dimensions. Continuums can be used to guide the design of the physical environment of an inclusive classroom. Moreover, continuums can be used as an effective set of tools to monitor the physical environment on a daily basis. Teachers as mediators of the physical environment can use the continuums to identify possible ways to improve or adapt the physical learning environment for individual children in their inclusive classrooms.

Added Dimensions

Winter (1999) posited that additional continuums beyond those identified by Prescott might merit consideration for teachers interested in analyzing inclusive early childhood settings. The following are four additional dimensions proposed for addition to the list of previously identified dimensions:

- Accessibility/inaccessibility
- High-sensory stimulation/low-sensory stimulation
- Predictibility/unpredictability
- Novelty/familiarity

These additional dimensions give the inclusive education team opportunities to adapt the complex early childhood ecology of the classroom to meet the diverse needs of children (Winter, 1999).

Accessibility/inaccessibility. All children benefit when the environment is sufficiently accessible to foster independence of children in play and learning activities. Children gain control over their environment and have choices of activities when they have freedom and access to the materials in their learning environment. Providing a highly accessible learning environment supports children in acquiring responsibility for their decisions (Kostelnik, Whiren, Soderman, Stein, & Gregory, 2002).

The concept of ensuring all children access is a foundational premise of inclusion. Addressing the accessibility end of this continuum reminds the inclusive education team to check the physical environment so that areas intended for children's use both indoors and outdoors are accessible to all children. It is vital to make whatever special provisions are necessary to include children with mobility challenges who might require special accommodations. Check all areas of the room to ensure that a minimum of 36 inches of space is available for maneuvering a wheelchair through the classroom. Check pathways where people walk, entrances, and exits.

Another key area to check for accessibility is learning centers, if they are used in the classroom. Avoid overfurnishing and crowding learning centers with too many items and pieces of equipment. All children, including those with mobility problems will benefit from adequate space to move and interact within all learning areas of the classroom. This is particularly true when there is a computer in the classroom. Leave enough space for two or three children to gather around the computer to play or solve problems together. When a child uses a computer as an alternative means of communicating or preparing assignments, being able to involve a peer will help keep the technological activity from isolating the child from others.

Part of the accessibility continuum can be viewed as social accessibility. Socially, teachers are key mediators of the environment who facilitate interactions by helping all children have access to interaction with peers. Further, teachers can take care to make themselves available to children. Administrators of schools and programs can help in that regard by keeping the teacher-child ratios low, so that teachers can be readily available to interact with children. Another way administrators can assist is to provide teachers with professional development opportunities so teachers can improve their skills in arranging the environment for accessibility and increasing cooperation and social interaction within the classroom.

On the other end of the continuum, we know that some areas of environments must be inaccessible to preserve the safety of children. Local health and safety codes usually dictate the kinds of materials and areas from which children's access must be restricted to protect them from harm.

High-sensory stimulation/low-sensory stimulation. Children with disabilities and special needs in inclusive classrooms may require different levels of sensory stimulation from the physical environment to optimize their skill development and learning. In addition to the traditional five senses of tactile, olfactory, gustatory, visual, and auditory, it is important to consider the proprioceptive and vestibular senses. Proprioceptive senses give children an awareness of their muscle movements, and vestibular is associated with balance and body position in space (Lynch & Simpson, 2004).

The Neurological Thresholds Behavioral Response Continuum Model (Dunn, 1997) explains the interaction of sensory processing and children's behavior and may have implications for teachers planning the sensory stimulation aspects of children's physical environments. According to this model, young children's sensory problems may range from a lack of sensitivity to overreaction or avoidance of stimuli in the environment. Teachers can observe children for patterns of behavior that develop, indicating that the child may have a neurological problem that interferes with processing sensory input from the environment. Four response patterns to environmental stimuli have been identified:

1. *Heightened sensitivity.* The child is easily distracted and overstimulated. Watch for a child who is highly reactive to stimuli in the classroom.
2. *Sensation avoidance.* The child withdraws from sources of stimulation in the classroom and avoids areas of moderate to high stimulation in favor of low stimulus areas.
3. *Sensation seeking.* The child gravitates toward sources of sensory stimulation and chooses activities that provide sensory experiences.
4. *Poor registration.* The child lacks sensitivity to stimulation and is not easily engaged in activities.

Becoming aware of these behavioral response patterns can help teachers detect sensory integration problems early, so children can receive early intervention services, if warranted. Furthermore, the presence of sensory issues in a child often has comorbidity with autism spectrum disorders. Consequently, the need to be observant and take note of specific behavior patterns as the child interfaces with the physical environment is important to consider because early detection of autism can improve the prognosis for a child with autism spectrum disorders (Dunn, Saiter, & Rinner, 2002; Strock, 2004). Further, there are implications of this research for teachers in designing the physical environment of their inclusive classrooms. Teachers can plan to provide a variety of situations in their inclusive classrooms. Some areas can provide high levels of one or more types of sensory stimulation for children who seek such stimulation or need high levels to respond, and other areas of the room can offer moderate or low levels of stimulation. Areas of the room with more privacy and less stimulation can be helpful to children needing a respite from higher levels of sensory stimulation they might experience in other areas of the physical environment.

Teachers can collaborate with specialists to create the sensory environment that best fits the children they serve. For example, seeking advice of an occupational therapist, who can lend expertise in sensory processing and integration, can recommend ways to tailor the physical environment to the individual child's pattern of response. Such accommodations will increase the likelihood that each child will receive the level of sensory stimulation they need from the physical environment of the inclusive classroom. Teaming with occupational therapists can help teachers learn to recognize sensory integration difficulties that are easily confused with problem behavior (Bakley, 2001; Lynch & Simpson, 2004). Recognizing sensory integration problems and finding ways to make the physical environment responsive to the sensory stimulation requirements of individual children enhance the success of children in an inclusive early childhood setting.

Predictability/unpredictability. Predictability can be an advantage for inclusive environments serving young children. An environment that is predictable can help young children feel secure while they gain independence through successful interaction with the indoor classroom and outdoor playground environments. Young children adjust more easily to changes in their environments when any variation is introduced gradually (Kostelnik et al., 2002; Marion, 2003).

Adjusting the degree of predictability of the physical environment and the features that compose the classroom space can be critical to inclusion of certain children with specific disabilities. For example, children who are blind or visually impaired require a more stable and predictable physical environment, both indoors and outside. Ensuring clear pathways that make traversing the classroom and playgrounds more certain can help children with visual impairments gain a sense of independence and security in their surroundings. Children with autism spectrum disorders will also feel more secure and may function better in environmental spaces that afford predictable spaces (Deiner, 1999).

Novelty/familiarity. Creating a balance between novel features in the physical environment and those that are more familiar is critical to the success of an inclusive classroom. Familiarity can be achieved by collaborating with families and neighborhood residents. Ask community members and parents to help collect artifacts, suggest colors, and provide materials that reflect the cultural heritage of children represented in the diverse membership of the inclusive classroom. These familiar features in the physical environment help children feel a sense of belonging and comfort in school. Families may provide photos or other items that personalize the surroundings for each child (Derman-Sparks & ABC Task Force, 1989; Winter, Bell, & Dempsey, 1994; York, 1992).

Facilitating and maintaining engagement of children in tasks that will enhance their learning are vital goals for teachers in inclusive classrooms (Odom & Wolery, 2003). Increasing the novelty of materials available in the classroom can peak children's curiosity and increase their motivation to learn. Teachers can introduce novelty simply by changing materials in centers periodically. Introducing new materials as new themes or units of study are introduced is a natural way to renew the environment with novel items. Novelty can also be added to social aspects of the classroom ecology. Visitors can be invited to the classroom to add new perspectives. Moreover, media and technology offer many ways for children to experience different people and cultures (Lynch & Simpson, 2004; Seefeldt, 1997; Winter, 1994/95).

Flexible/Fixed

A last continuum that is suggested for learning environments is composed of permanent features and objects that are static or fixed aspects of the space. Our perception of the environment and objects in it is influenced by our experience, interaction, and the focus of our attention (von Glasersfeld, 1996). The physical learning environment also has flexible and dynamic components that are more easily changed to accommodate special needs of individual children. When the inclusive classroom and outdoor spaces have features that allow for flexibility, it requires less effort to enact changes for individual children. Characteristics that afford flexibility enable teachers to make adjustments and adaptations as needed or to accommodate new children as the classroom membership changes, a common occurrence in neighborhoods characterized by high mobility among families.

SUMMARY

This chapter explained the importance of the physical environment in inclusive classroom environments. The classroom environment was explained as an ecology of physical and social factors that can influence learning. These variables also interface with characteristics of teachers and learners. The reader was alerted to the constellation of variables that can exert an impact on teachers and children. The geography of the classroom influences learning and behavior in the inclusive early childhood classroom. Ideas were presented for teachers to adjust and adapt the physical learning environment to optimize the classroom for individual children.

Discussion Questions

1. Explain how the physical aspects of learning environments are critical factors in influencing learning in inclusive classrooms.
2. Discuss how to use continuums to plan for optimal learning environments for children.
3. How does classroom layout or geography affect learning and teaching practices?
4. Describe ways families can be involved in planning the learning environment.
5. Discuss collaboration of teachers with other specialists to plan the learning environment.

Inclusive Activities

1. Visit an inclusive classroom and use Prescott's dimensions to evaluate the physical environment. Next, evaluate the environment using the added dimensions: accessibility/inaccessibility, high-sensory stimulation/low-sensory stimulation, predictibility/unpredictability, novelty/familiarity.

2. Visit several inclusive early childhood classrooms and draw sketches of the geography of the classroom space. Decide what you believe are the best ideas and draw an ideal classroom geography. Justify your design based upon the research presented in the chapter.

3. Visit an inclusive early childhood classroom and evaluate the use of wall space. How could you improve wall use? Is the environment personalized for the children in the classroom?

References

Altman, I., & Wohlwill, J. F. (1978). *Children and the environment.* New York: Plenum.

Bakley, S. (2001). Through the lens of sensory integration: A different way of analyzing challenging behavior. *Young Children, 56*(6), 70–76.

Bamford, S. (1844). *Passages in the life of a radical.* London: London Simpkin Marshall.

Berner, M. M. (1993). Building conditions, parental involvement, and student achievement in the District of Columbia public school system. *Urban Education, 28,* 6–29.

Blau, D., & Mocan, H. (2002). The supply of quality in child-care centers. *The Review of Economics and Statistics, 84,* 483–496.

Boyd, W. L. (Ed.). (1962). *Translation: Emile; or, education by Jean-Jacques Rousseau.* New York: Teachers College Press by arrangement with Heinemann of London.

Boyer, E. L. (1991). *Ready to learn: A mandate or the nation.* Princeton, NJ: The Carnegie Foundation for the Advancement of Teaching.

Brauner, J., Gordic, B., & Zigler, E. (2004). Putting child back into child care: Combining care and education for children Ages 3–5. *Social Policy Report, 18*(3), 3–15.

Chawla, L. (1992). Childhood place attachments. In I. Altman & S. M. Low (Eds.), *Place attachment (Human behavior and environment: Advances in research and theory Vol. 12)* (pp. 63–86). New York: Plenum Press.

Cohen, S. & Trostle, S. L. (1990). Young children's preferences for school-related physical-environmental setting characteristics. *Environment and Behavior, 22*(6), 753–766.

Crampton, F. E., Thompson, D. C., & Vesely, R. S. (2004). The forgotten side of school finance equity: The role of infrastructure funding in student success. *NASSP Bulletin, 88*(640), 29–56.

Deci, E. L., & Ryan, R. M. (1985). *Intrinsic motivation and self-determination in human behavior.* New York: Plenum Press.

DeGuimps, R. (1890). *Pestalozzi: His life and work.* New York: Appleton.

Deiner, P. (1999). *Resources for educating children with diverse abilities* (3rd ed.). Fort Worth, TX: Harcourt Brace.

Delefes, P., & Jackson, B. (1972). Teacher-pupil interaction as a function of location in the classroom. *Psychology in Schools, 9,* 119–123.

Derman-Sparks, L., & ABC Task Force. (1989). *Antibias curriculum: Tools for empowering young children.* Washington, DC: National Association for the Education of Young Children.

Desouza, E. R., & Sivewright, D. (1993). An ecological approach to evaluating a special education program. *Adolescence, 28*(111), 517–525.

Dreeben, R., & Gamoran, A. (1986). Race, instruction, and learning. *American Sociological Review, 51,* 660–669.

Dunn, W. (1997). The impact of sensory processing abilities on the daily lives of young children and their families: A conceptual model. *Infants and Young Children, 9*(4), 23–35.

Dunn, W., Saiter, J., & Rinner, L. (2002). Asperger syndrome and sensory processing: A conceptual model and guidance for intervention. *Focus on Autism and Other Developmental Disabilities, 17*(3), 172–185.

Dyck, J. A. (2002). The built environment's effect on learning: Applying current research. *Montessori Life, 14*(1), 53–56.

Ellis, J. (2002). The importance of attending to children and place. *International Journal of Educational Policy, Research, and Practice, 3*(3), 69–88.

Ellis, J. (2004). Researching children's place and space. *JCT, 20*(1), 83–99.

Feitler, F. C., Weiner, W., & Blumberg, A. (1970). *The relationship between interpersonal relations orientations and preferred classroom physical settings.* Paper presented at the American Research Association, Minneapolis.

Fujiura, G. T., & Yamaki, K. (2000). Trends in demography of childhood poverty and disability. *Exceptional Children, 66*(2), 187–199.

George, A. E. (Ed.). (1967). *Translation: The Montessori method by Maria Montessori.* Cambridge, MA: Bentley.

Gifford, R. (1997). *Environmental psychology: Principles and practice* (2nd ed.). Boston: Allyn & Bacon.

Greenwood, C., & Carta, J. (1987). An ecobehavioral interaction analysis of instruction within special education. *Focus on Exceptional Children, 19,* 1–12.

Greenwood, C. R., Delquadri, J. C., & Hall, R. V. (1984). Opportunity to respond and student academic performance. In W. L. Heward, T. E. Heron, J. Trap-Porter, & D. S. Hill (Eds.), *Focus on behavior analysis in education.* Columbus, OH: Merrill.

Hale, J. E. (1994). *Unbank the fire: Visions for the education of African-American children.* Baltimore: Johns Hopkins Press.

Hansen, S. J. (1993). The schools children are forced to attend. *The Journal of School Business Management, 5*(4), 30–36.

Harter, E. A. (1999). How educational expenditures relate to student achievement: Insights from Texas elementary schools. *Journal of Education Finance, 24,* 281–302.

Hayes, M. L. (1986). Resource room: Space and concepts. *Academic Therapy, 21*(4), 453–464.

Heller, K. (1990). Social and community intervention. *Annual Review of Psychology, 41,* 141–168.

Horm, D. M. (2003). Preparing early childhood educators to work in diverse urban settings. *Teachers College Record, 105*(2), 226–244.

Johnson, S. M. (1990). *Teachers at work: Achieving success in our schools.* New York: Basic Books.

Jones, E. J. (1977). *Dimensions of teaching-learning environments: Handbook for teachers.* Pasadena, CA: Pacific Oaks College.

Katz, L. G., & Chard, S. C. (1989). *Engaging children's minds: The project approach.* Norwood, NJ: Ablex.

Keating, M. W. (Ed.). (1967). *Translation: The Great Didactic of John Amos Comenius by John Amos Comenius.* New York: Russell & Russell.

Kostelnik, M. J., Whiren, A. P., Soderman, A. K., Stein, L. C., & Gregory, K. (2002). *Guiding children's social development: Theory to practice* (4th ed.). Albany, NY: Delmar Thomson Learning.

Lackney, J. (1994). *Educational facilities: The impact and role of the physical environment of the school on teaching, learning and educational outcomes.* Milwaukee, WI: University of Wisconsin-Milwaukee.

Landry, S. H., Smith, K. E., Swank, P. R., Assel, M. A., & Veliet, S. (2001). Does early responsive parenting have a special importance for children's development or is consistency across early childhood necessary? *Developmental Psychology, 37,* 387–403.

Lucas, D., & Thomas, G. (1990). The "geography" of classroom learning. *British Journal of Special Education, 17*(1), 31–34.

Lynch, S. A., & Simpson, C. G. (2004). Sensory Processing: Meeting individual needs using the seven senses. *Teaching Exceptional Children, 7*(4), 2–9.

Magnuson, K. A., Meyers, M. K., Ruhm, C. J., & Waldfogel, J. (2004). Inequality in preschool education and school readiness. *American Educational Research Journal, 41*(1), 115–157.

Marion, M. (2003). *Guidance of young children* (6th ed.). Upper Saddle River, NJ: Merrill/Prentice Hall.

Martin, S. H. (2002). The classroom environment and its effects on the practice of teachers. *Journal of Environmental Psychology, 22,* 139–156.

Moore, G., & Lackney, J. (1993). School design: Crisis, educational performance and design applications. *Children's Environments, 10*(2), 99–112.

Nelson, R. F. (2000). Personal and environmental factors that influence early childhood teachers' practices. *Journal of Instructional Psychology, 27*(2), 95–103.

NICHD Early Child Care Research Network. (1999). Child outcomes when child care center classes meet recommended standards for quality. *American Journal of Public Health, 89,* 1072–1077.

Nidditch, P. H. (Ed.). (1975). *Translation: An essay concerning human understanding by John Locke.* Oxford: Oxford University Press.

Odom, S. L., & Wolery, M. (2003). A unified theory of practice in early intervention/early childhood special education: Evidence-based practices. *The Journal of Special Education, 37*(3), 164–173.

Piaget, J. (1952). *The origins of intelligence in children.* New York, NY: International Universities Press.

Piaget, J. (1962). *Play, dreams and imitation in childhood.* New York: Norton.

Piccigallo, P. R. (1989). Renovating urban schools is fundamental to improving them. *Phi Delta Kappan, 70,* 402–406.

Prescott, E. (1984). The physical setting in day care. In J. Greenman & R. Fuqua (Eds.), *Making day care better: Training, evaluation, and the process of change.* New York: Teachers College Press.

Rathunde, K. (2001). Montessori educational optimal experience: A framework for new research. *NAMTA Journal, 26*(1), 10–43.

Richarz, S. (1993). Innovations in early childhood education: Models that support the integration of children of varied developmental levels. In C. Peck,

S. Odom & D. Bricker (Eds.), *Integrating young children with disabilities into community programs: Ecological perspectives on research and implementation* (pp. 83–107). Baltimore: Paul H. Brookes.

Safford, P. L. (1989). *Integrated teaching in early childhood: starting in the mainstream.* White Plains, NY: Longman.

Saur, R. E., Popp, M. J., & Isaacs, M. (1984). Action zone theory and the hearing impaired student in the mainstreamed classroom. *Journal of Classroom Interaction, 19*(2), 21–25.

Schloss, P. J., & Smith, M. A. (1994). *Applied behavior analysis in the classroom.* Boston: Allyn & Bacon.

Schumm, J. S., Vaughn, S., Gordon, J., & Rothlein, L. (1994). General education teachers' beliefs, skills, and practices in planning for mainstreamed students with learning disabilities. *Teacher Education and Special Education, 17*(1), 22–34.

Seefeldt, C. (1997). *Social studies for the preschool-primary child* (5th ed.). Upper Saddle River, NJ: Merrill/Prentice Hall.

Strock, M. (2004). *Autism spectrum disorders (Pervasive Developmental Disorders)* [No. NIH Publication No. NIH-04–5511]. Bethesda, MD: National Institute of Mental Health, U.S. Department of Health and Human Services.

Taylor, A., & Gousie, G. (1988). The ecology of learning environment for children. *Educational Facility Planner, 26*(4), 23–28.

Trancik, A. M., & Evans, G. W. (1995). Spaces fit for children: Competency in the design of daycare center environments. *Children's Environments, 12,* 311–319.

von Glasersfeld, E. (1996). Introduction: Aspects of constructivism. In C. T. Fosnot (Ed.), *Constructivism: Theory, perspectives, and practice.* New York: Teachers College Press.

Vygotsky, L. (1978). *Mind in society: The development of higher psychological functions.* Cambridge, MA: Harvard University Press.

Vygotsky, L. (1986). *Thought and language.* Cambridge, MA: MIT Press.

Wang, M. C., Reynolds, M. C., & Walberg, H. J. (1994/1995). Serving students at the margins. *Educational Leadership, 52*(4), 12–16.

Weinstein, C. S. (1979). The physical environment of the school: A review of the research. *Review of Educational Research, 49*(4), 577–610.

Weinstein, C. S., & Weinstein, N. D. (1979). Noise and reading performance in an open space school. *Journal of Educational Research, 72,* 210–213.

Wheldall, K. (1988). The forgotten A in behaviour analysis: The importance of ecological variables in classroom management with particular reference to seating arrangements. In G. Thomas & A. Feiler (Eds.), *Planning for special needs.* Oxford: Blackwell.

Widerstrom, A. H. (1986). Educating young handicapped children: What can early childhood education contribute? *Childhood Education, 63*(2), 78–83.

Winter, S. M. (1994/95). Diversity: A program for all children. *Childhood Education, 71*(2), 91–95.

Winter, S. M. (1999). *The early childhood inclusion model: A program for all children.* Olney, MD: Association for Childhood Education International.

Winter, S. M., Bell, M., & Dempsey, J. (1994). Creating play environments for children with special needs. *Childhood Education, 71*(1), 28–32.

Wright, C., Diener, M., & Kay, S. C. (2000). School readiness of low-income children at risk for school failure. *Journal of Children & Poverty, 6*(2), 99–117.

York, S. (1992). *Developing roots and wings.* St. Paul, MN: Redleaf Press.

Chapter 8

Managing, Guiding, and Organizing the Classroom

Key Principle

- Provide safe, challenging learning environments

Objectives

After reading this chapter, you will be able to:

1. Plan a schedule with flexible blocks of time and few transitions.
2. Describe various coteaching relationships and how teachers articulate their roles.
3. Discuss ways to collaborate with specialists to structure the classroom for inclusion.
4. Understand the impact that classroom organization has on children's learning.
5. Plan an organizational scheme for children with disabilities in inclusive classrooms.

Manage	■	Guide	■	Organize	
Organizing Curricular Activities			Time Schedules		
		Organizing Equipment and Materials			
Guide Transitions			Manage Environment		
Planning for Accessibility				Use of Learning Centers	

INTRODUCTION

The complexity of inclusive early childhood environments requires serious attention to managing and organizing the physical space, time, and routines of the classroom. Inclusive early childhood classrooms are busy places. Teachers and related service professionals, as well as parents, may make several interchanges during the day. It is important for children to know the routines and feel comfortable with the time-frames established. Teachers must plan with all the stakeholders, especially parents and families, to ensure the child has a well-organized daily routine. Spaces in the classrooms are carefully planned, and accessibility of all materials needed for learning must be assured to every child.

COLLABORATIVE MANAGEMENT STRATEGIES

The responsibility for managing, guiding, and organizing an inclusive early childhood classroom demands collaboration among professionals. A key ingredient is to build cohesion among all the teachers and professionals involved. Good working relationships among team members is fundamental to the smooth running of an inclusive classroom. Research on forming those relationships and maintaining good relations among team members is relatively sparse. Yet, most experts contend that roles and relationships are foundational to success in managing the inclusive classroom.

Articulation of Roles and Responsibilities

One of the initial decisions that must be made is whether specialists, such as the special education teacher, speech therapist, or behavioral interventionist, will coteach in the classroom or pull children out of the classroom for short spans to provide services. The preferred arrangement is coteaching, a relationship thought most conducive to children's social and academic inclusion and consistent with the philosophy of inclusion overall. However, coteaching situations require carefully coordinated disposition of instructional and organizational responsibilities. The teaching team must articulate roles that are comfortable for them and decide how to meet the instructional needs of children (Weiss & Lloyd, 2003).

Flexibility of roles. Flexibility is recommended so that the focus is on the roles and responsibilities providing proper support for children's learning and good management of the classroom. Roles that are too well-defined may confine teaching and allow for

Articulating roles and responsibilities is critical to effective collaboration.

little flexibility. Consequently, inflexibility may be just as inefficient as the lack of good relationships and organization. Unfortunately, flexibility may be difficult once the school year has begun. General education teachers tend to establish routines for classroom management and instruction within the first month of the school year, and these routines tend to persist (Fuchs, Fuchs, Hamlett, Phillips, & Karns, 1995). Any changes that need to be made to accommodate children with special needs or preferences of coteaching inclusive education partnerships may need to be discussed at the beginning of the year before rules and routines are institutionalized (Fuchs et al., 1995; Weiss & Lloyd, 2003). On the positive side, teachers of younger children may be more flexible and willing to collaborate to meet the diverse needs of children. Elementary teachers have been more willing to collaborate with special education teachers to accommodate children with special needs compared to teachers of older students (Schumm et al., 1995).

There are many options for interactions between coteachers; however, specifying the nature of the role can save time and help the classroom activities to progress efficiently during the daily schedule. Teachers must plan which activities necessitate one teacher in a primary leadership, with the other teacher serving an ancillary role. Teachers in the latter role can accomplish important responsibilities, such as observing children for assessment data and offering individually appropriate support to children as they participate. Another arrangement is for teachers to assume parallel roles with children split into different groups formed for specific purposes. The advantage of this arrangement is that cooperative learning groups can explore along complementary lines that are differentiated to match their interests. Differentiation is based upon the curriculum and children's interests rather than ability (Vaughn, Schumm, & Arguelles, 1997; Weiss & Lloyd, 2003).

Although many different teaching arrangements have been reported to be successful, understanding roles and coordination of efforts is considered critical. True professional collaboration can result in more effective inclusion and increased efficiency. However, when teachers are in conflict over ownership of roles and responsibilities, lack of partnership is detrimental to children's learning and the social emotional atmosphere of the classroom. Building a partnership between teachers takes a commitment of time, effort, and administrative support. Professional development aimed at acquisition of a common set of teaching strategies that are a good match for both teachers may help solidify a coteaching partnership. Administrative support is needed to allow for extra time for coteachers to plan, reflect on their roles, and share insights about children's progress (Cook & Friend, 1998).

ORGANIZING CURRICULAR ACTIVITIES

Organization Influences Learning

Research indicates that a variety of factors influence children's performance in school. A child's capacity and motivation to learn are influential. Family variables, such as socioeconomic status and the stimulation provided in the children's home, are related to school readiness and success. However, the teacher's classroom management also has a bearing on school success. Studies suggest that the effects of classroom management on children's achievement in school and metacognitive skills are also robust (Wang, 1993). Consequently, the ability to manage and organize an inclusive early childhood classroom is an essential skill for teachers. Keeping physical space organized, managing activities, and maintaining order are demanding tasks, given the complex ecology of most inclusive early childhood classrooms.

Good management promotes inclusion. In early childhood classrooms, children learn through experiences planned to help children acquire concepts and skills. It is a social learning environment where children engage in learning processes together. Several studies suggested that the organizational structure that teachers bring to learning experiences provided in classrooms can exert an influence on the degree of participation that children with disabilities are able to achieve with their peers.

Organizing for children with disabilities. Managing and organizing an inclusive early childhood classroom serving children with disabilities may necessitate additional training. Collaborating with a special education teacher who is familiar with ways to manage and organize classrooms to support use of specific teaching practices and techniques is often effective. Special education teachers receive training in specialized instruction needed to promote learning for specific children with disabilities. Whereas the efficacy of certain strategies have been established, implementing these validated strategies in real classrooms requires adherence to standards and conditions similar to those used in the efficacy studies for the specific strategy. Otherwise, positive results achieved in the efficacy studies on the strategy are not guaranteed. Further, some types of instruction require teachers to organize their materials and instructional space in advance of the activity so that children will gain the most benefit from the instruction. For example, when discrete trial training was used in inclusive classrooms, teachers reported the need to plan and organize to ensure positive results (McBride & Schwartz, 2003).

Culturally competent management. Cultural and linguistic diversity is on the rise, with over one third of school-aged children representing minority status (National Center for Educational Statistics, 1996). Increased diversity presents new challenges to teachers when deciding how to manage the classroom. Cultural differences influence how to organize activities, set limits, and communicate expectations to children. Even though cultural diversity is on the rise in classrooms, there are a number of challenges to ensuring that teachers will use culturally sensitive management techniques. A serious challenge is the lack of valid information to guide teachers in providing culturally competent management of their classroom. Many of the topics surrounding organization and management of the diverse classroom have garnered little or no attention from research investigators. Consequently, empirical study is limited in certain topics, such as organizing the physical environment, defining standards for participation, and communicating expectations to children and their families from a culturally sensitive perspective (Weinstein et al., 2004).

Lack of an empirical base has kept educators from describing the practices teachers will need to acquire and use. Moreover, educators have had difficulty in arriving at universally agreed upon definitions for "cultural competence" and "culturally responsive classroom management." The lack of a research base for management pedagogy and the

Guiding in culturally acceptable ways and considering organization for children with disabilities facilitates inclusion of all children.

lack of a definition for identifying culturally responsive classroom management are problems for teacher educators charged with preparing teachers to effectively manage their inclusive classrooms (Obegi & Ritblatt, 2005; Powell, McLaughlin, Savage, & Zehm, 2001; Weinstein et al., 2004). Teachers and the teacher educators who prepare them are generally not minority group members. Furthermore, school cultures and management routines are usually representative of the White majority culture, and as a result, the usual style of classroom management is not culturally neutral. Rather, most children of minority families are asked to fit into management systems that represent White, middle-class cultures with monolingual, English-speaking teachers (Bowers & Flinders, 1990; Howard, 1999; Ladson-Billings, 2001). The implication is that teachers who wish to include all children will need to carefully evaluate their preferred management routines and methods to ensure a good fit for all children and families they serve. Strong lines of communication are essential for matching the management strategies and classroom structure to the expectations and customs of families.

Communicating Rules and Procedures for Activities

Teachers are most effective in managing their inclusive early childhood classrooms when they formulate rules and procedures for the classroom that consider the rules and procedures that families with diverse backgrounds follow with their children at home. Creating continuity between home and school makes it easier to communicate to families and allows for a better understanding from the parents. Teachers need family cooperation to enact policies for attendance, completion of homework, and punctuality to school or parent meetings. Teachers will also be more successful in implementing school policies regarding acceptable behavior and discipline when there is agreement between home and school. A method called mutual accommodation has been suggested as a management procedure to adapt to individual children and foster collaboration with parents and families. Mutual accommodation is a process whereby teachers both accept a child and the family's culture and, simultaneously, build upon their beliefs and customs. Introducing routines and management structure of the classroom and school equips children for success in the culture of the school (Nieto, 2000). Boxes 8.1 and 8.2 contain suggested collaboration tips.

It is also important to communicate with classroom assistants and volunteers. When teachers articulate the rules and procedures for operation in the classroom with all instructional assistants and others, children are provided with a more consistent

COLLABORATION TIPS*   BOX 8.1

Parent Orientation Packet

1. Transportation form—please return BEFORE you leave. Thank you.
2. Always make sure to sign in at the office before coming to the classroom—for your child's safety!
3. Daily schedule (attached)
4. Library day—every Wednesday from 1:25–1:40 PM. Please remember to send back the library book so your child can check out a new one!
5. Computer day—every Tuesday from 1:30 PM–2:15 PM.
6. Book orders
7. Tardies . . . if you come in late, stop by the office and pick up a tardy slip.
8. Snacks—We have snacks after our specials. There is a new list of snacks we can and cannot have (new state law). Please make sure to look over the list—sent home in the PTA packet.
9. Student of the week—After Labor Day, we will begin to have a student of the week. I will send home a questionnaire that you can help him or her fill out, and I'll write the information on a poster.
10. Discipline management—Class rules were included in the letter I sent home on the first day of school, as well as when you registered your child for kindergarten (Responsibility section of folder and 10 charts).
11. Cafeteria—send lunch money in an envelope with your child's name and teacher written on it.
12. REMEMBER to always send a note with your child when he or she has been absent. These will be kept in our room, but the office will ask for them if your child has a lot of absences or tardies.

* See Appendix C for the full text.

COLLABORATION TIPS   BOX 8.2

To learn about home culture and management routines, try asking families questions about the following topics:

- Family. Who are the family members living in your home? Does your child have contact with extended family members? How long has the family lived in this country?

- Education. How does your child learn best? How do children learn in your home country? How would you describe the teacher's role?

- Discipline. What rules do you have for your child at home? What do you do when a child does not follow the rules?

- Time and scheduling. What tasks is your child responsible for completing at home? How long does finishing a task usually take? Is your child told when you expected the job to be completed?

- Food and health. What are your child's favorite foods? Are there foods your child may not eat? Who takes care of your family when they are ill?

Adapted from Weinstein, Tomlinson-Clarke, & Curran, 2004, p. 30–31.

Integrating therapy into daily routines provides multiple opportunities for improvement.

learning environment. The behaviors expected from children are clear and fewer interruptions occur. Box 8.3 is an example of one teacher's handout to her assistants. Super-
vising the interaction of assistants with children in the classroom was easier once
expectations were clearly articulated to the instructional assistants. Box 8.4 contains
instructional notes and a schedule for the teacher's substitute.

Integrating Therapy into the Curriculum

Provisions of IDEA enable specialists, such as occupational therapists, physical therapists, and speech pathologists, to provide services to eligible children in school. Part B
provisions allow these related specialists to provide services to preschoolers in natural

COLLABORATION WITH ASSISTANTS   BOX 8.3

Circle Time

Purpose: Developing prereading and phonemic awareness skills
through: rhyming, singing, poems, counting, and reading

What children should be doing: Actively engaged in music, movement, singing, and
answering/asking questions, and helping to read books.

Adults should: Facilitate learning by modeling the desired behavior and be fully
engaged in the activities. Adults should engage children in discussions that promote
further reflection and deeper understanding of the concepts and skills being taught.

Teacher/Staff-Directed Extension Activities

Purpose: To extend specific lessons and continue to facilitate a deeper understanding of concepts in pre-academic areas.

Children should: Be given the opportunity to discuss what they are doing and
hopefully how it is related to what is being studied.

Adults should: Be focused on the children and give clear short step directions.
Adults should engage children in discussions that promote further reflection and
deeper understanding of the concepts and skills being taught.

Free Choice Centers

Purpose: To allow children the opportunity to learn through play and the interaction with peers. This child-directed activity helps promote the use of language, pre-
academic, and social skills.

Children should: Be visiting centers and interacting with their peers, while following class rules.

Adults should: Visit centers with children and model desired behavior, as well as
engage children in discussions that promote further reflection and deeper understanding of the concepts and skills being taught. Adults should also remind students to clean up before moving on to another center.

---

*SUBSTITUTE NOTES: MS. SMITH'S KINDERGARTEN**   BOX 8.4

I usually have the things we are doing for the week in the Monday-Friday folders in the hanging files by my desk. Also, see lesson plans on my computer table.

Behavior Management

Students get their individual clips moved up—if you catch student doing a good job—or groups for whole groups doing a good job. If they get to 10, they pick a prize from prize box (just write down who did and I'll take care of it when I come back). A stamp is received in folder for appropriate behavior. If behavior was not appropriate, write what child did in the space and NO stamp!

7:40–8:15	Pick up my class from the cafeteria. Students know to walk quietly in the halls. Once in the room, students hang up backpacks and put folders on my computer desk tray. Then they sit quietly on the carpet until after the announcements.
	After announcements—check students' folders for notes, etc., then take attendance and lunch count. I usually have students raise their hands if they brought a lunch. Jane eats alternate choice on Wednesday and Thursday due to diet restrictions.
	CALENDAR—use CD labeled morning routine—#4 and #5 songs (months of year, days of week). Then say today's date and add number. Ask students: "Today is ___. What was yesterday? Today is ___. What will tomorrow be?" Then count the dates on calendar (if today is the 10th, you count to 10). Change over the number on the 100 chart and count how many days we have been in school so far. Count to 100. MORNING MESSAGE: Write on chart in on front table: Dear Class, Today is . . . Ms. Smith is not here today. My name is . . .
8:15–8:55	MATH—Put math manipulatives on the tables and the students can have choice time—they can go to the table they want and "play/manipulate" with them.
8:55–10:15	PREDICTABLE CHART—Day 1 and 2 is writing out the students' sentences on chart paper—see examples hung in room. I emphasize capital letter at beginning, period at end, and ask students to help me sound out the words. Check my plans for starter. Days 3–5: since I am not here, the students may just come up one at a time to read their sentences. Make sure they point to correct words (you may have to read sentences first, before student reads.

* See Appendix C for the full text.

---

settings, such as homes and child-care centers. Integrating therapeutic interventions into the daily routines of home, child care, and school contexts offers the advantage of making a difference on a daily basis for children. Specialists can help to make each context the child experiences more meaningful and can also help children with disabilities improve their functioning within the settings that influence their development and learning. There are a number of advantages for integrating therapy into the curriculum of the inclusive classroom. Specialists can embed intervention strategies into activities and daily routines of children, making differences among children less apparent. Integration of therapy affords a chance for coaching teachers and parents, so that follow-up and generalization of therapy into the natural settings experiences is more likely to occur. Working in these natural settings, specialists can better determine whether interventions are culturally relevant. Flexibility may be necessary so that adjustments can be made, accordingly, to achieve a better match between the cultural values of home and school. Collaboration of specialists with teachers and parents can result in responsive treatment of children and improved communication between home and school contexts. In terms of classroom management, specialists will consider schedules of the classroom routines, size, and composition of the group of children to ensure smooth integration of therapy into the usual routines (Hanft & Anzalone, 2001).

TIME MANAGEMENT AND SCHEDULING

Efficient Use of Time

Typical classrooms use 50% or less of the time children attend in a usual school day for instructional purposes; yet, time dedicated to learning activities is closely associated with children's achievement and performance (Evertson & Harris, 1992). It is critical to maximize every minute of time available in the inclusive classroom, especially since it is very time-consuming to meet the learning needs of each child. Children with developmental disabilities often require extra time to complete tasks or learn a concept or

Scheduling offers predictability and planning large, flexible blocks of time for activities ensures sufficient time for children to learn.

LESSON PLAN EXAMPLE					**BOX 8.5**
Jenny Smith Lesson Plans Week of: 2/2-6 Weekly Theme: Dental Health/Healthy Me					
Objectives: see TEKs		PPCD	Café	PPCD	Kinder
	7:30–7:35	7:40–7:50	7:55–8:25	8:25–8:55	9:00–10:15
Monday	Get off bus Unpack Get folder out	Pledge Announce. Line up Bathroom	Breakfast	Math: Rote counting & number recog. (CLASS Testing)	Phonemic Awareness/Letter Intro letter D Mr. D; letter tub, song Big book work jobs: Writing: Trace/glue dots on D like, beads and tweezer, lite brite
Tuesday	Get off bus Unpack Get folder out	Pledge Announce. Line up Bathroom	Breakfast	Speech	Phonemic Awareness/Letter Magic book: write letter D review d work jobs: Letter: cut & paste D, sandwich letter, magnet letters, etc.
Wednesday	Get off bus Unpack Get folder out	Pledge Announce. Line up Bathroom	Breakfast	Nurse comes to talk to kids about brushing teeth	Phonemic Awareness/Letter Popcorn words Letter song work jobs: Math: sort bad/good foods

skill. Further, some children may require more supervision or facilitation by teachers and their assistants. Children who are gifted may also need more time to complete activities that provide them with sufficient challenge to stimulate their learning (Freiberg & Driscoll, 1996). Box 8.5 shows a time-scheduled lesson plan example.

Establishing a Schedule with Flexible Blocks of Time

Large blocks of time are critical to offer ample opportunity for children to become fully engaged in learning tasks and maintain their efforts for sufficient time to result in success. Further, blocks of flexible time allow teachers more time for rich interactions with children, to guide and facilitate learning of individuals. Children of minority backgrounds who live in impoverished households may be further disadvantaged when schedules fail to allow adequate time to promote proper engagement and interaction, which are critical to the learning process (Espinosa & Laffey, 2003).

Scheduling the day into flexible blocks of time allows the teacher to be flexible in meeting the needs of individual children, as well as the group. If a child needs a few extra minutes to finish a task, a large block of time makes it easier to accommodate the time requirements of individual children. Teachers can break the day into manageable time frames and establish meaningful routines. With large, flexible blocks of time, children can learn to pace their own activities and begin to develop a concept of time. Children gain in independent learning skills when they learn to use their time efficiently. Teachers can help children learn to intersperse active periods with more restful times to prevent overstimulation or exhaustion, conditions that can aggravate behavioral problems (Gareau & Kennedy, 1991; Hendrick, 1998).

Flexible block scheduling allows for child-initiated activities so that children can follow their own curiosity. Children have the opportunity for play that is rich, and they can end their play or activities at a natural conclusion (Christie & Wardle, 1992; Frost, 1992; Frost, Wortham, & Reifel, 2001). Urging children to complete tasks may actually extend the time needed due to the distraction that the urging creates. Further, rushing children may

---

SCHEDULE   BOX 8.6
Preschool Program Daily Schedule

7:30–7:50	Bus arrival/Unpack/organize/bathroom
7:55–8:25	Breakfast **(teacher's planning)**
8:30–8:55	Goal-related activities or related services
*9:00–10:15	Kinder inclusion (letters/phonemic awareness and work job activities)bathroom
*10:15–10:30	Recess
10:37–11:07	Lunch
11:15–12:40	Social skills lesson; Circle time (ABC's counting, calendar, weather, morning message, etc.); Centers including: math, extension activities (fine motor, IEP goal-related, computers, etc.). Free centers.
12:40–1:00	Rest time: students self-selected reading, soft music
12:10–1:00	**Teacher's planning/conference period/lunch**
*1:00–2:00	Kinder Inclusion: STAR book, Free centers
2:00–2:15	Snack/Clean-up; pack-up/Dismissal—take students to parent for pick-up or to bus

* Inclusion times with kindergarten class in room #4.

Motor Lab	Speech	Bilingual Speech	OT/PT
Fridays	Tues./Thurs.	Tues./Thurs.	Monday
8:25–8:50	8:25–8:55	8:25–8:55	8:25–8:55

SCHEDULE   BOX 8.7
KINDERGARTEN

7:45–8:15	Announcements/attendance/lunch count
	Big group: Calendar/songs/morning message
8:15–8:55	Math
8:55–10:15	Predictable chart/shared writing (interactive writing/Shared reading/Literacy centers/guided reading
10:15–10:50	Recess/restroom
10:55–11:25	Lunch
11:30–11:35	Restroom break
11:40–12:30	P. E./Music/other
12:30–1:00	Story time/quiet time/snacks/restroom break
1:00–2:15	Science/Social studies/Choice centers
2:15–2:20	Clean up
2:20–2:40	Journals/prepare to be dismissed
2:40–2:45	Dismissal

Mon/Wed	Tues.	Thurs.	Friday						
PE	Music	FYI	PE	(A)	Music	(B)	PE	(C)	FYI (D)

Computer every Tuesday from 8:15–9:00 AM
Library every Thursday from 12:45–1 PM

---

result in children exhibiting resistant and noncompliant behaviors (Miller, 1996). Boxes 8.6 and 8.7 are examples of daily schedules for preschool and kindergarten, respectively.

Varying the Pace of Activities for Individual Children

Teachers who have established good lines of communication with families can gain valuable information that will help set a comfortable pace for individual children. Asking about the child's usual routines and activities at home and the time frames that parents schedule at home will help teachers to create good fit for all children. Culturally competent teachers take the influences that the family's culture has on the parent's scheduling and management decisions into account (Gonzalez-Mena & Eyer, 2001). For children with disabilities, it is vital for teachers to spend time being careful observers. Teachers can manage instruction more efficiently when they determine what situations and situational characteristics seem to improve children's performances. Children's preferences for working alone or with their peers can help teachers choose groupings that assist children in achieving success. Overcoming barriers and limitations to children's success and favoring children's strengths is a critical part of organizing and managing the inclusive classroom (Prater, 2003).

Collaboration with consultants. Teachers may benefit from outside help to plan for classroom management routines for children with special learning needs. Collaboration with consultants can be extremely helpful for classroom teachers wishing to match the circumstances of instructional activities to the needs of children with specific learning

COLLABORATION TIPS FOR TEACHER   BOX 8.8
CONSULTATION/COLLABORATION*

I am a preschool program for children with disabilities (PPCD) teacher. This year, my class will be going into a regular education kindergarten class for three hours daily. The kindergarten teacher and I met over the summer to discuss how we would run the class. We also met several times the week before school started, and set a weekly time that we could meet throughout the year. The kindergarten teacher has taught kindergarten for 5 years and prekindergarten for 5 years. She has worked with a PPCD class in the past and is familiar with all that inclusion involves. She is very open and willing to do whatever it takes to see her students, as well as mine, succeed. During our meetings, we devised a schedule and decided that we would coteach the activities.

After school started, we quickly realized the coteaching was turning more into the kindergarten teacher just teaching while my assistants and I guided my five PPCD students in her class. My students range from attention deficit hyperactivity disorder (ADHD) to moderate autism. We also realized our schedule—the times I brought my class in—was not the most appropriate for my five students or her kindergarten students. On top of all our realizations, we also discovered the kindergarten teacher had about 7 students in her class (2 of whom are in special education) who needed extra help. We decided to meet during our planning period to discuss how we could make our classroom more productive.

With all the distractions, we had to figure out a schedule that would meet the needs of all the students in the class. We also needed to discuss taking some of her students out of the class for some extra one-on-one help. We were/are hoping to change the schedule in a way that the kindergarten teacher could get some of those major components taught when my students were not present—since all of her students take a state-mandated test in the spring, and mine are exempt. We hoped that by changing the schedule, my children will be in kindergarten at more appropriate social times to gain social skills and that the kindergarten teacher's class can have a less distracting environment for learning.

We agreed to meet in the kindergarten teacher's room at 12:10 PM. I wanted to discuss changing the schedule with her first. This would involve a discussion of how we could change the components around in a logical/reasonable way. Some components of her schedule must de done for a certain amount of time.

* See Appendix C for the full text.

disabilities. Often, teachers associate attention deficit problems with learning disabilities. This assumption is not true for all children. Consultation with an educational psychologist can help teachers determine whether special accommodations would be beneficial in managing the time frame scheduled and the pacing of learning activities for an individual child with learning disabilities. Consultants can compare engagement behaviors of children in different sets of circumstances to help determine ways to maximize the learning of each child. Different groupings for instruction can have varying affects on children's engagement. Whole-group direct instruction can result in higher engagement than engagement levels when a teacher asks the child with a specific learning disability to work independently. Peers can also influence engagement of children with learning disabilities, so management of the group appears to matter as well as management of individual children's learning situation (Harris & Cancelli, 1993). Box 8.8 details collaboration tips for a teacher consultation and collaboration.

Avoiding Interruptions and Planning Transitions

Another reason for planning large, flexible time frames is to reduce the interruptions and need for transitions from one activity to another. Each transition that a child must negotiate fragments the day and requires psychological energy to meet the new demands of the next activity. Frequent transitioning is mentally taxing to children and teachers. Further, the stress caused by frequent changes is associated with behavioral problems (Hendrick, 1998). Children who are gifted may react with anxiety or become overexcited (Tucker & Hafenstein, 1997). The attention span of children is lengthened when teachers encourage completion of tasks within reasonable time frames (Gareau & Kennedy, 1991).

MANAGING OPEN SPACE ENVIRONMENTS

Learning Center Environments

Learning centers are an efficient way to accommodate children with a wide range of abilities. Arranging space and materials into learning centers provides a variety of learning contexts for children. The flexibility of learning centers allows specialists to easily integrate therapeutic interventions into children's natural activities and explorations. Careful management of learning center activities can reduce time for transitions of the whole class to different activities (Freiberg & Driscoll, 1996). Children who have difficulty making transitions gain practice, and teachers can supervise their transitions on an individual basis. Children can begin activities immediately upon entering the classroom and spend more time interacting with other children during the school day.

Managing the physical environment affects children's learning and behavior. Manipulation of the environment is critical to cognitive and social emotional development (Bailey & McWilliam, 1990; Marion, 2003). Poorly organized learning environments with insufficient space and materials contribute to aggressive behavior in children (Bailey, Harms, & Clifford, 1983). It is critical to ensure that all children with disabilities have

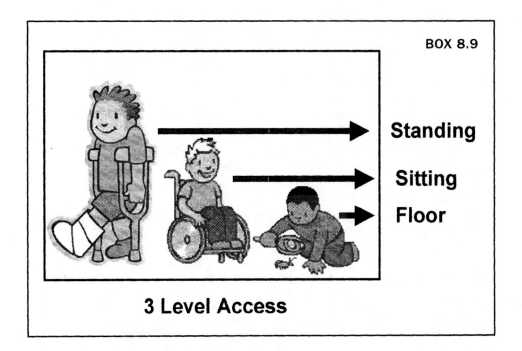

BOX 8.9

Standing

Sitting

Floor

3 Level Access

physical access to all learning centers and areas of the inclusive classroom. Children with certain disabilities may require more open floor space for mobility than typical children. Children with mobility problems may also need consideration when arranging materials and equipment in the learning centers. The mobility equipment that children use, their developmental levels and their range of vision are considerations in organizing materials in learning centers and other areas of the classroom. Three height ranges are recommended for full accessibility. Box 8.9 provides a visual aid for these three levels. Some materials can be placed at the shoulder level of a standing child to prevent bending or overreaching. This level keeps children from loosing their balance when they are in a standing position. Sitting- or table-level storage permits children in wheelchairs to obtain materials independently. Some children will need floor- or sitting-level material storage so they can crawl to shelves or reach from floor sitting levels (American Public Health Association & American Academy of Pediatrics, 2002).

Language and literacy across all areas. Managing the learning center environment is effective when language and literacy are stimulating and meaningful print helps children function productively in the classroom. For stimulating emergent literacy of young children, literacy experts have recommended that teachers incorporate print meaningfully into the visual environment of early childhood classrooms (Goodman & Goodman, 1979; Morrow, 2001; Purcell-Gates, 1996; Teale & Sulzby, 1988). A national survey of reading supervisors revealed they believed that creating a literate environment for children in kindergarten and the early grades was considered evidence of a commendable teacher (Pressley, Rankin, & Yokoi, 1996). Whether experts recommend teachers "litter with print" (Harste, Woodward, & Burke, 1984), or create a "print-rich" (Miller, 2000) or "literacy-rich" (Morrow, 2001) environment, they clearly

Functional use of print helps children see the value of words for communicating and organizing the learning environment.

favor offering children a variety of opportunities to view printed words in functional contexts. Labels and messages that serve the purpose of helping children identify and use equipment, materials, and spaces in the classroom environment are appropriate ways to integrate print. Print-rich environments provide children with opportunities to develop concepts about print that are essential to advancement, as literacy emerges during childhood. Moreover, some believe offering a print-rich environment may be especially beneficial for children who are at risk because their home environment is lacking in both printed materials to stimulate interest in reading and in chances to develop concepts about print. Literacy-rich environments are believed crucial for all children, including those with special needs (Miller, 2000).

Mediating the Learning Environment

What can teachers do to improve the fit of their classroom environment to their teaching and children's learning, despite limited tools to assess the quality of their classroom environment? Teachers who develop environmental competence can become mediators at attempting to achieve classroom environments that accommodate the learning needs of diverse groups of children. Mediation is the carefully planned, goal-oriented actions of the teacher that are designed to help children actively learn from their environment. Giving instruction denotes a more passive learner who is the recipient of knowledge delivered by the teacher (Odom & Wolery, 2003). The first step in mediating the learning environment is to determine which features are static (Desouza & Sivewright, 1993), in comparison to variables that might be dynamic or changeable, such as teacher-child interaction. Using ecobehavioral measurements to examine children's behaviors associated with features in the learning environment can help identify influential variables, static or dynamic, that may affect learning. Formally, ecobehavioral measurements can be used to detect patterns in the relationship between children's behavior and environmental variables (Desouza & Sivewright, 1993). Informally, teachers can use an ecological approach when observing children. Observing what a child is doing and taking notes about the environmental circumstances, materials used, and other people involved in the activity can help teachers decide which variables might be used in mediation strategies. Observing children is another opportunity for collaboration with other teachers or specialists. Partnering with another teacher to observe individual children in her or his classroom in exchange for that teacher to observe a few children with behavioral or learning difficulties of concern in your classroom is an informal way to collaborate. Create an observational scheme that includes the following questions:

- What is the child doing?
- What materials and equipment is he or she using?
- Where is he or she located?
- What are the conditions at that location (temperature, colors, furnishings, lighting, etc.)?
- Who is interacting with the child (teachers, assistants, other children, specialists)?

Using the observational checklist with time sampling improves the quality of the information gained. For example, observe five children for one minute each.

Identifying environmental features that are flexible and most likely to influence children's learning, and finding relationships to children's behavior and learning holds promise for better mediating the learning environment. With better information on these relationships, teachers may be more successful in altering the classroom ecology

Asking parents about the conditions that are most comfortable for their children can help teachers match the learning environment to individual children.

DAILY SCREENING   **BOX 8.10**

- How are children reacting to the room temperature?
- Do children have clothing appropriate for the weather and temperature?
- Is the lighting adjusted to reduce glare?
- What is the noise level in the room? Is it matched to the activity?
- Do children have space to move and engage in activity without bumping into one another?
- Is there any item or equipment that blocks pathways across the room?

---

in an effort to improve the learning environment and more positively affect outcomes for children. The goal is to achieve a match between the child and the learning environment. Parents may notice a child seems agitated by the noise level of the room, or the child might comment to parents that they are not comfortable in his or her surroundings. Families can also provide materials and decorations that bring the cultures of individual children into the classroom space. Teachers can ask families for information about the conditions in which they feel their child works best. Some children need quiet for their work, and others seem to work equally well when there is much activity around them. Box 8.10 lists suggested ecological screening questions.

SUMMARY

In this chapter, the reader learned how to manage time and create time schedules for inclusive early childhood classrooms. It is important to find ways to collaborate with other teachers and specialists who will be involved with children throughout the day. The relationship of coteachers and collaboration with specialists in the inclusive classroom was explored. Articulation of roles and responsibilities is a key part of managing an inclusive classroom to ensure minimal disruption. A good working relationship among professionals is fundamental to supporting the learning of each child. The structure and time schedule of the classroom must support the teacher's and other support professionals' work and meet the needs of all children. Planning large blocks of time afford flexibility and encourages children to work independently. Children can monitor their own use of time and become more efficient in self-regulation.

Discussion Questions

1. Discuss ways to collaborate with other professionals and specialists to ensure comfortable time frames and scheduling.
2. Why is organization critical in an inclusive early childhood classroom?

3. How can you ensure all children access to learning materials in the classroom?

4. How can you accommodate culturally and linguistically diverse children in the inclusive classroom?

5. What do you believe is important for accommodating individual differences of children in inclusive classrooms?

6. What supports do coteachers need to facilitate their planning and collaboration in structuring the classroom?

7. Describe different kinds of coteaching relationships. Discuss the importance of teachers articulating their roles and responsibilities toward managing their inclusive classroom.

Inclusive Activities

1. Observe an inclusive classroom where teachers are in a coteaching relationship. Look for ideas on creating a good working relationship. Make a list of things that each teacher does to facilitate learning in the classroom. Considering the actions you observe, describe what you think the role of each teacher might be, and write a description.

2. Ask teachers you know for a copy of their daily classroom schedules for their inclusive classrooms. Develop a set of criteria based upon the information in the chapter. Evaluate the schedules using your criteria. What would you do the same? What might you do to improve the schedule for children?

3. Visit an inclusive classroom serving children with physical disabilities. Observe children and take note of how accessible the classroom is for each child. Use the concept of three levels of access in your evaluation. Plan what you might do to improve accessibility for all children.

4. Interview a teacher or a coteaching team in an inclusive classroom. Ask the teachers to articulate the rules, routines, and procedures they have taught children so the classroom is convenient and easy to manage.

References

American Public Health Association & American Academy of Pediatrics. (2002). *Caring for our children: National health and safety performance standards: Guidelines for out-of-home care.* Washington, DC: American Public Health Association.

Bailey, D. B., Harms, T., & Clifford, R. M. (1983). Matching changes in preschool environments to desired changes in child behavior. *Journal of the Division of Early Childhood, 7,* 61–68.

Bailey, D. B., & McWilliams, R. A. (1990). Normalizing early intervention. *Topics in Early Childhood Special Education, 10*(2), 33–47.

Bowers, C. A., & Flinders, D. J. (1990). *Responsive teaching: An ecological approach to classroom patterns of language, culture, and thought.* New York: Teacher's College Press.

Christie, J. F., & Wardle, F. (1992). How much time is needed to play? *Young Children, 47*(3), 28–32.

Cook, L., & Friend, M. (1998). Co-teaching: Guidelines for creating effective practices. In E. L. Meyen, G. A. Vergason & R. J. Whelan (Eds.), *Educating students with mild disabilities: Strategies and methods.* Denver, CO: Love.

Desouza, E. R., & Sivewright, D. (1993). An ecological approach to evaluating a special education program. *Adolescence, 28*(111), 517–525.

Espinosa, L. M., & Laffey, J. M. (2003). Urban primary teacher perceptions of children with challenging behaviors. *Journal of Children & Poverty, 9*(2), 135–156.

Evertson, C. M., & Harris, A. H. (1992). What we know about managing classrooms. *Educational Leadership, 92*, April, 74–78.

Freiberg, H. J., & Driscoll, A. (1996). *Universal teaching strategies* (2nd ed.). Boston, MA: Allyn & Bacon.

Frost, J. L. (1992). *Play and playscapes.* Albany, NY: Delmar.

Frost, J. L., Wortham, S., & Reifel, S. (Eds.). (2001). *Play and child development.* Upper Saddle River, NJ: Merrill/Prentice Hall.

Fuchs, L., Fuchs, D., Hamlett, C., Phillips, N., & Karns, K. (1995). General educator's specialized adaptation for students with learning disabilities. *Exceptional Children, 61*(5), 440–459.

Gareau, M., & Kennedy, C. (1991). Structure time & space to promote pursuit of learning in the primary grades. *Young Children, 46*(4), 46–51.

Gonzalez-Mena, J., & Eyer, D. W. (2001). *Infants, toddlers, and caregivers* (5th ed.). London: Mayfield.

Goodman, K. S., & Goodman, Y. (1979). Learning to read is natural. In L. B. Resnick, & P. Weaver (Eds.), *Theory and practice of early reading* (Vol. 1, pp. 137–154). Hillsdale, NJ: Erlbaum.

Hanft, B. E., & Anzalone, M. (2001). Issues in professional development: Preparing and supporting occupational therapists in early childhood. *Infants and Young Children, 13*(4), 67–78.

Harris, A. M., & Cancelli, A. A. (1993). Academic engagement of students with learning disabilities in mainstream classrooms: Challenging conventional wisdom. *Journal of Educational & Psychological Consultation, 4*(4), 385–389.

Harste, J. C., Woodward, V. A., & Burke, C. L. (1984). *Language stories and literacy lessons.* Portsmouth, NH: Heineman.

Hendrick, J. (1998). *Total learning: Developmental curriculum for the young child* (5th ed.). Upper Saddle River, NJ: Merrill.

Howard, G. R. (1999). *We can't teach what we don't know: White teachers, multiracial schools.* New York: Teacher's College Press.

Ladson-Billings, G. (2001). *Crossing over to Canaan: The new teachers in diverse classrooms.* San Francisco: Jossey-Bass.

Marion, M. (2003). *Guidance of young children* (6th ed.). Upper Saddle River, NJ: Merrill/Prentice Hall.

McBride, B. J., & Schwartz, I. S. (2003). Effects of teaching early interventionists to use discrete trials during ongoing classroom activities. *Topics in Early Childhood Special Education, 23*(1), 5–17.

Miller, R. (1996). *The developmentally appropriate inclusive classroom in early education.* Albany, NY: Delmar.

Miller, W. H. (2000). *Strategies for developing emergent literacy.* Boston: McGraw-Hill.

Morrow, L. M. (2001). *Literacy development in the early years: Helping children read and write* (4th ed.). Boston: Allyn & Bacon.

National Center for Educational Statistics. (1996). *Digest of educational statistics.* Washington, DC: Government Printing Office.

Nieto, S. (2000). *Affirming diversity: The sociopolitical context of multicultural education* (3rd ed.). New York: Longman.

Obegi, A. D., & Ritblatt, S. N. (2005). Cultural competence in infant/toddler caregivers: Application of a tri-dimensional model. *Journal of Research in Childhood Education, 19*(3), 199–213.

Odom, S. L., & Wolery, M. (2003). A unified theory of practice in early intervention/early childhood special education: Evidence-based practices. *The Journal of Special Education, 37*(3), 164–173.

Powell, R. R., McLaughlin, H. J., Savage, T. V., & Zehm, S. (2001). *Classroom management: Perspectives on the social curriculum.* Upper Saddle River, NJ: Merrill/Prentice Hall.

Prater, M. A. (2003). She will succeed! Strategies for success in inclusive classrooms. *Teaching Exceptional Children, 35*(5), 58–64.

Pressley, M. C., Rankin, J., & Yokoi, Y. (1996). A survey of instructional practices of primary teachers nominated as effective in promoting literacy. *Elementary School Journal, 96*(4), 363–384.

Purcell-Gates, V. (1996). Stories, coupons, and the "TV Guide": Relationships between home literacy experiences and emergent literacy knowledge. *Reading Research Quarterly, 31*(4), 406–428.

Schumm, J. S., Vaughn, S., Haager, D., McDowell, J., Rothlein, L., & Saumell, L. (1995). General education teacher planning: What can students with learning disabilities expect? *Exceptional Children, 61*(4), 335–352.

Teale, W., & Sulzby, E. (1988). *Emergent literacy: Writing and reading.* Norwood, NJ: Ablex.

Tucker, B., & Hafenstein, N. L. (1997). Psychological intensities in young gifted children. *Gifted Child Quarterly, 41*(3), 66–75.

Vaughn, S., Schumm, J., & Arguelles, M. E. (1997). The ABCDEs of co-teaching. *Teaching Exceptional Children, 30*, 4–10.

Wang, A. Y. (1993). Cultural-familial predictors of children's metacognitive and academic performance. *Journal of Research in Childhood Education, 7*(2), 83–90.

Weinstein, C. S., Tomlinson-Clarke, S., & Curran, M. (2004). Toward a conception of culturally responsive classroom management. *Journal of Teacher Education, 55*(1), 25–38.

Weiss, M. P., & Lloyd, J. (2003). Conditions for co-teaching: Lessons from a case study. *Teacher Education and Special Education, 26*(1), 27–41.

PART III

Effective Teaching in an Inclusive Classroom

Chapter 9

Identifying Effective Teaching Strategies and Practices

Key Principle

Apply recommended strategies and practices

Objectives

After studying this chapter you should be able to:

1. Understand why it is important to know a variety of instructional strategies and practices to accommodate individual children.

2. List the advantages of differentiated instruction.

3. Differentiate between implicit and explicit teaching strategies.

4. Define naturalistic strategies and give examples of the use of this type.

5. Describe sociocontextual strategies and explain the use of this type of strategy.

6. Summarize what brain research has revealed about the importance of varying instructional strategies and practices.

INTRODUCTION

The previous chapter described how to manage and organize an inclusive classroom to promote the active learning of children. Another serious step for teachers who wish to teach more inclusively is to learn about best practices that have been identified by research as most likely to be effective in facilitating children's growth, development, and learning. Consequently, this chapter introduces categories of research-based strategies and their foundational principles. Proven strategies underlie the most effective teaching in inclusive classrooms, and teachers who are well-equipped with a palette of fundamental strategies are prepared to foster the acquisition of knowledge, skills, and attitudes toward learning for each child.

One important principle is that teachers who use effective strategies that are deliberately planned and thoughtfully selected to differentiate instruction can enhance the learning of all children. To ensure each child has the best possible chance for success, it is critical to identify and become proficient in using strategies that have a proven record of effectiveness. When practices do not yet have an accumulated body of research to establish their efficacy, the strategies should, at least, have emerged from solid instructional theory. Further, when these strategies are matched to the learning needs of individual children, teachers are taking great strides toward providing inclusive learning environments. Teachers who masterfully use a set of effective teaching strategies can influence children's success in school and affect each child's lifelong pursuit of learning.

GOALS AND OBJECTIVES FOR USING INCLUSIVE TEACHING STRATEGIES

There are two overall goals for using carefully selected inclusive teaching strategies:

1. **Successful learners:** to help all children experience success in learning
2. **Independent learners:** to assist children in gaining independence as learners

The major goal of inclusive education in early childhood is to promote the success of all children in their early learning experiences. The importance of achieving this goal cannot be overstated; it is paramount that each child be offered the best possible opportunities to meet challenges and succeed in learning. Prospects are very dim for children whose preschool education and early schooling result in repeated frustration and failure. The window of opportunity to acquire skills and abilities that are foundational to academic and personal success is narrow. Research is clear that children who are not proficient learners by the end of the primary grades have a very poor prognosis for attaining acceptable achievement in school and experiencing lifelong success. Reading and literacy acquisition is one area of development that exemplifies the short window of time children have to catch up with their peers academically. Studies indicated that children who are not reading by the end of third grade are unlikely to perform well through the remainder of their formal schooling (Good, Simmons, & Smith, 1998; Gunn, Biglan, Smolkowski, & Ary, 2000). However, children who are at risk of school failure are not doomed to poor outcomes. Accumulated research underscores the success of early detection of children with social and learning difficulties and, most of all, prevention of failure through skilled use of teaching strategies. The remainder of this chapter explores strategies that are universal and aimed at assisting all children to gain independence and proficiency in learning.

There are several objectives teachers in inclusive classrooms seek to accomplish through careful and deliberate use of learning enhancement strategies. Among various reasons, teachers use inclusive teaching strategies to:

- Encourage children's engagement
- Improve the quality of play and learning opportunities
- Streamline learning processes of children
- Activate children's prior knowledge
- Facilitate children's social and learning interactions

Assisting children in acquiring efficient learning strategies requires vigilant teachers who favor teaching strategies and practices backed by scientific research and avoid unproven teaching fads. The next section discusses what we know about the importance of adult-child interaction for helping children become independent and proficient learners.

SELECTING INCLUSIVE TEACHING STRATEGIES AND PRACTICES

Chapter 5 discussed the content of curricula designed for inclusive early childhood education. However, there is abundant evidence indicating that "how" children are taught is just as critical as "what" they are taught. Teachers tend to spend time planning the curricular activities or units of activities that present children with the curriculum content or "what" is to be learned. Less time is spent planning the teaching strategies the teacher will use to facilitate the learning of children. Yet, the selection and use of teaching strategies to facilitate learning are crucial areas in inclusive classrooms with children who represent a wide range of abilities and learning styles. Children who are better equipped with strategies for learning have increased chances to gain more from the content of the curriculum.

Insight from Brain Research

Why are interactive teaching strategies a critical focus of teachers in inclusive early childhood classrooms? Insights gained from recent discoveries in the neurobiological sciences have revealed that the instructional interactions of teachers with children can be instrumental in fostering learning and can affect development of the brain in young children. This section discusses some key findings of brain research that support the contention that the use of strategies for enhancing learning is a significant feature of inclusive programs.

Nature and nurture. Advances in technology have provided high-tech tools, such as position emission tomography (PET) brain scans, that have permitted scientists to delve into new frontiers for examining and understanding the way the brain grows and develops. Through neurobiological research, we learn that brain development is a dynamic process that involves a unique interplay between nature and nurture. A longstanding assumption of scientists has been that nature, the biological and genetic characteristics of individuals, affects how a child's brain grows and develops. Current brain research, however, reveals that nature is not the sole influence on brain development. Scientists are finding evidence that several complex environmental variables that constitute what is commonly referred to as nurture also exert a profound influence on the growth and development of the human brain. Moreover, some environmental variables exert an influence on the brain of a fetus still in utero; for example, substances such as cocaine, nicotine, and other drugs can have a detrimental affect on brain development prior to birth. The type of stimulation children receive, the adequacy of their

Experiences and playful interactions with the environment early in life stimulate neural growth and development.

nourishment, the kind of care they are given, and the social interactions children experience are among the types of environmental conditions identified as influential in the development of the amazing organ that we call the brain (Bergen & Coscia, 2001).

Critical periods. There are windows of time and opportunity for environmental variables to exert an influence. Critical periods for the development of certain abilities, such as language acquisition, have been identified, and several of these critical periods exist during the early years of a child's life. Scientists have determined that the brains of infants and toddlers are far more active compared to the brains of adults. Although the human brain continues to change throughout life, the brain is astonishingly more active and pliable during the first three years of life. During these years of growth, children's interaction with the environment is thought to be mandatory for the process of brain development to continue. Neural growth is highly dependent upon the type and amount of stimulation that is received from various sources present within the child's home and learning environments. Some of these sources of stimulation are encountered through a child's natural experiences and manipulation of objects in the physical environments of home and school. Further, a significant source of stimulation is attributable to the social environment created by interactions with parents, teachers, siblings, and peers.

Research also suggested that the environmental contexts in which a child grows and develops can exert either a positive or negative influence on brain development and learning. Safe, healthy indoor and outdoor environments that are rich with opportunities for manipulating the toys, household items, and natural materials provide many sources for positive stimulation. Conversely, physical environments that fail to provide materials to explore in safe and healthy circumstances are likely to negatively affect brain development (Nash, 2002). We also know that warm, responsive caregiving is essential for optimizing brain development, especially during critical periods for specific types of learning.

Research has helped scientists to better understand the neurobiological process that results in neural development and brain growth. Neurons in the brain are designed to promote the establishment of connections or synapses with other neurons. A neuron is equipped with an axon to send signals and dendrites to receive electrical signals. These signals travel across a pathway via chemical neurotransmitters, such as serotonin, dopamine, or endorphins. As a result of this process, connections or synapses are formed at a phenomenal rate during the first three years of life. Following this initial period of high neural activity and synapse productivity, the brain continues during childhood to organize neural connections and prune away unneeded connections. Through this process, the density of neural connections is reduced, as the brain discards approximately one half of the unneeded connections by adolescence.

Early experience and social interactions of children are believed to play a critical role in cueing the brain to retain some connections as vital, while pruning away other neural connections that are no longer needed. When neural pathways are stimulated through a child's experience with the physical environment or social interactions with teachers, parents, and others, the brain is signaled to retain those synapses or connections that form that pathway. Repeated stimulation and activation of these connections further strengthens the chemical signal the brain receives and makes it even more likely that the neural connection will be retained as a permanent component of the brain circuitry. Conversely, neural pathways that fail to receive sufficient stimulation are eliminated, as the brain efficiently organizes its circuitry based upon usage of connections that were formed. Furthermore, emotions appear to play a role in the amount of stimulation obtained to retain neural pathways (Bergen & Coscia, 2001; Shore, 1997).

Implications for parents and teachers. Mounting evidence implies that interactions, such as those that occur as a result of efforts to teach children, can have extraordinarily powerful affects on the brain development of children. Specifically, these interactions can exert a direct and very precise impact on the wiring of a child's brain for learning. Consequently, the kinds of teaching strategies and practices used in the home, child-care, and school settings are serious decisions. The type and number of different strategies and practices teachers and parents use may affect the quality of interactions and experiences of children during periods of growth that are prime for the development of the brain and the acquisition of knowledge and skills. Unfortunately, all children may not be involved in sufficient interactions with caring adults. Elkind (1987) reported that mothers spend an average of 11 minutes a day with their children during the week in quality interactions.

Early is best. Another important implication of brain research is that early childhood is a critical time in brain development in which teaching strategies appear to be highly influential in facilitating the development of the brain's circuitry system.

Consequently, it makes sense for early childhood teachers to be especially conscientious in planning their roles in facilitating children's learning in the classroom. Planning time can be well spent trying to identify best practices for use in their inclusive classrooms. Further, it is important to plan beyond the activities and materials that will be offered to children daily. Equally important is the facilitation of learning by caring teachers; daily planning should include careful attention to planning of the teaching strategies and techniques teachers will use to support the natural learning processes of children. Early childhood teachers should aim for selecting teaching strategies that are matched to the learning style and specific learning needs of individual children, so opportunities for acquiring knowledge and skills within the curriculum are optimized.

Implications for teaching children with special needs. Recent brain research holds a number of significant implications for children with special needs. Of key importance is the prevention of conditions that are the result of an illness, the child's environment, or incidents. It is most efficient to ensure proper brain development through attention to adequate nutrition, care, health, and safety for all children. However, when trauma and negative influences on children's brain development have not been averted, it is critical to focus on providing these children with access to prompt and intensive intervention during the early years when the brain is most likely to recover (Shore, 1997; Thompson & Nelson, 2001).

Implications for inclusion. Findings of brain research to date supports differentiated instruction that is keyed to optimize the learning of individual children. Howard Gardner and others have long contended that "one size fits all" teaching fails to reach all children. Effective teachers adjust their teaching strategies to the learning styles of individual children in their classrooms, which is particularly true of inclusive early childhood settings. Box 9.1 offers suggested reflection questions.

The interactive role of teachers and parents as learning facilitators who help children take full advantage of learning opportunities is also supported by brain research. In particular, the tendency of these "expert" learners to provide support, or scaffolding, to help novice learners learn how to learn.

When children with identified special needs are included, planning the teaching strategies that will be used to facilitate learning becomes extremely important. For example, children with sensory impairments, such as children who are deaf, hard of hearing,

---

MY REFLECTION **BOX 9.1**

- What do I know about the development of the brain and what that means for learning?
- What do I already know about teaching strategies and practices for enhancing learning?
- What do I want to know about how children learn?

or blind, receive less sensory stimulation or input, which might interfere with or diminish the formation of neural connections in the brain. To counteract any possible negative effects on children's learning from reduced sensory input, teachers can use strategies that help these children to attend to and use the sensory input that they are able to receive. The high stimulation of being served in inclusive classrooms with typically developing peers is thought to be an advantage offered by inclusive settings for children with special needs.

Professional Recommendations Across Disciplines

An interdisciplinary approach is essential to meet the challenge of teaching in inclusive education settings. A commitment to teach inclusively requires dedication to remain knowledgeable regarding theory and practice across multiple related fields of study, such as general early childhood education, early childhood special education, multicultural and multilingual education, language and literacy, and developmental psychology, to name a few. Staying informed is not an insurmountable task when teachers are savvy about resources for obtaining valid information. Professional organizations are also reliable sources of information about teaching strategies and practices that are effective.

As mentioned previously, professional organizations prepare position papers, recommendations, standards, and sets of guidelines in an effort to provide leadership to their respective fields of study. In addition to periodically publishing these formal statements, professional organizations often serve as a source of ongoing research-based information

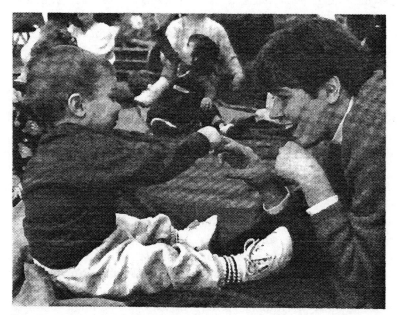

Parents and teachers can help children use sensory experiences to learn concepts and language.

BOX 9.2

Steps To Identifying Inclusive Teaching Strategies
➜ Join Organizations
➜ Read Journals
➜ Talk to Teachers
➜ Attend Workshops
➜ Observe Children

---

for teachers. Newsletters, journals, electronic journals, books, and other publications keep teachers informed about research developments and applications in the classroom.

Guiding preparation and practice. Professional standards and guidelines serve a dual purpose in early childhood education. First, these documents provide a solid research basis for guiding practice in early childhood settings. Second, professional guidelines provide a framework for personnel preparation. The extent that these documents are used for these purposes influences the cohesiveness among professionals in the field and the effectiveness of services provided to children and families. In early intervention, the specifications for serving children at each age range differ. For example, personnel and practices for serving in infant and toddler intervention will vary from those in preschool programs, and, similarly, elementary personnel preparation differs from preparation for serving younger children. As a result, personnel preparation must address the unique qualifications and specifications for teaching children at each age span.

Another consideration is whether the content of personnel preparation varies across disciplines and, if so, to what extent. A national survey of personnel preparation programs revealed a common emphasis on family-centered practices. However, two areas, service coordination and teaming, received only nominal attention. Adoption of national standards for practice and personnel preparation has been suggested as a needed reform to improve the quality of early intervention across the United States (Bruder & Dunst, 2005).

Staying informed. Early childhood teachers in inclusive classrooms are obligated to stay apprised of accepted strategies and practices across disciplines and fields of study. In addition to journals and publications in early childhood education, teachers in inclusive classrooms should check for relevant information in multicultural, special education, giftedness, and bilingual education literature to name a few. Another source of information is attending conferences of professional organizations. Often, these conferences offer staff development training sessions, seminars, and workshops that introduce new teaching strategies to participants. Teachers can prepare for inclusive settings by acquiring new techniques and discussing the implementation of strategies with experts and other practitioners. Box 9.2 lists steps to aid in identifying inclusive teaching strategies.

DEVELOPING A REPERTOIRE OF STRATEGIES AND PRACTICES
Importance of Acquiring a Full Palette of Strategies

Acquiring a variety of teaching strategies and techniques helps prepare teachers for enhancing the learning of all children in inclusive early childhood settings. Abundant research has suggested that teachers who possess a full repertoire of strategies are more successful at matching their instruction to the individual strengths, characteristics, and learning styles of children (Baker & Zigmond, 1990; Joint Committee on Teacher Planning for Students with Disabilities, 1995; Schumm & Vaughn, 1991). Attaining competence in a wide range of strategies helps teachers make good judgments about the feasibility of using a particular strategy with an individual or group of children. Teachers who have acquired expertise in using a variety of instructional strategies are more confident in their ability to effectively teach all children.

A continuum of strategies: naturalistic to explicit. Instructional strategies recommended for inclusive classrooms represent a continuum in terms of the degree of intrusiveness and the amount of support offered to children during learning activities. At one end of the continuum are implicit or naturalistic instructional strategies that are minimally intrusive, and toward the other end are explicit strategies that require teachers to intervene in ways that are more intrusive. Another way to view this continuum is from the perspective of child-centered and teacher-centered strategies. Naturalistic strategies are the least intrusive and, therefore, the most child-centered approach. Explicit strategies involve a more teacher-initiated approach that might be effective to support children's learning under specific circumstances (Karp & Voltz, 2000).

Naturalistic strategies involve scaffolding and other mild forms of intervention embedded in play, classroom routines, social interactions, and other usual activities that naturally occur in the learning environment. These teaching strategies can be spontaneous, but are usually based upon teachers' observations of children's activities. In contrast, explicit strategies tend to be more deliberate, intrusive interventions that are often planned in advance. Teachers implement explicit strategies in a more exact manner, with specific directions to children and verbalizations that may be scripted. Explicit strategies elicit specific behaviors or performance from children as a direct result of the intervention. For example, seeking to change a child's behavior through a training sequence with a prescribed set of steps is a highly intrusive approach. Such behavior analysis techniques can be effective with certain children, but these methods represent an intensive form of intervention. For children with disabilities or special learning needs, teachers carefully avoid bringing undue attention to their differences. Moreover, supporting the autonomy of learners to construct knowledge within their community of learners is also important. For these reasons, many experts agree that the goal for teachers in inclusive classrooms is to use the least intrusive strategies possible to help each child reach his or her learning goals (Atwater, Carta, Schwartz, & McConnell, 1994; Bailey & McWilliam, 1990; Bailey & Wolery, 1992).

Tips for acquiring strategies. Developing a repertoire of strategies is a process that begins when a teacher is introduced to a strategy or set of techniques. Once the basic steps to using a strategy are understood, use of the strategy helps teachers attain a level of comfort and automaticity that comes with practice. It has been recommended that teachers adopt new techniques and strategies gradually (Silberman, 1996). The pace of trying new practices should be comfortable for the teacher and introduced slowly in the inclusive classroom. Avoiding dramatic or rapid shifts will help preserve the sense of stability that is critical in inclusive classrooms. Teachers' undue stress or nervousness is easily transmitted to children. Prudent teachers delay trying new strategies until the acquisition phase is complete and they feel fully prepared and confident to proceed with implementation. Novice teachers may be more prone to rush into implementation than more experienced teachers. It is always a good idea to discuss using a new strategy with fellow teachers who may have some valuable advice.

There has been some research exploring whether the providing feedback on performance affects teachers' implementation of embedded strategies or children's performance. A study in 2000 suggested no feedback was necessary to gain positive results from training (Horn, Lieber, Li, Sandall, & Schwartz, 2000). Other studies suggest it may be important for teachers to receive feedback following their attempts to implement embedded strategies. These studies found that when feedback was provided as a training follow-up, teachers were more likely to continue to embed strategies into routines and activities in early childhood settings (Mudd & Wolery, 1987; Schepis, Reid, Owenby, & Parsons, 2001; Tate, Thompson, & McKerchar, 2005). Although more studies are needed to provide definitive answers, the latter studies may hold tentative implications for inclusive classrooms involving teaching teams. Team members might serve as sources of feedback for one another as they implement new teaching strategies. Having another professional available to encourage and remind of strategy use might be an advantage of coteaching or other collaborations that are available to teachers in inclusive classrooms.

Selecting effective practices. How does a teacher who wants to be prepared to promote the learning of all children choose from the plethora of research-based strategies described in professional literature? The number of strategies and practices teachers will find can be overwhelming. To avoid confusion, teachers can aim toward acquiring a core set of strategies or tools for teaching inclusively that can be expanded as needed. Keeping in mind the continuum that goes from naturalistic strategies to those that are explicit, the goal can be to acquire a few key types of strategies along different points in the continuum. This variation can help teachers gain sufficient breadth to address a wide range of learners—individuals who, at times, may need minimal intervention or, at other times, may require intensive support. To support children representing a full span of ability, teachers may be wise to develop a balanced set of strategies in several major areas or categories, rather than selecting a narrow band of strategies that are very similar. A core set of strategies might include naturalistic strategies, such play-based and activity-based intervention. To address the middle of the continuum, teachers might prepare to use sociocontextual strategies, such as cooperative learning and peer-mediated strategies. Explicit strategies, at the other end of the continuum, could include teaching learning strategies to children, task analysis, and using technology-based intervention strategies (Winter, 1999). Although there is no specific place on the continuum where each kind of strategy lies, the notion of a continuum can help teachers plan. Some of the variables that can influence the degree of intensity or intrusiveness of the strategy are the way the strategy is used and whether it is embedded in a context, such as a routine activity or play. Considering these variations, the concept of a continuum makes sense in helping us think about the relative orientation of a strategy and the approximate degree of intensity or intrusiveness.

Teachers who are capable of using several strategies from each category of this common core will have flexibility in meeting individual needs and the breadth to stimulate learning of all children. Gaining competence in using evidence-based instructional practices prepares teachers to effectively assist all children in inclusive classrooms to become proficient learners. The following sections introduce strategies toward the naturalistic end of the continuum and key characteristics that require minimal intrusion into children's learning. Box 9.3 gives an overview of naturalistic strategies.

NATURALISTIC STRATEGIES

What are Naturalistic Strategies?

Naturalistic strategies are implicit teaching strategies and practices that naturally occur within the typical contexts of early childhood settings. Strategies in this category include incidental or milieu teaching, a type of naturalistic strategy where teachers embed strategies as incidents occur to enhance learning within the usual milieu of the classroom activities and functions (Harper-Whalen, Walmsley, & Moore, 1991). Strategies at the naturalistic end of the continuum are minimally invasive, meaning these strategies are among the least intrusive of teaching strategies. Naturalistic strategies can refer to strategies and practices that are embedded within

---

NATURALISTIC STRATEGIES   **BOX 9.3**

- Respect a child's way of learning
- Value play as a natural catalyst for learning
- Maximize transitions and routines
- Are unobtrusive
- Foster learning in a relevant context

Using naturalistic strategies helps maximize learning through daily routines and activities at home and school.

the natural stream of routines, such as arriving and departing, eating meals and snacks, clean-up times, dressing, and other personal care activities. Teachers can embed group and individual learning objectives in these typical activities to create authentic opportunities for learning. The naturally occurring routines and play activities of young children offer many opportunities for teachers to reinforce and enhance the emerging concepts and skills of young children. Embedding the practice of skills that children are acquiring in daily routines and activities helps children who require chances for repetition to enhance their learning. Box 9.4 describes a routine practice for daily use.

The Importance of Naturalistic Strategies

Naturalistic strategies are vital tools that afford teachers opportunities to maximize precious minutes each day toward the goals of enhancing all children's development and boosting skills abilities related to school readiness. Use of naturalistic strategies permits teachers to significantly increase the chances for children to learn without adding undue pressure. The high degree of influence that play has on the growth,

---

ROUTINE PRACTICE FOR ADAM	**BOX 9.4**

Adam, a child with Down syndrome, practices his colors with his teacher each day, as they set out plastic cups for milk at each child's place setting for lunch. As a child with mental retardation, Adam benefits from daily opportunities to name colors as he and his teacher perform a routine task.

development, and learning of children makes play a powerful context for learning in inclusive early childhood classrooms. Naturalistic and play-based strategies offer many advantages and benefits when used in inclusive early childhood education classrooms. A distinct advantage of the strategies in this category is that these techniques are the least intrusive to children because they are woven into their usual activities and interests. Less intrusion may be particularly important to children who are at risk or who have disabilities, as these children are thought to benefit from engaging in sustained, natural interactions with their peers (Bailey & McWilliam, 1990). Further, because of the inherent relevance of these activities, children are more likely to be motivated to engage in them. In sum, naturalistic strategies, including those embedded in play contexts, are consistent with the tenets of developmentally appropriate practice (Bredekamp & Copple, 1997) and early childhood inclusion models built upon constructivist theoretical foundations (Winter, 1999).

Play-based strategies. Children's play activities offer a variety of opportunities for teachers to enhance children's learning. Research has indicated that play has characteristics that relate to all areas of development. From infancy, the motor components of play are present, as infants learn to maneuver and control their bodies. As children progress through preschool, so does their ability to perform more complex movements. Language acquisition is also influenced by play with other children and adults. Play has identifiable social characteristics that have been examined by researchers and categorized according to the degree of social involvement of children with their peers (Parten, 1933). Jean Piaget recognized the symbolic nature of play. Play involves cognitive development, as children learn to reason and problem solve through increasingly complex play activities, and it can be categorized into stages that correspond to a child's intellectual development through childhood (Piaget, 1962). In fact, children deprived of play suffer serious consequences to their developmental progress (Frost, Wortham, & Reifel, 2001).

Play is also linked to culture and is present in every society across the globe. Play appears to serve a cultural function of creating a cohesive bond between children and their society. From an anthropological perspective, cultural values are expressed through children's play (Schwartzman, 1978). A growing body of evidence has suggested that culture influences the kinds and degree of interactions teachers and parents might have with children during play activities. Some studies reveal Mexican mothers do not value play as critical to development and do not view their role as participatory in children's play activities (Farver & Howes, 1993). In contrast, Chinese mothers and American mothers tend to be highly engaged in promoting and participating in the play activities of their preschool children. American mothers influence their children's play both directly, through prompting and elaborating on what children do, and indirectly, such as providing play environments and encouragement for play (Chin & Reifel, 2000; Haight, 1998; Haight & Miller, 1992). Cultural beliefs influence the value attached to play activities, whether play is encouraged, who can participate, and the degree and kind of participation deemed acceptable (Rogoff, Mistry, Goncu, & Mosier, 1993; Saville-Troike, 1978).

KEY NATURALISTIC STRATEGIES   BOX 9.5

- Schedule time daily for children to play indoors and outside.
- Use learning or interest centers for active learning experiences in meaningful contexts.
- Observe children in play and routines to find opportune moments to interact and stimulate learning.
- Scaffold children's learning in careful, unobtrusive ways.
- Embed interventions or therapy into daily contexts.

How To Apply Naturalistic Strategies

Use naturalistic and play-based strategies. Naturalistic strategies are teaching strategies and techniques that are embedded in existing contexts or naturally occurring routines that are typical in classrooms. The power of naturalistic strategies is that children are learning in a meaningful context that is relevant to them. Sometimes teachers plan to embed their strategies in usual classroom routines. Other times, teachers seize spontaneously arising opportunities and maximize these chances for learning. The key is that teachers are maximizing every minute of the school day for learning without wasting precious time (see Box 9.5). Learning is also maximized because children can

Play and naturalistic settings provide a meaningful context for learning.

make connections between concepts and apply their skills in meaningful ways. Play and simple routines are turned into valuable learning experiences through the thoughtful interactions of teachers. Typical intents of teachers are to introduce new vocabulary, give opportunities for children to practice skills, and to assess understanding.

Maximize routines. One way to foster learning in authentic circumstances is to embed strategies and practices into various routines and activities the child experiences throughout the day. This implementation method ensures children will have multiple exposures to concepts and many opportunities to practice skills. Most importantly, embedding strategies and practices into daily routines and activities guarantees the child opportunities for learning within familiar contexts of the early childhood classroom and the playground. Children with mild to moderate retardation or learning disabilities may benefit from repetitive activities embedded in their daily routines.

Teaching Through Routines: David Gets Ready for Breakfast

At breakfast, Mr. Halverson involves David, age 5, in setting the table. David is a child with moderate developmental delays. He works with different peer partners each day and requires some supervision from Mr. Halverson to perform the tasks of this routine activity. However, after several months, David is showing progress in learning to count the correct number of cereal bowls, spoons, and cups needed for the children present. Although David cannot count independently, he is beginning to anticipate the next number and will sometimes say it before his partner. He and his partner also organize the dishes and utensils into a set for each child. David takes pride in being able to complete this task each day and enjoys getting to know his classroom peers through this duty.

- What mathematical concepts or skills does David have an opportunity to practice repeatedly during this routine?
- How would you facilitate this learning experience?
- What social skills can David learn through working with the peer partner?
- Is it fair for David to always have a turn at this routine?
- What does differentiated instruction mean in regard to this task?

Using activity-based intervention techniques. Activity-based intervention (ABI) was first introduced as an early intervention technique for infants, toddlers, and preschoolers with developmental delays or identified disabilities. Later, Bricker and Cripe (1992) recommended this technique for use in inclusive early childhood classrooms because of the compatibility of these strategies with developmentally appropriate practices. Emphasis is placed on enhancing authentic classroom activities with logical antecedents and consequences. Teachers plan the activities that give all children opportunities for participation. The clear advantages of this approach are that children are allowed to initiate their own participation, and they learn concepts and skills at their own pace but holistically, through authentic experiences rather than piecemeal in isolation (Bricker, 2000; Bricker & Cripe, 1992; Bricker, Pretti-Frontczak, & McComas, 1998).

Using Naturalistic Strategies in an Activity: The Snowy Day

Most of the children in Ms. Dottie's class had never experienced snow in their warm, southwestern climate. After reading *The Snowy Day* by Ezra Jack Keats, Ms. Dottie let the children play in activity centers. The children who went to the water table were surprised to find that instead of water, the table was filled with shaved ice that resembled snow. Ms. Dottie had added a variety of small toys, containers of different sizes and shapes, and kitchen spoons and utensils. The teacher invited the children to put on their mittens to play in the snow. Vanessa, a child with delayed language and conceptual development, was delighted to participate. Ms. Dottie encouraged the children to explore by asking questions such as, "How does the snow feel?" "What can you do with the snow?" and "What happens when you hold it in your hands for a while?" Vanessa had an opportunity to increase her vocabulary and learn how to explore and extend her conceptual development regarding properties of water. Box 9.6 lists some reflection questions for this activity.

Naturalistic Strategies in Preschool

Washing hands

- Sensory awareness: "Feel the water running over your hands? Is it cool or warm? How does the soap make your hands feel? How does the soap smell? Tell me how the water sounds."
- Vocabulary: "Let's see how many words we can use to tell about water. Water is . . . wet, cool, warm. It splashes, sprinkles, drops."
- Mathematics: "How much water do you think you will use to wash your hands?" Have various sized containers by the sink (e.g., cup, pint, quart, half gallon, etc.). Let the child make a prediction. Then pour water from the container over the child's hands or have another child help. The child begins to have a concept of measurement and volume of liquids.

Walking to playground

- Motor: "Be very careful so you won't fall or bump anyone. Can you walk tall? Walk small? Can you walk BIG? Can you be quiet as a mouse? If you are wearing blue, walk on tiptoes. If you are wearing red, take tiny steps."

MY REFLECTION   **BOX 9.6**

- What characteristics of the Snowy Day activity as described are congruent with activity-based instruction?
- Think about how you would facilitate the exploration of the children. What might you say? What could you do?
- How would you manage this activity?

- Finding a Bug Outdoors: "Let's pretend we are scientists who study bugs. What is this bug doing? Walking, running? Is it fast or slow? Does it have antennae? What do you think it eats?" Encourage children to remain engaged in observing by asking questions. Better yet, encourage children to ask questions and observe to find the answers to their own questions.

Embedding Strategies and Practices into Daily Routines

Embedding therapy into routines and play activities. Another way to implement naturalistic strategies is to embed therapeutic interventions into natural routines and play situations planned for all children in the inclusive classroom. This method of application maximizes the usefulness of typical activities by addressing the objectives targeted for individual children without making their needs obvious to their peers.

Embedding Therapy in a Typical Activity: The Puppet Theater

Ms. Gardner, a speech therapist from an elementary school, visited Melissa, age 4, twice a week in her child-care center. Melissa had difficulty with the articulation of a number of phonemes and had an overall language delay. The child-care center was not spacious and it was difficult to find a private area for individual therapy. Ms. Gardner thought it would be a good idea to integrate her therapy sessions with Melissa into the regular classroom activities. Ms. Sills, the teacher of Melissa's class, agreed to plan with Ms. Gardner, and they used various ways to plan for each week. Sometimes, Ms. Sills would give Ms. Gardner a copy of her lesson plans for the activities and learning centers planned around the children's interests or themes. Other times, they talked by telephone or e-mailed each other to plan which activities would be most suitable for integrating Melissa's speech goals. This week, Ms. Gardner spent time in an activity center set up as a puppet theater. She brought props with names that began with "b" or "d" for the puppeteers to use while they played. Ms. Gardner donned a puppet and played along with Melissa and the other children. All the children had a chance to practice their language skills and Melissa improved her articulation. Ms. Gardner also had an opportunity to screen a new child who Ms. Sills believed might be delayed in language development.

SOCIOCONTEXTUAL STRATEGIES

What are Sociocontextual Strategies?

Sociocontextual strategies and practices are a type of naturalistic strategy that involve children with others in authentic situations or contexts (see Box 9.7). The power of these strategies is derived in part from the social interchanges that occur. These strategies are also effective because they draw upon the relevance and authenticity of the context for the participants. Sociocontextual strategies capitalize on the social aspects

---

SOCIOCONTEXTUAL STRATEGIES   BOX 9.7

- Help children acquire collaborative interaction skills
- Foster group thinking to learn
- Enhance social interaction
- Provide opportunities for practicing expressive language and communication skills

---

of a learning situation to increase communication, socialization, and contemplation. Strategies in this category often involve teacher interactions with a single child or a group of children. Teachers can use sociocontextual strategies to promote child-to-child interactions. The social interchange and learning of children with a peer or group of peers also constitutes a powerful inclusion strategy.

The Advantages of Sociocontextual Strategies

One of the main benefits of inclusive settings is the wealth of opportunities these classrooms can offer all children for acquiring social interaction skills. This advantage is well-substantiated by research targeting children with disabilities and their typically developing peers (Guralnick, 1993; Peterson & McConnell, 1993; Sapona & Phillips, 1993). Further, social benefits of inclusive settings have been touted as a way to improve children's intercultural competence when classrooms are diverse (Grant, 1995; Solomon, 1995).

Research has shown that social and collaborative skills are learned. Children learn their social skills and acquire attitudes through interactions with others, especially their peers. An inclusive classroom with ample opportunities for play with a peer or groups of children serves as a social laboratory for children to explore the social realm with relative safety. This is especially true when a responsive teacher is available to guide children through any conflicts they are not yet equipped to resolve independently. Box 9.8 lists suggested key sociocontextual strategies.

KEY SOCIOCONTEXTUAL STRATEGIES   BOX 9.8

- Select games and activities that promote interaction.
- Encourage children to work and play in pairs or small groups.
- Reduce materials for some activities to foster sharing and cooperation.
- Assist children in delineating roles for group activities or play.
- Scaffold children's interactions.
- Interact with children frequently during their activities.
- Stimulate peer mediated play and learning.

COLLABORATIVE PROBLEM SOLVING IN THE   BOX 9.9
BLOCK CENTER

Two five-year-old children in the block center are trying to build a bridge for the toy train to cross. Tommy remembers that his Dad used a block that was curved into an archway. He tells his friend Kevin about this idea and they look for an arched shaped piece of wood in the block bin. They find an arched block and find that it can stand upright. Kevin tells Tommy that the bridge he crosses to come to school is curved but it has a flat roadway on top. They try several different blocks until they find one that balances on the arched block. Their ability to use language and communication effectively allows the boys to consider prior knowledge and experiences of both. They can work together cooperatively to find a solution to the problem.

The optimal period for social development is from birth to age 12 when critical social skills and characteristics, such as trust, self-esteem, prosocial skills, self-discipline, ability to form friendships, and coping skills, are acquired (Kostelnik, Whiren, Soderman, Stein, & Gregory, 2002). These skills and abilities are critical for all children currently and in the future. Predictions are that future jobs are more likely than ever to require high levels of reasoning, communication, group effort, and cooperation rather than individual work performed independently (Darling-Hammond, 1996; Iran-Nejad & Marsh, 1994). Therefore, inclusive classrooms that currently seek to prepare all children for success in school, as well as success in the workforce later, regularly incorporate peer and group strategies.

Social learning opportunities. In addition to providing fertile ground for the development of social competence, an inclusive classroom in which teachers liberally use peer and group strategies is conducive to cognitive development. Creating a social context or situation for young children increases the opportunity for cognitive development to be enhanced and conceptual learning to occur. Strategies in this category aim at fostering collaboration of peers or groups of children centered around a common purpose or problem. Strategies that foster the interaction of peers or the collaboration of groups of children to engage in common tasks or problem-solving activities are important sociocontextual strategies (Winter, 1999). Box 9.9 demonstrates a collaborative approach to problem solving.

Lev Vygotsky proposed a view of mental processing, which was different from the Western idea of cognition, that considered such processing as an individual, internal phenomenon. Vygotsky viewed the construction of knowledge as a socially mediated process that is influenced by interactions with others in a shared social context. The notion of shared cognition is one in which the thinking and processing of information, ideas, and thoughts by individuals is profoundly influenced by the thinking expressed by others in the group. Language and communication are key elements of sharing mental processes (Vygotsky, 1978).

More advanced forms of learning take place in a social context when there are possibilities for communication and shared thought with a peer or among a group of children. The collaborative activities of children and efforts toward cooperation are prized. The formation of a community of learners is an important goal for inclusive early childhood settings. When using strategies in this category, teachers promote social skills and learning through shared thought and language interactions. Evidence suggests that knowledge is not acquired passively but rather through an active process that occurs within the social realm in which humans live and work (Luria, 1979).

Sociocontextual Strategies in Kindergarten

Adapting materials and equipment to promote interaction. When early childhood teachers wish to reach every child and advance his or her learning, adapting materials or equipment used for activities and experiences may be a necessary step. Some children, especially those with identified disabilities or special learning needs, are more likely to achieve success if the equipment and materials support their efforts. Changes to adapt materials are often simple and inexpensive. As discussed previously, it is extremely important to avoid unnecessary adaptations that reduce the challenges for children. Subtle adaptations make a child's need for accommodations less obvious to their peers, which increases the child's acceptance into the group (Salisbury, 1991; Schumm & Vaughn, 1991; Wolery, 1991).

Adapting materials and increasing accessibility. Jody and Russell enjoyed the small motor manipulatives in their kindergarten classroom. Their teacher, Ms. Detrick, noticed that Matthew often joined them in the center; he would smile at the boys and play near them. However, Matthew was not very successful in this activity center because he had poor motor control due to cerebral palsy. He had only limited use of one arm and used a walker to move around the room, which meant he had difficulty taking puzzles or the large, open bins of plastic snap blocks off the shelves without spilling them. He often knocked several bins to the floor as he used his entire arm to sweep his chosen activity off the shelf, which tended to annoy the other children in the center who liked to play on the carpeted floor. Ms. Detrick decided it was time to remodel the activity center. First, she added several sets of manipulatives that would be easier for Matthew to handle, including larger snap blocks and jumbo plastic foam puzzles. 'All the children would enjoy these jumbo versions of their favorites,' she thought. Next, she placed the new materials in deep baskets with upright handles. Matthew could scoop the basket up with his arm and carry it as he used his walker to move around the center. Mrs. Detrick also put lids on the existing bins and put fewer items on each shelf to minimize spillage. The baskets of new items were moved to shoulder level on the shelves so Matthew could reach them easily from his walker. Jody and Russell loved the changes to the center, and they interacted with Matthew more frequently as they tried out the new materials in the center.

SUMMARY

This chapter discussed the importance of teachers acquiring competence in using a variety of teaching strategies and practices. Information was provided about the implications of brain research, underscoring the advantages of using a variety of teaching strategies and practices in inclusive early childhood classrooms. Reasons for the importance of the early years in the development of children were offered. This chapter also provided ideas on how to identify effective strategies and practices and ways to acquire them. The role of professional organizations in teachers' acquisition of strategies and practices was discussed. The concept of teaching strategies representing a continuum from naturalistic, implicit strategies to more overt, explicit strategies was introduced. The fundamental concept of using naturalistic practices in authentic early childhood home and school contexts was a key theme. Two major categories of teaching strategies were introduced: naturalistic and sociocontextual, and examples and ideas were provided for implementing each type of strategy.

Discussion Questions

1. What are some of the implications of recent findings in brain research for teachers in inclusive early childhood classrooms?
2. How can teachers find resources and identify effective strategies for enhancing children's learning?
3. What is a naturalistic strategy? Name a key advantage of this method.
4. Give an example of a naturalistic teaching strategy.
5. Explain how you would use a naturalistic strategy to facilitate the learning of young children.
6. What kinds of sociocontextual strategies involve peers and groups of children to implement?
7. Why are strategies aimed at developing efficient thinking and processing of information important in inclusive classrooms?
8. Which strategies are well-suited for classrooms with children speaking languages other than English?
9. What advantages can strategies differentiated for individuals bring to inclusive early childhood classrooms?
10. What are some of the thinking and processing strategies teachers can use to enhance learning during interactions with children?
11. What are the advantages of peer and group strategies for enhancing the learning of young children in inclusive settings?
12. Can individual children's learning be enhanced in a group setting?

13. How can teachers use typical classroom routines to promote learning for all children?

14. Give an example of a strategy for enhancing peer interactions among children who are diverse in language, culture, and ability.

15. How would you use peer and group strategies in a linguistically diverse classroom with children who are learning English as a second language?

Inclusive Activities

Try these activities to extend your knowledge and examine ways to apply key practices:

1. Select one of the categories of inclusive teaching strategies introduced in the chapter. Perform a literature search using professional Internet search engines to locate articles describing research that has been conducted on the use of strategies in the chosen category.

2. Write a brief one-paragraph synopsis for each category of inclusive teaching strategies introduced in this chapter.

3. Arrange to interview a teacher in an inclusive early childhood classroom. Send the teacher your one-paragraph synopsis of the categories of inclusive teaching strategies by mail or e-mail 1-2 days before your scheduled visit. Ask the teacher to discuss her thoughts about these strategies. Which ones interest her? Which strategies would she want to become more familiar before using? What kind of staff development does she participate in to increase her teaching skills for inclusive classrooms?

References

Atwater, J. B., Carta, J. J., Schwartz, I. S., & McConnell, S. R. (1994). Blending developmentally appropriate practice and early childhood special education: Redefining best practice to meet the needs of all children. In B. L. Mallory & R. S. New (Eds.), *Diversity and developmentally appropriate practices: Challenges for early childhood education* (pp. 185–201). New York: Teachers College Press.

Bailey, D. B., & McWilliams, R. A. (1990). Normalizing early intervention. *Topics in Early Childhood Special Education, 10*(2), 33–47.

Bailey, D. B., & Wolery, M. (1992). Strategies for intervention: teaching procedures and options. In D. B. Bailey & M. Wolery (Eds.), *Teaching infants and preschoolers with disabilities* (pp. 161–196). New York: Macmillan.

Baker, J., & Zigmond, N. (1990). Are regular education classes equipped to accomodate students with learning disabilities? *Exceptional Children, 56*(6), 515–526.

Bergen, D., & Coscia, J. (2001). *Brain research and childhood education: Implications for educators.* Olney, MD: Association for Childhood Education International.

Bredekamp, S., & Copple, C. (Eds.). (1997). *Developmentally appropriate practice in early childhood programs* (rev. ed.). Washington, DC: National Association for the Education of Young Children.

Bricker, D. (2000). Inclusion: How the scene has changed. *Topics in Early Childhood Special Education, 20*(1), 14–19.

Bricker, D., & Cripe, J. J. W. (1992). *An activity-based approach to early intervention.* Baltimore: Brookes.

Bricker, D., Pretti-Frontczak, K., & McComas, N. (1998). *An activity-based approach to early intervention* (2nd ed.). Baltimore: Brookes.

Bruder, M. B., & Dunst, C. J. (2005). Personnel preparation in recommended early intervention practices: Degree of emphasis across disciplines. *Topics in Early Childhood Special Education, 25*(1), 25–33.

Chin, J. C., & Reifel, S. (2000). Maternal scaffolding of Taiwanese play: Qualitative patterns. In S. Reifel (Ed.), *Play and culture studies: Vol. 3. Play in and out of context.* Stamford, CT: Ablex.

Darling-Hammond, L. (1996). The right to learn and the advancement of teaching: Research, policy, and practice for democratic education. *Educational Researcher, 25*(6), 5–17.

Elkind, D. (1987). *Miseducation.* New York: Knopf.

Farver, J., & Howes, C. (1993). Cultural differences in American and Mexican mother-child pretend play. *Merrill-Palmer Quarterly, 39,* 344–358.

Frost, J. L., Wortham, S., & Reifel, S. (2001). *Play and child development.* Upper Saddle River, NJ: Merrill/Prentice Hall.

Gardner, H. (1983). *Frames of mind: The Theory of multiple intelligences.* New York: Basic Books.

Good, R. H., Simmons, D. C., & Smith, S. B. (1998). Effective academic interventions in the United States: Evaluating and enhancing the acquisition of early reading skills. *School Psychology Review, 27*(45–56).

Grant, R. (1995). Meeting the needs of young second language learners. In E. E. Garcia, B. McLaughlin, B. Spodeck & O. N. Saracho (Eds.), *Meeting the challenge of linguistic and cultural diversity in early childhood education* (Vol. 6, pp. 1–17). New York, NY: Teachers College Press.

Gunn, B., Biglan, A., Smolkowski, K., & Ary, D. (2000). The efficacy of supplemental instruction in decoding skills for Hispanic and non-Hispanic students in early elementary. *The Journal of Special Education, 34*(2), 90–103.

Guralnick, M. J. (1993). Developmentally appropriate practice in the assessment and intervention of children's peer relations. *Topics in Early Childhood Special Education, 13*(3), 344–371.

Haight, W. (1998). Adult direct and indirect influences on play. In D. Bergen (Ed.), *Play from birth to twelve and beyond: Contexts, perspectives, and meanings* (pp. 259–265). New York: Garland.

Haight, W., & Miller, P. J. (1992). The development of everyday pretend play: A logitudinal study of mothers' participation. *Merrill-Plamer Quarterly, 38*(3), 331–349.

Harper-Whalen, S., Walmsley, T., & Moore, K. (1991). *An introduction to teaching through play* (No. 4). Washington, DC: Montana University at Missoula.

Horn, E., Lieber, J., Li, S., Sandall, S., & Schwartz, I. (2000). Supporting young children's IEP goals in inclusive settings through embedded learning opportunities. *Topics in Early Childhood Special Education, 20*(4), 208–223.

Iran-Nejad, A., & Marsh, G. E., II. (1994). Discovering the future of education. *Education, 114*(2), 249–256.

Joint Committee on Teacher Planning for Students with Disabilities. (1995). *Planning for academic diversity in America's classrooms: Windows on reality, research, change, and practice.* Lawrence, KS: The University of Kansas Center for Research on Learning.

Karp, K. S., & Voltz, D. L. (2000). Weaving mathematical instructional strategies into inclusive settings. *Intervention in School and Clinic, 35*(4), 206–215.

Kostelnik, M., Whiren, A., Soderman, A., Stein, L., & Gregory, K. (2002). *Guiding children's social development: Theory to practice.* Albany, NY: Delmar.

Luria, A. R. (1979). *The making of mind: A personal account of Soviet psychology* (M. Cole, & S. Cole, Trans.). Cambridge, MA: Harvard University Press.

Mudd, J., & Wolery, M. (1987). Training head start teachers to use incidental teaching. *Journal of the Division of Early Childhood, 11,* 124–134.

Nash, J. M. (2002, November 11). Inside the womb. *Time,* 68–78.

Parten, M. (1933). Social play among preschool children. *Journal of Abnormal and Social Psychology, 28,* 136–147.

Peterson, C. A., & McConnell, S. R. (1993). Factors affecting the impact of social interaction skills interventions in early childhood special education. *Topics in Early Childhood Special Education, 13*(1), 38–56.

Piaget, J. (1962). *Play, dreams and imitation in childhood.* New York: Norton.

Rogoff, B., Mistry, J., Goncu, A., & Mosier, C. (1993). Guided participation in cultural activity by toddlers and caregivers. *Monographs of the Society for Research in Child Development, 58*(Serial No. 236).

Salisbury, C. (1991). Mainstreaming during the early childhood years. *Exceptional Children, 58*(2), 146–155.

Sapona, R., & Phillips, L. (1993). Classrooms as communities of learners: Sharing responsibility for learning. In A. M. Bauer (Ed.), *Children who challenge the system* (pp. 63–87). Norwood, NJ: Ablex.

Saville-Troike, M. (1978). *A guide to culture in the classroom.* Rosslyn, VA: National Clearing House for Bilingual Education.

Schepis, M. M., Reid, D. H., Owenby, J., & Parsons, M. B. (2001). Training support staff to embed teaching within natural routines of young children with disabilities in an inclusive preschool. *Journal of Applied Behavior Analysis, 34,* 313–327.

Schumm, J., & Vaughn, S. (1991). Making adaptations for mainstreamed students: General classroom teachers' perspectives. *Remedial and Special Education, 12*(4), 15–24.

Schwartzman, H. G. (1978). *Transformations: The anthropology of children's play.* New York: Plenum.

Shore, R. (1997). *Rethinking the brain: New insights into early development.* New York: Families and Work Institute.

Silberman, M. (1996). *Active learning: 101 strategies to teach any subject.* Boston: Allyn & Bacon.

Solomon, R. P. (1995). Beyond prescriptive pedagogy: Teacher inservice education for cultural diversity. *Journal of Teacher Education, 46*(4), 251–258.

Tate, T. L., Thompson, R. H., & McKerchar, P. M. (2005). Training teachers in an infant classroom to use embedded teaching strategies. *Education and Treatment of Children, 28*(3), 206–221.

Thompson, R. A., & Nelson, C. A. (2001). Developmental science and the media: Early brain development. *American Psychologist, 56*(1), 5–15.

Vygotsky, L. (1978). *Mind in society: The development of higher psychological functions.* Cambridge, MA: Harvard University Press.

Winter, S. M. (1999). *The early childhood inclusion model: A program for all children.* Olney, MD: Association for Childhood Education International.

Wolery, M. (1991). Instruction in early childhood special education: "Seeing through a glass darkly . . . . knowing in part". *Exceptional Children, 58*(2), 127–135.

Chapter 10

Differentiated Instruction with Individually Appropriate Support

Key Principle:

- Foster success of individuals within group contexts

Objectives

After reading this chapter you will be able to:

1. Discuss how to provide differentiated instruction with individually appropriate levels of support.
2. Describe how to embed teaching strategies into naturalistic contexts of an inclusive classroom.
3. Discuss ways to use explicit strategies at different levels of intensity to promote social, communication, and academic learning.
4. Explain the importance of teaching cognitive learning strategies.
5. Discuss how to implement opportunities for children to practice cognitive learning strategies.
6. Ensure that English language learners receive adequate support for their learning.
7. Evaluate the effectiveness of inclusive teaching strategies.

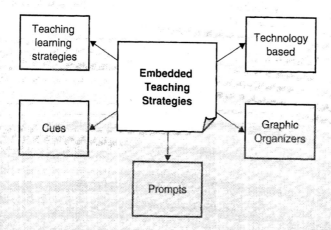

INTRODUCTION

This chapter discusses how to provide differentiated instruction in an inclusive classroom through the use of responsive teaching to accommodate individual children. Building a repertoire of effective instructional strategies and practices helps teachers provide differentiated instruction for all children in inclusive classrooms. However, gaining proficiency in using effective strategies and practices, alone, is not enough to promote the success of all children. When teaching diverse groups of young children, sensitivity to the learning styles and strengths of individual children is critical. Matching the types of strategies and intensity of support provided to individual children in specific learning situations is vital. Teachers who are most effective in fostering the learning of all children have competence in using a full repertoire of strategies and are astute at making good matches between those strategies and individual children.

Chapter 9 presented the conceptualization of teaching strategies as a continuum from naturalistic to more explicit. This chapter emphasizes embedding strategies into naturalistic activities of early childhood classrooms to accommodate individual learners. Of particular concern is the ability to match the level or intensity of instructional support with individual children's needs so each can benefit from differentiated curricular activities and achieve his or her learning goals. Application of developmentally and individually appropriate strategies and support as children participate in shared activities of a differentiated curriculum is the goal of inclusive early childhood classrooms.

INDIVIDUALLY APPROPRIATE SUPPORT

Differentiated instruction in an inclusive classroom is accomplished through the use of teaching strategies that are responsive to individual children who vary in culture, language, ability, and demographic characteristics. Child-centered or child-initiated learning matched to the child's development is commonly associated with developmentally appropriate practice (DAP) and embraced by educators in early childhood and early intervention (Division for Early Childhood Council for Exceptional Children, National Association for the Education of Young Children, & Association of Teacher Educators, 1995). DAP guidelines also specify that learning experiences should also be individually appropriate for children (Bredekamp & Copple, 1997; Carta, 1994). Whereas some children require minimal facilitation of their learning using naturalistic strategies, others benefit from more intensive support. The goal is to teach responsively by providing the level of support necessary for each child in the inclusive classroom to have full access to curriculum and instruction.

As mentioned in Chapter 5, matching the level of support to the needs of individuals is essential to providing differentiated curriculum and instruction (Tomlinson, 2004). All children, including those with disabilities, have better opportunities to learn when teachers continually embed individually supportive and responsive strategies into their developmentally appropriate activities. In essence, by providing different input modes and options for response and varying levels of support to children in their classroom, teachers effectively differentiate their instruction. Offering individual support with appropriate strategies customized to the child, helps children in inclusive classrooms benefit from each new learning experience (Broderick, Mehta-Parekh, & Reid, 2005; Tomlinson, 2004).

Earlier debates between proponents of DAP and those advocating more traditional early childhood special education teaching strategies based on behaviorist foundations have resulted in a blending of practices across fields (Udell, Peters, & Templeman, 1998). It is widely recognized that there is a need for both sets of practices so teachers can apply powerful teaching strategies that are also individually appropriate. Research has indicated that teachers in inclusive early childhood classrooms can be accepting of both sets of practice, and teachers schooled in DAP principles can accept and learn to effectively embed more explicit, teacher-mediated instructional support strategies in their inclusive early childhood classrooms (Malmskog & McDonnell, 1999). Corroborating these findings, surveys revealed few differences in the perceptions of early childhood teachers in self-contained and inclusive classrooms regarding implementation of explicit strategies. Teachers in both settings indicated remarkable similarity in their positive views regarding the feasibility of implementing social interaction interventions in their classrooms (Rheams & Bain, 2005). These studies suggested that gaps between teachers who have early childhood education backgrounds and those prepared in early intervention programs may be narrowing in some areas. It certainly suggests increasing acceptance for embedding individually appropriate support into differentiated learning activities in DAP classroom contexts; however, acceptability and actual implementation could be very different. Even though teachers indicated acceptability of more active intervention, more research is needed to determine to what extent they implement these strategies in the classroom. One study examining social skill development reported teachers in inclusive early childhood classrooms tend to choose more passive and indirect facilitation strategies (Buysse, Goldman, & Skinner, 2003).

Embedded Teaching Approaches

An overarching approach to pedagogy in early childhood education is an embedded teaching method. In this approach to teaching, teachers implement teaching strategies within routines or usual activities of the child (Venn, Werts, Morris, DeCesare, & Cuffs, 1993). The embedded approach contrasts with clinical teaching approaches in which children are "pulled out," away from typical settings, to receive instruction for a targeted skill under a structured set of conditions. Naturalistic and milieu approaches are among the types of teaching methods considered in the embedded teaching category. Using embedded teaching approaches, teachers try to match their support strategies to best accommodate the individual child and enhance that child's chances for success in typical activities and play (Harper-Whalen, Walmsley, & Moore, 1991; Tate, Thompson, & McKerchar, 2005).

Identifying strategies for individual children. Observing children as they work and play is one way that teachers can plan teaching strategies that are well-matched to individual children. Teachers can focus observations toward the identification of each child's areas of strength, with the aim to notice some of the conditions and strategies for learning that appear to result in a child's success. Pinpointing a few of the ways individual children are successful in learning can provide a basis for planning future scaffolding, as a child is introduced to new concepts and skills. While watching and working with each child, the teacher can use the following questions to guide observing and recording of information:

- What conditions seem to help the child learn best?
- Can you describe the strategies the child tries?
- How does the child solve problems?
- During what kinds of activities is the child most successful?

- Is the child most successful learning alone or with others?
- What kind of teacher assistance seems to work best?

Remember that there is probably not one best way for a child to learn. The conditions for success will vary somewhat depending upon the nature of the task or what is to be learned, children's interest, novelty of the task, personal preferences, and a variety of other factors. Nevertheless, teachers who are observant while children are learning can often identify some preferences for learning, and the usual ways children approach tasks can provide a basis for choosing teaching strategies.

Range and intensity. Matching teaching strategies to the children in inclusive classrooms needs thoughtful consideration. The range of abilities represented by children in such classrooms is often broad; consequently, there is evidence to suggest that using different kinds of strategies will be needed to produce beneficial effects for individual children. Further, teaching inclusively will require attention to variations in the amount of structure provided and the intensity level used to support the learning of individual children (Rose & Rose, 1994; Sears, Carpenter, & Burstein, 1994).

Evaluating the effectiveness of strategies. It has often been said that teaching is both an art and a science. Teachers must have a fund of scientific, research-based knowledge from which to draw upon during teaching situations. Whereas teachers can become knowledgeable about the various strategies that can be used, it is critical that they gain expertise in applying strategies to situations where the techniques are most likely to have a positive outcome. The latter, the art of applying the strategies, has been examined and pondered by educators. Lay-Dopyera and Dopyera (1992) contend that early childhood educators are rather automatic in their strategy use. Without much forethought, they instinctively use strategies and practices as situations arise in early childhood classrooms. For most teachers, these spontaneously chosen strategies generally do produce the desired results. However, early childhood teachers are often unable to describe their actions and tend not to think about why these strategies were successful (Lay-Dopyera & Dopyera, 1992). Donald Schon (1983, 1987) has explained this phenomenon as a teacher "knowing in action" that the strategy works. He believes, however, that teachers should strive for a more conscious orientation toward strategy use. A teacher who is monitoring her actions and whether the strategy is working has achieved a level of awareness that may allow her to be even more effective in strategy use. Schon says a teacher who is conscious of her actions is "reflecting in action" and is able to evaluate the effectiveness of the strategies she is using in the learning situation. This evaluation process allows the teacher to alter the strategy or use different strategies during the teaching and learning interaction to help a child achieve greater success (Schon, 1983, 1987).

An early childhood teacher who wishes to provide an inclusive learning environment for all children must be willing to move beyond the automatic use of strategies toward thoughtful, deliberate, and planned implementation. Arriving at the state of deliberate application of strategies requires conscious forethought and planning, in-process evaluation, and active decision making. Teachers base their planning on observation of children and careful scrutiny of their own teaching behaviors.

Explicit Teaching Strategies

Explicit teaching strategies are deliberate, planned support strategies to facilitate a child's understanding, learning processes, or skill acquisition. However, explicit strategies require more than rote memorization by the learner. Using explicit teaching can create an apprenticeship relationship between the teacher and child. For example, a teacher may demonstrate a cognitive strategy for solving a mathematical problem. As the child learns the strategy, less support is provided by the teacher (Karp & Voltz, 2000; Stein, 1998). A variety of strategies fall into the explicit category from simple cues and prompts to more complex sets of strategies designed to help children learn skills and streamline learning processes.

Prompts. Prompts and cues are among the commonly used types of explicit strategies routinely used in inclusive classrooms. Teachers use prompts to help the child respond accordingly, which promotes a child's learning. Prompts and cues offer the learner additional information or turn the child's attention toward relevant features of a task. The following are usual types of prompts and cues that offer varying levels of support to the child:

- Cue: a command or direction that helps a child know that a response is necessary
- Physical or manual prompts: the providing of physical assistance to cue a child to respond, accordingly. This type of prompt is also called hand-over-hand prompting.
- Verbal prompts: the use of words or voice inflections to help a child gain information
- Visual prompts: the use of pictures, words, or graphics to convey information or help a child learn concepts
- Gestural prompts: the use of nonverbal signs or gestures to convey information and invite responses
- Modeling: the demonstrating of the desired performance or set of behaviors

Prompts and cues are among the actions teachers can take to help children learn behaviors or responses needed to participate in early learning contexts with their peers. These forms of intervention are specific and can be repeated to help children learn a task or concept (Cavallaro, Haney, & Cabello, 1993; Polloway & Patton, 1997; Schloss & Smith, 1994).

Graphic information and organizers. Providing visual information and organizing curriculum content with graphic advance organizers is beneficial for children who are English language learners (ELLs). Advance organizers help these children access their prior knowledge and make links to the newly introduced content knowledge. Visual scaffolding is another method of supporting ELLs as they progress across the curriculum. Visual information that is organized and sequenced can help children comprehend the language of instruction so they acquire knowledge and concepts along with their peers (Herrell & Jordan, 2004). Visual organizers embedded in authentic

Individually appropriate support for a child might be a demonstration of how to use specialized equipment or how to perform a task.

contexts contribute to the comprehensibility of language necessary for acquisition of knowledge (Krashen, 1982; Krashen & Terrell, 1983).

Some children with disabilities, especially those with cognitive delays or hearing impairments, benefit from explicit strategies that are visual in character. A graphic organizer exemplifies an explicit strategy designed to organize key information for children into a visual cueing system. A graphic organizer can be used in advance of an activity to activate prior knowledge or to stimulate the motivation of children. Graphic organizers can also be used during an activity to guide the participation of children with learning disabilities. For example, an outline of a story can guide children's comprehension as the teacher reads a story. The outline could be filled in with story details during story reading, making the graphic organizer an effective method of teaching children how to organize pertinent thoughts and ideas as they read by following the story line of the book (Gross & Ortiz, 1994).

Children, especially those who are deaf and hard of hearing, may need to be taught explicit strategies for gaining meaning from graphic information presented in storybooks or texts. In preschool, teachers can begin explicit modeling of telling a story using pictures. Learning this technique when they are young may help these children with the maps, charts, diagrams, and other graphics in expository texts that they will use in elementary grades. In addition, children's responses to literature can help them comprehend text and gain more explicit answers to questions. Dramatic reenactments with puppets or role-playing can make books more accessible to children who are deaf and hard of hearing (Cerra, Watts-Taffe, & Rose, 1997).

Reenactments with puppets helps children who are deaf or hard of hearing comprehend textual information.

Corrective feedback. Providing a child with specific information regarding his or her performance on a task can help the child improve subsequent attempts. Offering feedback to correct a child's mistakes is best when information is specific and offered immediately following performance of the task. It is crucial to establish a positive atmosphere when providing the child with corrective feedback. Teachers can use an encouraging tone of voice and positive facial expressions to provide reassurance and motivate the child to try again (Eggen & Kauchak, 1996; Polloway & Patton, 1997).

Individualized reinforcement. Certain children may require reinforcement to encourage their participation in learning activities. For example, children with developmental delays may need systematic reinforcement of their participation. Teachers can identify a child's preference by presenting items to the child and noting the child's reaction. Categories of reinforcement items may include sensory reinforcement, such as visual, social, tactile, and gustatory reinforcers. Preferred items identified for each child can be kept in a box with the child's name. This individualized method of assessing and using reinforcement for each child encourages children to participate fully in the activities offered in inclusive classrooms (Mason & Egel, 1995).

Common misconceptions. It is important to distinguish between explicit strategies and other teaching practices based upon behaviorist tenets. Explicit strategies refer to a variety of teacher-mediated techniques that may be used to provide systematic instruction to children when individually appropriate. However, it is important to note that while explicit strategies can be used in systematic instruction, explicit strategies alone do not constitute direct instruction. Confusion surrounding the term direct instruction stems from Rosenshine's use of the term in a review of behaviorist teaching practices (Rosenshine, 1976). Rosenshine emphasized two explicit strategies, task analysis and teacher modeling, used in the direct instruction model (Bereiter & Englemann, 1966). Although the direct instruction model (DI) includes the two strategies Rosenshine highlighted, it is actually a far more comprehensive system of teaching. The DI model uses various program components, such as curriculum analysis to identify relevant content, scripted lessons, and assessment, to achieve individually appropriate instruction and student mastery of the curriculum (Kim & Axelrod, 2005; Stein, 1998).

Embedding Explicit Strategies

As mentioned previously, explicit teaching strategies can be used before authentic learning opportunities as advance organizers, during a learning activity to guide responses, and after an experience to provide feedback and reinforcement. These strategies are an application of a behaviorist theory involving stimulus-response methodology and used in clinical approaches to teach skills outside of authentic contexts. Explicit strategies vary in intensity, and these strategies are more intrusive compared to naturalistic strategies at the other end of the continuum. Consequently, for early childhood settings, experts recommend embedding explicit strategies in authentic learning situations so children with special needs can learn alongside their peers. When embedded in naturally occurring routines or the authentic contexts of an early learning experience, explicit learning strategies can help certain children gain skills needed to participate more fully in their inclusive classroom (Cavallaro et al., 1993; Malmskog & McDonnell, 1999; Polloway & Patton, 1997).

Intensifying child-focused support. To achieve individually appropriate practices, teachers may use explicit strategies, singly or in combination, within natural activities and routines that occur. Experts in early intervention recommend child-focused interventions as intentional actions to intensify intervention and help some children gain greater benefits from natural contexts, such as homes, child-care centers, and inclusive classrooms. Child-focused strategies can be effective when they are adapted for individual children based on skills targeted on their IEPs. Consistency is achieved when teachers systematically apply the intervention strategies across children's learning activities and experiences. Hierarchical intervention models offer flexibility to match a child's needs for support as they progress in learning skills and accomplishing tasks. Teachers using hierarchical approaches embed child-focused strategies at different levels of intensity from simple environmental changes to specifically planned trial sequences. The type and amount of support is planned based on data teachers collect through observation and performance-based assessment (Bricker, Pretti-Frontczak, & McComas, 1998; Wolery, 2000).

However, for some children, embedding naturalistic strategies into routines and activities, such as activity-based interventions (ABIs), may lack sufficient intensity or consistency to improve behavior or learning. Certain children may require more opportunities for practice on targeted behaviors and more intensive support for their learning (Carta, Schwartz, Atwater, & McConnell, 1991). Individually appropriate practice for these children may involve embedding the use of a planned, instructional strategy called a learning trial or a discrete learning trial into an activity-based or DAP classroom environment. Learning trials involve implementation of specifically planned explicit strategies, such as preselected prompts or specific reinforcement. Teachers using this form of embedded instruction follow the child's lead; however, they watch for opportunities to implement the learning trial. Studies of specifically planned learning trials using explicit strategies embedded in ABI contexts have reported success. Preschoolers have demonstrated improvements in targeted skills, such as peer interaction skills and peer engagement in learning tasks (McBride & Schwartz, 2003; VanDerHeyden, Snyder, Smith, Sevin, & Longwell, 2005).

Embedding social and communication strategies. Children learn social interaction skills during infancy and early childhood through opportunities in various contexts. They gain in social skills through feedback from family and others they encounter within their school and community. The acquisition of social skills is critical foundation for development of meaningful and effective communication (Trent, Kaiser, & Wolery, 2005). Teachers can use explicit strategies to expand the opportunities for individual children to learn social interaction skills within the natural contexts of the inclusive classroom. Children who learn to interact well with their peers are reported to be less aggressive and more prosocial than those who are withdrawn or fail to interact successfully. Peer interactions can be difficult for young children with cognitive disabilities or language disorders who lack good conversational skills. Research has revealed that teachers may observe children who:

- Usually play alone
- Wander and avoid participation
- Tend to be aggressive—hitting, kicking, biting, or verbally abusive
- Lack friends

Children with these symptoms might benefit from explicit strategies used to help them acquire social skills needed for communication and interaction (Girolametto, Weitzman, & Greenberg, 2004).

Explicit strategies can be applied within naturalistic play contexts to make communicative peer interactions more productive. Teachers can learn to apply both direct and indirect explicit strategies to offer verbal support to children who experience difficulty in play interactions with peers. Direct strategies clearly tell the child what to say or do to elicit interaction with a peer. Indirect strategies cue the child to salient information about the social situation or give encouragement. Using verbal prompts, offering suggestions, and giving children verbal invitations can facilitate

Teachers may use explicit strategies to teach children to resolve conflicts and improve social interaction skills.

children's communications and interactions with one another. In fact, this method of embedding explicit strategies into a naturalistic setting may better enhance generalization of the acquired social skills to other settings than explicit strategies used in isolation outside a situational context (Girolametto et al., 2004).

Embedding explicit strategies can help children with depression or mood disorders to learn better strategies for interacting with peers, which can improve their feeling of depression and lessen isolation. For example, some children may need to learn strategies for initiating a conversation or making a bid to participate in an activity with their peers. Embedding these strategies into the natural social contexts of the classroom allows children to practice and gain confidence. Peers can play a role in cueing the child to use new social skills. As children with depression receive feedback and experience success, they connect with their peers and these interactions may lead to formation of friendships (Abrams, Theberge, & Karan, 2005). Children with oppositional and defiant behaviors are also reported to benefit from direct social skill teaching to help them establish relationships with peers and interact more cooperatively in the classroom. Establishing and teaching rules and routines can foster more compliant behaviors (Salend & Sylvestre, 2005).

Embedding reading and literacy strategies. Explicitly teaching instructional strategies and routines has been reported successful in helping children with learning disabilities improve their performance in reading and literacy. Teachers model specific strategies for planning and conducting tasks and provide guidance until students can perform the routines independently. Guidance is customized for individual children, and teachers calibrate their support so that less support is provided as the child gains efficiency in using the inculcated strategies. Self-regulated writing strategies, such as semantic webbing and reading to locate information, have been taught to children in elementary grades and beyond. The results of more than two decades of research has indicated that explicitly taught strategy use improves their writing skills (Troia & Graham, 2002).

Explicit teaching of phonetic analysis to children with and without mental retardation has been a topic of research study for many years. Following a review of more than a decade of studies, Joseph and Seery (2004), recommended inculcating explicit phonetic strategies into the literacy activities in the curriculum for young children with mental retardation. These authors recommended incorporating phonemic awareness into literacy activities initially, followed by explicit teaching of letter-sound relationships. Learning these strategies may enhance children's later word recognition performance, although studies are needed to provide verification. Nevertheless, children with mental retardation do appear to gain some benefit from instruction in explicit phonetic analysis strategies, and studies have suggested these children can generalize their skills to new reading tasks (Joseph & Seery, 2004).

The practice of combining explicit reading strategies with whole-language instruction in authentic contexts has shown promise in helping children in elementary school improve their spelling and reading skills. The power of combining these two types of strategies appears to supercede using whole-language instruction alone (Butyniec-Thomas & Woloshyn, 1997). For some children, such as those who are deaf and hard of hearing, teachers can explicitly model how to make an inference by asking questions and thinking aloud to ponder the answer. Another way to use explicit strategies with children who are deaf is to use direct explanation. Using this strategy, children in early elementary who are reading are told to use prior knowledge to help them make sense of the new information presented in the narrative (Cerra et al., 1997).

Embedding strategies for the English language learner. Children learning a second language will gain an understanding of words in their new language before they feel comfortable attempting to communicate using their newly acquired vocabulary. Teachers can use the total physical response (TPR) method embedded in naturalistic activities in the classroom to help ELLs learn to communicate in the second language. To introduce new words, teachers identify vocabulary words used in learning activities or classroom routines and demonstrate word meaning through physical demonstration and gestures. Simple commands used for classroom management, such as sit down or stand up, will help the child understand the cueing system. As the child learns the words or commands, the teacher fades the physical prompts and introduces the next set of words. Embedding TPR in games and other authentic, naturalistic contexts will give the child practice and help build confidence in using the second language. Because this strategy is performance based, it is easy for teachers to assess the progress of children (Asher, 1982; Herrell & Jordan, 2004).

The Significance of Explicit Teaching Strategies

Certain children may require more overt and intensive intervention to promote their learning. Naturalistic teaching strategies may not provide sufficient support for children with severe disabilities. Children with autism, those with severe mental retardation, or those with multiple disabilities may lack the skills to participate in classroom activities independently. Consequently, the effectiveness of naturalistic strategies alone may be limited for these children, and they may miss critical opportunities for learning (Carta et al., 1991). Embedding explicit strategies into naturalistic classroom contexts can help children with severe disabilities acquire social interaction skills and may help all children improve their literacy skills (Butyniec-Thomas & Woloshyn, 1997). Whereas explicit strategies are individually appropriate options for mediating the learning of certain children, it is still wise to use the least intrusive explicit strategies necessary to promote the learning of these individual children (Drinkwater & Demchak, 1995).

Implications for collaboration. Use of embedded explicit strategies has implications for collaboration among professionals and family members. Collaborative team planning and involvement of families is important to maximize the positive effects of embedded teaching. Classroom teachers are critical team members who provide ongoing data on each child's behavior and learning. These data are valuable in planning and evaluating the success of embedded strategies. When intensive embedded strategies, such as learning trials, are needed, the team may benefit from special education teachers and school psychologist. Collaboration with these experts can help teachers validate and use effective learning trials that are individually appropriate for certain children. Families can contribute to planning, implementing, and evaluating embedded strategies since their role is critical in generalizing children's learning to home contexts and helping to maintain a child's skills.

Peer modeling influence on the behavior of children with special needs has long been fundamental to the pro-inclusion argument. Although findings indicate peer modeling has positive effects on social behaviors, less is known about the outcomes of peer modeling as an instructional strategy to explicitly teach novel behaviors. A study comparing adult models to sibling models for preschool children with autism suggested both types of modeling can be effective for teaching language skills (Jones & Schwartz, 2004). Modeling tasks that were focused on increasing the functional vocabulary for the preschooler with autism were successful. Whereas the relationship of models and the ability of the children with special needs to attend to the model are among the factors that may influence the effectiveness of peer modeling, the results of this study are promising. Use of peer modeling for instructional purposes within the natural contexts of inclusive preschool classrooms is supported by this study; preschoolers with autism can engage in observational learning, and modeling was effective for increasing their functional vocabulary (Jones & Schwartz, 2004).

Recent evidence has suggested that older siblings can learn to use explicit strategies to promote social interaction skills in young children with developmental disabilities.

Siblings of children with Down syndrome were trained to use responsive interaction strategies to foster social communication interactions. The training involved modeling, role-playing, and oral feedback to help the sibling gain proficiency in using the responsive interaction strategy. Follow-up revealed the siblings were able to use the strategy a month after training, and the children with Down syndrome made modest gains in communicative skills (Trent et al., 2005).

Approaches emphasizing family-centered practices are compatible with the strategy of involving parents in the explicit instruction of young children. The new emphasis on building a collaborative relationship with parents, rather than simply providing services to families, opens up the option of sharing the teaching responsibilities with parents. Modeling has potential as a strategy for explicitly teaching skills across both home and school contexts. Research supports the involvement of parents as instructional models for young children at risk or those with identified special needs. Consequently, parent education, focused on how parents can teach skills to their children, has the advantage of providing more opportunities for children to learn within naturalistic contexts of home and neighborhood. Further, maintenance of skills is enhanced when parents provide ongoing modeling and reinforcement in authentic home situations. Experts have called for attention to be focused on the potential of parent education for explicit modeling and teaching, and more emphasis on research about the potential effects of these strategies is warranted (Mahoney et al., 1999). In pursuit of such inquiry, an extensive review of previous early childhood programs found encouraging results for parent involvement aimed at improving school success of children. Programs with parent education focused on teaching parents to assume a coaching role with their young children reported yielding positive effects on a child's cognitive development (Blok, Fukkink, Gebhardt, & Leseman, 2005).

TEACHING COGNITIVE LEARNING STRATEGIES

This category of explicit teaching strategies encompasses techniques and practices teachers use to facilitate each child's learning and promote the development of a child's own strategies for learning (see Box 10.1). Some refer to this category as strategies instruction or cognitive interventions (Owen & Fuchs, 2002). Strategies instruction or teaching learning strategies can range from providing children with a framework for problem solving to the application of specific routines or sets of strategies (Wong, 1994). This category of explicit strategies can be used successfully in inclusive education settings with young children; however, whole-group instruction may be less effective for teaching learning strategies. Teaching strategies in small groups or asking children to work in pairs while using the strategy taught may be more effective in improving children's performance (Fuchs, Fuchs, & Karns, 2001; Fuchs, Fuchs, Prentice, Burch, & Paulsen, 2002).

Children with typical development naturally become strategic learners, gaining knowledge and skills from their experiences and interactions with others in their social

```
┌─────────────────────────────────────────────────────────────────────┐
│                                                                       │
│                    LEARNING STRATEGIES              BOX 10.1          │
│     • Acquisition helps children become independent learners.         │
│     • Expert learners can model learning strategies.                  │
│     • Teachers can encourage children to develop and try new strategies.│
│                                                                       │
└─────────────────────────────────────────────────────────────────────┘
```

and physical environment. Some children with disabilities can learn functional skills through instruction embedded in routine activities (Bricker et al., 1998; Hemmeter, 2000). Other children with developmental disabilities or autism seem to need explicit or direct instruction with high interaction with the teacher to acquire the functional life skills that peers with typical development learn independently or with minimal assistance (McBride & Schwartz, 2003).

Defining Cognitive Learning Strategies

From birth, children embark on a lifelong mission to learn *how* to learn. As infants, children are immersed in a barrage of sensory information. There are sources of visual stimulation, such as colors, shapes, and images, moving across their field of vision. Children hear a cacophony of sounds produced by objects, animals, and people in their environment. They feel different temperatures and textures. How do infants make sense of the confusing and complex sources of sensory input in their world? They begin to make associations and see relationships among the stimuli they receive. Within the context of social interactions, children devise and use a variety of thinking strategies for processing sensory input and gaining information about their world and the people in it, as they develop and learn throughout childhood. The child takes an active role in making sense of their world (Bakley, 2001; Dunn, 1997; Lynch & Simpson, 2004).

Brain research not only offers a better understanding of how the brain grows and develops, but also permits a greater understanding of how brain development and learning are related. Scientists have found evidence that aspects of intelligence once thought to be inborn are, in fact, learned. This finding casts a different light on the role of teachers and the mission of educational settings, especially regarding evidence that has suggested that thinking skills, or metacognition, are learned (Abbott & Ryan, 1999). Teachers, parents, and other expert learners can influence the acquisition of thinking skills in young children.

Mediated problem solving. Vygotskian theory explains that children first learn their metacognitive and problem-solving skills in social interactions with others (Vygotsky, 1978). Children benefit from teachers and parents who are good mediators of their experiences. Evidence has suggested that interaction with parents and teachers is instrumental in shaping the thinking processes children use as they explore and learn. Being able to explore freely within the security of a caring adult as a safety net affords children more opportunities to take risks during their interactions and problem solving attempts. The security of a nurturing adult as a mediator of tasks may also contribute to the level of persistence that children show in staying engaged in tasks (Bowlby, 1969; Klein, 1992). A child is more likely to benefit when an adult assists the child in solving a problem rather than solving the problem for the child. It appears to be even more beneficial when the adult talks about the strategies they are using while helping children solve a problem. Children with a mediating adult who regularly talks about the metacognitive information they used as they engage in joint problem solving appear to acquire more sophisticated thinking strategies (Moss, 1992).

Evidence has also suggested that mathematical problem solving of children with learning disabilities can be improved using strategies instruction. Moreover, strategies for problem solving can be effectively implemented in inclusive classrooms serving a diverse group of children in typical elementary school classrooms. Learning strategy interventions planned for use in real-life classrooms can be effective when teachers consider the developmental appropriateness of strategies and the strategies are used to solve authentic problems. Strategies that have found to be effective are:

- Simple
- Explicit
- Concrete examples
- Developmentally appropriate
- Peer mediated

Pairing children with each other, peer mediation, provides children with immediate feedback and may be particularly beneficial for young children with and without disabilities. The success of using strategies instruction with peer mediation in inclusive classrooms provides further substantiation that children with disabilities can learn with their peers who have typical development. Finding strategies that enhance the learning of all young children does provide a boost to inclusive education. These findings are important because the avoidance of strategies that single out children is always preferable to preserve the self-esteem of children with disabilities (Owen & Fuchs, 2002).

Modeling cognitive learning strategies. Children benefit when teachers model strategies to enhance thinking and processing information. Teachers can act as coaches, showing how, helping the child attempt the strategy, and evaluating the results. In this way, teachers help children construct higher level strategies than children can devise on their own. It is important to provide children with effective feedback to keep them motivated to complete the task. Repeated modeling and practice of thinking process strategies helps children learn to become self-regulated, independent learners.

Studies have indicated that parents and teachers can be very influential models of strategic learning for children; gifted preschoolers were found to acquire learning strategies during casual play with parents when their parents modeled learning strategies (Moss, 1992).

Supporting Child Acquisition and Use of Strategies

A lifelong process of becoming a successful learner begins at birth. As mentioned previously, the early childhood years is an extremely important time in brain development. Moreover, children are acquiring strategies for learning through their experiences with the physical environment and social interactions within their learning environment. Children are gaining competence in developing strategies that will help them to learn. Further, childhood is a time when children can practice using various strategies for learning through play and routine activities. Practice helps children gain proficiency and learn to apply strategies efficiently as they acquire concepts and skills.

The socioconstructivist theory of Lev Vygotsky is relevant to the goals for inclusive classrooms. Through scaffolding, teachers provide children with help and support so they can move beyond what they can do independently. The term scaffolding refers to actions of teachers intended to assist or facilitate a child's learning. These actions include use of an array of instructional strategies, both planned and spontaneous, used by the teacher to support a child's attempts to acquire skills and knowledge. Through

---

SORTING ATTRIBUTE BLOCKS   BOX 10.2

Ms. Fernandez placed a set of attribute blocks in the table-toys center for her inclusive class of three-year-old children to explore. The blocks were different shapes, such as circles, triangles, and squares cut into different sizes. All the shapes of a particular size were the same color. Before making this activity available to the children, she had spent some time planning how she could enhance the thinking processes of children as they played with the blocks. Ms. Fernandez thought of all the problems she might pose to children using the blocks. She tried to imagine ways children might respond to the problems and how she could assist them in finding solutions.

As Ms. Fernandez supervised children in the learning centers, she took notice that Vanessa was sitting on the floor with the blocks spread out on the carpet. Observing for a few minutes to see what Vanessa might do on her own, she noticed that Vanessa seemed to know her basic colors. Careful not to disrupt Vanessa's activity, Ms. Fernandez moved to the center so she could watch Vanessa more closely. She watched as Vanessa finished arranging the blocks by color (teacher observes child). "Vanessa, can you tell me why you put these blocks together? Ms. Fernandez asked as she pointed to a pile of red triangles. "They're red!" she replied. "Yes, you are right! You have grouped them together because all the blocks are red in this stack." "Can you find another way to group some blocks?" asked Ms. Fernandez. Vanessa looked at blocks and moved a few around with her finger. Soon, she looked toward the teacher and shook her head. "Let's see, if I were grouping the blocks, I might put all the circles together (teacher introduces a problem). Can you do that?"

strategies such as modeling, assisting the child, providing cues and prompts, the teacher supports a child's efforts to learn what is just beyond his independent level of performance. Vygotsky believed the role of a teacher was to draw a child out into the zone of proximal development, where the child requires assistance to perform tasks and activities. Within this zone, the teacher and child would coconstruct knowledge through discussion, questioning, and explanations (Fosnot, 1996).

Helping child activate prior knowledge. Another objective teachers aim to accomplish is to activate the prior knowledge of the learner. Children can more easily grasp new information if they can establish a link between the new information and what is already known. Teachers are instrumental in helping children remember their experiences and knowledge that relate to the new facts and concepts. Activating prior experiences is especially important when children are young, with a limited experiential and conceptual knowledge base. Children will learn best when they are helped to see the relationship of new experiences and information to previous experiences (Bodrova & Leong, 1996). Box 10.2 provides an example of sorting blocks by attributes.

Help child identify and use strategies. In inclusive classrooms, the distinction between teaching strategies and learning strategies is blurred. Teachers realize that the goal is to help children acquire and effectively use a variety of strategies to learn (see Box 10.3 for key learning strategies). Children naturally develop strategies for learning; however, some children are more efficient at acquiring learning strategies than others. Although some children easily develop strategies for learning, it is not an automatic process that teachers can take for granted. Many children struggle and need the inter-

---

KEY LEARNING STRATEGIES   BOX 10.3

- Increase children's motivation for learning.
- Involve children in active learning.
- Help children become aware of salient sensory cues.
- Encourage children to hypothesize and make predictions.
- Ask different types of questions, especially open-ended questions.
- Stimulate children to find alternatives and creative solutions.
- Offer opportunities to recognize and solve problems.
- Promote collaborative thinking and problem solving.
- Model use of learning strategies and problem solving.
- Help children recognize their emerging strategies for learning.
- Provide activities to develop memory strategies.
- Activate children's prior knowledge.
- Think aloud and foster children's metacognitive awareness.
- Provide time, space, and props to support cognitive play.
- Foster increased attention to tasks and sustained on-task behavior.

Explicit strategies can help children learn problem-solving skills and efficient ways to learn.

vention of more skilled learners, such as teachers and parents, to acquire strategies needed for proficient learning. Further, evidence is accumulating that indicates learners who are more expert than children, such as adults and older children, can assume a role as a coach or mentor. Research and theory in the fields of cognitive psychology and neurobiology have helped us better understand thought and memory. With technology, scientists have explored the brain, and research has revealed new information about thinking and learning processes and how they develop in children. We know more about how children come to know, learn to think, and develop an awareness of their own thinking. Children make conscious decisions about their actions, solving problems, and creating new products or ideas.

Teachers can use cognitively guided instruction (CGI) with children in the early grades as a way to support strategy development of children. CGI is a method that is akin to strategies instruction in that it seeks to streamline the cognitive and problem-solving processes of children. However, CGI is different from strategies instruction because the focus is on identifying strategies children are using or usually use to solve problems and teachers seek to improve the children's strategies. Using this method, teachers receive professional development to gain an understanding of children's cognitive processes and their mathematical thinking. Teachers learn typical ways children try to solve problems, particularly related to mathematics, and use that knowledge within the context of their own classroom by observing children. Within an atmosphere of inquiry and experimentation, teachers facilitate children's thinking toward the development of more efficient problem-solving strategies. Teachers plan their facilitation strategies by thinking about:

- Ways to present problems
- Types of questions to ask
- Ways to promote interactions with peers and teachers

Children's thinking and inquiry takes the lead in CGI and becomes the basis for the teacher's practices (Franke & Kazemi, 2001). This method is representative of a true child-centered approach that is recommended by DAP guidelines (Bredekamp & Copple, 1997). It may also be an advantage in culturally diverse classrooms where learners might approach problem solving and learning from different cultural perspectives.

Encourage engagement. The amount of time children spend exploring physical and social aspects of their environment is referred to as engagement. Children vary in their adeptness in gaining meaningful information and learning from these interactions (McWilliam & Bailey, 1992). Engagement is considered fundamental to learning and skill development (Reinhartsen, Garfinkle, & Wolery, 2002), is a good predictor of a child's achievement, and is purported to serve as one indicator of the worth a child's program (Gettinger & Stoiber, 1999; McWilliam, Trivette, & Dunst, 1985). Consequently, a key objective to keep in mind when selecting teaching strategies is to identify ones that are likely to promote a child's prolonged engagement in a task or interaction with others. The quality of the activity generally increases as a child becomes more deeply involved. Consequently, prolonged engagement in an activity is usually the objective, since increased time spent is generally associated with greater benefits to the learner (Polloway & Patton, 1997; Wang, Haertel, & Walberg, 1993/94).

The nature of the task, the goals the learner is pursuing, and the ability and experience the learner brings to bear can be factors in the amount of time needed to maximize learning. Children present a variety of social and cognitive variations that influence their ability to establish and maintain sufficient engagement that will result in learning. For example, children with ADHD may find it difficult to initiate engagement or to maintain engagement for a sufficient period of time to allow for learning (Altman & Kanagawa, 1994).

Remember, however, that children vary in the amount of time they need to learn, and the type of task may also influence the amount of engagement time needed for learning. Young children who are gifted may learn certain tasks in shorter time frames than their typically developing peers. Conversely, these children sometimes benefit from an extension of the usual time periods when they find a task more absorbing than their peers. Although prolonged engagement generally improves learning outcomes for most learners, differentiation of time intervals for engagement in tasks may need to be more flexible for gifted children (Kennedy, 1995; Sternberg & Zhang, 1995).

Improve quality of engagement. An important part of the teacher's role is to make decisions about the degree and quality of the child's engagement in a task. Engagement is the degree to which the child is persistent and maintains attention on the task or activity. Strategies that help a child remain focused and attentive to the task may improve engagement and increase the potential for the child to learn in the situation. Therefore, teachers in inclusive classrooms need to be prepared to use strategies designed to assist children in developing patterns of high quality engagement in a variety of tasks and interactions. McWilliam and Bailey (1992) advised teachers to analyze engagement both temporally and in terms of the quality of engagement simultaneously. These researchers recognized that children tend to progress through a gradual process of lengthening levels of engagement. This continuum begins with nonengagement and advances to the attainment of sustained or prolonged engagement across a span of time. Moreover, they noticed that the quality of a child's engagement tends to correspond with the length of time the child remained engaged. McWilliam and Bailey described the quality of engagement in terms of a child's ability to elaborate on tasks, overcome challenges, or use various strategies for problem solving. Increased engagement appears to be associated with greater use of strategies by children and results in more successful learning (McWilliam & Bailey, 1992).

For early childhood teachers, efforts to promote engagement are gentle and carefully done to avoid putting undue pressure on children. Trying to require or force prolonged engagement constitutes punishment rather than encouragement. Instead, for some children, simply allowing the opportunity for uninterrupted time may be sufficient for lengthening engagement time and improving the quality of the activity. Limiting interruptions and curbing the disruptive behavior of other children can foster children's concentration and engagement in their activities. Children who learn more slowly or those with ADHD may require a planned strategy for gradually lengthening time of engagement.

Well-managed classroom environments are conducive to children's engagement in tasks; however, alone, classroom management strategies may not yield optimal engagement for all children. Teachers may need to use more explicit strategies with some preschoolers with special needs to promote a sufficient level and quality of engagement so learning can occur (Malmskog & McDonnell, 1999). Teachers can monitor the activities of children in the inclusive classroom to detect individuals who may need specific assistance or special conditions to help prolong time and increase the quality of their engagement with activities and interactions. Encouraging high-quality engagement of children is critical to children's learning. Therefore, some of the strategies teachers use should be selected with the intent of promoting prolonged, high-quality interactions with activities, children, and the teacher in the inclusive classroom setting.

INCLUSION STORIES FOR COGNITIVE LEARNING STRATEGIES

Promoting Thinking and Learning Strategies: Sorting Seashells

Ms. Tovar's class of 2- and 3-year-old children was interested in the ocean after several families returned from beach vacations. She filled the sand table with beach items borrowed from the families including seashells of various sizes, shapes, and colors. Several

Encouraging prolonged engagement in activities alone or with others helps children gain knowledge and skills.

children gathered around the table to sift the sand and examine the beach items buried in the sand. Ms. Tovar joined the children as they played. As she dug up items, Ms. Tovar sorted the seashells into one pile and plastic beach toys into another. Amy noticed and followed her teacher's modeling. "Amy, you have 2 groups like I do," commented Ms. Tovar. "What do you think we should call this group?" she asked as she pointed to the seashells. Amy said "Seashells!" "Good idea," responded Ms. Tovar. "Now, what shall we call the other group?" The other children joined Amy in suggesting names, such as not seashells or toys. "Let's make some other groups," Ms. Tovar challenged, and she began to categorize shells by different characteristics and verbally named the groups she had formed. "I am making a group of shells that are flat and another group that are pointed. I will call this group red-spotted shells and this group the gray-spotted shells." Soon, the children were grouping and regrouping their shells. They helped each other label the groups by salient characteristics, such as color, shapes, size, and other attributes. As the children sorted seashells or beach toys into piles, Ms. Tovar asked them questions, encouraged collaboration, and stimulated talk. "David, tell me what you call this group of shells?" and "Tell me about this group," "How are these shells alike?" "In what ways are these shells different?"

Problem-Solving Strategies: The Green Balloon

The children in Ms. Cook's 3-year-old classroom were learning to discriminate among different primary and secondary colors. To help motivate the children, Ms. Cook arranged a visit by a circus clown, Dottie, who brought a bunch of colorful mylar balloons. While entertaining the children, Dottie used color names and asked individual children to identify their favorite colors. Dottie was able to call on children by name because Ms. Cook had planned ahead and taped a name tag on each child's shirt. The children were motivated to participate by the clown's animated presentation and silly antics. Before she left the classroom, Dottie had taped the balloons on a special bulletin board about colors. However, one of the most valuable lessons occurred later in the day. Ryan was taking a turn at moving a length of yarn on the bulletin board to connect a colored card with the printed word green to the balloon of the corresponding color. The helium-filled mylar balloon suddenly pulled loose from the tagboard background and soared to the top of the 9-foot ceiling. Ryan was mildly annoyed that the loss of the balloon kept him from completing the task. Yet, he and a few of his friends were becoming fascinated with the predicament of the balloon floating gently against the ceiling tiles. Ms. Cook noticed the small group of children forming beneath the stray balloon. "The balloon is up on the ceiling. How do you think we can get it down?" asked Ms. Cook. Ryan pushed on the wall nearest the balloon and turned to see if he had jarred the balloon loose. He tried again, but to no avail. Ms. Cook challenged Ryan and the others, "Can anyone think of another way? What could we try?" Jacob thought they should try to blow it down. First, the children tried with their own breath then, with Ms. Cook's help, they used an electrical fan. The balloon moved to a new position when the fan was turned on, but still hovered near the ceiling. Marta suggested throwing something at the balloon to knock it down. They tried a foam rubber ball and a beanbag, but the balloon wouldn't budge. Finally, David suggested a ladder. He remembered that his Dad used one to retrieve his balloon once when it escaped his grasp. The children clapped with glee as the custodian stepped up the ladder and reached the balloon.

Testing Predictions: Outdoor Inquiry

A group of kindergarteners were watching a large beetle scurry across the playground sidewalk. "What do you think it will do if we gently turn him on his back?" their teacher, Ms. Kameron, asked. The children made various predictions, including "He will just flip back over", "The beetle will stay there and wiggle his legs", and "I think he will go to sleep." Ms. Kameron jotted down their predictions on a large notepad as the children observed. They watched with eager anticipation while Ms. Kameron moved the large beetle with her finger. The beetle wiggled a few seconds, scooted onto his side, and then righted himself to a standing position. The children talked excitedly about their hypotheses as the beetle scampered along. "Julie and Kate were both right!" said Ezra. "I wonder if it would have made a difference if the beetle had been on grass rather than the concrete sidewalk. What do you think?" Ms. Kameron thought aloud. "I think it would be harder for the beetle to flip over!" yelled Sam. "I say it would be the same!" stated Daniel. Ms. Kameron wrote down their predictions again. With Ms. Kameron's help, they gently turned the beetle over in the grass and watched. "It is taking longer," observed Julie. "He gets on his side, but he can't flip over," noticed Ezra. Finally, the

Encouraging observation and predictions helps children gain conceptual knowledge.

beetle maneuvered to his feet just as the recess bell rang. In the classroom, Ms. Kameron put the prediction notepad on the easel, and they assembled for group time to finish talking and writing about their experience.

- What strategies did Ms. Kameron use to promote the thinking and learning processes of children?
- How did making the prediction chart help children use strategies for thinking?

TECHNOLOGY-BASED STRATEGIES

Another category of strategies commonly used to provide individually appropriate instruction to children is technology-based strategies or those that involve the use of technological tools (see Box 10.4). Technological tools and strategies using technology embedded in natural contexts of an inclusive early childhood classroom can enhance learning opportunities for children and can be particularly beneficial for at-risk children (Duttweiler, 1992). The term technology is often used to mean computers and software; however, in inclusive classrooms technological tools might range from low to high technology. At the low end of the spectrum, special grips for writing utensils, tape recorders, and videotapes are generally so familiar that these items are taken for granted. New and more sophisticated items are constantly being developed in our high-tech society. Some high-technological devices, such as voice-activated computers,

---

KEY PRACTICE: TECHNOLOGY   BOX 10.4

- Equalizes playing field for some children
- Fosters collaboration
- Promotes problem solving
- Permits saving work to re-examine later
- Offers flexibility and wealth of options

---

are becoming widely used in workplaces, and these tools can be used in early educational settings as well. Assistive technology is a particular subset of technological aids, equipment, or devices that were developed specifically to serve a compensatory purpose for individuals with disabilities.

Significance of Technological Strategies for Inclusion

A major emphasis of the Goals 2000 Initiative was to promote children's acquisition of computer skills (Goals 2000: Educate America Act, P. L. 103-227, 1994). Subsequently, instructional strategies and practices involving the use of technological equipment and software represent an emerging area of teaching. The rapidly accumulating research base has indicated that these tools can positively facilitate children's learning and social skills. There are several reasons why technological strategies are drawing increasing interest among teachers in inclusive classrooms. One reason is that technological equipment can offer increased independence for all learners. For children with certain disabilities, technological tools, including assistive devices, can better equalize their educational experiences with those of their typically developing peers. Technology benefits children with special needs by ensuring that they have a more level playing field in early learning environments (Hutinger & Johansen, 2000; Pittman, 2003).

Computers and young children. Acceptance of computers for young children in early childhood education settings was not immediate. Initially, early childhood teachers and professionals were wary, and professional organizations voiced their concerns. It was feared that computers would isolate children from interactions with their peers. Further, teachers were cautioned that computers were poor substitutes for a child's interaction with authentic, concrete materials in the physical environment. Professional organizations were also prudent in their recommendations, and urged teachers to be judicious in the use of computers for small children until sufficient research was conducted to elucidate the possible benefits or disadvantages of computers and technology in early childhood classrooms.

Research has helped to dispel early concerns about technology. Evidence has suggested that wise use technology can result in benefits for all children. The worth of technology in early childhood settings has received endorsement from professional organizations and experts in the field (Bredekamp & Rosegrant, 1994; National Association for the Education of Young Children, 1996, 1999). Although integration of technology has gradually increased in early childhood settings, children do not have equal access to technology, and the reasons for which might be related to costs associated with technology or lack of training for teachers and administrators (Martin, Forsbach-Rothman, & Crawford, 2004). Access to computers and technology is a serious issue with ramifications for society. One large study of more than 1,600 African American children in kindergarten and first grade found a positive correlation between academic achievement and access of these children to computers and software in their homes and schools (Judge, 2005).

Social emotional advantages emerge. Many of the initial concerns about computer use socially isolating children in early childhood have now dissipated. Accumulating research studies have substantiated numerous positive contributions of technological strategies to acquisition of social interaction skills. Rather than socially isolating children, research has shown that computers serve as social catalysts attracting children to cooperate, talk, and create together. One study reported that toddlers and preschool-aged children used computers as a form of play. These children also exhibited increased engagement in social pretend play in noncomputer related activities (Howard, Greyrose, Kehr, Espinosa, & Beckwith, 1996). Moreover, studies have revealed that social interaction changes with the type of software used, with open-ended types of programs promoting cooperative efforts (Clements, 1994; Clements & Sarama, 2002).

In addition to social advantages, computer use in inclusive classrooms can also offer children motivational and emotional benefits. Children are highly motivated by technology and use computers with ease and confidence. When children experience success in manipulating the computer and software, they are imbued with self-confidence and pride (Clements & Nastasi, 1993; Papert, 1980). These kinds of benefits are particularly significant for children with disabilities who may experience far less success with traditional school tasks and activities. Computers are flexible, adaptable tools that allow children with disabilities to exert control over their environment and learning. These motivational benefits result in an increased sense of self-esteem and motivation to learn for children with special needs (Oddone, 1993; Ryba, Selby, & Nolan, 1995; Schery & O'Connor, 1992).

Studies also revealed that computer use fosters social interaction between preschoolers with disabilities and their nondisabled peers. Teachers can help children with disabilities acquire social and communicative skills by embedding carefully sequenced opportunities for social interaction into computer activities with peers (Lau, 2000). Offering children with disabilities varied opportunities for structured and unstructured computer play activities increased social skills and interactions with peers (Hobbs, Bruch, Sanko, & Astolfi, 2001). Dramatic gains in social and emotional development have been reported for children with special needs when computer activities were included in the educational program (Hutinger & Johansen, 2000; Spiegel-McGill, Zippiroli, & Mistrett, 1989).

Cooperative use of technology enhances learning for all children.

Benefits for learning. The opportunities to advance various learning skills abound with technological tools. Different kinds of software will foster opportunities to practice and learn an array of skills across the curriculum. Computer activities offered in conjunction with a full range of hands-on, developmentally appropriate learning activities create many learning options. Combining technological activities with manipulative activities in math is an approach that shows promise; monolingual and bilingual young children were motivated and successful with counting and numerical activities when hands-on and computer applications were used (Ainsa, 1999). Technological tools allow all children, even those with special needs, to achieve success in their learning.

Studies reported that open-ended software in early childhood classrooms can stimulate inquiry and problem-solving processes. Mathematical operations conducted using computer manipulatives can afford children more flexible tools than traditional concrete math manipulatives. Further, the ability to save results and re-examine these manipulations can be very advantageous (Clements & Sarama, 2002). Computer-based interventions contributed to effective programs to develop reading and literacy skills in young children. Children at risk for reading difficulties demonstrated improvement in reading skills, such as phonological awareness, word recognition, and letter naming when computer activities were used as a part of their instructional program (Mioduser, 2000; Moxely, 1992; Steg, Lazar, & Boyce, 1994).

Legal provisions for assistive technology. For children with disabilities, technological strategies can be crucial to their success in learning. The critical need for some children to access to assistive technology was underscored in provisions of the Individuals with Disabilities Education Act (IDEA, P.L. 101-476). The mandate requires schools to provide any technological devices a child needs to achieve success in the learning environment and to have the technological devices available across all contexts of the school setting (Parette, Hourcade, & VanBiervliet, 1993). Assistive technology can permit some children to circumvent their weaknesses and use their inherent strengths to propel their learning (Winter, 1997; Winter, Bell, & Dempsey, 1994). Using adaptations or assistive technological devices when warranted, children with disabilities can also be highly successful with computers as tools to stimulate and support their learning (Clements & Sarama, 2002). Cases of children with special needs demonstrating unexpected capabilities through computer use have been reported (Ryba et al., 1995). In 1998, The Assistive Technology Act (P.L. 105-394, S. 2432) was passed, which made it clear that it is the right of eligible children to have access to technology. For children who qualify, technology is elevated from the status of a tool of choice to that of a necessity to properly support their learning.

Planning the Use of Assistive Technology

Assistive technology, also called adaptive technology, can help children with certain disabilities gain access to content of the curriculum (Broderick et al., 2005) (see Box 10.5). As stated previously, some children have the right to use assistive technology when it is deemed critical to their success in learning. In these cases, it is designated as an instructional accommodation in the child's Individualized Education Program (IEP). When assistive technology is listed as such, teachers are legally obligated to ensure the child has access to use the specified devices in all learning settings. Collaboration of

---

KEY TECHNOLOGY STRATEGIES   **BOX 10.5**

- Provide carefully selected assistive technology to support learning of children who are likely to benefit.
- Integrate technology across the curriculum.
- Combine technological activities with manipulative activities.
- Promote cooperative use of computers.
- Use technology to create more relevant, meaningful learning opportunities.
- Select a variety of software types for different instructional purposes.
- Choose software that allows latitude and flexibility to accommodate a full range of learners.
- Use technology to stimulate thinking, learning, and problem-solving processes.
- Monitor, interact, and scaffold children's technological activities.
- Ensure equitable computer access to all children, including those who are culturally and linguistically diverse.

IEP team members is critical to ensure that the team is aware of all options and the assistive technology selected is a good match for the child. Assistive technology can be highly technical. Consequently, decisions about the types of assistive devices from which a child may benefit sometimes requires specialized knowledge and expertise. Seeking consultation of professionals in assistive technology may be warranted in some cases, and IDEA does provide for procurement of assistive technological equipment. The ultimate goal is to use universal design principles to create a classroom where technology can be seamlessly embedded into instruction or used as an instructional tool unobtrusively (Male, 2003; Parette et al., 1993).

Collaborative Planning for Technology Integration

Technology advances at a fast pace, making it difficult for educators to stay current on the latest trends. Developing communities of practice to help teachers acquire knowledge and gain competence in using technology is a concept that has proven highly successful. The U.S. Department of Education's Office of Special Education funded a five-year model professional development program to promote the integration of technology. Supporting Teacher to Achieve Results by Integrating Technology into the Curriculum (STAR Tech) was designed to provide technical assistance to teachers, help them acquire knowledge, and develop leadership in classroom technology use. A community of learners was formed, with general and special education teachers collaborating with specialists in technology and curriculum. A cycle of integration involved teamwork and intensive teacher training. A social learning system of support was created to facilitate technology use. The STAR participants gained valuable insights about the abilities of children through team collaboration and planned activities. Teachers reported greater awareness of children's needs and increased confidence in finding technological solutions to address the identified needs and strengths of individual children. The amazing success of the STAR project for children with and without disabilities indicated that collaboration is imperative to integration of technology use to improve outcomes for all children (Zorfass & Rivero, 2005).

INCLUSION STORIES FOR TECHNOLOGY-BASED STRATEGIES

Technology for Inclusion: Piya's Journal

After reading the story *The Very Hungry Caterpillar* by Eric Carle, the children in Piya's kindergarten class were divided into pairs to write in their response journals. First, each pair talked about their favorite part of the story and then the children collaborated on the type of response they would make to the story. Most of the children drew or wrote, using large sheets of unlined paper. A few of the pairs were using computers. Piya, who has visual impairments and poor fine-motor control worked with her partner at a computer with a large trackball instead of the usual mouse. Using a children's word processing and drawing software package, Piya was able to respond to the story with

---

MY REFLECTION   **BOX 10.6**

- Do I have sufficient experience with children that I am likely to notice the children being inattentive?
- How would I react? Would I stay calm or might I be likely to panic?
- What strategies might I use to gain children's attention?

---

her partner. Piya used the trackball to draw a big, red apple, and her partner helped by typing in large font letters underneath.

- Discuss how the technology strategies the teacher used ensured that Piya would have an opportunity to participate in the journal writing activity.
- Why did the teacher pair the children?
- Why did other pairs also have the option to use the computer to prepare their journal responses?

A Demonstration of Reflecting in Action: Mrs. Castillo at Story Time

Mrs. Castillo noticed the children in her prekindergarten class were not paying attention to the story she was reading (see Box 10.6). Some of the children were staring out the window, one child yawned, and others whispered and giggled with one another.

To help regain their attention, Mrs. Castillo became more animated in her reading. She changed her voice to simulate that of the story character speaking and she increased her vocal expression. She also made deliberate attempts to gain eye contact with individual children. Periodically, Mrs. Castillo asked questions that helped children relate their lives to those of the story characters. "Have you ever been afraid of doing something new? How did you feel?" Sometimes she asked, "What would you do if you were Big Anthony? How would you get rid of all that spaghetti?" See Box 10.7 for follow-up reflection questions.

MY REFLECTION   **BOX 10.7**

- Do some teachers you have observed seem unaware of children who are inattentive?
- What strategies did Mrs. Castillo use to regain children's attention?
- How did this teacher help children access their prior knowledge?
- Can you give an example of when Mrs. Castillo involved children in problem solving?

APPLYING STRATEGIES IN TYPICAL INCLUSIVE CLASSROOMS

Typical early childhood classrooms are usually inclusive, whether planned or incidental by membership of children enrolled. Preschool classrooms are frequently the first learning environments outside the home that children experience. Whereas some children may have disabilities or other special needs that were detected during infancy or toddlerhood, many children's conditions are not identified until preschool or even later in their schooling. Consequently, preschools have always been on the frontlines in identifying children who may be at risk of school failure or those with special learning needs. Approaching all early childhood classrooms as inclusive is not only prudent, but an effective way to teach all children. Therefore, it is vital for teachers to ensure the inclusion of all children and meet the needs of diverse groups with a wide span of ability.

It is always helpful to visit inclusive classrooms where teachers are knowledgeable regarding inclusive teaching strategies. Observing teachers interacting with children and applying effective inclusion strategies is an ideal way of learning how to teach in inclusive classrooms. The following descriptions of inclusive classrooms will provide examples of the kinds of inclusive classrooms one might see in typical neighborhood settings. Increasing numbers of classrooms are becoming more inclusive, as teachers learn from inclusive teaching strategies and apply these techniques in their classrooms. The following sections describe two model inclusive education classrooms serving children at preschool and kindergarten. These scenarios will provide insight into how inclusive teaching strategies can be applied with classrooms of children at different ages. These examples are intended to provide a gestalt or overall view of ideal implementation of inclusive teaching strategies. These sample classrooms can serve as a guide for teachers and prospective teachers as they visit classrooms in their own neighborhoods to observe inclusive education in action.

The Neighborhood Context

The location of these classrooms is an urban neighborhood in a large metropolitan area. Typical of many areas in the United States, the families in the neighborhood are culturally and linguistically diverse. Caucasian families represent slightly more than one half of the families in the neighborhood. Many of the families are members of minority groups, with the largest number being Latino. Other families represent continents and countries from across the globe, including Asia, Africa, Eastern Europe, Pacific Islands, and the Middle East, to name a few. Most children have working parents with low- to middle-income levels. Some of the families have income levels at or below poverty levels.

Crime in the neighborhood is moderately high with some gang violence and drug use evident, primarily among adolescents. There is some toxic chemical contamination in the area and blood tests of some children living in older homes in the area have revealed unacceptably high levels of lead. The educational attainment of parents is generally a high school education, but a few have earned some college credits or additional

---

MY REFLECTION   **BOX 10.8**

1. How is this neighborhood similar to ones in the area where you live? How is it different?
2. How would you plan to work with the children and families in this neighborhood? What skills and strategies would a teacher need?

---

professional training. Most families in this neighborhood have some level of involvement in their child's education, and their involvement in school activities varies from moderately to occasionally involved. Parents in this neighborhood value education and are interested in their children achieving success in school. However, low-income levels, poverty, and detrimental social and environmental factors have resulted in some children having a higher risk of school failure. Teachers in the neighborhood are committed to inclusive education to provide all children with the best possible chance for educational success. See Box 10.8 for reflection questions.

A Day in the Life at Preschool

Mrs. Torres teaches in a neighborhood child-care center. Her preschool classroom serves children, aged 3 and 4 years, who arrive at the center early in the morning and remain until late in the day while their parents work in nearby businesses. Today, the theme is "How Things Move." As children arrive, she invites each child to choose an activity center to begin his or her day. Children find their friends and begin to work and play while Mrs. Torres greets parents and helps children with their coats. Adelina arrives with tear-streaked cheeks. Her grandmother explains that Adelina's teenaged mother dropped her off very late last night. Adelina is tired and confused. While the other children play in the activity center, Mrs. Torres spends a few minutes comforting Adelina and helping her find a book in the library area. There is a shelf with a variety of picture books related to the day's theme, and to promote emergent literacy, there are books about transportation vehicles, how animals move, and different ways children move, too. Children can listen to audiotaped stories or look at books together on a comfortable rug. When all the children have arrived, Mrs. Torres circulates around the room, making sure all children are engaged in an activity of their choice. Many of the centers have activities that help children gain the concept of locomotion and how people, animals, and things move. Mrs. Torres talks with children in the block center, where they are playing with wooden planks and a collection of vehicles. The children are building ramps and racing the cars down to see which one is the fastest. To help children recall related experiences, she asks, "Have you ever ran down a hill? Can you move faster down a hill than on a flat road? Which is easier?" She challenges the children to build ramps of different heights. Before the children have a chance to race the vehicles, she encourages them to make predictions. "Will the blue car on the tall ramp move

Children with disabilities may need specialized equipment to support their learning and school achievement.

faster than the red car on the lower ramp?" she asks. When that race is over, Mrs. Torres says, "What do you think made the blue car win the race?" and "Can you think of any other way to build a ramp?" Mrs. Torres helps Amanda to the block center in her wheelchair. On the tray table of her wheelchair, Mrs. Torres places a smaller set of cars and blocks for ramps. She invites two of Amanda's friends to explore the movement of the toy cars on Amanda's tray table. During the cooperative play, one of the children notices the wheels on Amanda's wheelchair. With Mrs. Torres, they discuss how hard it is to push Amanda's wheelchair up the ramp to the classroom and how the wheels make it easier. "What if Amanda's wheelchair had no wheels?" Mrs. Torres asks. The children discuss their ideas as Mrs. Torres encourages them to think of alternatives.

In the table toys and manipulative center, children are encouraged to build things that move with wooden and plastic building pieces. "I see you have found a wooden piece that looks like a wheel. How many do you need to make your truck?" When Juan indicates he doesn't know, Mrs. Torres sends Yao, who is learning to speak English, to the block center to borrow a toy truck. Together, the teacher and children examine the truck. Mrs. Torres encourages them to see and touch the car and its wheels. "Let's touch each one as we count," she says and then demonstrates the counting strategy. Mrs. Torres helps Yao by touching his finger to each wheel as she counts with him. First she counts in Chinese, then in English. Then she helps Juan touch the wheels and count. She encourages them to repeat the task on their own. Mrs. Torres prompts the counting when each child needed assistance until they could do it independently. "What happens if we don't have four wheels?" Mrs. Torres asks? After a few minutes of thinking and conjecturing, they join the children at the block center to find out. Mrs. Torres helps the children remove one of the plastic wheels from the toy car. The children send

---

MY REFLECTION   **BOX 10.9**

1. Identify the kinds of strategies Mrs. Torres used to stimulate children's learning.
2. Can you think of other strategies she could use?
3. Why is each of the strategies you identified useful in classrooms with diverse learners?

---

the car down one of the ramps and find that the car's movement down the ramp is impaired. The children continue to experiment by removing the wheels and trying to move the car. Mrs. Torres introduces the words friction, speed, and smooth as the conversation continues.

Later in the morning Mrs. Torres, reads a storybook called *The Wheels on the Bus* to a small group of children in the library area. Adelina is feeling better after the restful activity and responds favorably to Mrs. Torres' invitation to sing the song that accompanies the book. Some of the children decide they want to draw pictures about their activities, exploring movement of the toy cars in the block center so they move to the art center to make their own big books with large sheets of paper. Mrs. Torres wrote words and sentences they dictated to tell others about their pictures.

Mrs. Torres noticed a few of the children in the block area had difficulty naming simple shapes and colors. Later in the day, she loaded early learning activities software on the computer that includes color and shape games to give them more practice. Yao joined the children. He already knew the color names in Chinese and the computer activities reinforced his knowledge of the English name for each color. See Box 10.9 for reflection questions.

A Day in the Life at Kindergarten

Around the corner from Mrs. Torres' preschool classroom is a public elementary school where Mrs. Adams teaches kindergarten. This class is also involved in a unit on How Things Move. The children begin the day with a short, large-group activity. Each child had brought a picture or an object illustrating the theme of things that move. Each child was encouraged to name the object and to say a few words about his or her experiences with the things that move examples. Children are working in learning centers. Just before lunch, children gather for a large-group reading of the 1981 Caldecott Honor Book *Truck* by Donald Crews. They enjoyed answering questions Mrs. Adams posed and thought of many uses of trucks in their neighborhood. In fact, they thought of so many uses that Mrs. Adams suggested that they make a list of all the ways they saw trucks being used, such as at grocery stores, delivering mail, and hauling garbage out of the city streets. They posted the chart paper list on a bulletin board so children could review it later. At the computer, several children gathered to record their responses to the shared story reading. They used the word processing software to write and illustrate their thoughts. Tanikka, who has cerebral palsy, was a member of this group. The computer is equipped with a large trackball and an adaptive keyboard to assist Tanikka because she has difficulty with fine-motor control.

SUMMARY

Responsive teaching with the differential use of individually appropriate support strategies was the focus of this chapter. An embedded approach to teaching was defined and the use of such approaches was described. Ways to provide a full spectrum of individual accommodations and support was presented. Explicit teaching strategies can be applied at different levels of intensity to match the individual learner's strengths and needs for support. The chapter introduced how to teach cognitive learning strategies to promote better thinking and problem-solving skills in children. The chapter concluded with information on the use of technology in teaching. Technology-based teaching strategies were illustrated and presented as a way to enhance learning. The chapter ended with usage of assistive technology needed by certain children, which is sometimes required by law as an accommodation to provide individually appropriate support for eligible children.

Discussion Questions

1. Explain the construct of differentiated instruction. What are the main ideas that underlie this idea? What is the research basis that is foundational to differentiated instruction?
2. Define an embedded approach to teaching. What does this mean and how can teachers implement an embedded approach?
3. Discuss embedding explicit strategies and give examples to illustrate their use.
4. Discuss the use of total physical response techniques in inclusive classrooms where children are linguistically diverse. What other strategies can teachers use to ensure that children who are English language learners are able to participate in learning activities?
5. Describe a strategy involving technology that would help to ensure the inclusion of a child with a physical disability in an early childhood classroom.
6. Why is the use of technology an important strategy for helping diverse groups of children access a differentiated curriculum?
7. Analyze a few of the inclusive stories presented in the chapter. How was differentiated instruction provided? What did the teacher do to ensure each child had individually appropriate support?
8. How does differentiated instruction contribute to a community of learners in the inclusive classroom?

Inclusive Activities

1. Observe a teacher in an inclusive early childhood classroom. Describe several incidents in which strategies were used to provide individually appropriate support. Evaluate whether the strategies used seemed to be effective. Why or why not?

2. Interview a teacher who has experience teaching in an inclusive early childhood classroom. Ask the teacher to discuss what strategies they have used successfully to facilitate the learning of all children. Ask about strategies the teacher has found appropriate for certain individual children.

3. Plan a lesson using one of the strategies discussed in the chapter. Make arrangements to present the activity with a small group of children in an inclusive early childhood classroom. Reflect on your experience afterward. Did you feel comfortable using the strategy? Do you think the strategy was helpful? If you were to use this strategy again, what would you do differently?

4. Make a list of ways to enhance the language development and literacy skills of young children from diverse backgrounds. Interview a teacher and ask them to add strategies to your list.

5. Explore Websites on assistive technology and plan a strategy involving technology that would help to ensure the inclusion of a child with a physical disability in an early childhood classroom.

6. Locate and read an article written from a teacher's perspective that describes the use of strategies in inclusive early childhood settings. Some professional journals to examine are:
   - *Young Children*
   - *Young Exceptional Children*
   - *Childhood Education*
   - *Topics in Early Childhood Special Education*
   - *Early Childhood Research Quarterly*
   - *Journal for Early Intervention*
   - *Journal of Research in Childhood Education*

References

Abbott, J., & Ryan, T. (1999). Learning to go with the grain of the brain. *Education Canada, 39*(1), 8–11.

Abrams, K., Theberge, S. K., & Karan, O. C. (2005). Children and adolescents who are depressed: An ecological approach. *Professional School Counseling, 8*(3), 284–292.

Ainsa, T. (1999). Success of using technology and manipulatives to introduce numerical problem solving skills in monolingual/bilingual early childhood classrooms. *The Journal of Computers in Mathematics and Science Teaching, 18*(4), 361–369.

Altman, R., & Kanagawa, L. (1994). Academic and social engagement of young children with developmental disabilities in integrated and nonintegrated settings. *Education and Training in Mental Retardation and Developmental Disabilities, 29,* 184–193.

Asher, J. (1982). *Learning another language through actions: The complete teachers' guidebook.* Los Gatos, CA: Sky Oaks.

Bakley, S. (2001). Through the lens of sensory integration: A different way of analyzing challenging behavior. *Young Children, 56*(6), 70–76.

Bereiter, C., & Englemann, S. (1966). *Teaching disadvantaged children in the preschool.* Upper Saddle River, NJ: Prentice Hall.

Blok, H., Fukkink, R. G., Gebhardt, E. C., & Leseman, P. P. M. (2005). The relevance of delivery mode and other programme characteristics for the effectiveness of early childhood intervention. *International Journal of Behavioral Development, 29*(1), 35–47.

Bodrova, E., & Leong, D. (1996). *Tools of the mind: The Vygotskian approach to early childhood education.* Upper Saddle River, NJ: Merrill/Prentice Hall.

Bowlby, J. (1969). *Attachment and loss: Vol. I. Attachment.* New York: Basic Books.

Bredekamp, S., & Copple, C. (Eds.). (1997). *Developmentally appropriate practice in early childhood programs* (Rev. ed.). Washington, DC: National Association for the Education of Young Children.

Bredekamp, S., & Rosegrant, T. (1994). Learning and teaching with technology. In J. L. Wright & D. D. Shade (Eds.), *Young children: Active learners in a technological age* (pp. 53–61). Washington, DC: National Association for the Education of Young Children.

Bricker, D., Pretti-Frontczak, K., & McComas, N. (1998). *An activity-based approach to early intervention* (2nd ed.). Baltimore: Brookes.

Broderick, A., Mehta-Parekh, H., & Reid, D. K. (2005). Differentiating instruction for disabled students in inclusive classrooms. *Theory Into Practice, 44*(3), 194–202.

Butyniec-Thomas, J., & Woloshyn, V. E. (1997). The effects of explicit-strategy and whole-language instruction on student's spelling ability. *The Journal of Experimental Education, 65,* 293–302.

Buysse, V., Goldman, B., & Skinner, M. L. (2003). Friendship formation in inclusive early childhood classrooms: What is the teacher's role? *Early Childhood Research Quarterly, 18*(4), 485–501.

Carta, J., Schwartz, I., Atwater, J., & McConnell, S. (1991). Developmentally appropriate practice: Appraising its usefulness for young children with disabilities. *Topics in Early Childhood Special Education, 11*(1), 1–20.

Carta, J. J. (1994). Developmentally appropriate practices: Shifting the emphasis to individual appropriateness. *Journal of Early Intervention, 18*(4), 342–343.

Cavallaro, C. C., Haney, M., & Cabello, B. (1993). Developmentally appropriate strategies for promoting full participation in early childhood settings. *Topics in Early Childhood Special Education, 13*(3), 293–307.

Cerra, K. K., Watts-Taffe, S., & Rose, S. (1997). Fostering reader response and developing comprehension strategies in deaf and hard of hearing children. *American Annals of the Deaf, 142*(5), 379–386.

Clements, D. H. (1994). The uniqueness of the computer as a learning tool: Insights from research and practice. In J. L. Wright & D. D. Shade (Eds.), *Young children: Active learners in a technological age* (pp. 31–49). Washington, DC: National Association for the Education of Young Children.

Clements, D. H., & Sarama, J. (2002). The role of technology in early childhood learning. *Teaching Children Mathematics, 8*(6), 340–343.

Clements, D. H., & Nastasi, B. K. (1993). Electronic media and early childhood education. In B. Spodeck (Ed.), *Handbook of research on the education of young children* (pp. 251–275). New York: Macmillan.

Division for Early Childhood Council for Exceptional Children, National Association for the Education of Young Children, & Association of Teacher Educators. (1995). *Personnel standards for early education and early intervention: Guidelines for licensure in early childhood special education.* Pittsburgh, PA: Division for Early Childhood Council for Exceptional Children.

Drinkwater, S., & Demchak, M. (1995). The preschool checklist: Integration of children with severe disabilities. *Teaching Exceptional Children, 28*(1), 4–8.

Dunn, W. (1997). The impact of sensory processing abilities on the daily lives of young children and their families: A conceptual model. *Infants and Young Children, 9*(4), 23–35.

Duttweiler, P. C. (1992). Engaging at-risk students with technology. *Media & Methods, 12,* 6–8.

Eggen, P. D., & Kauchak, D. P. (1996). *Strategies for teachers: Teaching content and thinking skills* (3rd ed.). Boston: Allyn & Bacon.

Fosnot, C. T. (1996). Constructivism: A psychological theory of learning. In C. T. Fosnot (Ed.), *Constructivism: Theory, perspectives, and practices* (pp. 8–33). New York: Teachers College Press.

Franke, M. L., & Kazemi, E. (2001). Learning to teach mathematics: Focus on student thinking. *Theory Into Practice, 40*(2), 102–109.

Fuchs, L. S., Fuchs, D., & Karns, K. (2001). Enhancing kindergarteners' mathematical development: Effects of peer-assisted learning strategies. *Elementary School Journal, 101*(5), 495.

Fuchs, L. S., Fuchs, D., Prentice, K., Burch, M., & Paulsen, K. (2002). Hot math: Promoting mathematical problem solving among third-grade students with disabilities. *Teaching Exceptional Children, 35*(1), 70–73.

Gettinger, M., & Stoiber, K. (1999). Excellence in teaching: Review of instructional and environmental variables. In C. R. Reynolds & T. Gutkin (Eds.), *The handbook of school psychology* (3rd ed., pp. 933–958). New York: Wiley.

Girolametto, L., Weitzman, E., & Greenberg, J. (2004). The effects of verbal support strategies on small-group peer interactions. *Language, Speech, and Hearing Services in Schools, 35*(3), 254–268.

Goals 2000: Educate America Act, Pub. L. No. 103–227, 20 U.S.C. 5811, 5812, §§101–102 (1994).

Gross, A. L., & Ortiz, L. W. (1994). Using children's literature to facilitate inclusion in kindergarten and the primary grades. *Young Children, 49*(3), 32–35.

Harper-Whalen, S., Walmsley, T., & Moore, K. (1991). *An introduction to teaching through play* (No. 4). Washington, DC: Montana University at Missoula.

Hemmeter, M. L. (2000). Classroom-based interventions: Evaluating the past and looking toward the future. *Topics in Early Childhood Special Education, 20*(1), 56–61.

Herrell, A., & Jordan, M. (2004). *Fifty strategies for teaching English language learners* (2nd ed.). Upper Saddle River, NJ: Pearson Merrill/Prentice Hall.

Hobbs, T., Bruch, L., Sanko, J., & Astolfi, C. (2001). Friendship on the inclusive electronic playground. *Teaching Exceptional Children, 33*(6), 46–51.

Howard, J., Greyrose, E., Kehr, K., Espinosa, M., & Beckwith, L. (1996). Teacher-facilitated microcomputer activities: Enhancing social play and affect in young children with disabilities. *Journal of Special Education Technology, 13*, 36–47.

Hutinger, P. L., & Johansen, J. (2000). Implementing and maintaining an effective early childhood comprehensive technology system. *Topics in Early Childhood Special Education, 20*(3), 159–173.

Jones, C. D., & Schwartz, I. S. (2004). Siblings, peers, and adults: Differential effects of models for children with autism. *Topics in Early Childhood Education, 24*(4), 187–198.

Joseph, L. M., & Seery, M. E. (2004). Where is the phonics?: A review of the literature on the use of phonetic analysis with students with mental retardation. *Remedial and Special Education, 25*(2), 88–94.

Judge, S. (2005). The impact of computer technology on academic achievement of young African American children. *Journal of Research in Childhood Education, 20*(2), 91–101.

Karp, K. S., & Voltz, D. L. (2000). Weaving mathematical instructional strategies into inclusive settings. *Intervention in School and Clinic, 35*(4), 206–215.

Kennedy, D. M. (1995). Plain talk about creating a gifted-friendly classroom. *Roeper Review, 17*(4), 232–234.

Kim, T., & Axelrod, S. (2005). Direct instruction: An educators' guide and a plea for action. *The Behavior Analyst Today, 6*(2), 111–120.

Klein, P. S. (1992). Mediating the cognitive, social, and aesthetic development of precocious young children. In P. S. Klein & A. J. Tannenbaum (Eds.), *To be young and gifted* (pp. 245–277). Norwood, NJ: Ablex.

Krashen, S. (1982). *Principles and practice in second language acquisition*. Oxford: Oxford Pergamon.

Krashen, S., & Terrell, T. (1983). *The natural approach: Language acquisition in the classroom*. Oxford: Pergamon Press.

Lau, C. (2000). How to take turns and other important early childhood lessons helped along by computers. *Teaching Exceptional Children, 32*(4), 8–13.

Lay-Dopyera, M., & Dopyera, J. E. (1992). Strategies for teaching. In C. Seefeldt (Ed.), *The early childhood curriculum: A review of current research* (2nd ed., pp. 16–41). New York: Teachers College Press.

Lynch, S. A., & Simpson, C. G. (2004). Sensory Processing: Meeting individual needs using the seven senses. *Teaching Exceptional Children, 7*(4), 2–9.

Mahoney, G., Kaiser, A. P., Girolametto, L., MacDonald, J., Robinson, C., Safford, P., et al. (1999). Parent education in early intervention: A call for a renewed focus. *Topics in Early Childhood Special Education, 19*(3), 131–140.

Male, M. (2003). *Technology for inclusion: Meeting the special needs of all students* (4th ed.). Boston: Allyn & Bacon.

Malmskog, S., & McDonnell, A. P. (1999). Teacher-mediated facilitation of engagement by children with developmental delays in inclusive preschools. *Topics in Early Childhood Special Education, 19*(4), 203–216.

Martin, S., Forsbach-Rothman, T., & Crawford, C. (2004). Computer availability and use by young children in childcare settings. *Information Technology in Childhood Education*, 121–134.

Mason, S. A., & Egel, A. L. (1995). What does Amy like? Using a mini-reinforcer assessment to increase student participation in instructional activities. *Teaching Exceptional Children, 28*(1), 42–45.

McBride, B. J., & Schwartz, I. S. (2003). Effects of teaching early interventionists to use discrete trials during ongoing classroom activities. *Topics in Early Childhood Special Education, 23*(1), 5–17.

McWilliam, R. A., & Bailey, D. B. (1992). Promoting engagement and mastery. In D. B. Bailey & M. Wolery (Eds.), *Teaching infants and preschoolers with disabilities* (pp. 229–255). New York: Macmillan.

McWilliam, R. A., Trivette, C. M., & Dunst, C. J. (1985). Behavior engagement as a measure of the efficacy of early intervention. *Analysis and Intervention in Developmental Disabilities, 5,* 59–71.

Mioduser, D., Tur-Kaspa, H, & Leitner, I. (2000). The learning value of computer-based instruction of early reading skills. *Journal of Computer-Assisted Learning, 16*(1), 54–63.

Moss, E. (1992). Early interactions and metacognitive development of gifted preschoolers. In P. S. Klein & A. J. Tannenbaum (Eds.), *To be young and gifted* (pp. 278–318). Norwood, NJ: Ablex.

Moxely, R. (1992). Writing strategies of three pre-kindergarten children on the microcomputer. *Journal of Computing in Childhood Education, 3*(2), 137–179.

National Association for the Education of Young Children. (1996). NAEYC position statement: Technology and young children—ages three through eight. *Young children, 51*(6), 11–16.

National Association for the Education of Young Children. (1999). Position statement: Technology and young children—ages three through eight. *Information Technology in Childhood Education, 1,* 281–286.

Oddone, A. (1993). Inclusive classroom applications. *Teaching Exceptional Children, 26,* 74–75.

Owen, R. L., & Fuchs, L. S. (2002). Mathematical problem-solving strategy instruction for third-grade students with learning disabilities. *Remedial and Special Education, 23*(5), 268–278.

Papert, S. (1980). *Mindstorms: Children, computers and powerful ideas.* Brighton, England: Harvester.

Parette, H. P., Hourcade, J. J., & VanBiervliet, A. (1993). Selection of appropriate technology for children with disabilities. *Teaching Exceptional Children, 26,* 18–22.

Pittman, J. (2003). Preparing teachers to use technology with young children in classrooms. *Information Technology in Childhood Education, 2003,* 261–287.

Polloway, E. A., & Patton, J. R. (1997). *Strategies for teaching learners with special needs* (6th ed.). New York: Merrill/Macmillan.

Reinhartsen, D. B., Garfinkle, A. N., & Wolery, M. (2002). Engagement with toys in two-year old children with autism: Teacher selection versus child choice. *Research & Practice for Persons with Severe Disabilities, 27,* 175–187.

Rheams, T. A., & Bain, S. K. (2005). Social interaction interventions in an inclusive era: Attitudes of teachers in early childhood self-contained and inclusive settings. *Psychology in the Schools, 42*(1), 53–63.

Rose, D., & Rose, C. (1994). Students' adaptations to task environments in resource room and regular class setting. *The Journal of Special Education, 28*(1), 3–26.

Rosenshine, B. (1976). Recent research on teaching behavior and student achievement. *Journal of Teacher Education, 27,* 61–64.

Ryba, K., Selby, L., & Nolan, P. (1995). Computers empower students with special needs. *Educational Leadership, 52*(2), 82–84.

Salend, S. J., & Sylvestre, S. (2005). Understanding and addressing oppositional and defiant classroom behaviors. *Teaching Exceptional Children, 37*(6), 32–39.

Schery, T. K., & O'Connor, L. C. (1992). The effectiveness of school-based computer language intervention with severely handicapped children. *Language, Speech, and Hearing Services in Schools, 23,* 43–47.

Schloss, P. J., & Smith, M. A. (1994). *Applied behavior analysis in the classroom.* Boston: Allyn & Bacon.

Schon, D. A. (1983). *The reflective practitioner: How professionals think in action.* New York: Basic Books.

Schon, D. A. (1987). *Educating the reflective practitioner.* San Francisco: Jossey-Bass.

Sears, S., Carpenter, C., & Burstein, N. (1994). Meaningful reading instruction for learners with special needs. *The Reading Teacher, 47*(8), 632–638.

Spiegel-McGill, P., Zippiroli, S., & Mistrett, S. (1989). Microcomputers as social facilitators in integrated preschools. *Journal of Early Intervention, 13*(3), 249–260.

Steg, D., Lazar, I., & Boyce, C. (1994). A cybernetic approach to early education. *Journal of educational computing research, 10*(1), 1–27.

Stein, L. C. (1998). Direct instruction: Integrating curriculum design and effective teaching practice. *Intervention in School and Clinic, 33*(4), 227–234.

Sternberg, R. J., & Zhang, L. (1995). What do we mean by giftedness? A pentagonal implicit theory. *Gifted Child Quarterly, 39*(2), 88–94.

Tate, T. L., Thompson, R. H., & McKerchar, P. M. (2005). Training teachers in an infant classroom to use embedded teaching strategies. *Education and Treatment of Children, 28*(3), 206–221.

Tomlinson, C. A. (2004). Sharing responsibility for differentiating instruction. *Roeper Review, 26*(4), 188–189.

Trent, J. A., Kaiser, A. P., & Wolery, M. (2005). The use of responsive interaction strategies by siblings. *Topics in Early Childhood Special Education, 25*(2), 107–118.

Troia, G. A., & Graham, S. (2002). The effectiveness of a highly explicit, teacher-directed strategy instruction routine: Changing the writing performance of students with learning disabilities. *Journal of Learning Disabilities, 35*(4), 290–305.

Udell, T., Peters, J., & Templeman, T. P. (1998). From philosphy to practice in inclusive early childhood programs. *Teaching Exceptional Children, 30*, 44–49.

VanDerHeyden, A. M., Snyder, P., Smith, A., Sevin, B., & Longwell, J. (2005). Effects of complete learning trials on child engagement. *Topics in Early Childhood Special Education, 25*(2), 107–118.

Venn, M. L., Werts, M. G., Morris, A., DeCesare, L. D., & Cuffs, M. S. (1993). Embedding instruction in art activities to teach preschoolers with disabilities to imitate their peers. *Early Childhood Research Quarterly, 8*, 277–294.

Vygotsky, L. (1978). *Mind in society: The development of higher psychological functions.* Cambridge, MA: Harvard University Press.

Wang, M. C., Haertel, G. D., & Walberg, H. J. (1993/94). What helps students learn? *Educational Leadership, 51*(4), 74–79.

Winter, S. M. (1997). "Smart" planning for inclusion. *Childhood Education, 73*(4), 212–218.

Winter, S. M., Bell, M., & Dempsey, J. (1994). Creating play environments for children with special needs. *Childhood Education, 71*(1), 28–32.

Wolery, M. (2000). Recommended practices in child-focused interventions. In S. Sandall, M. E. McLean & B. J. Smith (Eds.), *DEC recommended practices in early intervention/early childhood special education* (pp. 29–37). Longmont, CO: Sopris West.

Wong, B. (1994). Instructional parameters promoting transfer of learned strategies in students with learning disabilities. *Learning Disability Quarterly, 17*, 110–120.

Zorfass, J., & Rivero, H. K. (2005). Collaboration is key: How a community of practice promotes technology integration. *Journal of Special Education, 20*(3), 51–67.

Chapter 11

Assessing the Effectiveness of the Inclusive Classroom

Key Principle

- Use assessment to fuel instruction

Objectives

After reading this chapter you will be able to:

1. Understand the difference between assessment and testing.
2. Discuss the reasons that assessment is necessary in inclusive early childhood classrooms.
3. Plan ways to involve families in the assessment process.
4. Explain processes and tools to help measure children's progress.
5. Plan for evaluation of your inclusive program.

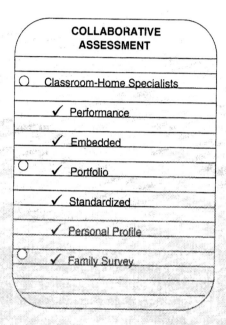

COLLABORATIVE ASSESSMENT

○ Classroom-Home Specialists

✓ Performance

✓ Embedded

○ ✓ Portfolio

✓ Standardized

✓ Personal Profile

○ ✓ Family Survey

INTRODUCTION

Assessment is a critical component of an inclusive early childhood classroom. Curricular planning depends on accurate assessment to ensure a good match for children. Providing differentiated instruction requires careful attention to gathering assessment data on children, formally and informally. Families can collaborate with teachers to obtain accurate information about their children's skills and performance in both home and neighborhood contexts. Teachers in inclusive classrooms use many different ways to communicate the results of classroom-based assessments to parents. Establishing a reciprocal relationship with families for assessment purposes can result in more accurate information upon which to base learning experiences and instructional activities.

USES OF ASSESSMENT AND RELATED ISSUES

What Is the Difference Between Testing and Assessment?

Assessment is a term that is usually more broadly defined than testing. It is the ongoing process of gathering data and artifacts over a span of time and the analysis of the collected information. The goal of assessment is to provide an accurate view of the child's progress, allowing teachers to make informed decisions about instruction or strategies to stimulate a child's learning. Testing, on the other hand, is generally defined more narrowly as a method of checking for skill mastery, content knowledge, or determining performance of a task. The process of assessment may include testing using various types of instruments, including standardized measures and criterion-referenced tests prepared by teachers following a unit of study. Assessment is viewed as fundamental to planning in early childhood and guiding decisions about early intervention strategies. However, it is equally important to ensure that assessment is purposeful and is conducted judiciously as needed to guide planning (Linn & Gronlund, 2000; McConnell, 2000).

Reasons for Assessment

Assessment practices are an integral component of inclusive early childhood classrooms that contribute to success of the program. Both improved services for children and their families and instructional support that are closely matched to children's strengths and abilities are key outcomes of an effective scheme of assessment in inclusive classrooms. Assessment contributes to decisions about best methods of intervention for individual children and the intensity level of those strategies that is likely to prompt success. For these reasons, emphasis on assessment for the purpose of monitoring children's progress is likely to continue (McConnell, 2000).

High-quality assessment instruments are vital to inclusive classrooms for a number of important reasons. Assessments aid teachers to:

- Identify strengths of individual children or gaps in their skills and knowledge base.
- Help monitor children's progress toward meeting individual or IEP targeted goals.
- Inform curricular planning.
- Ensure the child's goals are realistic and attainable with an appropriate level of challenge.
- Identify effective accommodations for individual children.
- Create data to follow the child during transition to the next setting (Hampton & Fantuzzo, 2003).

Accountability is another valid reason for assessing children. Some misconstrued assessment for accountability as high-stakes testing. To the contrary, others point out the obligation to monitor the services rendered to children, especially those with disabilities or developmental delays. It may be more cost-effective to monitor the quality of services rather than limiting accountability and suffering the consequences. Failure to provide children with effective early intervention and school readiness programs will be more costly in the long run in terms of financial expenditure and, more importantly, loss of potential capacity for learning. Children who already suffer economic disadvantages or developmental delays are most likely to be further jeopardized when programs of poor quality slip through the system undetected (Ramey & Ramey, 2004).

Developmental screening and early identification. Children with developmental delays are usually identified later than those with diagnosed conditions (Scarborough et al., 2004). Consequently, teachers in early childhood settings who become familiar with screening tools and assessments can help identify children with potential who might benefit from early intervention services. It has been estimated that early detection and intervention could have resolved or averted the majority of reading problems suffered by today's adults (Snow, Burns, & Griffin, 1998). Language is a sensitive indicator often associated with disorders or delays in other domains of development. Children with hearing loss, neuromotor difficulties, learning disabilities, and specific language disabilities can be identified through language screening using valid instruments. Identifying language problems early and providing immediate intervention can change the trajectory of a child's development. Language affects other areas of development and the learning and socialization of young children. Consequently, if language disorders fail to be detected, children are likely to be at risk of developing other difficulties as they grow and develop. Yet, detecting early language problems is a complex undertaking with no simple answer. Language is a multidimensional system composed of many subcomponents that interplay with one another, resulting in the ability to comprehend, express, and produce communication in various forms. Single tests are insufficient for obtaining a comprehensive view of children's language skills and abilities. Batteries of assessments or tests with multiple subtests provide more accurate profiles of children's language abilities. Use of multiple formal and informal assessment measures, including norm-referenced tests, have been recommended to gain a valid perspective of a child's language abilities. Accuracy of the linguistic profiles developed for individual children are critical in making predictions about the future literacy development of children. Accurate diagnosis and early intervention can improve the chances for a child to develop typical patterns of oral language functioning and reading skills and abilities (Dockrell, 2001).

Parents and families can cooperate with professionals during the language assessment process. Informal methods of assessment, such as collecting and analyzing language samples, administering parent questionnaires, or observing parent-child interactions are good ways to gain insight into children's functional language use in the home context.

The sociocultural theory of child development explains children's learning as an apprenticeship with adults or more expert learners. Interactions between children and their parents allow children to acquire learning strategies, knowledge, and skills more efficiently than the child could do on their own. There is evidence children gain

Observing children and charting their progress on a developmental checklist is a simple way to detect problems early in life.

language, cognitive, and social skills as a result of interactions within sociocultural contexts of their home and community (National Institute of Child Health and Human Development Early Child Care Research Network, 1999; Rogoff, 1990; Vygotsky, 1986).

Abundant research substantiates the relationship between the early language abilities of children and their later performance in language and reading. The more information gained from examining the language of children in different contexts, such as home, school, and child care, the more predictive the data is likely to become. Observing the kind of linguistic support parents provide to infants and toddlers has been found to be predictive of later language skills. An instrument to capture those interactions for later analysis has been developed and validated. The Parent-Infant/Toddler Interaction Coding System (PICS) was developed to measure key aspects of these interactions:

- Child language
- Parent language
- Emotional tone
- Joint attention
- Parental guidance
- Parental responsivity

Results have indicated a strong relationship between these parent behaviors and a child's early literacy skills. Further, measurement of these parent supportive behaviors was found to be a better predictor of child literacy skills than parent report measures (Dockrell, 2001; Dodici, Draper, & Peterson, 2003).

Health screening. Poor general health of children is also a risk factor that can alert teachers to potential developmental problems that might require early intervention services. Children who qualify for early intervention services are eight times more likely to have poor health, which increases their risk of developmental and learning difficulties (Scarborough et al., 2004). Moreover, strong correlations exist between low socioeconomic status of families and their children's risk of health problems and poor developmental outcomes (Chen, Matthews, & Boyce, 2002; Park, Turnbull, & Turnbull, 2002).

Daily health screenings can be conducted by teachers as children enter the classroom each day. Simple observational approaches using a sensory approach allows teachers to gather data about the state of each child's health. Teachers can look for physical symptoms of illness and check for fever (Lakin, 1994). A daily scan can detect a contagious disease before it spreads to other children and may help identify health problems that might interfere with learning. Periodic health screenings by professionals can be scheduled during the year. In public school early childhood and early elementary classrooms or Head Start Centers, teachers can cooperate with a school nurse or other designated health care professionals to perform routine growth and health screening, such as measuring height, weight, vision, and hearing of children. For community-based early childhood programs, it is recommended that teachers cooperate with health care professionals in their area. It is vital to enlist the aid of a health consultant to assess the health and well-being of all children. Typical health consultants available in the community are physicians, nurse practitioners, or registered nurses, with the health care expertise and training to screen children and serve as a resource person to teachers and parents (American Public Health Association & American Academy of Pediatrics, 2002).

In areas with a serious lead toxicity problem in the environment, screening might include checking for elevated blood levels of lead. When teachers in inclusive classrooms have concerns about children's difficulty in learning, inability to concentrate, or behavioral problems, factors other than development may be influential. Lead toxicity is a problem that cuts across income levels and can affect children of all cultures and racial backgrounds. One in six children under the age of six has elevated levels of lead in their bloodstream (Jaroff & Blackman, 1991). Brain and neurological development can be impaired leading to difficulty in cognitive, motor, and socio-emotional areas of development. Children may evidence difficulty in these key learning skills and behaviors:

- Reading
- Writing
- Math
- Motor skills
- Hand-eye coordination
- Hearing
- Irritability
- Aggression

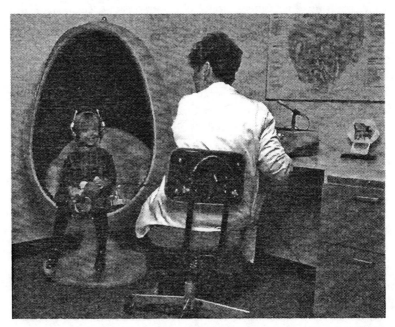

Early screening can ensure good health and development fundamental to learning.

Decreased intelligence and slowed development can result from exposure to even low levels of lead in the environment (Ryan, Levy, Pollack, & Walker, 1999). Lead poisoning may be responsible for behavioral problems that result in antisocial patterns of behavior and can later manifest as delinquency (American Academy of Pediatrics, 1998).

Standards-based testing. Standards-based legislation, particularly NCLB Act in 2002, has raised many issues relevant to assessment in elementary school settings. Concerns regarding the valid assessment of English language learners (ELL) are being revisited, as mandated high-stakes testing requires the inclusion of all learners with virtually no exceptions. A long history of antidiscrimination legislation and case law have contributed to the change in the long-standing pattern of excluding children whose performance might reflect poorly on their school's overall achievement profile. With the current mandates to include all children regardless of ability, ethnicity, language, gender, or other characteristics, it is critical to address ways to include all children in assessments with adaptations and accommodations that level the playing field without invalidating the test. The challenge is to make accommodations that are fair, but avoid giving undue advantages to certain children. For English language learners, these accommodations might make changes to the:

- Testing process
- Test itself
- Test item response model

The necessity to make accommodations for ELL or limited English proficiency (LEP) children raises many important issues about which adjustments are scientifically valid, who makes decisions about the accommodations, how will accommodations be implemented, and other considerations. A critical question is who qualifies for accommodations and how are the adjustments going to be monitored. Whereas laws govern the accommodations for children who qualify for special services, namely through decisions made by the IEP committee, ELL children have no such assurances (Abedi, Hofstetter, & Lord, 2004). Policies are likely to be generated locally within administrative structures selected by the school. Another serious issue reported by school psychologists is the overemphasis on high-stakes testing that has led to the phenomenon of "teaching to the test" (Harrison et al., 2004).

Eligibility for Services, Placement Decisions, and Retention Issues

Some experts believe a paradigm shift has occurred, changing priorities in the assessment of children. Currently, more emphasis is being given to assessment for the purpose of planning individualized early intervention, rather than changing diagnostic testing solely to determine whether children are eligible for services (Harrison et al., 2004). Other experts argue that early childhood has historically been viewed as a time period for detecting potential developmental delays without the obligation of assigning specific labels or categories to the child (McConnell, 2000). Nevertheless, most experts agree that the current emphasis is definitely in favor of prevention and early intervention. Considerable energy and resources are being focused on documenting the characteristics of children and families who access early intervention services and the outcomes gained through preventative strategies. For example, The U.S. Department of Education's National Early Intervention Longitudinal Study (NEILS), was launched to collect comprehensive descriptive data about children who receive early intervention services initiated before age 3. A nationally representative sample of children were followed through kindergarten entry to gain insight into early intervention outcomes. Findings have indicated that there is considerable variability in the characteristics of children who receive early intervention services. Children were representative of a full range of income levels; although, children in low-income families were represented in a higher proportion compared to other income levels. Given the well-substantiated risks associated with poverty, the overrepresentation of children from impoverished homes receiving early intervention services might be viewed as beneficial and could help prevent more pervasive disorders later (Scarborough et al., 2004).

Differences in philosophy can influence the interpretation of diagnostic tests and the designation of eligibility for services. The existence of philosophical variations among professionals can lead to exclusionary practices in schools. There are reports of speech services being denied to children with severe communication delays because of the belief that oral communication was not feasible for children who lacked prerequisite skills to benefit from speech therapy. Further, some philosophies hold that some children are too young to benefit from speech therapy, yet, research has indicated that some persons with severe delays in communication can continue to gain skills well into adulthood. Parents and teachers should be aware of such exclusionary practices, so they can advocate for children with severe communication deficits (Snell et al., 2003).

ASSESSMENT TO INFORM PLANNING

Selecting Assessment Tools

To derive positive benefits from the time and effort used to administer assessments, it is important to select measurement instruments carefully. Assessment tools and instruments must have psychometric properties that meet criteria set forth by respected measurement organizations, such as the American Educational Research Association, American Psychological Association, and the National Council on Measurement in Education. Validity is the major criterion to consider when selecting an assessment instrument; otherwise, one cannot be sure the test is measuring the phenomena it is purported to measure (Hampton & Fantuzzo, 2003). Professional groups of researchers have published evaluations of assessments available in early childhood, which can be helpful in selecting instruments that match the type of information desired and the characteristics and age of the children being assessed (see Box 11.1).

Varying Assessment Methods and Instruments

Teachers using a variety of assessment methods and tools are more likely to obtain an accurate view of each child's strengths and how to help the child progress. A balanced selection of assessment instruments and methods can yield information to provide a well-rounded view of all aspects of a child's competence and ability. New assessment

COLLABORATION TIPS   BOX 11.1

COOPERATING WITH TEACHERS

When planning with your age- or grade-level team of teachers:

- First, discuss what information about children's skills and abilities was gleaned from previous assessments.
- Next, plan ways to assess each objective for new units of study or themes.
- Brainstorm ways that assessment techniques might need to be changed or adapted for individual children.
- Embed methods of assessment in activities whenever possible.

instruments are being developed that point to novel ways of predicting children's future school performance. For example, the Penn Interactive Peer Play Scale (PIPPS) instrument was developed to assess the social interaction of children in play circumstances, which was also reported to be valuable in predicting the later social competence and school success of young children (Hampton & Fantuzzo, 2003).

Establishing a Scheme of Ongoing Assessment

If a child qualifies for special services, ongoing monitoring of those services is necessary to ensure appropriate fit, so benefits can continue to be derived from the designated services (Snell et al., 2003). Whereas assessment information is useful to monitor the gains children are making, schools also have an obligation to ensure all children have ample opportunities to grow and develop. The new concept of school readiness focuses upon the reciprocal relationship between the child and the school setting. Whereas parents and teachers collaborate to build a foundation of pre-academic skills and abilities related to successful functioning in classrooms, the school is also obligated to ensure that environments and practices support the development of school readiness skills and abilities in children (Hampton & Fantuzzo, 2003). A scheme of ongoing assessments can also inform teachers about whether the match between the child and the school is robust.

ALTERNATIVE ASSESSMENT TECHNIQUES

Child Performance Assessments

Monitoring children's progress by evaluating their performance on specific learning tasks is widely accepted as an alternative assessment method in early childhood and early childhood special education (McConnell, 2000).

Portfolio and Work Sample Systems

An assessment and documentation method that is beneficial for all children is the portfolio system. Teachers using this method find it is a versatile system for assessing children's progress and keeping tangible records documenting their work samples. In an inclusive classroom, portfolios represent a strengths-based system that highlights a child's abilities rather than disabilities. Whereas norm-referenced tests give families and teachers a tool for understanding a child's progress compared to other children, a portfolio assessment chronicles an individual child's progress across a span of time. Children's progress is viewed as a pattern of their own accomplishments; their achievements are not compared to the gains of others (Smith, Brewer, & Heffner, 2003). Experts advise that norm-referenced assessments augmented with alternative methods of assessment are needed for obtaining an accurate view of the accomplishments and progress of children with disabilities and those with potential delays in development.

Portfolio or work sample systems enhance collaborative assessment of children by families and teachers.

For example, norm-referenced tests do not capture children's progress in mastering functional skills necessary for daily living. A comprehensive appraisal of the skills and abilities of children with special needs is essential to ensure the recommendation of appropriate placements that will properly support and advance the development of these children (Greenspan, Meisels, & Work Group on Developmental Assessment, 1994).

Another advantage of the portfolio system in inclusive classrooms is the value of this method to foster communication and collaboration between teachers and families. Portfolios are an effective vehicle for stimulating communication, making parent conferences a reciprocal interchange of information. Together, teachers and parents can share anecdotes and examine concrete evidence of accomplishments for signs of progress in a child's development. There are opportunities for collaboration in assessing children when families are invited to contribute to samples of children's progress evidenced at home or when families offer their interpretation of their children's work for consideration along with teacher's interpretation. Families can use home videos to document a child accomplishing a task or interacting with peers in the neighborhood. Pictures the child has drawn or invented spelling and story writing can be contributed to the portfolio.

Videotaped performance of tasks in the classroom can uncover detailed information useful in curriculum planning. Videos can reveal environmental factors in the classroom and how classroom attributes influence a child's performance. Teachers can look for factors that might exert an influence:

- Noise
- Lighting

- Visual cues
- Materials

Videos can reveal how children approach difficult tasks and ways they attempt to overcome obstacles. Teachers can use videos to identify learning strategies the child uses successfully (Smith et al., 2003). For example, some children rely on visual cues, whereas others may respond better to a combination of peer modeling with auditory instructions.

Observational Methods and Ecobehavioral Assessment Tools

As discussed in Chapter 5, a host of factors in the physical and social aspects environment can affect a child's learning and day-to-day performance of academic and functional tasks in the classroom. It is vital to gain a contextualized view of children's behavior, learning, and developmental progress. Ecobehavioral assessment continues to evolve from its roots in ecobehavioral research, a method of examining behavior in light of contextual variables that may contribute to performance or influence behavior. An ecobehavioral approach to assessment permits teachers to gain perspective on the environmental characteristics present in their classroom that might play a role in either fostering or impeding the learning of children. Ecobehavioral methods of assessment hold promise for better understanding the processes of how naturalistic contexts influence child behaviors to promote development (Arreaga-Mayer, Utley, Perdomo-Rivera, & Greenwood, 2003; McConnell, 2000).

Role of Collaboration in the Assessment Process

When teachers use collaborative methods that bring others into the assessment process, the resulting information will likely be more comprehensive and accurate. Families might have vital information to share about their children, especially when there are medical routines that must be conducted or medications that must be administered. Paraprofessionals, frequently assisting teachers in inclusive classrooms, can be involved in the day-to-day routines of monitoring children's performance and progress toward goals. However, it is important to ensure that paraprofessionals are properly trained in assessment techniques. One survey of paraprofessionals indicated that 60% perceived a need for additional training in service delivery, including the monitoring of children's progress and performance on tasks so they could assist in adjusting the program to fit children's needs (Killoran, Templeman, Peters, & Udell, 2001).

Personal profile. Increasingly, children with moderate to severe disabilities are being included in early childhood classrooms. Traditional methods of assessment typically reveal the weaknesses and deficits of children with serious disabilities and rarely offer a full view with their interests and areas of strength. Compiling an individual personal profile for these children is a child-centered method of rapidly obtaining a balanced view of the whole child in a short period of time. Involving families in developing the profile at the beginning of the school year can inform the teacher of pertinent information about the child and how he or she functions best. Profiles can be an effective method of initiating a reciprocal flow of information between home and school, which is essential for a true partnership. The personal profile is an efficient way of obtaining information that might be critical to a child's adjustment to the new setting.

The personal profile is similar to a case study; however, it is a greatly abbreviated form with bulleted categories of information. Whereas categories can reveal strategies for supporting and accommodating a child, a strengths-based approach is intended to emphasize positive attributes and successful ways the child has approached learning. With this method, teachers can involve parents and families of the child with disabilities to decide on relevant categories of information to include in the profile. Teachers and family members can participate in gathering information to add in the bulleted format, resulting in a concise overview of the child's strengths, interests, preferences, and favorite activities. Parents can share information about the challenges their children face, as well as their parental expectations and goals. Parents and the child can communicate to the teacher the accomplishments that are a source of pride for the child and family. Teachers can gain valuable information about the home life and personal characteristics of the child that might help them plan ways to optimize the learning experiences.

Research suggests personal profiles can help teachers and other professionals have positive feelings toward a child through the sense of familiarity the imparted information brings. Parents reported a favorable response to this method because it was less technical compared to other assessments and helped them communicate key facts and information to all personnel working with their children (Kelly, Siegel, & Allinder, 2001).

CULTURE-FAIR AND GENDER-FAIR PRACTICES
Selecting Assessment Techniques and Instruments

Living in poverty can impede a child's chances for success in school. For example, the economic disadvantage can narrow options for families and limit access to high-quality care and early education for their children. Children of disadvantaged families, who are often minorities, are less likely to enroll in preschool or child-care centers prior to formal school entry. Lack of preschool experience can have an affect on later academic performance. Children who attended child-care centers or preschools have been reported to demonstrate higher scores on reading and math compared to children with no preschool enrollment. This reported gap in the school readiness of children related to family income appears to persist into the early grades (Magnuson, Meyers, Ruhm, & Waldfogel, 2004). Home-learning environments of children in poverty have been reported to influence their scores on developmental tests. Findings have suggested that one-half the gap in developmental scores between preschoolers from low-income homes and those from more affluent families is attributable to the quality of the home environment (Smith, Brooks-Gunn, & Klebanov, 1997).

These findings have potential implication for the selection of assessment instruments and the interpretation of children's scores. Selecting validated instruments and culture-fair assessment tools ensures reliable, accurate data for decision making. Such steps will help ensure that the test, itself, does not place limitations on the performance of children. With accurate data, teachers can better plan instruction at the intensity level needed for each child to succeed and learn. An ongoing scheme of cultural-fair assessments to guide instruction may help close the academic gaps precipitated by poverty, lack of preschool experience, or other factors.

Collaborative Approaches with Professionals

Children of cultural and linguistic minority families present particular challenges to professionals involved in assessment and early intervention programming. Suspected developmental delays may be difficult to detect in these children, especially delays in language, when the family's primary language is not the majority language in their residence area. Collaboration of families and professionals can be instrumental in obtaining valid diagnostic data and ongoing assessment information. Sometimes, diagnoses are tentative due to the young age of the child and difficulty in gaining a diagnosis. Suspected language barriers may also contribute to difficulty in properly assessing a child. Frequently, medical professionals, such as pediatricians, are among the first professionals involved in a child's case and may provide initial referrals for diagnosis. The cultural competence of medical professionals and their knowledge of second-language acquisition can be critical in early identification. Discerning true language delays from typical patterns of second-language acquisition can be challenging. Research has suggested that acquiring a second language does not slow language development. If pediatricians wrongly attribute language delays to the process of second-language acquisition, early intervention may also be deferred. On the other hand, pediatricians can be powerful allies with early childhood professionals and members of diagnostic teams (see Box 11.2 for collaboration tips). Trusted pediatricians can encourage parents to seek further assessment and diagnosis, and they can be strong advocates for children in the school setting. Further, medical professionals who understand family belief systems and folk-illnesses or know of folk-cures that families might have used can enlighten teachers and schools about the physical aspects of a child's behavioral or learning problems. For example, some folk-cures have been reported to contain high levels of lead that can impair a child's cognitive functioning and limit learning potential. Information about the use of such cures by families is highly relevant to diagnosis and assessment of children by school teams (Stein, Flores, Graham, Willies-Jacobo, & Magana, 2004).

IDEAS AND TIPS   BOX 11.2
COLLABORATION WITH PROFESSIONALS

- Establish contact with professionals already involved with the children in your inclusive classroom.
- Identify professionals not yet in your network who can contribute ways to assess the child's skills and abilities.

PROGRAM EVALUATION

Ongoing Evaluation of Program Effectiveness

Maintaining a high-quality inclusive program requires systematic evaluation of key program components. Formal evaluations scheduled periodically can reveal programmatic strengths or areas in need of improvement. Between scheduled formal evaluations, informal evaluation techniques can provide teachers with a method of reckoning to keep the program on target with established goals. Box 11.3 demonstrates a sample progress report.

Informal evaluation. Three key program indicators have proven reliable as barometers for estimating the overall quality of an early childhood program:

1. The educational attainment of teachers is associated with high-quality programs.
2. Low child-to-staff ratios are likely to signal effective programs.
3. Low class size has been reported to have a high correlation with quality programs.

Although these indicators are structural in nature, large national studies have corroborated the association of these variables with global high-quality programs that are likely to result in positive outcomes for children (National Institute of Child Health and Human Development Early Child Care Research Network, 2002; Phillips, Mekos, Scarr, McCartney, & Abbott-Shim, 2000).

The quality of an early childhood program can be evaluated using criteria established by the National Association for the Education of Young Children (NAEYC) (Bredekamp & Copple, 1997). When first published, the NAEYC's developmentally appropriate practice (DAP) guidelines (Bredekamp, 1987) stirred much controversy regarding the applicability of the guidelines for inclusive early childhood settings. The debate centered upon differences in the recommended best practices subscribed to by the fields of early childhood and early childhood special education. These two fields

---

05-21-04   **BOX 11.3**

Progress Report for Juanita:

Juanita is doing well in the Prekindergarten class. She is able to identify and tell me the entire alphabet in capital and lowercase, as well as numbers 1-15. She is able to pattern, count 1-1 correspondence and we are working on letter sounds. We have also worked on rhyming—which is hard for her.

Juanita was a pleasure to have in class and has really progressed throughout the year in acquiring some of the academics skills taught. My hope for her next year is to see her apply some of these skills and also see her language and communication skills progress.

Ms. Smith
Prekindergarten Teacher

evolved from separate and distinct theoretical and philosophical backgrounds. Special education teachers espouse to a range of instructional practices, including those heavily influenced by behaviorist theory, and historically have accepted more intrusive, direct teaching models of practice as necessary and effective for children with certain disabling conditions. Teachers with an early childhood education background tend to eschew such practices in favor of child-centered methods that encourage children to learn through play and exploration. The debates tempered extreme views in both fields and resulted in more agreement toward blending of recommended practices, with emphasis on matching instruction to individual needs of children, both disabled and nondisabled. A revised version of the DAP guidelines was published, reflecting more emphasis on accommodating individual needs of children and matching the intensity of practices to what a child needs to succeed. Increased cultural sensitivity and competence of teachers in teaching practices was also urged (Bredekamp & Copple, 1997). The result is a set of guidelines that can be useful in guiding informal evaluation of practices adopted by an inclusive program.

Involving families in evaluation. Providing families with an opportunity to give feedback on their perceptions of program effectiveness enables the teacher to make changes that respond to family expectations. Teachers can formulate simple surveys with carefully worded questions or compile a group of multiple choice response items stated in positive terms. The idea is to capture family feelings, perceptions of teacher commitment, and satisfaction with learning activities. Guaranteeing anonymity to parents will increase the likelihood of accuracy and voicing of honest opinions. Making

Families play a key role in assessing children and the impact of programs that serve young children.

small changes in the program or procedures can make a big difference in parental satisfaction. Ask families to comment on the following major program areas:

- Communication. Is there sufficient contact? Are the methods of contact convenient?
- Satisfaction with program strategies. What meets the needs and goals of the family and which strategies do not fit family goals.
- Child's satisfaction with the program. Does child want to attend and seem happy with the activities?
- Child's progress in learning new skills. Is the parent satisfied with the child's progress? Does child's progress meet the parental expectations? Do the skills, behaviors, and concepts the child is learning match family goals and values? (Moore, 2003).

Another innovative assessment tool that has potential for increasing the collaboration of teachers with families is the Asset-Based Context (ABC) matrix. This tool is designed to assess the functional participation of a child in the home, early childhood program, and community contexts. Examining a child's participation in these three activity settings can help identify opportunities for children to learn, demonstrate strengths, and develop interests within each context. The matrix asks families to respond to questions about their children's activities as they play, learn, and carry out functional routines for daily living, such as what their children do, what they enjoy, and how they respond to people in their family and neighborhood. Ideas for expanding the possibilities for interactions and expanding on learning opportunities in the home and community contexts are elicited from parents.

COLLABORATION TIPS   BOX 11.4

WITH DIVERSE FAMILIES

- Plan how to involve families in assessment before, during, and after the unit activities.
- Ask parents about other professionals who may be providing services to the child and family (e.g., social worker, pediatrician, public health nurse, religious education teacher).
- Let families know you value their role in gathering information about their children (e.g., newsletters, parent conferences, thanking parents for contributing information).
- Plan simple, fun data gathering activities for families to do with their children.
- During conferences, allow ample time for parents to tell you about what they see as progress and what they still wish to know about their children's strengths and abilities.

The ABC matrix can inform teachers and families about the type and range of activities in which a child is able to engage. The information gleaned from this assessment tool fosters collaborative decision making between teachers and family members. The concept of the individualized family service plan (IFSP) necessitates tools that carry assessment activities beyond the classroom and into the home and family contexts. (Wilson, Mott, & Batman, 2004). Tools, such as the ABC matrix, promote the establishment of links between home and classroom contexts that can facilitate greater continuity for children. This tool stimulates learning of children in all the contexts in which they grow and learn and brings parents and families into fuller participation as the first teachers of their children. Boxes 11.4 through 11.6 offer collaboration tips and activities for families.

FAMILIES GATHERING DATA   BOX 11.5
Healthy Lifestyle

Scavenger Hunt

Provide a list of healthy foods and items that promote healthy lifestyles. Ask parents to check off each item as they find it around the house.

- **Fresh vegetables**
    - **Broccoli**
    - **Green Beans**
    - **Tomatoes**
    - **Carrots**
- **Fresh fruits**
    - **Apples**
    - **Oranges**
    - **Bananas**
    - **Grapes**
- **Whole grains foods**
    - **Oatmeal**
    - **Whole wheat bread**
    - **Corn tortillas**
- **Protein sources**
    - **Lean meat**
    - **Chicken**
    - **Fish**
    - **beans**

COLLABORATION TIPS   BOX 11.6

Photo Diary

Give each family a disposable camera and invite them to take pictures of indoor and outdoor sports and exercise activities:

- Cleaning the house
- Yardwork and outdoor chores
- Dancing to music
- Participating in team sports
- Visiting a neighborhood park or playground
- Individual sports and practice

  - Pitch and catch
  - Skating
  - Walking in neighborhood
  - Family games

SUMMARY

This chapter emphasized the importance of ongoing assessment routines in the inclusive early childhood classroom in which teachers can gather daily information about children. It is critical for family members to collaborate with teachers and specialists to collect information about the child in the home context. When teachers devise fun and interesting assessment activities families can do together, parents are glad to cooperate. It is also important to have a variety of different ways to communicate assessment information to parents. Establishing partnerships with parents and family members can help to gain an accurate view of a child's performance and the child's ability to generalize skills to contexts other than school.

Discussion Questions

1. Summarize the key elements of a good program of assessment in an inclusive early childhood classroom.
2. What is the distinction between testing and assessment?
3. How can families be helpful in gathering data on children's performance, interests, and skills?

4. What are alternative assessments and how are these tools used in the inclusive classroom?

5. Describe ways assessment can support early identification and early intervention.

6. How can you be fair and unbiased when assessing children in the classroom?

7. Are there effective ways to find out what parents already know about their child?

8. How can you find out what kinds of experiences and opportunities children have to learn in their homes or neighborhoods?

Inclusive Activities

1. Look for samples of family surveys designed to help teachers find out more about family activities and the activity preferences of children. You may wish to design your own based on the sample instruments you find. Remember to keep it short to be respectful of parents' time. You may need to have the instrument translated into several languages for the convenience of families.

2. Meet with a teacher in an inclusive classroom to ask about tests used by the school and assessments used in the classroom to evaluate young children's progress.

3. Locate a school counselor, diagnostician, or other personnel involved in determining eligibility of children for special education services. Ask your resource person to discuss the process and diagnostic instruments used. Look for checklists that screen for child abuse and mental health problems.

4. Make a list of steps a classroom teacher can take to participate in prereferral processes and collect data for children who may need early intervention.

5. Talk with a school nurse or community health professional about ways to screen young children for health problems. Make a list of resources and checklists for teachers to use.

6. Explore electronic portfolio software packages. Download a sample and practice designing a portfolio for a child.

References

Abedi, J., Hofstetter, C. H., & Lord, C. (2004). Assessment accommodations for English language learners: Implications for policy-based empirical research. *Review of Educational Research, 74*(1), 1–28.

American Academy of Pediatrics. (1998). Screening for elevated blood lead levels. *Pediatrics, 101*(6), 1072–1078.

American Public Health Association & American Academy of Pediatrics. (2002). *Caring for our children: National health and safety performance standards: Guidelines for out-of-home care.* Washington, DC: APHA.

Arreaga-Mayer, C., Utley, C. A., Perdomo-Rivera, C., & Greenwood, C. R. (2003). Ecobehavioral assessment of instructional contexts in bilingual special education programs for English language learners at risk for developmental disabilities. *Focus on Autism and Other Developmental Disabilities, 18*(1), 28–40.

Bredekamp, S. (Ed.). (1987). *Developmentally appropriate practice in early childhood programs serving children from birth through age 8.* Washington, DC: National Association for the Education of Young Children.

Bredekamp, S., & Copple, C. (Eds.). (1997). *Developmentally appropriate practice in early childhood programs*

(Rev. ed.). Washington, DC: National Association for the Education of Young Children.

Chen, E., Matthews, K. A., & Boyce, W. T. (2002). Socioeconomic differences in children's health: How and why do these relationships change with age? *Psychological Bulletin, 128*(2), 295–329.

Dockrell, J. E. (2001). Assessing language skills in preschool children. *Child Psychology & Psychiatry Review, 6*(2), 74–85.

Dodici, B. J., Draper, D. C., & Peterson, C. A. (2003). Early parent-child interactions and early literacy development. *Topics in Early Childhood Special Education, 23*(3), 124–136.

Greenspan, S. I., Meisels, S. J., & Work Group on Developmental Assessment. (1994). Toward a new vision for the developmental assessment of infants and young children. *Zero to Three, 14*(6), 22.

Hampton, V. R., & Fantuzzo, J. (2003). The validity of the Penn Interactive Peer Play Scale with urban, low-income kindergarten children. *School Psychology Review, 32*(1), 77–91.

Harrison, P. L., Cummings, J. A., Dawson, M., Short, R. J., Gorin, S., & Palomares, R. (2004). Responding to the needs of children, families, and schools: The 2002 multisite conference on the future of school psychology. *The School Psychology Review, 33*(1), 12–33.

Jaroff, L. & Blackman, A. (1991, February 25). Controlling a childhood menace. *Time 137*(8), 68–69.

Kelly, K. M., Siegel, E. B., & Allinder, R. M. (2001). Personal profile assessment summary: Creating windows into the worlds of children with special needs. *Intervention in School and Clinic, 36*(4), 202–210.

Killoran, J., Templeman, T. P., Peters, J., & Udell, T. (2001). Identifying paraprofessional competencies for early intervention and early childhood special education. *Teaching Exceptional Children, 34*(1), 68–73.

Lakin, M. (1994). Observing from a different point of view. *Child Care Information Exchange, 95* (Jan.–Feb.), 65–69.

Linn, R. L., & Gronlund, N. E. (Eds.). (2000). *Measurement and assessment in teaching*. Upper Saddle River, NJ: Merrill/Prentice Hall.

Magnuson, K. A., Meyers, M. K., Ruhm, C. J., & Waldfogel, J. (2004). Inequality in preschool education and school readiness. *American Educational Research Journal, 41*(1), 115–157.

McConnell, S. R. (2000). Assessment in early intervention and early childhood special education: Building on the past to project into our future. *Topics in Early Childhood Special Education, 20*(1), 43–48.

Moore, K. B. (2003). Evaluating your program at mid-year: Doing a mid-year evaluation goes a long way toward making long-term program improvements. *Scholastic Early Child Today, 17*(4), 12–13.

National Institute of Child Health and Human Development Early Child Care Research Network. (2002). Child care structure, process, outcomes: Direct and indirect effects of child-care quality on young children's development. *Psychological Science, 13*, 199–206.

National Institute of Child Health and Human Development Early Child Care Research Network. (1999). Child-care and mother-child interaction in the first 3 years of life. *Developmental Psychology, 35*, 1399–1413.

Park, J., Turnbull, A. P., & Turnbull, H. R. (2002). Impacts of poverty on quality of life in families of children with disabilities. *Exceptional Children, 68*, 151–170.

Phillips, D., Mekos, D., Scarr, S., McCartney, K., & Abbott-Shim, M. (2000). Within and beyond the classroom door: Assessing quality in child care centers. *Early Childhood Research Quarterly, 15*(4), 475–496.

Ramey, C. T., & Ramey, S. L. (2004). Early learning and school readiness: Can early intervention make a difference? *Merrill-Palmer Quarterly, 50*(4), 471–491.

Rogoff, B. (1990). *Apprenticeship in thinking: Cognitive development in social context*. New York: Oxford University Press.

Ryan, D., Levy, B., Pollack, S., & Walker, B. (1999). Protecting children from lead poisoning and building healthy communities. *American Journal of Public Health, 89*(6), 822–824.

Scarborough, A. A., Spiker, D., Mallik, S., Hebbeler, K. M., Bailey, Jr., D. B., & Simeonsson, R. J. (2004). A national look at children and families entering early intervention. *Exceptional Children, 70*(4), 469–483.

Smith, J., Brewer, D. M., & Heffner, T. (2003). Using portfolio assessments with young children who are at risk for school failure. *Preventing School Failure, 48*(1), 38–40.

Smith, J. R., Brooks-Gunn, J., & Klebanov, P. K. (1997). Consequences of living in poverty for young children's cognitive and verbal ability and early school achievement. In G. J. Duncan & J. Brooks-Gunn (Eds.), *Consequences of growing up poor* (pp. 132–189). New York: Russell Sage Foundation.

Snell, M. E., Cave, K., McLean, L., Mollica, B. M., Mirenda, P., Paul-Brown, D., et al. (2003). Concerns regarding the application of restrictive "eligibility" policies to individuals who need communication services and supports: A response by the National Joint Committee for the Communication Needs of Persons with Severe Disabilities. *Research and Practice for Persons with Severe Disabilities, 28*(2), 70–78.

Snow, C., Burns, M. S., & Griffin, P. (Eds.). (1998). *Preventing reading difficulties in young children.* Washington, DC: National Academy Press.

Stein, M. T., Flores, G., Graham, E. A., Willies-Jacobo, L., & Magana, L. (2004). Cultural and linguistic determinants in the diagnosis and management of developmental delay in a 4-year-old. *Pediatrics, 114*(5), 1442–1447.

Vygotsky, L. (1986). *Thought and language.* Cambridge, MA: MIT Press.

Wilson, L. L., Mott, D. W., & Batman, D. (2004). The asset-based context matrix: A tool for assessing children's learning opportunities and participation in natural environments. *Topics in Early Childhood Special Education, 24*(2), 110–120.

Appendixes

WORKING WITH YOUR CHILD AT HOME

Dear Parents:

I have compiled a packet of ideas, activities, and materials for you to use with your child at home. In our weekly newsletter, you will see the concepts and letters your child will be working on at school. This packet provides you with the tools to work on those same key concepts at home.

LETTERS

Please make sure you only introduce the letters we have already introduced at school—check our weekly newsletter to see what letter we'll be introducing or reviewing. When teaching your children letters:

1. Hold up lowercase and capital letter flash cards—one at a time.
2. Say the letter and then give the sound.
3. Have your child repeat the letter and sound.
4. When your child is familiar with the letters, you can hold the flash cards up and have the child tell you the letter and sound.
5. You can also ask your child what words start with the letter.
6. Put several letters on the table and have your child pick out the letter you say.
7. Write the letter as you say the name and sound. Have your child repeat.

WRITING NAME

Use the enclosed sentence strip and D'Nealian letter guide to write your child's name.

1. Have the child trace the letters with his or her finger.
2. Have the child trace the letters with a pencil.
3. Set the name in front of the child, and have him or her use it to try to copy his or her name.
4. You can use the single-letter flash cards and start with one letter at a time first.

NUMBERS

Start introducing numbers by:

1. Helping your child count to 10—while you hold up the flash cards and say numbers along with your child.

2. Put two numbers on the table and have the child pick out the one you ask for.

3. Hold up the cards one at a time and have your child tell you the number on the card.

Your child also needs to know how to count using 1-1 correspondence; 1-1 correspondence means that the child points to an object and counts it.

1. Put 2 objects on the table.

2. Demonstrate pointing to the first object and say "one." Then point to the second object and say "two."

3. Have your child try.

4. After your child is able to count two, try adding another object to make three—and so on up to 10.

SHAPES

1. Hold up a shape and tell your child what it is.

2. Have your child repeat the name.

3. After you go over all the shapes, have your child tell you each shape on his or her own.

4. The shapes are different colors so you can practice having your child tell you the color as well, "blue square."

5. Point out objects around the house and have your child tell you the shape.

COLORS

1. Hold up the flash card and say the color.

2. Have your child repeat the color.

3. After you have practiced with your child, have him or her repeat the names of the colors on his or her own.

PATTERNS

Patterns can be very difficult, so it is important to start with an easy one, and then move on to harder ones.

1. Make a simple ABAB pattern for your child to see—circle, square, circle, square.

2. Work with your child to create the pattern—asking him or her, "What comes next?"

3. When you think your child has the concept, let him or her make a pattern by him or herself.

4. You can eventually introduce an AABAA (circle, circle, square, circle, circle) or BBABB (square, square, circle, square, square) pattern.

HELP YOUR CHILD WITH HIS OR HER FINE MOTOR SKILLS

- Practice holding pencils properly.
- Pick pinto beans out of play dough.
- Practice coloring in the lines.
- Trace shapes, letters, etc.
- Cut out things—coupons or find printables online: www.dltk-kids.com.

Appendix B **COLLABORATION TIPS**

PARENT CONFERENCE I

I. Identifying Information

- *Class:* Preschool program for children with disabilities (PPCD) class
- *Child:* A child with attention deficit hyperactivity disorder (ADHD) and mild Cerebral Palsy affecting left side of body. The child is bright and academically, performs near his peers, but has some behavior problems. The child has a hard time spending time in the general education classroom.
- *Parents:* The child's mother was in attendance at the conference. She is a working mom who is involved in the child's education. She is very willing to collaborate with me and tries to make sure to help the child at home.
- *Conference Manager:* The PPCD teacher.
- *Time:* This conference was held four weeks after school started.

II. Rationale of Conference

- *Purpose/Intent:* I held this conference to discuss the child's behavior. I would like to discuss with the mother the results of the behavior interventionist's visit. I want to tell her and show her some of the ideas the interventionist had, as well as talk about holding an admission, review, and dismissal (ARD) meeting to reduce the child's time in general education kindergarten. I believe these measures will help to reduce and hopefully eliminate some of the behavior problems. (Unplanned: We also ended up discussing some recent problems the mother has had and a new behavior management system she implemented at home that seems to be helping.)
- *Type:* Planned.
- *Initiation:* I initiated the conference.

III. Preconference Preparation

- I prepared a folder of work samples, as well as my notes on his behavior. I was prepared to show the mother examples of the strategies suggested by the interventionist: a picture schedule system, first/then cards, and the reward system. I also provided the mother a copy of the behavior interventionist's report.

IV. Conference Topography, Demographics

- *Where:* In the conference room. *Who:* Mother and I.
- *Seating:* We sat at a small table, with two chairs.
- *Proximity:* We sat across from each other.
- *Arrangement:* This was a rather large room, but I made it more personal by sitting at a small table very close to the mother.
- I offered her a beverage. Mom and I both took a few notes of the meeting—just to jot down any ideas we had or issues/concerns for the ARD.

V. Process/Content

- The conference began by the mother asking me how the child's day was so far today. I told her we had already had a few behavior problems. Mom was concerned, but I told her not to worry. She seemed very tense—and definitely worried. She explained to me about some of the problems she'd been having at home with her child. She has tried everything. Then I began to tell her about the interventionist's visit. (I did not go into detail about his behavior, etc., because I send home notes daily, and we have been in contact over the phone.) I explained to her how there is no pattern when the behavior occurs, although the kindergarten time is very tough for the child. The child is easily frustrated and needs an environment with a smaller class size at the moment. Mom agreed. We decided to go back to ARD and change the time the child was going to be included in kindergarten. I wanted her to know that we would word the paperwork so that her child may spend more time in kindergarten when the behavior improved. At this point, I gave the mother a copy of the behavior interventionist's report. This was her copy to take home. I highlighted some of the important parts of the report for her. I then showed her examples of the picture schedule system and first/then cards. I also explained to her we were going to reward the other children in the class for their appropriate behavior when her child was exhibiting behavior problems, but also reward everyone, including her child when appropriate behavior was exhibited. Rewards could vary from a fun activity to a small piece of food. I told her we needed to give these strategies some time to work. I told her the interventionist said the behaviors might get worse before they get better. Mom then relaxed a little more. She then told me about how they started a token economy at home and it seemed to be working well. I agreed to start one at school as well. We then talked about when a good time for the ARD would be for her. Then, I asked her if she had any other questions or concerns. She said no. I assured her that we were going to find something that would work for her child, and told her not to worry. I, again, let her know she could call, e-mail, etc. me any time. I told her I'd get her the paperwork soon for the upcoming ARD. I shook her hand and told her to have a nice rest of the day.

VI. Evaluation of Results

- *Process:* This conference was substantiated. I had plenty of data to back up my ideas and information—including data from the behavior interventionist. I think the conference went well. The mother is very easy to talk with and I value her opinions as the child's mother, just as she values mine as his teacher. We work well together to come up with solutions. I gained information about how the child's behaviors are still continuing at home—not just at school. I feel it is always important to keep the parent involved in his or her child's education. I felt this conference did that.

- *Conference outcomes:* The parent is following through at home with the reward system. I also write in the child's folder if the child gets tokens for appropriate behavior at school. I am also following through at school with a token economy reward system (the picture schedule system), and I even created social stories for him to follow. As a result of the conference and implementing the strategies, the child is no longer having behavior fits at home or at school.

- *Follow-Up:* I think the conference went smoothly. I really like it when the parents think the same way and are willing to follow through at home. This conference put my mind at ease, in a way, because the mother was having the same problems at home. I was hoping it was not my teaching and discipline management failing. I believe this parent will continue to stay involved in her child's education. I am also happy to report the behaviors have stopped for the most part. Mother reports her child is doing better at home as well. The child has worked his way up to attending regular education kindergarten for a half day so far since the conference.

COLLABORATION TIPS

PARENT CONFERENCE II

I. Identifying Information

- *Class:* Preschool program for children with disabilities (PPCD) class.
- *Child:* A five-year-old child with attention deficit hyperactivity disorder (ADHD) and processing problems. The child, for the most part, is well behaved in my class. He has, on occasion, been a little impulsive or hyperactive due to switching medications. His main issue is processing. He often stares off into space and is behind academically.
- *Parents:* The child's father was in attendance at the conference. He is a working dad who is very involved in his child's education. He is very willing to collaborate with me and make sure to match that what is being done at school is also done at home. Also, our school speech pathologist (who provides speech for the child), the school's occupational therapist, and the child's private speech pathologist were present.
- *Conference Manager:* The PPCD teacher and the school speech pathologist.
- *Time:* This conference was held six weeks after school started from 2:30 to 3:30 PM.

II. Rationale of Conference

- *Purpose/Intent:* This conference was held as per a request from the child's father. He had several topics that he wanted to discuss. First, he wanted to request another admission, review, and dismissal (ARD) meeting to change some of the child's goals. He also wanted to have a discussion on what some more appropriate goals would be. Last, he wanted the private and school speech pathologists to meet, so they could compare notes and collaborate their efforts.
- *Type:* Planned pre-ARD conference. The conference went as planned.

III. Preconference Preparation

- I prepared a folder of work samples, as well as my notes on the child's academics. I met ahead of time with the occupational therapist to discuss ideas for objectives and came up with some we thought would be academically beneficial for the child. I also gave the child a formal test to assess knowledge and skills. I waited to give the test until a week before the conference. I did this because I knew the child needed time to recover from being out for the summer. I was prepared to show the child's father the test scores, as well as my ideas for new goals. The school speech pathologist also prepared some new objectives.

IV. Conference Topography, Demographics

- *Who:* Myself, father, school speech pathologist and occupational therapist, and the private speech pathologist
- *Seating:* We sat at a small table, with enough chairs for all.
- *Proximity:* We sat across from each other.
- *Arrangement:* This was a rather large room, but I made it more personal by sitting at a small table. There was enough room for all to spread out paperwork and so forth
- We all took notes during the meeting. My notes consisted of the changed individualized education program (IEP) goals and other information that the father requested.

V. Process/Content

- Father asked for our (mine and school speech pathologist) input on how his child was progressing on his goals. I talked about how he had mastered most, but that we were still working on a few. The speech pathologist then gave her update for the father. In the middle of the update, the private speech pathologist came in and apologized for being late. Father introduced the private speech pathologist to us. The school speech pathologist proceeded to finish talking about her goals. When she was finished, the father asked the private speech pathologist to explain what she was working on. The private speech pathologist explained the areas she was working on with the child and expressed she was glad she was able to work on other areas of speech weakness in the child (not the same areas as the school speech pathologist). We all agreed that was good news. I then asked the father what ideas he had for new goals. He had a list of items. We went through each one. The occupational therapist jumped in a few times to tell the father that certain goals really needed to focus on academics and less on self-help and at-home skills. When working with this father, I really try to accommodate him. We tried to figure out a way to include most of his ideas—we combined some and helped the father to determine which ones he really needed extra help to accomplish. I then proceeded to give the father my ideas. I also let him know that we really needed to choose 10 or fewer objectives—that way we are not inundated with objectives and we can better serve the child. As usual, I explained to him that just because an objective is not on the IEP, does not mean we do not work on it. The occupational therapist and I agreed to get back with the father on a more finalized draft of objectives within one week. I also asked the father when a good time and day would be for him to come to the ARD, knowing his busy work schedule. He gave me a few times and dates. I began to close the meeting by thanking all in attendance for coming. I asked the father if he had any further questions. I assured him that we would be back in touch within a week. I walked the father and the private speech pathologist to the door. The occupational therapist, school speech pathologist, and I set up a time to meet to finish working on the child's IEP.

VI. Evaluation of Results

- *Conference outcomes:* I know the parent is following through in coming up with ideas and working with his child at home. I know this is true because I see a tremendous improvement in the skills he is working on at home with the child. We also e-mail each other on a regular basis. He tells me about any important information I should know about the child, and I update him on the child's progress. As a result of the conference and constant parental communication, I see major improvements in the child's academics.
- *Follow Up:* As I have said, the father and I e-mail each other often. I also write a little note in the folder daily. As a result of our constant communication, I have learned to tailor progress reports to all parents' needs. I think the conference, as a whole, was very effective and efficient. I was prepared and the father was prepared. I predict this parent will always be very involved in his son's education. I think future teachers will need to make sure to follow through with this parent.

Appendix C COLLABORATION TIPS

PARENT ORIENTATION PACKET

1. Transportation form—please return BEFORE you leave. Thank you.
2. Always make sure to sign in at the office before coming to the classroom—for your child's safety!
3. Daily schedule (attached)
4. Library day—every Wed. from 1:25–1:40 PM. Please remember to send back the library book so your child can check out a new one!
5. Computer day—every Tues. from 1:30–2:15 PM.
6. Book orders
7. Tardies . . . if you come in late, stop by the office and pick up a tardy slip.
8. Snacks—We have snacks after our special classes. There is a new list of snacks we can and cannot have (new state law). Please make sure to look over the list, which was sent home in the PTA packet. Birthdays—you may bring cupcakes during snack time only.
9. Tying shoes—Stops after December break!
10. Student of the week—After Labor Day, we will begin to have a student of the week. I will send home a questionnaire that you can help him or her fill out, and I'll write the information on a poster.
11. Discipline management—Class rules were included in the letter I sent home on the first day of school, as well as when you registered your child for kindergarten (in the Responsibility section of folder and 10 charts).
12. Cafeteria—Send lunch money in an envelope with your child's name and teacher written on it.
13. Sodas in lunches—I would appreciate it if you would not send caffeinated sodas for lunch with your child.
14. REMEMBER to always send a note with your child when he or she has been absent. Notes will be kept in our room, but the office will ask for them if your child has numerous absences or tardies.
15. Change of clothes—Please send a change of clothes to keep in the cubbies.
16. Dress code—Tennis shoes are the best type of shoe for your child to wear at school. We do have recess every day, even if it is not a PE day!
17. Return take-home folders daily. This way we can communicate. Your child can earn a stamp every day. Also check for important notes, etc.
18. Kindergarten report cards will be done on computer every nine weeks.
19. Conference sign-up—In late September, we will hold conferences to talk about your child's progress. Please sign up before you leave. Thank you!
20. Math program—All math is hands on exploration.
21. Field trips—Usually one bus trip per semester. We also have presenters come to the school. If any of you are doctors, dentists, nurses, police officers, fire fighters, etc., we'd love to have you come in and talk to the children.
22. Parent volunteers—You can schedule a regular time to come in and volunteer—usually outside the classroom—or you may volunteer to take things home and return them. Thank you!

23. As children begin wearing jackets, etc., be sure to put their names in them. Talk to your child about remembering his or her jacket!

24. Background check and forms—Please make sure you have returned all your school forms. Also, don't forget to fill out the background check form if you would like to work here for the PTA or to go on field trips (it takes at least 2 weeks for form to go through!).

25. If you ever have any questions, problems, etc., please make sure to contact the teacher before you contact the office.

SUBSTITUTE NOTES: MS. SMITH'S KINDERGARTEN

I usually have the things we are doing for the week in the Monday-Friday folders in the hanging files by my desk. Also, see lesson plans on my computer table.

BEHAVIOR MANAGEMENT

Students get their individual clips moved up—if you catch student doing a good job—or groups for whole groups doing a good job. If they get to 10, they pick a prize from prize box (just write down who did and I'll take care of it when I come back). A stamp is received in folder for appropriate behavior. If behavior was not appropriate, write what child did in the space and NO stamp!

7:40–8:15   Pick up my class from the cafeteria. Students know to walk quietly in the halls. Once in the room, students hang up backpacks and put folders on my computer desk tray. Then they sit quietly on the carpet until after the announcements.

          AFTER ANNOUNCEMENTS—check students' folders for notes, etc., then take attendance and lunch count. I usually have students raise their hands if they brought a lunch. Jane eats alternate choice on Wednesday and Thursday due to diet restrictions.

          CALENDAR—Use CD labeled morning routine: #4 and #5 songs (months of year, days of week). Then say today's date and add number. Ask students: "Today is ___. What was yesterday? Today is ___. What will tomorrow be?" Then count the dates on calendar (if today is the 10th, you count to 10). Change over the number on the 100 chart and count how many days we have been in school so far. Count to 100.

          MORNING MESSAGE—Write on chart on front table: Dear Class, Today is . . . . Ms. Smith is not here today. My name is . . . .

8:15–8:55   MATH—Put math manipulatives on the tables and the students can have choice time. They can go to the table they want and play/manipulate with them.

8:55–10:15   PREDICTABLE CHART—Days 1 and 2 are writing out the students' sentences on chart paper; see examples hung in room. I emphasize capital letter at beginning, period at end, and ask students to help me sound out the words. Check my plans for starter. Days 3-5, since I am not here, the students may just come up one at a time to read their sentences. Make sure they point to correct words (you may have to read sentences first, before student reads).

          INTERACTIVE WRITING (Wed.–Fri. only)—Check theme in my lesson plans— usually something about our curriculum theme for the week. I get out dry erase markers and white boards. Students come up with sentence to write, then we write letters/words together. They hold up the boards and check to see that the letters were written correctly.

SHARED READING—See big book on front table—usually the lessons are right there with it. If not, read the book, then read and have students repeat after you.

PHONEMIC AWARENESS—See book on computer table (you may skip this if necessary).

LITERACY CENTERS—Make sure to move the color groups on the chart clock-wise (unless it is Monday). One student from each group brings the yellow basket to the table. Then you call the groups one at a time to tables. This is an independent work time—students need to stay at their tables. If they have a question, they can ask someone at their table. You work with the teacher group at their table. At about 10:30, I start calling one group at a time to go to the bathroom. Remind students to put names on papers. At clean-up time (CD with orange cover, song #1), students put their work in "YES" box if finished or "NO" box if not.

10:15–10:50 RECESS—Put block in door—ask kids to show you how. Students may ask to get a drink of water and use bathroom at this time. I usually don't let too many go in at once (1 to 2). When students come in, they sit quietly on carpet.

10:55–11:25 LUNCH—Students line up and walk with NO talking in hallway. After lunch, I call one side at a time to walk in a line to trash can and then sit quietly on numbers.

11:25–11:40 SPECIALS—Mon./Wed. = PE, Tue. = Music, Thur. = FYI (library), Fri. = (A week), PE (B), Music (C), PE (D), FYI. We usually wait in hallway until 11:40—by our special—if PE or Music, wait in that hall; FYI, wait by that door. Students know that we do not talk in hallway. We sing songs (whisper), play the quiet game, or take a 10-minute recess.

11:40–12:30 Planning time

12:30 Pick up students at their special classes. We walk quietly back to class. It is quiet when students enter room.

12:30–1:00 QUIET TIME—Students may sit at tables for snack. See top of cubbies and just give students a small handful of something. If a book is on the front table (a chapter book), you may read it until 1:00. I usually let the students draw pictures while I read (they make their own pictures to go with story). If book is not there, you can pick one from library or just have students lie on the floor quietly, and they can have a self-selected reading time. I call groups one at a time to use the bathroom and get a drink of water—usually when most are finished eating snack.

1:00–2:15 THEME/SCIENCE—See folder for book and activity. Have students clean up and join you back on carpet.

FREE-CHOICE CENTERS—Students can choose center they wish to go to. Only 3 students per center, and they must be wearing a clip. Students must also clean up before switching centers. Do folders: stamp and ink in basket by front door of room. Call students to put folders in backpack as you finish them. Use clean up song ("If You're Happy and You Know It" on orange CD case song #1).

2:20–2:35 JOURNALS—Students write date at top of paper and they can write or draw pictures of what they did today.

2:35–2:40 Clean up and line up for dismissal. See folder on black shelf by door for how students go home. Walk down the hall at 2:40—students going to after-school care, day care, or the bus know where to go—they are at front of line. Other students go with you and sit in kindergarten spot in the front until parents come. They must tell you before they go—I always watch until they are safely in vehicles.

COLLABORATION TIPS

TEACHER CONSULTATION/COLLABORATION

I am a preschool program for children with disabilities (PPCD) teacher. This year, my class will be going into a regular education kindergarten class for three hours daily. The kindergarten teacher and I met over the summer to discuss how we would run the class. We also met several times the week before school started and set a weekly time that we could meet throughout the year. The kindergarten teacher has taught kindergarten for 5 years and prekindergarten for 5 years. She has worked with a PPCD class in the past and is familiar with all that inclusion involves. She is very open and willing to do whatever it takes to see her students, as well as mine succeed. During our meetings, we devised a schedule and decided that we would coteach the activities.

After school started, we quickly realized the coteaching was turning more into the kindergarten teacher teaching, while my assistants and I guided my five PPCD students in her class. My students range from attention deficit and hyperactivity disorder (ADHD) to moderate autism. We also realized our schedule—the times I brought my class in—was not the most appropriate for my five students or her kindergarten students. On top of all our realizations, we also discovered the kindergarten teacher had about seven students in her class (two of which are in special education) who needed extra help. We decided to meet during our planning period to discuss how we could make our classroom more productive.

Several major concerns came about after the first couple of weeks. First, the kindergarten teacher was not able to get some of the major learning components into her day. We were coming in during important learning components for her class: math, reading, and journal writing. She really wanted to make sure the students had very few distractions during those times of learning. Plus, my students were not learning anything from those components because they had a hard time staying focused for that long period of time. We also felt it was important for my students to have more time in which they could socialize with the other students and we were not coming in the class during free-choice centers. I also had time constraints as to when we could come into the kindergarten class due to related services and breakfast. Second, most of my students should not have been placed in kindergarten for three hours in a six-hour day. These students were having a difficult time getting used to the new environment, as well as the large number of students. The previous teacher made the ARD decisions last year. The children were not exposed to prekindergarten inclusion last year, so they did not know what to expect. Also, my five students need a smaller class size than the overcrowded kindergarten. Too many children and no prior exposure to the regular education environment overwhelmed my students, causing them to act up (crying, getting up, noises, and aggressive behavior) in the kindergarten class. Last, we worried about the quality of learning that was taking place in the room. With all the distractions and interruptions, we worried the children were not learning enough. After an informal test of certain concepts, given by the kindergarten teacher one-on-one, her students were not grasping the key concepts taught in the class so far.

With all the distractions, we had to figure out a schedule that would meet the needs of all the students in the class. We also needed to discuss taking some of her students out of the class for some extra one-on-one help. We were/are hoping to change the schedule in a way that the kindergarten teacher could get some of those major components taught when my students were not present, because all of her students take a state-mandated test in the spring, and mine are exempt. We hoped that by changing the schedule, my children will be in kindergarten at more appropriate social times to gain social skills and that the kindergarten teacher's class can have a less distractive environment in which to learn.

We agreed to meet in the kindergarten teacher's room at 12:10 PM. I wanted to discuss changing the schedule with her first. This would involve a discussion of how we could change the components around in a logical/reasonable way. Some components of her schedule must de done for a certain amount of time.

Next, I wanted to discuss pulling out certain children in her class for some extra reinforcement of some key concepts. We needed to figure out which children would benefit from some extra small-group instruction. We had to decide who would provide the extra help, where, what time, and which activities.

First, we sat down to discuss the schedule. With lesson plans and our master schedules in hand, we wrote down the major components and their allotted times needed. Then, we looked at the times I needed to be in the room with my class. We decided to keep the mornings the same, but instead of coming back after lunch, we would return from 1 to 2 PM. The kindergarten teacher then filled into her schedule the components that she wanted to complete without my class present. We talked about some of her components to decide which ones would be best for my five students. We decided that presenting the letter people and puppets was fun—since my students enjoy and participate in singing/dance activities. So, we decided to include phonemic awareness and the letter component in our inclusion time schedule. Because my students work better in small groups, we decided work jobs—where small groups work together to complete tasks in math, writing, letter recognition and art—would be an appropriate setting for my students. We also included recess and lunch for socialization. This took care of our morning inclusion time. For the afternoon, the kindergarten teacher really had to get one more component in: STAR book time. So, we decided to join in during that time (where a book was read) and then do free-choice centers (children can play at any center they choose). To arrive at an agreement on the schedule, we had to work together to find the best solution to meet the most children's needs. It took quite a bit of time and plenty of erasing and changing to come up with the best solution.

Last, I wanted to discuss what the kindergarten teacher thought about pulling out some of her students into a small group. I explained to her that it would help not only the students, but also their scores on the spring state-mandated tests. She thought the idea was wonderful. We first discussed which kids would benefit from the extra help. We decided seven students would need to have extra help. I thought the group would be too large, so I suggested that we divide the group into two. I could work with one on Monday/Wednesday and the other on Tuesday/Thursday. We discussed the time possibilities. When could we pull the children out? We decided during work jobs: 9:30–10:00 AM. We also discussed where we should have the small groups. Now that my five PPCD students know the kindergarten teacher, she volunteered to help my two assistants with my students, along with hers, so I could take the kindergarten students to my room. In an informal progress report test that the kindergarten teacher administered, it showed the seven kindergarten students needed help with letter and sound recognition, rhyming, and syllables. I gave her some ideas for helping the students and she also gave me a book of activities. We decided it would be my responsibility to plan and carry out these activities. By the time we finished, our planning period was over. We both felt better about our new ideas and hoped they would help the children succeed.

We are currently (and have been) evaluating our efforts through observation and informal testing. The kindergarten teacher and I have both informally tested all the students, including my PPCD students. Formal testing will be given in the spring. I also give a formal test to my PPCD students in the spring.

The outcomes of this collaboration with the kindergarten teacher have been better than expected. We have noticed my PPCD students are behaving more appropriately and benefiting from the social interactions. While we still have some distractions, including some from her kindergarten students, it is significantly less than before. According to our informal testing, the students are grasping more of the concepts than before the schedule change and small-group instruction. These small groups may also help these seven students move onto first grade next year—instead of repeating kindergarten. I am hoping the small groups I teach will also result in higher scores on the state-mandated testing. I hope to continue meeting with the kindergarten teacher every week.

Author Index

Subject Index